PENGUIN BOOKS

A SKELETON KEY TO *FINNEGANS WAKE*

Joseph Campbell was for many years a member
of the Literature Department at Sarah Lawrence
College. He wrote numerous books, inlcuding
*The Hero with a Thousand Faces, Myths to Live By,
The Flight of the Wild Gander, The Mythic Image,* and
the four-volume study *The Masks of God.* He
edited *The Portable Arabian Nights* and *The Portable
Jung.* Professor Campbell died in 1987.

Henry Morton Robinson's many published works
include poetry, nonfiction, and novels, including
the bestselling *The Cardinal* and *Water of Life.*

A SKELETON
KEY TO
Finnegans Wake

by

JOSEPH CAMPBELL &
HENRY MORTON ROBINSON

PENGUIN BOOKS

PENGUIN BOOKS

Viking Penguin Inc., 40 West 23rd Street,
New York, New York 10010, U.S.A.
Penguin Books Ltd, Harmondsworth,
Middlesex, England
Penguin Books Australia Ltd, Ringwood,
Victoria, Australia
Penguin Books Canada Limited, 2801 John Street,
Markham, Ontario, Canada L3R 1B4
Penguin Books (N.Z.) Ltd, 182–190 Wairau Road,
Auckland 10, New Zealand

First published in the United States of America by
Harcourt Brace Jovanovich, Inc., 1944
Viking Compass Edition published 1961
Reprinted 1961, 1964, 1966, 1967, 1968, 1969, 1972, 1973, 1975
Published in Penguin Books 1977
Reprinted 1980, 1986

Published by arrangement with Harcourt Brace Jovanovich, Inc.

Printed in the United States of America

Set in Garamond

To

JEAN AND GERTRUDE

*Two sparkling daughters of
Anna Livia Plurabelle*

ACKNOWLEDGMENTS

We wish to thank the Viking Press for permission to paraphrase and quote from *Finnegans Wake*.

Grateful acknowledgment is made of help derived from the following: *Our exagmination round his factification for incamination of Work in Progress* (Faber and Faber, Ltd., London, no date), *transition,* edited by Eugene Jolas (Paris, The Hague, New York, 1927, etc.), Frank Budgen, *James Joyce and the Making of Ulysses* (Grayson and Grayson, London, 1934), Stuart Gilbert, *James Joyce's Ulysses* (Alfred A. Knopf, N. Y., 1934), Herbert Gorman, *James Joyce* (Farrar and Rinehart, Inc., N. Y., 1939), Edmund Wilson, *The Wound and the Bow* (Houghton Mifflin Co., Boston, 1941), Harry Levin, *James Joyce* (New Directions Books, Norfolk, Conn., 1941), Thornton Wilder, *The Skin of Our Teeth* (Harper and Brothers, N. Y., 1942).

We have quoted from Eleanor Hull, *Folklore of the British Isles* (Methuen and Co., Ltd., London, 1928), Sir Edward Sullivan, *The Book of Kells* (4th edition, The Studio, Ltd., London, 1933), and have given references to John Arnott MacCulloch, *Celtic Mythology* (*The Mythology of All Races,* Vol. III, Marshall Jones Co., Boston, 1918).

Mr. Edmund Wilson kindly supplied us with a copy of James Joyce's corrections of *errata* for the 1939 edition of *Finnegans Wake*.

Mrs. Helen McMaster carefully studied the manuscript at an early and questionable stage, revived our confidence in it, and improved the work with her valuable suggestions. And throughout the entire period of our labors the intelligence and ever fresh co-operation of Betty Brown Parsons were of inestimable value in helping us prepare the manuscript.

FOREWORD

Five years ago James Joyce released for publication the great manuscript of *Finnegans Wake,* on which he had labored a third of his life. Apart from some penetrating critiques by a handful of reviewers, and the enthusiasm of the faithful few who had long awaited the work, the public reception was one of massive indifference. "What does it all mean?" "Why should we bother about a book so hard to read?" were questions quite generally asked. Even normally responsive readers dismissed the book as a perverse triumph of the unintelligible. When James Joyce suddenly died a few months later, it was freely prophesied that *Finnegans Wake* would never be explained, and could look forward only to an undusted career as a piece of literary *curiosa.*

There existed, however, the possibility that *Finnegans Wake* might be the keystone of the creative arch that Joyce had been constructing carefully since youth. That its language was difficult and its structure complex were readily admitted by everyone who seriously attempted to read it. Yet sincere efforts to unravel its meaning were rewarded so generously that some readers continued to struggle for the unimaginable prize of complete understanding.

Provoked by the sheer magnitude of the work, we felt that if Joyce had spent eighteen years in its composition we might profitably spend a few deciphering it. Our qualifications for this task were not such as to set us apart from the average reader of decent literacy. Although we were students of Joyce's previous work, and admirers of his genius, we had never met him or any members of his circle. Nor, totally unfamiliar with Dublin, were we exceptionally prepared to recognize the thousand local references to places and persons. Our only equipment was a shelf of dictionaries, the *Blue Guide* to Ireland, and a general knowledge of literature and history which widened and deepened as our task progressed.

The chief contribution of the present volume is its thin line tracing of the skeletal structure of *Finnegans Wake*. Here for the first time the complex and amazing narrative of Joyce's dream-saga is laid bare. Avoiding temptations to amplify, and indicating briefly only the most important themes, we have sought to follow page by page the progress of Joyce's story. Our purpose has not been to elaborate any passage or group of images, but merely to indicate the fundamental narrative itself.

We have not been entirely true to our purpose. Many passages were so charming and amusing that we could not forbear to let them contribute to the life and color of our own pages. Other passages, darker and more difficult, have been rendered more fully than the original plan required. Furthermore, from sentence to sentence we had to select and again select (among the crowding, curiously melting nuances of implication) precisely the one or two lines to be fixed and rendered. Wherever possible we have clung to Joyce's own language, but in order to stress the narrative we have freely condensed, simplified, and paraphrased the heavily freighted text. No one can be more conscious than ourselves of our numberless inept decisions. Nevertheless, even through our failures the great skeleton structure emerges, and clearly enough to disclose the majestic logic of *Finnegans Wake*.

If the present book does nothing else, it should make henceforth impossible the easy rejection of Joyce's work as remote from the interests and problems of the modern world. The *Wake*, at its lowest estimate, is a huge time-capsule, a complete and permanent record of our age. If our society should go to smash tomorrow (which, as Joyce implies, it may) one could find all the pieces, together with the forces that broke them, in *Finnegans Wake*. The book is a kind of terminal moraine in which lie buried all the myths, programs, slogans, hopes, prayers, tools, educational theories, and theological bric-a-brac of the past millennium. And here, too, will be found the love that reanimates this debris. Joyce's moraine is not brickdust but humus: as he never tires of telling us, "The same returns."

Finnegans Wake is above all else an essay in permanence. From its perspective, the hopeful or fearful may learn to behold with a vast sympathy the prodigious upsurging and dissolution of forms, the continual transvaluation of values, the inevitable ambiguities, which are the stuff of life and history. Through notes that finally become tuneable to our ears, we hear James Joyce uttering his resilient, all-enjoying, all-animating "Yes," the Yes of things yet to come, a Yes from beyond every zone of disillusionment, such as few have had the heart to utter.

J. C.

H. M. R.

New York City
February 1, 1944

PREFACE TO THE PENGUIN EDITION

After seventeen years of rugged service between hard covers, *A Skeleton Key to Finnegans Wake* now enters a new phase of usefulness. We take this opportunity to thank the editors of the Penguin Edition for giving our *Key* its present format, thereby making it more readily available to an ever widening audience of students and general readers.

In the course of preparing this new preface we were profoundly struck by the tone of our original Foreword. Its utter lack of pretension is broken by a singularly prophetic sentence: "There existed [we wrote in 1944] the possibility that *Finnegans Wake* might be the keystone of the creative arch that Joyce had been constructing carefully since youth."

Seldom does a critical forecast predict with greater accuracy the shape, size and striking power of things to come. Today the *Wake* is universally regarded not as a *coda* to fame already secured by *Ulysses,* but as the integration, total and complete, of Joyce's personality and creative powers.

This unexpected emergence of the *Wake* as "literature" caused a tremendous flutter among academic dovecotes. The cap-and-gown set presumably knew of Joyce's existence; indeed, a doctoral thesis on some aspect of his earlier work was considered a bold short-cut to promotion and pay. But the generally accepted notion that *Finnegans Wake* has produced a ripe harvest of critical commentary is a serene piece of wishful thinking. Schoolmen, terrified by the difficulties of Joyce's "root language," have been raking leaves in Phoenix Park for the past twenty years.

While the scholarly *Drang nach Finnegans* was petering out, the *Wake* began to find its own audience. Joyce's big black book caught on simply because its author bespeaks the human predicament.

Underneath the verbal ambiguities and philologic traps of the *Wake,* deep speaks to deep about such everyday matters as marital discord, sibling strife, military slaughter, racial violence, theological differences and financial thimblerigging—fascinating material that academicians (at their peril) fail to discuss or continue to ignore. The general cry, "Tell us more about *Finnegans Wake*!" has caused many a professor to begin looking for his glosses—which sometimes turn up, oddly enough, between the pages of *A Skeleton Key.*

There exists, of course, no substitute for the richly rewarding experience of plunging headlong into the *Wake* and wrenching loose some trophy of meaning from its still-unexplored deeps. Not until a sufficient number of readers have survived thousands of independent plunges will our *Key* become obsolete. Meanwhile, we offer the aid and comfort of its pages to those who are preparing themselves for the trial-and-error ordeal of understanding the secret that james Joyce wishes—oh, so desperately—to disclose.

J. C.
H. M. R.

New York City
November 1, 1960

TABLE OF CONTENTS

A SKELETON KEY TO
Finnegans Wake

INTRODUCTION TO A STRANGE SUBJECT

Running riddle and fluid answer, *Finnegans Wake* is a mighty allegory of the fall and resurrection of mankind. It is a strange book, a compound of fable, symphony, and nightmare—a monstrous enigma beckoning imperiously from the shadowy pits of sleep. Its mechanics resemble those of a dream, a dream which has freed the author from the necessities of common logic and has enabled him to compress all periods of history, all phases of individual and racial development, into a circular design, of which every part is beginning, middle, and end.

In a gigantic wheeling rebus, dim effigies rumble past, disappear into foggy horizons, and are replaced by other images, vague but half-consciously familiar. On this revolving stage, mythological heroes and events of remotest antiquity occupy the same spatial and temporal planes as modern personages and contemporary happenings. All time occurs simultaneously; Tristram and the Duke of Wellington, Father Adam and Humpty Dumpty merge in a single percept. Multiple meanings are present in every line; interlocking allusions to key words and phrases are woven like fugal themes into the pattern of the work. *Finnegans Wake* is a prodigious, multifaceted monomyth, not only the *cauchemar* of a Dublin citizen but the dreamlike saga of guilt-stained, evolving humanity.

The vast scope and intricate structure of *Finnegans Wake* give the book a forbidding aspect of impenetrability. It appears to be a dense and baffling jungle, trackless and overgrown with wanton perversities of form and language. Clearly, such a book is not meant to be idly fingered. It tasks the imagination, exacts discipline and tenacity from those who would march with it. Yet some of the difficulties disappear as soon as the well-disposed reader picks up a few compass clues and gets his bearings. Then the enormous map of *Finnegans Wake* begins slowly to unfold, characters and motifs emerge, themes become recognizable, and Joyce's vocabulary falls more and more familiarly on the accustomed ear. Complete understanding is not to be snatched at greedily at one sitting; indeed, it may never come. Nevertheless the ultimate state of the intelligent reader is certainly not bewilderment. Rather, it is admiration for the unifying insight, economy of means, and more-than-Rabelaisian humor which have miraculously quickened the stupendous mass of material. One acknowledges at last that James Joyce's overwhelming macro-microcosm could not have been fired to life in any sorcerer furnace less black, less heavy, less murky than this, his incredible book. He had to smelt the modern dictionary back to protean plasma and re-enact the "genesis and mutation of language" in order to deliver his message. But the final wonder is that such a message could have been delivered at all!

The first clue to the method and mystery of the book is found in its title, *Finnegans Wake*. Tim Finnegan of the old vaudeville song is an Irish hod carrier who gets drunk, falls off a ladder, and is apparently killed. His friends hold a deathwatch over his coffin; during the festivities someone splashes him with whisky, at which Finnegan comes to life again and joins in the general dance. On this comedy-song foundation, Joyce bases the title of his work. But there is more, much more, to the story. Finnegan the hod carrier is identifiable first with Finn MacCool, captain for two hundred years of Ireland's warrior-heroes, and most famous of Dublin's early giants. Finn typifies *all* heroes—Thor, Prometheus, Osiris, Christ, the Buddha—in whose life and through whose inspiration the race lives. It is by Finn's coming again (Finn-again) —in other words, by the reappearance of the hero—that strength and hope are provided for mankind.

By his death and resurrection, hod carrier Finnegan comically refigures the solemn mystery of the hero-god whose flesh and blood furnish the race with spirit-fructifying meat and drink. At the wake of Finnegan, the watchers eat everything that belongs to the dead hero. Not only do they devour all the edibles in the house, but they partake of his very body, as of a eucharist. By its fall, the shell of the Cosmic Egg has been shattered, but the essential egg substance has been gathered and served for the nutriment of the people, "sunny side up with care."

Finnegan's fall from the ladder is hugely symbolic: it is Lucifer's fall, Adam's fall, the setting sun that will rise again, the fall of Rome, a Wall Street crash. It is Humpty Dumpty's fall, and the fall of Newton's apple. It is the irrigating shower of spring rain that falls on seeded fields. And it is every man's daily recurring fall from grace. These various fallings (implying, as they do, corresponding resurrections) cause a liberation of energy that keeps the universe turning like a water wheel, and provide the dynamic which sets in motion the four-part cycle of universal history.

But why a "four-part" cycle? This reference is to a conception of the eighteenth-century Italian philosopher Giambattista Vico, whose *La Scienza Nuova* provides the philosophic loom on which Joyce weaves his historical allegory. Essentially, Vico's notion is that history passes through four phases: theocratic, aristocratic, democratic, and chaotic. The last phase is characterized (like our own) by individualism and sterility, and represents the nadir of man's fall. It is terminated by a thunderclap, which terrifies and reawakens mankind to the claims of the supernatural, and thus starts the cycle rolling again with a return to primeval theocracy.[1]

In Joyce's composition, the comical Finnegan episode is only the prologue to the major action. It is related to the later episodes as

---

[1] Oswald Spengler's *The Decline of the West* (Alfred A. Knopf, one volume edition, 1932) presents a fourfold cycle of history comparable to that of Joyce. Indeed, Spengler's "Tables of Historical Epochs" (Vol. 1, facing p. 428) considerably elucidate *Finnegans Wake*. The Spenglerian and Joycean analyses of modern times essentially agree, though the attitudes of the two men toward the inevitables of history greatly differ.

Spengler's four-part cycle is derived from Goethe, as Joyce's from Vico. Both Goethe and Vico developed the idea from the Greek mythological sequence of the Four Ages (Gold, Silver, Bronze, Iron), which in turn is a counterpart of the Hindu Round of the Four Yugas (Krita, Treata, Dvāpara, Kali). Joyce amalgamates all in his colossal tragicomical vision of the Morphology of Human Destiny.

prehistory is related to history; or (to use a Viconian image) as the giants of the dawn-chaos are related to the patriarchs of orderly history. In *Finnegans Wake* the transition from the earlier to the later hero takes place on pages 24 to 29,[2] where the company at the wake forcibly hold Finnegan down and bid him rest in peace. They tell him that a newcomer, his successor, has just sailed into Dublin Bay. This newcomer is HCE, or more specifically, Humphrey Chimpden Earwicker, who thereafter dominates the work.

As the tale unfolds, we discover that this H. C. Earwicker is a citizen of Dublin, a stuttering tavernkeeper with a bull-like hump on the back of his neck. He emerges as a well-defined and sympathetic character, the sorely harrowed victim of a relentless fate, which is stronger than, yet identical with, himself. Joyce refers to him under various names, such as Here Comes Everybody and Haveth Childers Everywhere—indications of his universality and his role as the great progenitor. The hero has wandered vastly, leaving families (that is, deposits of civilization) at every pause along the way: from Troy in Asia Minor (he is frequently called "the Turk") up through the turbulent lands of the Goths, the Franks, the Norsemen, and overseas to the green isles of Britain and Eire. His chief Germanic manifestations are Woden and Thor; his chief Celtic, Manannán MacLir. Again, he is St. Patrick carrying the new faith; again, Strongbow, leading the Anglo-Norman conquest; again, Cromwell, conquering with a bloody hand. Most specifically, he is our Anglican tavernkeeper, HCE, in the Dublin suburb, Chapelizod.

As in *Ulysses*, the principal action takes place in Dublin and its environs. We are introduced at once to Howth Castle, Phoenix Park, the River Liffey, Wellington Monument, Guinness's Brewery, and other important landmarks, all of which have allegorical significance. Phoenix Park, for example, is reminiscent of the Garden of Eden. And the product of Guinness's Brewery is the magic elixir of life, the immortal drink of heroes and gods. Many an allusion

---

[2] References are to the Viking Press edition of *Finnegans Wake*, New York, 1939.

is clarified by consulting a detailed map of Dublin. For example, "the knock out in the park" (p. 3) is Castle Knock, in a cemetery near the west gate of Phoenix Park. The neighboring hillocks are figuratively the upturned toes of the giant whose head is the Hill of Howth. This giant, whose belly is the city of Dublin itself, is none other than the prostrate comical hero-god of the wake. Indeed, all the living, loving, fighting, and dying of Dublin is precisely the hurly-burly of *Finnegans Wake*.

But to return to HCE. He is a man who has won his place in society, a place not of high distinction but of decent repute. He is a candidate in a local election. Gossip, however, undoes his campaign and his reputation as well.

It was in Phoenix Park (that Garden of Eden), near his tavern, that he committed an indecorous impropriety which now dogs him to the end of his life-nightmare. Briefly, he was caught peeping at or exhibiting himself to a couple of girls in Phoenix Park. The indiscretion was witnessed by three drunken soldiers, who could never be quite certain of what they had seen; from them it went out to the world. Earwicker's anxiety to justify himself riddles his every utterance with incriminating slips of the tongue, and contributes to his bulky presence a flavor of slightly rancid butter, exposing him to further gossip on every hand. The rumors grow. He is said to suffer from an obscure disease, suspiciously venereal, a physiological counterpart of his psychological taint.

Unquestionably his predicament is of the nature of Original Sin: he shares the shadowy guilt that Adam experienced after eating the apple. It is akin also to the bewilderment and confusion that paralyze Hamlet, and is cognate with the neurotic misease of modern times. Stephen Dedalus, who suffers from an analogous malady in *Ulysses,* calls it the "agenbite of inwit," the incessant gnawing of rat-toothed remorse. Earwicker, suffering from this taint, yet aware of his claims to decency, is torn between shame and aggressive self-satisfaction, conscious of himself both as bug and as man (an earwig is a beetlelike insect, popularly supposed to creep into the human ear). Worm before God and giant among

7

men, he is a living, aching arena of cosmic dissonance, tortured by all the cuts and thrusts of guilt and conscience.

A very specific ramification of the Guilt motif crops out constantly in the old-man, young-girl situations sprinkled throughout the book. In the Swift-Vanessa, Mark-and-Iseult episodes, gray-beards are passionately fired with a half-incestuous, half-lyrical yearning for young love. Earwicker himself is troubled by a passion, compounded of illicit and aspirational desires, for his own daughter, Isabel, whom he identifies with Tristram's Iseult, and who is the sweet little reincarnation of his wife. Himself he envisions now as gallant Tristram and now as cuckolded King Mark.

Although Earwicker is a citizen of Dublin, he is resented by the populace as an intruder, even a usurper. Why? Because, springing from Germanic rather than Celtic stock, he typifies all the invaders who have overrun Ireland—Danes, Norsemen, Normans, and English. The clash of arms that resounds through the first pages of the book recalls the battles of all Irish history and furnishes a background to the battlefields of the tavern—and the battlefields of Earwicker's own soul.

The rumors about HCE are started by a native Dubliner, smoking a pipe, who encounters Earwicker at midnight in Phoenix Park. This Cad with a pipe asks HCE for the time, and is surprised when the great personage exhibits uneasiness and launches into an elaborate self-defense. The Cad goes home, broods over a bottle, and mumbles what he has heard. His wife, catching the suspicious words, communicates them to her priest, who, in turn, passes them on at the racetrack. Three down-and-outers pick up the tale, exaggerate it comically, and finally turn it into a scurrilous lampoon ("The Ballad of Persse O'Reilly," p. 44).

The rumor runs through the city like a virulent infection. Several pages (51–61) are devoted to round robins of public opinion. The plague of evil gossip that encircles the present Mr. H. C. Earwicker races back through the past—touches and contaminates every likeness of the unforgettable great citizen through all the annals, not only of Ireland, but of man. Thus the inquirer finds it impossible to distinguish between the tumultuous earwigging (gossiping) of the present and that of remoter days. The scandal-stew boils gloriously with ingredients from every moment of human time.

While the man in the street gossips, twelve stately citizens of the jury sit in formal though tipsy session. These twelve are, locally, the twelve constant customers of Mr. Earwicker's tavern. They are also leading mourners at Finnegan's wake. They are also the twelve signs of the zodiac. Their presence betrays itself with sonorous sequences of words terminating in "-ation"; as, for instance, on page 6, "all the hoolivans of the nation, prostrated in their consternation, and their duodisimally profusive plethora of ululation."

In addition, there are four slobberishly senile judges who remember and rehearse the anecdotes of old times. They are identified with the four winds, the Four Master Annalists of Ireland, the Four Evangelists, the four Viconian ages, and so forth. Their principal charge is to care for a Donkey, which, in its better moments, is revealed as an archaic incarnation of the Logos. Pages 383 to 399 are devoted largely to the recollections of the Four. They themselves, in younger days, were protagonists of the great life-roles which they can now only regard and review. Life once stirred in them and shaped them; but it has moved on, so that they now are but cast-off shells. Crotchety, brittle crystallizations out of the past, they have only to await disintegration. Meanwhile, however, they sit in judgment over the living present.

A dim-witted policeman, crony of the Four, arrests HCE for disturbing the peace, and gives testimony against him (pp. 62–63, and 67). But he has many of the traits of the hero himself—as have, indeed, all the male characters of the populace-opposition. For, in the last analysis, the universal judgment against HCE is but a reflection of his own obsessive guilt; and conversely, the sin which others condemn in him is but a conspicuous public example of the general, universally human, original sin, privately effective within themselves. Thus, throughout the work, there is a continual intermelting of the accused and his accusers. All these characters, moving around and against one another, are but facets of some prodigious unity and are at last profoundly identical—

9

each, as it were, a figure in the dream complex of all the others. One is reminded of Schopenhauer's wonderful image of the world in his essay *On an Apparent Intention in the Fate of the Individual:* "It is a vast dream, dreamed by a single being; but in such a way that all the dream characters dream too. Thus everything interlocks and harmonizes with everything else."

Earwicker has a wife, the psyche of the book—bewitching, ever-changing, animating, all-pervading. She appears typically under the name of Anna Livia Plurabelle, abbreviated to ALP. Just as Earwicker is metamorphosed into Adam. Noah, Lord Nelson, a mountain, or a tree, so ALP becomes by subtle transposition, Eve, Isis, Iseult, a passing cloud, a flowing stream. She is the eternally fructive and love-bearing principle in the world—a little crone who goes about gathering fragments into a basket; Isis picking up the dismembered body of her brother-husband, Osiris. She is the widow who serves the feast at the wake: "Grampupus is fallen down but grinny sprids the boord" (p. 7). Again, she is a mother hen that scratches out of a dung heap the torn scrap of a gossipacious letter filled with all the secrets of a woman's heart (pp. 110–11), a bewitching letter, which, only partially recovered, tantalizes with its life riddle through every page of *Finnegans Wake:* the entire book, in fact, is but a dreamlike emanation of this "untitled mamafesta memorialising the Mosthighest" (p. 104), written (time and place unknown) by ALP herself.

But above all, Anna is a river, always changing yet ever the same, the Heraclitean flux which bears all life on its current. Principally, she is the river Liffey, running through Dublin, but she is also all the rivers of the world: the heavenly Ganges, the fruitful Nile, the teeming Irrawaddy, the mysterious Nyanza. She is the circular river of time, flowing past Eve and Adam in the first sentence of the book, bearing in her flood the debris of dead civilizations and the seeds of crops and cultures yet to come.

The circular course of the river Liffey illustrates her cycle of transformation. Her brooklet source in the Wicklow Hills finds her as a young girl, free, dancing gaily, a delicious nymph. Passing the Chapelizod of HCE's tavern, she is a comely, matronly stream.

Still farther on, running through the city of Dublin, she is an old haggard scrubwoman, carrying away the filth of the city. At last she flows back to Father Ocean, from whence she rises again in mist, to descend in showers and become once more the sparkling mountain stream. Anna's cycle is a perfect example of the Viconian *corso* and *recorso*—the circular ground-plan on which *Finnegans Wake* is laid.

It is the role of the *younger* Anna to shatter HCE as the container of fixed energy. It becomes the function of the *older* Anna, the widow, to gather up the remains of her broken lord and consign them again to a fresh start. As Joyce says, "she puffs the blaziness on," converts past into future, and displays the female's typical concern for the future of her race. Among her younger manifestations are Earwicker's daughter and her twenty-eight little companions (the days of the month), seven beaming rainbow-colored girls, and the two temptresses in the Park. Among her older incarnations are the writer and receiver of the letter, and the garrulous housekeeper of the Earwicker establishment, Kate the Slop, "built in with bricks." The roles are continually shifting and mingling into each other. Anna is the principle of vivid movement, ever setting in motion and keeping in motion the river-flow of time.

Earwicker and his wife have two sons, called in their symbolic aspect Shem and Shaun, and in their domestic aspect Jerry and Kevin. They are the carriers of a great Brother Battle theme that throbs through the entire work. Just as HCE and ALP represent a primordial male-female polarity, which is basic to all life, so Shem and Shaun represent a subordinate, exclusively masculine battle polarity which is basic to all history. Opposing traits, which in their father were strangely and ambiguously combined, in these sons are isolated and separately embodied. As characters, therefore, these boys are very much simpler than their father; accordingly, the chapters of the work devoted to the delineations of their caricature-portraits (Bk. I, chap. 7 (pp. 169–95) for Shem; Bk. II, chaps. 1 and 2 (pp. 219–308) for Shaun) are comparatively easy reading, excellent places for trial spins.

Shem (Jerry), the introvert, rejected of man, is the explorer and discoverer of the forbidden. He is an embodiment of dangerously brooding, inturned energy. He is the uncoverer of secret springs, and, as such, the possessor of terrific, lightning powers. The books he writes are so mortifying that they are spontaneously rejected by the decent; they threaten, they dissolve the protecting boundary lines of good and evil. Provoked to action (and he must be provoked before he will act), he is not restrained by normal human laws, for they have been dissolved within him by the too powerful elixirs of the elemental depths; he may let loose a hot spray of acid; but, on the other hand, he can release such a magical balm of forgiveness that the battle lines themselves become melted in a bacchanal of general love. Such absolute love is as dangerous to the efficient working of society as absolute hate. The possessor of the secrets, therefore, is constrained to hold his fire. Nobody really wants to hear what he has to say; the shepherds of the people denounce him from their pulpits, or else so dilute and misrepresent his teachings as to render them innocuous. Thus Shem is typically in retreat from society; he is the scorned and disinherited one, the Bohemian, or criminal outcast, rejected by Philistine prosperity. Under the title of Shem the Penman, he is the seer, the poet, Joyce himself in his character of misunderstood, rejected artist. His characteristic behavior is to take refuge in his own room, where, on the foolscap of his own body, he writes a phosphorescent book in a corrosive language which Shaun cannot understand.

The character of Shaun (Kevin), the folk-shepherd brother, the political orator, prudent, unctuous, economically successful favorite of the people, policeman of the planet, conqueror of rebels, bearer of the white man's burden, is developed by Joyce elaborately and broadly. He is the contrapuntal opposite of Shem: the two brothers are the balanced ends of the human dumbbell. And if it is the typical lot of Shem to be whipped and despoiled, Shaun is typically the whipper and despoiler.

When he turns from making empires and preserving the peace of the world to the writing of best sellers, the favored son does not himself descend to those dangerous, obscene, and forbidden depths from which the other brings forth his mad productions; his works are never in danger of censorship and rejection; they are the censors and rejectors. Indeed, Shaun is not concerned with spiritual or esthetic matters except in so far as he can exploit them; the life of the flesh and the senses is good enough for him. In a diverting passage beginning on page 429, Shaun addresses the little daygirls of St. Bride's Academy, smiting their tender ears with admonitions of good counsel and very practical advice. "Collide with man, collude with money," is a typical Shaunian saw. In sum: Shaun is man naïvely and shrewdly outgoing, whereas Shem, his brother, has been touched by the "agenbite" which probes back again to the source. Shaun execrates Shem, maligns him, with the frank but not altogether unfearful disdain of the man of action for the man of thought. Under the title of Shaun the Postman, he delivers to mankind the great message which has been actually discovered and penned by Shem, and enjoys thereby all the rewards of those who carry good tidings.

Shem's business is not to create a higher life, but merely to find and utter the Word. Shaun, on the other hand, whose function is to make the Word become flesh, misreads it, fundamentally rejects it, limits himself to a kind of stupid concretism, and, while winning all the skirmishes, loses the eternal city.

HCE, the father of this pair, represents the unity from which their polarity springs. Compared with the rich plasticity of HCE, the boys are but shadow-thin grotesques. Their history plays like a strange mirage over the enduring core of the basic presence of HCE. The energy generated by their conflict is but a reflex of the original energy generated by the father's fall. Furthermore, antipodal as the brothers may be, they are both easily embraced by the all-inclusive love of their wonderful mother ALP. (See, for instance, the charming passages on pages 194 to 195.)

Toward the close of the work (specifically during the third chapter of Book III (pp. 474–554)), the forms of the son's world dissolve and the everlasting primal form of HCE resurges. The all-father is reunited with his wife in a diamond-wedding anniversary, as if to demonstrate that behind the complexity of their

13

children's lives, they still continue to be the motive-givers. Together, they constitute the primordial, androgynous angel, which is Man, the incarnate God.

What, finally, is *Finnegans Wake* all about? Stripping away its accidental features, the book may be said to be all compact of *mutually supplementary antagonisms:* male-and-female, age-and-youth, life-and-death, love-and-hate; these, by their attraction, conflicts, and repulsions, supply polar energies that spin the universe. Wherever Joyce looks in history or human life, he discovers the operation of these basic polarities. Under the seeming aspect of diversity—in the individual, the family, the state, the atom, or the cosmos—these constants remain unchanged. Amid trivia and tumult, by prodigious symbol and mystic sign, obliquely and obscurely (because these manifestations are both oblique and obscure), James Joyce presents, develops, amplifies and recondenses nothing more nor less than the eternal dynamic implicit in birth, conflict, death, and resurrection.

SYNOPSIS AND DEMONSTRATION

SYNOPSIS

Finnegans Wake is divided into four great Parts, or Books, not named, but numbered from I to IV. In leaving these Books untitled, Joyce is not wantonly casting the reader adrift without such chart or compass as chapter headings ordinarily provide. Rather, he intends that the subject matter of each Book shall develop organically out of its own life cell, making known its nature and direction as the development proceeds. The titles we have assigned to these Books in the following synopsis are based on the relationship of Joyce's fourfold cycle to the Four Ages of the Viconian *Corso-Recorso*. As here presented, the titles, and the synopsis itself, are intended to serve as a handrail for the reader groping his way along unfamiliar galleries.

BOOK I: THE BOOK OF THE PARENTS

Chapter 1: Finnegan's Fall [1] (*pp. 3–29*)

The first four paragraphs are the suspended tick of time between a cycle just past and one about to begin. They are in effect an overture, resonant with all the themes of *Finnegans Wake*. The dominant motif is the polylingual thunderclap of paragraph 3 (bababadalgharaghtakamminarronnkonnbronntonnerronntuonn-thunntrovarrhounawnskawntoohoohoordenenthurnuk!) which is

---

[1] Our titles for the sixteen chapters into which the work is subdivided are adaptations from phrases in Joyce's text.

the voice of God made audible through the noise of Finnegan's fall.

Narrative movement begins with the life, fall, and wake of hod carrier Finnegan (pp. 4–7). The Wake scene fades into the landscape of Dublin and environs. Whereupon we review scenic, historic, prehistoric, and legendary evidences of Finnegan's all-suffusing presence (pp. 7–23). The Wake scene re-emerges. At the sound of the word "whisky" (*usqueadbaugham!*) the deceased sits up and threatens to rise, but the company soothes him back. The whole structure of the new day has been founded on the fact of his demise (pp. 23–28). Primeval Finnegan has already been supplanted by HCE, who has arrived by sea to set up family and shop (pp. 28–29).

Chapter 2: HCE—His Agnomen and Reputation (*pp.* 30–47)

A half-trustworthy account is given of the earliest days of HCE and of how he came by his curious name. The rumors of his misconduct in the Park are reviewed. We next are regaled with the story of how these rumors grew after his encounter with a certain tramp in Phoenix Park. The scurrilous tales culminate in a popular lampoon, "The Ballad of Persse O'Reilly," which fixes on HCE the blame for all local ills.

Chapter 3: HCE—His Trial and Incarceration (*pp.* 48–74)

Through the fog screen of scandal little can be clarified. As the author points out, it all happened a long time ago and the participants are no longer alive—yet their counterparts dwell among us. A series of personages voluntarily arise to explain HCE's case. Somehow they all resemble the accused. Passers-by are interviewed for their opinion of the celebrated wrongdoer (pp. 48–62). The story is told of his arrest. His fate is compared to that of an American sugar-daddy. The women in the case are said to have come to unhappy ends. After the hurly-burly is over, HCE, the eternal scapegoat, is incarcerated for his own protection and roundly insulted through the keyhole of his cell by a visiting hog-caller from the U.S.A. (pp. 62–74).

Chapter 4: HCE—His Demise and Resurrection (pp. 75–103)

Various thoughts pass through the mind of the captive HCE. Meanwhile, a subaqueous grave is prepared for him at the bottom of Lough Neagh, which, presently, he is induced to enter. During the general chaos that immediately ensues, phantom apparitions of HCE are variously reported from several battlefields (pp. 75–79).

The filthy paganism of his day and the origin of a certain mud mound in which a letter was deposited are described by the scrubwoman, Widow Kate. This is the first hint of the great Letter theme which foliates hugely throughout the book (pp. 79–80).

A fresh encounter and arrest, and the trial of a certain Festy King, reproduce with important variations the case of HCE. Festy King is Shaun the Postman; his accuser, Shem the Penman; they are the sons of the great figure. All now await a certain letter which, it is expected, may reveal the whole truth. Meanwhile, the Four Old Judges ruminate the days of HCE (pp. 81–96).

It is found that the inhabitant of the watery tomb has escaped and may be anywhere. He is perhaps incarnate in the newly elected Pope. But having heard his story, what we want to hear now is the history of the suffering and forgiving wife (pp. 97–103).

Chapter 5: The Manifesto of ALP (pp. 104–25)

This chapter discusses at length the origin and calligraphy of the Great Letter, which has gone by various names in various times and places. It was dug from a mud mound by a hen, was saved by Shem, but then passed off by Shaun as his own discovery. Scholarly analysis of the letter by a professor-figure shows it to be pre-Christian, post-Barbaric, and peculiarly Celtic. The scribe responsible for this letter manuscript, working under the dictation of ALP, is suggested to have been much like Shem the Penman.

(This letter, which is to go through many metamorphoses during the course of *Finnegans Wake,* is Mother Nature's partial revelation of the majesty of God the Father; simultaneously, it is the broken communication of that revelation through poetry and myth—ALP the Muse, Shem the scribe; finally, it is the germ and substance of *Finnegans Wake* itself.)

Chapter 6: Riddles—the Personages of the Manifesto (pp. 126–68)

In the form of a classroom quiz the professor who has just analyzed the letter manuscript now propounds a series of riddles touching the characters therein revealed: (1) The Father, (2) The Mother, (3) Their Home, (4) Their City, (5) The Manservant, (6) The Scrubwoman, (7) The Twelve Sleepy Customers, (8) The Temptresses, (9) The Man's Story, (10) His Daughter, dreaming Love into her Mirror, (11) The Battle Polarity of his Sons, (12) That Cursed Shem.

Question 11 is answered by a ponderous Professor Jones, who discusses at great length the history and metaphysics of the brother conflict and demonstrates the relationship of the Shem-Shaun-Iseult triangle to HCE-ALP. To aid those unable to follow his complex thesis he supplies the parable of "The Mookse and The Gripes" (pp. 152–59), wherein the conquest of Ireland by Henry II with the encouragement of Pope Adrian IV is presented as an Alice-in-Wonderland fable translated from the Javanese. Professor Jones is of the Shaun type and his speech is an *apologia pro vita sua.*

Chapter 7: Shem the Penman (pp. 169–95)

The low character, self-exile, filthy dwelling, vicissitudes, and corrosive writings of the other son of HCE comprise the subject matter of this chapter. This is a thinly veiled burlesque of Joyce's own life as an artist. It is a short chapter, highly amusing and comparatively easy to read.

Chapter 8: *The Washers at the Ford* (*pp.* 196–216)

Two washerwomen rinsing clothes on opposite banks of River Liffey gossip about the lives of HCE and ALP. Every garment reminds them of a story, which they recount with pity, tenderness, and ironic brutality. The principal tale is of ALP at her children's ball, where she diverts attention from the scandal of the father by distributing to each a token of his own destiny. The mind is thus led forward from recollections of the parents to the rising generation of sons and daughters. As the stream widens and twilight descends, the washerwomen lose touch with each other; they wish to hear of the children, Shem and Shaun; night falls and they metamorphose gradually into an elmtree and a stone; the river babbles on.

BOOK II: THE BOOK OF THE SONS

Chapter 1: *The Children's Hour* (*pp.* 219–59)

The children of the taverner play in the evening before the tavern. Shem and Shaun, under the names of Glugg and Chuff, battle for the approval of the girls. Glugg (Shem) loses out, and retreats with a rancorous threat to write a revenging Jeremiad. The children are summoned home to supper and to bed. Again playing before sleep, they are finally silenced by the thunderous noise of their father slamming a door.

Chapter 2: *The Study Period—Triv and Quad* (*pp.* 260–308)

Dolph (Shem), Kev (Shaun), and their sister are at their lessons. Their little tasks open out upon the whole world of human learning: Cabalistic Theology, Viconian Philosophy, the seven liberal arts of the Trivium and Quadrivium, with a brief recess for letter-writing and belle-lettristics. The mind is guided by gradual stages from the dim mysteries of cosmogony down to Chapelizod and the tavern of HCE (pp. 260–86).

While the little girl broods on love, Dolph assists Kev with a geometry problem, revealing to him through circles and triangles the mother secrets of ALP. Kev indignantly strikes him down; Dolph recovers and forgives (pp. 286–306).

The chapter concludes with a final examination and commencement. The children are ready to create their New World, which will feed upon the Old (pp. 306–8).

Chapter 3: *Tavernry in Feast* (pp 309–82)

This chapter, nearly one-sixth of *Finnegans Wake* in bulk, is ostensibly a great feast held in the tavern of HCE. Yarns go round and the radio breaks in constantly. We overhear the tavern customers telling the fabulous histories of a Flying Dutchman sea-rover whom we come to suspect is HCE in an earlier phase. The whole story of HCE's presence in the town, and of his misadventure in the Park, is being rehearsed under cover of the Flying Dutchman yarn (pp. 309–37).

As the drinks and stories go round, we reach the midpoint of *Finnegans Wake* with an installment of the television skit of "Butt and Taff." These vaudeville characters rehearse the story of how one Buckley shot a Russian General at the Battle of Sevastopol in the Crimean War. Amidst echoes of "The Charge of the Light Brigade" the figure of the Russian General appears on the television screen; he is the living image of HCE (pp. 338–55).

When the radio is shut off the entire company sides with Buckley. But the tavernkeeper arises to the support of the Russian General. The company agrees in a powerful condemnation of their host who, it appears, is running for public office. It is nearly closing time. From afar come sounds of an approaching mob, singing a ballad celebrating the guilt and overthrow of HCE. Feeling that he has been rejected by his people whom he came to rule, the tavernkeeper clears his place and is at last alone. In desperation he laps up the dregs of all the glasses and bottles, and collapses drunkenly on the floor. He now beholds, as a dream, the vision of the next chapter (pp. 355–82).

Chapter 4: Bride-Ship and Gulls (pp. 383–99)

HCE, dreaming on the floor, sees himself as King Mark, cuckolded by young Tristram who sails away with Iseult. The honeymoon boat is circled by gulls, i.e., the Four Old Men, who regard the vivid event from their four directions. HCE, broken and exhausted, is no better now than they.

BOOK III: THE BOOK OF THE PEOPLE

Chapter 1: Shaun before the People (pp. 403–28)

HCE has gathered himself up to bed with his wife. His dream vision of the future unfolds. Shaun the Post is seen to stand before the people recommending himself to their votes, and abusing his rival, Shem. To illustrate the brother contrast Shaun recounts the Aesopian fable of "The Ondt and the Gracehoper" (pp. 414–19). His principal point against Shem is that his language is beyond the pale of human propriety. The vision fades and a keen is lifted for the departed hero.

Chapter 2: Jaun before St. Bride's (pp. 429–73)

Shaun, now called Jaun (Don Juan), appears before the little girls of St. Bride's Academy, Iseult and her twenty-eight playmates. To them he delivers a long farewell sermon, shrewdly prudential and practical, cynical, sentimental, and prurient. He is about to depart on a great mission.

Jaun is an imperial-salesman parodist of the Christ of the Last

Supper, leaving advice to the little people of his Church. He introduces Shem, his brother, the Paraclete who will serve his bride while he is gone. Sped with pretty litanies, he departs—celebrated Misdeliverer of the Word.

Chapter 3: Yawn under Inquest (pp. 474-554)

Shaun (now Yawn) lies sprawled atop a ridge in the center of Ireland. The Four Old Men and their Ass arrive to hold an inquest. Ruthlessly they question the prostrate hulk, and it gradually disintegrates. Voices break from it, out of deeper and deeper stratifications. Shaun is revealed as the Gargantuan representative of the last and uttermost implications of HCE.

As the examination proceeds, it becomes more than the four old investigators can handle. The complaints of raped India and Ireland, the garbled reports of self-contradictory witnesses and juries, wild, fragmentary outcries of subliminal voices long forgotten, the primeval scene of *Finnegans Wake* itself, come forth from the expiring titan. A group of young Brain Trusters takes over, to press the inquest to conclusion. Their sheafs of questionnaires quickly co-ordinate the evidence. They summon Kate, the widow of earliest times, and finally evoke the father presence himself. The voice of HCE pours forth in a vastly welling, all-subsuming tide, and the entire scene is dissolved in the primordial substance of HCE.

Chapter 4: HCE and ALP—Their Bed of Trial (pp. 555-90)

The Four Old Inquisitors now are sitting around the parental bed. They are the posts of the four-poster. The long night is yielding to dawn; the dream figments are dissolving back into the furnishings of the room. Everybody is asleep. A little cry is heard from Jerry (Shem) who has been having a nasty dream (pp. 555-59).

The anxious mother leaps from bed, seizes the lamp, and, followed by her husband, hastens upstairs to the child's room. Child comforted, mother and father return downstairs to bed (pp. 559–82). Their shadows on the windowblind flash far and wide the copulation of HCE and ALP. The cock crows; it is dawn (pp. 582–90). The male and female relax for an early-morning nap (p. 590).

BOOK IV: *RECORSO*

Angelic voices herald the day. The sleeper has rolled over; a beam of light troubles the back of his neck. The world awaits the shining hero of the new dawn (pp. 593–601).

Issuant from the lake of night and celebrated by girly voices, arises the form of innocent St. Kevin. The idyllic moment is suggestive of Ireland's lovely Christian dawn of the fifth century (pp. 601–6).

Day is gaining. The sleepers are passing from sleep. The ambiguities of night will soon be dispelled (pp. 606–9).

The moment of the triumph of wakefulness over deep mythological dream is represented as the arrival of St. Patrick (*ca.* A.D. 432) and his refutation of mystical Druidism. All thereafter moves toward enlightenment. Yet things are not essentially changed, only refreshed (pp. 609–15).

The morning paper and ALP's letter in the mail will tell you all the news of the night just past (pp. 615–19).

The woman, during the morning sleep, has felt her husband turn away from her. Time has passed them both; their hopes are now in their children. HCE is the broken shell of Humpty Dumpty, ALP the life-soiled last race of the river as it passes back to sea. The mighty sweep of her longing for release from the pressing shores and for reunion with the boundless ocean swells into a magnificent final monologue (pp. 619–28). Anna Liffey returns to the vast triton-father; at which moment the eyes open, the dream breaks, and the cycle is ready to start anew.

The First Four Paragraphs of Finnegans Wake

The first page and a half of *Finnegans Wake* hold in suspension the seed energies of all the characters and plot motifs of the book. Here the Joycean volcano in full eruption vomits forth raw lumps of energy-containing lava, a mythogenetic river still aflame as it floods across the page. The first impression is one of chaos, unrelieved by any landmark of meaning or recognition. Unless James Joyce could be trusted as a wielder of the most disciplined logic known to modern letters, there would be little hope that these hurtling igneous blocks would eventually respond to the solvent of analysis. The fact is, however, that these opening paragraphs are choked with nutrient materials of sense and sustenance. The themes here darkly announced are developed later with such organic inevitability that the reader, having finished the book, gazes back with amazement at the prophetic content and germinal energy of the first page.

The first four paragraphs of *Finnegans Wake* remotely suggest the first verses of the Book of Genesis. On a darkened stage, and against a cosmic backdrop, terrestrial scenes and characters begin to emerge in a drama of creation. The landscape itself gropes its way into action, and in the primeval dawn we dimly descry a river and a mountain.

> *riverrun, past Eve and Adam's, from swerve of shore to bend of bay, brings us by a commodius vicus of recirculation back to Howth Castle and Environs.*

Appropriately, the first word of *Finnegans Wake* is "riverrun." Opening with a small letter, it starts the book in the middle of a sentence. "Riverrun," however, is *not* a beginning, but a continuation—a continuation among other things of the ecstatic, swiftly slipping and abruptly interrupted sentence with which the volume ends. For the book is composed in a circle; the last word flows into the first, Omega merges into Alpha, and the rosary of history begins all over again.

"Riverrun" is more than a clue to the circling plan of *Finnegans Wake;* it characterizes the essence of the book itself. For in this work, both space and time are fluid; meanings, characters, and vocabulary deliquesce in constant fluxion. The hero is everywhere: in the elm that shades the salmon pool, in the shadow that falls upon the stream, in the salmon beneath the ripples, in the sunlight on the ripples, in the sun itself. Three men looking at you through one pair of eyes are not men at all, but a clump of shrubs; not shrubs either, but your own conscience; and finally, not your private conscience, but an incubus of the universal nightmare from which the sublime dreamer of cosmic history will awaken, only to dream once more.

Alive to the depthless metaphor in which we are moving, let us begin by bringing into focus the composition of place indicated in the first sentence of *Finnegans Wake.* Specifically, "riverrun" refers to Dublin's River Liffey, flowing past a church called "Adam and Eve's" which is situated on its banks. As Adam and Eve stand at the beginning of human history, so they stand at the beginning of our book, suggesting Eden, sexual polarity, the fall of man, and the promise of redemption. "Riverrun" suggests, too, the river of time, on which these world events are borne.

from swerve of shore to bend of bay . . .

We follow the topography of the Irish shoreline from the mouth of River Liffey northward to a deep bend where the waters of Dublin Bay pound the Hill of Howth. The swerve of shore is the coy gesture of the pretty isle herself which invites the assault of the bay waters, thus hinting at a Seduction theme which will later emerge full of import. Again, the waters of Dublin Bay continually pounding the Head of Howth represent, on an elemental level, the perennial invaders of Ireland continually pummeling the head of the defender.

brings us by a commodius vicus of recirculation . . .

Joyce here announces in the word "recirculation" the Viconian **recorso** theme, the metaphysical pivot on which the Finnegan cycle

25

turns. The cunning key word, "vicus," means street or highway, but is at the same time the Latin form of the Italian Vico. "Commodius" sweeps the mind back to the Rome which showed its first severe symptoms of decay in the time of the emperor Commodus. It also suggests the broad and easy path that leads our present civilization to destruction.

back to Howth Castle and Environs . . .

This Dublin landmark (note the initials HCE peeping through the name) is a high headland crowned by a castle and guarding Dublin Bay. It is popularly regarded as the cranium of a recumbent giant whose belly is the city of Dublin and whose feet turn up amidst the hillocks of Phoenix Park. If the river Liffey is the heroine, this sleeping landscape giant is the hero. Historical associations crowd around his recumbent form. On this headland the sentinels of Finn MacCool stood guard against invaders from the sea. Centuries later, when the Anglo-Norman king Henry II subjugated the island, the present castle was founded by one of the invading company, Sir Almeric Tristram. That was in the century of the flowering of the Arthurian romances, with which are inseparably woven the names of Tristram and Iseult.

So now we read:

> Sir Tristram, violer d'amores, fr'over the short sea, had passencore rearrived from North Armorica on this side the scraggy isthmus of Europe Minor to wielderfight his penisolate war . . .

The basic sense is this: Sir Tristram, musician of love, from across Saint George's Channel,[2] had not yet rearrived [3] from North Brittany, which is on Ireland's side of rugged Europe,[4] to wage

[2] Tristram first arrived in Ireland by coracle from Cornwall, over the same sea crossed by the historical Sir Almeric Tristram, founder of Howth Castle.

[3] Note the curious implication of "rearrived." Joyce intends to indicate that in the courses of the Viconian cycle all has happened before and is on the point of happening again.

[4] North Armorica is North Brittany, the scene of the love-death of Tristram and Iseult of Ireland. It was the scene also of Tristram's morbid, unconsummated marriage with the second and younger Iseult, Iseult of Brittany.

again his war. The war is designated "penisolate," which suggests "late, or recent war of the penis," a designation not inappropriate to the gest of a Tristram. But the word may also be read, "pen-iso-late," whereupon it suggests a war waged with the pen, not by a robust extrovert, but by an isolated, introverted man of letters. The Tristram figure will later split into such antipodal characters, giving battle to each other. Finally, if we read "Peninsular War," we shall be reminded of the Anglo-Irish Dubliner, Arthur Wellesley, first duke of Wellington, who in the Peninsular War waged his first great battles against Napoleon.

With this sounding of the Tristram motif of guilty love, Joyce boldly strikes one of the major chords of *Finnegans Wake*. The legend of Tristram and the two Iseults is well known; its mold fits perfectly over HCE. He has a bewitching daughter whom he compares to the second Iseult, her of Brittany, whereas his wife in some of her transformations is identical with Iseult of Ireland. Torn between the two, the man is tempted and destroyed by the representatives of the younger, but he is gathered up and his wounds are healed by the older, whom he never ceases to cherish. This conflict which drives a wedge into HCE's heart is a manifestation of the ambiguous guilt neurosis that has troubled men of the western world since the medieval innovation of romantic love.

The double note of love and war is to become the pervasive theme of *Finnegans Wake:* key changes and modulations will break the simple statements into baffling congeries of dissonance and harmony. Ambiguous the love—ambiguous too will be the war, continually outcropping in the struggles between Shem and Shaun and their shadow extensions Butt and Taff, Mutt and Jute, the historical figures of Wellington and Napoleon, Cæsar and Brutus, Sigtrygg and Brian Boru, and those curiously inchoate personages, Buckley and the Russian General. Under many appearances, love and war are the constant life expressions of that polarized energy which propels the universal round.

"North Armorica" suggests North America. The phrase following develops this evocation of the New World Beyond the Sea, to which those Irish fled who took refuge from the English plunderer, and where many a canny Irishman has won money and prestige:

> *nor had topsawyer's rocks by the stream Oconee exaggerated themselse to Laurens County's gorgios while they went doublin their mumper all the time . . .*

Oddly enough there is a stream Oconee flowing through Laurens County, Georgia, U.S.A., and on the banks of this stream stands Dublin, the county seat. Thus an American duplication of Dublin on Liffey is Dublin on Oconee. The word Oconee resembles the Irish exclamation of grief, "ochone," undoubtedly uttered by many an Irishman leaving his home for America.

Numerous suggestions resound through this passage: Tom Sawyer, for instance, with his associations of Huck Finn and Mark Twain (Mark the Second).[5] When men are sawing timber over a saw pit, a top sawyer stands *above* the log; a pit sawyer stands *below*. This image carries forward the idea of the opposed brothers: the sawyer on top is the successful one; his "rocks" (slang for "money") "exaggerate themselves," that is to say, increase. Also the rocks transform themselves into property in Laurens County, Georgia; the citizens of this area are the "gorgios,"[6] fruit of Topsawyer's rocks—"rocks" now meaning "testicles."

The drift of this dense passage is as follows: A successful son of HCE emigrates from East to West, as his father before him. Settling in America he begets a large progeny and bequeaths to them a decent, even gorgeous prosperity. The idea of procreation and prosperity is carried forward by the expression "doublin their mumper[7] all the time," which may be read primarily as "doubling their number all the time."

[5] Mark Twain (Samuel Clemens) appears frequently in *Finnegans Wake*. Both he and his hero Huck Finn (Finn in America) were adventurers, rose to a height, and took a fall. Interestingly enough, Samuel Clemens called his wife "Livy."

[6] "Gorgio" is a gypsy word meaning "non-gypsy," also "youngster."

[7] Other hints rise from this word "mumper": "Mum," a sweet strong beer first brewed in 1492, the year of the discovery of America. HCE is identified with beer; he not only consumes and serves it in his tavern, he *is* beer. Finally, "doubling mum" introduces the Superfetation theme, the theme of

But the passage refers to Ireland, as well as to America, and precisely to Ireland of the time of the Anglo-Norman conquest. The bishop of Dublin, at that time, was Lawrence O'Toole; Dublin County would be Lawrence's County. Furthermore, in honor of his victory under the patronage of St. Lawrence, Sir Almeric Tristam, founder of Howth Castle, changed his family name to Lawrence.

> *nor avoice from afire bellowsed mishe mishe to tauftauf thuartpeatrick . . .*

The primary reference here is to St. Patrick and his Christianizing of Ireland. This saint baptizes (tauftauf) the peat rick, Ireland; *taufen* is German, "to baptize," which reminds us that St. Patrick's spiritual tutor was St. Germanicus. From a fire below comes the voice of the virgin lady of the isle—the goddess Brigit, who became St. Bridget when baptized. "Mishe mishe," she says in her native tongue, "I am, I am," thus affirming her character as the mother-substance of all being, namely, ALP. On the level of spiritual allegory, Patrick is HCE—the perennial invader—this time fructifying Mother Ireland with the gyzm of life eternal. The peat fire refers to the legendary miracle of St. Patrick's Purgatory. He drew a circle on the ground and the earth opened in flame; into this fire the most zealous of his converts descended. References to "Pat's Purge" occur several times in *Finnegans Wake*.

> *not yet, though venissoon after, had a kidscad buttended a bland old isaac . . .*

This brings us back to the Old Testament brother battle of Jacob and Esau, in which Father Isaac, wishing to bless the elder son, becomes the butt of the cadet's (younger son's) cunning. The passage may be read: Not yet, though very soon after, Jacob, disguised in the kidskin, duped his blind old father. There is also a local Irish suggestion in the juxtaposition of the words "butt" and "isaac." Isaac Butt, in 1877, was ousted from leadership of the Irish

one world burrowing on another, which is the great key to the dynamism of *Finnegans Wake*.

Nationalist party through the machinations of the younger Parnell, who himself then moved into command.

The word "venissoon" not only signifies the goat venison of the Biblical story, but points forward to the Swift-Vanessa theme, struck in the statement following:

> *not yet, though all's fair in vanessy, were sosie sesthers wroth with twone nathandjoe . . .*

"Nathandjoe" is an anagram for Jonathan (Dean Jonathan Swift) split in two and turned head over heels by his two young-girl loves, Stella and Vanessa. Not yet, though all's fair in the vain game of love, were these saucy sisters wroth with their father-sur-rogate, the two-in-one Wise Nathan and Chaste Joseph. (There exists a little riddle, attributed to Vanessa herself, which plays on Jonathan Swift's name in this way.)

"Sosie sesthers wroth" is also a transformation of the names Susannah, Esther, and Ruth, the heroines of three Biblical tales in-volving the loves of old men for young girls. "In vanessy" sug-gests Inverness, the name of the castle of Macbeth: Macbeth was seduced by the wiles of the Three Weird Sisters.

> *Rot a peck of pa's malt had Jhem or Shen brewed by arclight . . .*

One thinks of the moment after the ark had come to rest on Ararat, when Noah began to till the ground and plant a vineyard. Drinking of the wine, he became drunk and was seen naked by his son Ham. But Shem and Japheth, the other two sons, put a cloak on their shoulders, and going backward covered their father's nakedness. This passage should be construed in terms of the Fa-ther-castration theme and the superseding of the father by the sons. The three names, Shem, Japheth, and Ham, are telescoped to com-prise the Shem and Shaun duality of the Earwicker household. Instead of wine the intoxicant is beer, in keeping with the Ger-mano-Celtic pattern.

> *and rory end to the regginbrow was to be seen ringsome on the aquaface . . .*

30

And toward the orient (rory end to) the rainbow was to be seen casting its reflection on the face of the waters. This rainbow, the sign of God's promise and man's hope, with its seven hues of beauty, is one of the dominant images of *Finnegans Wake*. It balances the thunderclap, the signal of God's wrath and man's fear.

"Rory" connotes Rory O'Connor who was High King of Ireland when the royal brow of the conqueror, Henry II, came up over the eastern horizon. This brow was the coming of a new age, as was the rainbow in the time of Noah.

> *The fall (bababadalgharaghtakamminarronnkonnbronn-*
> *tonnerronntuonnthunntrovarrhounawnskawntoohoohoor-*
> *denenthurnuk!) . . .*

"The fall," and the strange polysyllable following it, introduce us to the propelling impulse of *Finnegans Wake*. The noise made by the thumping of Finnegan's body tumbling down the ladder is identical with the Viconian thunderclap, the voice of God's wrath, which terminates the old aeon and starts the cycle of history anew.

> *of a once wallstrait oldparr is retaled early in bed and later*
> *on life down through all christian minstrelsy. . . .*

"Old Parr" was the nickname of Thomas Parr (1483–1635!), of Shropshire, who lived to be one hundred and fifty-two years old. "Parr" and "wallstrait" are also plays on the rise and fall of stock-market values in the modern world. The fall of this Old Parr is the fall of Adam in the garden, Finnegan from the wall, HCE in Phoenix Park.

> *The great fall of the offwall entailed at such short notice*
> *the pftjschute* [8] *of Finnegan, erse solid man, that the hump-*
> *tyhillhead of humself prumptly sends an unquiring one*
> *well to the west in quest of his tumptytumtoes . . .*

Note the lumpishness of the wording, and the suggestion of the fall and scattering of Humpty Dumpty, the Cosmic Egg. Inquiring

[8] "Pftjschute" suggests "chute," also the hissing rush of a falling meteor— Lucifer falling into Hell.

tourists who wish to trace the anatomy of the fallen giant in the Dublin landscape must seek his head in the Hill of Howth and his upturned toes at Castle Knock in a cemetery in Phoenix Park. In this Park the Orangemen (invaders) have been laid to rest upon the Green since the first Dubliner loved Anna Liffey. This thought is concluded in the following lines:

> and their upturnpikepointandplace is at the knock out in the park where oranges have been laid to rust upon the green since devlinsfirst loved livvy.

In the next paragraph there rages around the upturned toes of the giant a turmoil comparable to that of the Roman twilight, when Ostrogoth battled Visigoth; comparable to the chaos of the deluge, where oyster battled fish; comparable to the disorder of the underworld, where an Aristophanic frog chorus croaks in a murk:

> What clashes here of wills gen wonts, oystrygods gaggin fishygods! Brékkek Kékkek Kékkek Kékkek! Kóax Kóax Kóax! Ualu Ualu Ualu! Quáouauh! Where the Baddelaries partisans are still out to mathmaster Malachus Micgranes and the Verdons catapelting the camibalistics out of the Whoyteboyce of Hoodie Head. Assiegates and boomeringstroms. Sod's brood, be me fear! Sanglorians, save! Arms apeal with larms, appalling. Killykillkilly: a toll, a toll. What chance cuddleys, what cashels aired and ventilated!

Clearly, the tone of the entire passage is brawling and primitive; early warriors are out to kill each other. This much is indicated by "clashes," "partisans," "arms," "catapelting," and "boomeringstroms." But who are these warriors? They are "wills gen wonts" —the have-not's vs. the have's—invaders vs. native inhabitants. There is a hint that the passage is symbolic of the fall of Rome; it also contains references to early Irish religious quarrels.

"Oystrygods gaggin fishygods": Ostrogoths vs. Visigoths; also a reference to the shellfish-eaters, said to have preceded the fish-eaters on the coasts of Ireland. "Gaggin" hints at the Germanic *gegen* meaning "against"; also conveys the idea that the conquest was rammed down the throats of the conquered.

"Brékkek Kékkek Kóax Ualu Quáouauh," etc.: The guttural sound "brékkek kóax," borrowed from Aristophanes' comedy, *The Frogs,* suggests a swampy, damp terrain where these early struggles took place. Allegorically, this passage hints at the post-Flood battles of primitive men.

"Ualu" and "Quáouauh": Welsh cries of lament.

"Mathmaster": *Math* is Anglo-Saxon for "mow" or "cut down," and Sanskrit for "annihilate." It is also Hindustani for "hut" and "monastery." This word says: "to overpower by cutting down men and annihilating their homes and monasteries."

"Badellaries; Malachus Micgranes": Apparently Celtic clans and families involved in early tribal wars.

"Catapelting the camibalistics": "Catapelting" suggests both "catapult" and "pelting." The first syllable of "*cami*balistics" is Celtic for "crooked and perverse." In the entire word double connotations of barbaric flesh-eating practices and ballistics are conveyed. The sentence now runs: "Certain tribes were hammering the perverse cannibalistic instincts out of their rivals by means of catapults and primitive weapons."

"Whoyteboyce of Hoodie Head": The "White-boys" were a band of religious fanatics who went about hooded much after the fashion of the Ku Klux Klan. "Hoodie Head" is perhaps, too, the Hill of Howth.

"Assiegates and boomeringstroms": The first two syllables of "assiegates" are identical with those of *assiéger* (French), "to besiege." Again, they suggest "assegai," a spear. The last part of the word being "gates," the sum becomes, "attempts by means of spears and darts to lay siege to city or castle gates." "Boomeringstroms" suggests both "boomerangs" and the booming sounds of cannon. *Strom* is a Scandinavian word for "whirlpool," which draws men down to death.

"Sod's brood, be me fear": "Sod" is "Old Sod" or Ireland. "Chil-

33

dren of Ireland, I fear for you"; also "I fear you." Sod's brood suggests "God's blood."

"Sanglorians, save": The first syllable of "sanglorians" is *sang*, French for "blood"; the first two syllables are "sanglo" which has the same sound as *sanglot*, French for "sob." Obviously, the word has overtones of blood and tears. Blood and tears for what? For "glori," which occurs in the very middle of the word. "Save" can be construed either as the Latin *salve*, meaning "hail," or the English "save," meaning "to protect." The whole expression is in the vocative: Joyce is addressing someone. "You who fought in blood and tears for glory's sake, I hail you." Or to use an alternative rendition of "save," the expression becomes: "May God protect you who fought in blood and tears for glory."

Always seek in a Joycean expression an antinomy or contradiction. He delights in saying two opposite things in the same words. Thus, while there was plenty of "blood and tears" in the obscure Irish wars, there was but little "glory." The first syllable of *"sanglorians"* suggests *sans*, French for "without." So it is quite possible that Joyce ironically says here, "You who fought in blood and tears *without* glory."

"Arms apeal with larms": *Larm[e]s*, French for "tears," repeats grief theme. *Lärm*, German for "noise," gives the din of battle.

"Killykillkilly, a toll, a toll": nothing but killing; a humorous half-reference to the two Kilkenny cats which fought till nothing was left but their tails. "Toll" hints at the sad ringing of bells for dead heroes. Also, the terrific cost in lives. The word "atoll" means a coral island. Ireland, of course, is an island. "A toll, a toll" echoes the Irish brogue, "a-tall, a-tall."

"What chance cuddleys": "Cuddleys" suggests "cudgels"; what an opportunity for cudgeling! The word also has overtones of softness and weakness. What chance would a weakling have? Or again, "cuddle" is suggested. What opportunities for chance lovemaking (in the lawless manner of the Viconian giants).

"What cashels aired and ventilated!" "Cashel": a circular wall enclosing a church or group of ecclesiastical buildings; a stone building. Turning to a gazetteer, we find "Cashel, population 3,000,

Tipperary County, at base of Rock of Cashel, 300 feet high, on which are ruins of a cathedral, a chapel, and a tower." Translated, the expression becomes, "What church walls were broken down, what fresh air was blown through musty religious institutions by these religious wars!"

> *What bidimetoloves sinduced by what tegotetabsolvers! What true feeling for their's hayair with what strawng voice of false jiccup!*

"Bid-me-to-loves" are temptresses; "tête-à-tête absolvers" are father confessors. "Teg" is a lamb or woman. "Goat" (got) is the animal of lechery. Things are so topsy-turvy that the preachers of God's word lead the prostitutes into sin.

"The voice is Jacob's voice, but the hands are the hands of Esau"; Isaac's words before blessing the usurper of the birthright are mingled with an echo of "Hayfoot, Strawfoot, bellyfull of beansoup!" Hayfoot and Strawfoot are the antagonistic brothers.

> *O here here how hoth sprowled met the duskt the father of fornicationists but, (O my shining stars and body!) how hath fanespanned most high heaven the skysign of soft advertisement! But waz iz? Iseut? Ere were sewers?* [9] *The oaks of ald now they lie in peat yet elms leap where askes lay. Phall if you but will, rise you must: and none so soon either shall the pharce for the nunce come to a setdown secular phoenish.*

The "father of fornicationists," a primordial man, has met the dust; but the rainbow, sign of the promise of his renewal, now emerges. The promise is here associated with the name and theme of Iseult, who enacts in *Finnegans Wake* a dual role; first, of tempting the all-father to his fall, and then, of gathering up and handing forward the reanimated remains. As mother, she will receive his substance and renew it in her children. As charming vir-

[9] In the list of errata that James Joyce prepared shortly before his death, he introduced these three question marks.

gin, she is the rainbow to beckon him forward again, in the coy, teasing game of expectation and despair.

With the image of Iseult and the theme of the rainbow hope, the motif of the Cycle comes before us. The oaks of the past have fallen into peat, yet where ashes lay there now spring living elms. And the phallic pun "Phall if you but will, rise you must" gives a Rabelaisian twist to the wheel of life. Nothing will end: apparent *Finish* will be converted to *Phoenix*-rebirth, as the Fall in the Phoenix Park of Eden entailed the miracle of Redemption.

These few lines of commentary are an admittedly inadequate gloss on the first four paragraphs of *Finnegans Wake*. All the literal and allegorical references compressed into these paragraphs would fill many volumes with historical, theological, and literary data. But even should the reader one day find himself in control of the entire bulk of this material, there would remain to be conquered the depths of moral and anagogical implication. Here no commentary could do more than furnish introductory clues; for it is impossible to exhaust the import of a poetical image or a mythological symbol. The present interpretation can only hint at some of the secrets of Joyce's language and indicate the great outlines of his method: the *experiencing* of the work must be left to the sensibilities of the apt reader.

Suffice it to say, that three great moments have presented themselves during the course of these opening paragraphs: (1) The Fall, (2) The Wake, (3) The Rise. The first is associated with the theme of the thunderclap and "pftjschute"; the second with the quarrels and loves of human history; the third with the sky sign, the elms, the phallus, and the phoenix. The Fall is, in a profound sense, prehistoric, and the Rise will take place at the end of time. Meanwhile, the living and quarreling of the Wake is a kind of fermentation or superfetation of maggot sons and daughters out of the body of the gigantic sleeper, "doublin their mumper" all the time. And no matter where we turn, if we regard carefully any phenomenon or complication of the world picture, we shall find that the surface configurations disintegrate to reveal, ever present, the foundation substance of the old World Father. As his initials emerge through the pattern of "*Howth Castle and Environs*," so through all the loves, all the brother betrayals, and all the ventilatings of cashels, he will go on. By a commodius vicus of recirculation, riverrun will bring us always, ever, and only back to Him.

BOOK I

THE BOOK OF THE PARENTS

Book I, Chapter 1: Finnegan's Fall

[The story of Finnegan, freed from the thematic entanglements of the first four paragraphs, now begins to run in a narrative style comparatively easy to follow. Henceforth a thin line tracing of the basic story of *Finnegans Wake* will suffice to guide the reader. It is not our purpose to elucidate fully any page or group of images, but to weld together the fundamental links of the narrative itself. Our comments are in brackets and in footnotes; the numbers in parentheses refer to the pages of the Viking Press edition of *Finnegans Wake,* 1939.

[The first twenty-five pages of Joyce's narrative (4–28) deal directly with the subject of the title theme: the fall, the wake, and the portended resurrection of the prehistoric hod carrier Finnegan.]

(4) Primordial Big Master Finnegan, free mason, lived, loved, and labored in the broadest way imaginable: piled buildings on the river banks, swilled ale, jigged with his little Annie, and would calculate the altitude of the skyscraper erections, (5) hierarchitec-titiptitoploftical,[1] rising under his hand.

---

[1] This is a good word on which to practice. Note the way in which it combines the words "hierarchy," "architect," "tipsy," and "toplofty," climbing up and up, beyond every expectation, like a skyscraper. In Joyce's text, the phrase "with larrons o'toolers clittering up and tombles a'buckets clottering down" refers to Lawrence O'Toole and Thomas à Becket, bishops respectively of Dublin and Canterbury in the time of Henry II. The former advanced his personal career, the latter was martyred.

He was of the first to bear arms and a name: Wassaily Booslaeugh of Riesengeborg. His crest, green, showed in silver a he-goat pursuing two maids, and bore an escutcheon with silver sun-emblem and archers at the ready. Its legend: Hohohoho! Hahahaha! Mr. Finn you're going to be Mr. Finn-again! In the morn you're vine, in the eve you're vinegar. Mr. Funn, you're going to be fined again!

What brought about that Thursday-morning tragedy? Our house still rocks to the rumor of it; there is a shabby chorus of those who would blame him; the evidence is difficult to evaluate.— Therefore, stay us (O Sustainer!) in our search for truth.—It may have been a misfired brick, or perhaps a collapse of back promises; but as sure as Adam bit the apple of Eve, what with the noise of the (6) traffic below, hod carrier Finnegan, high above, fell tippling full, his hod shook, he stumbled, he was dead. He is now fit for a mastaba-tomb.[2]

[We attend the Wake. Twelve dismal citizens, sighing his praises, lay him out:] "MacCool, MacCool, orra why did ye die?" There is a bottle of whisky at his feet, and a barrowload of Guinness's over his head.

[The scene begins to disintegrate. Outlines of the hills show through the lineaments of the wake.] Hurrah! It is all one and the same: Finnegan's form is that of the landscape. Let us peep at him, prostrate. From Shopalist to Bailywick he calmly extensolies. By the bay winds he is bewailed. (7) Annie's flutelike trochees wake him. Grace before glutton; Amen. Grampupus is fallen down but grinny sprids the boord.[3] Fish, bread, and ale are placed around the bier. But the moment you would quaff off the drink and sink tooth into the food (the communion drink and food of his flower-white body), behold, he is smolten in our midst. The Wake scene, like a fadeout, melts away.

[2] An Egyptian mummy tomb of stone.
[3] The key theme of the Wake: in a communion feast the substance of All-Father is served by All-Mother to the universal company.

Yet, we may still behold the brontoichthyan [4] form outlined in the contours of the land: a giant hill recumbent by the stream he loved, HCE beside his ALP.

[The Wake scene, having withdrawn into the world interior, is now to be thought of as constituting the substratum of all existence. It is the archetypal Form of all forms. Through the next seventeen pages (7–23) are to be studied various evidences, geographical and historical, of the fallen Finnegan's all-suffusing, all-feeding, slumberous presence. Not only the landscape is to be reviewed (7, 10, 12, 14, 23) but typical epochs of human history: modern history (8–10), medieval history (13–14), prehistory (15–20); also, a few fragments of folklore (20–23); a comical vaudeville song; and the dump heap in our own backyard (19). As the eye regards each, it slightly disintegrates to reveal an unmistakable trait or two of the grotesque Finnegan within.

[First, the landscape:]
The head of him can be seen at Ben Howth. His clay feet, swarded in grass, stick up, not far from Chapelizod, where he last fell on them—by the Magazine Wall, where the Maggies seen all, while the three spying soldiers lay in ambush.[5] From here a view (8) may be had of the little Wellington Museum in Phoenix Park, a charming waterloose country round about, and two pretty white villages, like the two saucy Maggies themselves, amidst the foli-

---

[4] *Bronte,* "thunder"; *ichthys,* "fish": thunder-fish. The reader will think of the Leviathan, whose flesh, together with the flesh of Behemoth, is the food of those in Paradise; also, the fish symbol of Christ, whose flesh is the food of the faithful.

[5] Finnegan's fall was on the identical spot where HCE is to become involved in his misadventure with two girls and three soldiers. On this spot there at present stands a museum dedicated to the memory of Wellington. Wellington is an incarnation of HCE. The three spying soldiers will bear various names in various parts of the text. The names will carry suggestions of one or another of England's imperialistic wars. Wellington, it will be remembered, served in India before his campaigns against Napoleon; hence a sepoy, Shimar Shin, appears as one of the three soldiers at the conclusion of the present episode.

ages. Penetrators are permitted into the museum. For her passkey supply to the janitrix, the mistress Kathe. Tip.[6]

[This Museum should be regarded as a kind of reliquary containing various mementoes symbolizing not only the eternal brother-conflict, but also the military and diplomatic encounters, exchanges and betrayals of recorded history.] An old woman conducts a party through the museum, pointing out relics from the battle career of her hero Wellington, the Iron Duke. There are exhibits under glass and pictures on the walls. A flag, a bullet, a military hat; Duke Wellington on his big white horse; three soldiers crouching in a ditch; a pair of Napoleon's jinnies,[7] making believe to read a book of strategy; and a sex-caliber telescope through which the Duke trains on the flanks of the jinnies. The reader begins to recognize through all the shooting-gallery noises and the smoke-confused scenes of battle the omnipresent story of a great man, two temptresses, and three soldiers.[8] Between the Duke and the jinnies dispatches go back and forth. This (9) is me, Belchum, bearer of the dispatches.[9] First, a dispatch from the jinnies to annoy the Willingdone: "Behold thy tiny frau, hugacting. Signed: Nap." This is me, Belchum, carrying the dispatch. And this is Wellington's answer, displayed on the regions rare of me, Belchum: "Figtreeyou! Damn

[6] The repetition throughout *Finnegans Wake* of the word "tip" finally turns out to be a dream transformation of the sound of a branch knocking against HCE's window as he sleeps beside his wife in the upper room. This branch is the finger of Mother Nature, in her desiccated aspect, bidding for attention.

[7] This word refers both to a couple of young mares on the battlefield, and to a pair of Napoleonic *filles du régiment*. These polymorphous beings correspond to the two temptresses of the Park episode.

[8] This is a reflex, of course, of the story of HCE, whose fall is to be but a variant of the fall of Finnegan. The fire water which intoxicated the ancient giant, and the two urinating girls who intoxicate HCE, are variant-aspects of the one eternal river-woman ALP.

[9] This entire passage is full of obscure references to England's many wars and must be regarded as an adumbration of the Empire theme. The characters are fluid and only half emergent, but constantly suggest Wellington, Napoleon, Blücher, and other personages of the battle of Waterloo. "Belchum" carries overtones of "Belgium," the country in which Waterloo is situated.

fairy Ann—*ça ne fait rien. Vôtre:* Willingdone." (That was the first joke of Wellington. Tit for tat.) This is me, Belchum, in his twelve-league boots, footing it back to the jinnies. [Napoleon and Wellington are exchanging insults, Napoleon being represented through the jinnies.]

Here now are some more exhibits: Balls, cannon fodder, other views of the jinnies, the soldiers, and the Willingdone. The Wellington cry is "Brum! Brum! Cumbrum!" The jinnies' cry is *"Donnerwetter! Gott straffe England!"* To the tune of "It's a long way to Tipperary," the jinnies run away. This is me, Belchum; poor the pay! This is Wellington, brandishing his telescope on the runaway jinnies. A (10) triad of soldiers is observing him; one of them is a Hindu sepoy, Shimar Shin. Suddenly Wellington picks up the half of a hat from the filth and hangs it on the crupper of his big white horse. (The last joke of the Willingdone.) The crupper wags with the hat to insult the sepoy, who, mad as a hatter, jumps up with a cry. Whereupon, Wellington, a born gentleman, tinders a matchbox to the cursing Shimar Shin. The do-for-him sepoy blows the whole of the half of the hat off the top of the tail on the back of Wellington's big wide harse. (Bullseye! Game!) This way out of the museum.

Phew, but that was warm.

[Dense with figures half lost in the dust of war, the turbulent Museum scene amplifies the private sin of HCE into an image of the hero throughout the course of history. Toward the middle of *Finnegans Wake* (338–55) an even denser, dustier episode, namely, that of the Russian General at Sevastopol, will culminate the development of this blood-and-tears theme. In the wild heat of battle, life discloses its most shameful secret—i.e., HCE's sin in the Park.

[We turn from the museum to the countryside, now a silent field after battle. Round about are twelve pilfering little birds, metamorphosed duplicates of the citizens at the Wake. The janitrix herself, in a bird transformation, moves through the twilight, gathering relics (as widowed Isis gathered the scattered fragments of her dismembered husband, Osiris).]

(10) We know where she lives: it's a candle-little house of a month and one windies.[10] The vagrant wind's awaltz around the piltdowns and on every blasted knollyrock there's a gnarlybird ygathering. Old Lumproar is lying under his seven red shields;[11] our pigeon pair has flown; (11) the three crows have flapped away. She never comes out when the thunder is roaring, she is too moochy afreet; but tonight is armistice; here she comes: a peace-bird, picking here, picking there. All spoiled goods go into her nabsack: with a kiss, a kiss cross, cross criss, unto life's end. Amen.

In this way she serves the future: stealing our historic presents from the postprophetical past, so as to will to make us all lordly heirs and lady mistresses of a pretty nice kettle of fruit. Greeks may rise and Trojans fall, (12) young heroines come and go, but she remembers her nightly duty: she'll puff the blaziness on. Though Humpty Dumpty fall frumpty times, there'll be eggs for the croaking company that has come to wake him.

[This fragment-gathering crone is identical with old grinny who spreads the feast after the Fall (7). The shell fragments of Humpty lie scattered about, but she gathers what she can of the old fellow's substance, which she will serve to the generations of the future, to sustain them and carry them forward.]

Let us, meanwhile, regard the two mounds and all the little himples, these hillocks, which are like so many boys and girls of a smaller generation sitting around playing games, Bridget with

[10] A month and one windies; 28-plus-1 windy windows. The 1 is the leap-year girl Iseult, 28 the number of her little girl companions. These represent the younger, Kate the older, manifestations of ALP. Where the one is apparent, the other is implicit. There would be no fragments lying about for old Kate to collect and cherish, had there been no seduction to precipitate a fall.

[11] In the text is a pun on the Rothschilds. Was it Byron who said that not Wellington but the House of Rothschild defeated Napoleon? The seven superimposed shields carry the suggestion, also, of the seven "sheaths" (physical, astral, mental, buddhic, nirvānic, anupādakic, and ādic) which, according to the occultists, clothe the essence of the soul.

Patrick, on his chest—his very presence urging them to love. They are hopping around his middle like kippers on a griddle as he lies dormant. And nearby is the Magazine Wall. [An echo is heard of Dean Jonathan Swift's verse on the futility of this military structure in a land picked bare by English masters:]

> Behold a (13) proof of Irish sense!
> Here Irish wit is seen!
> Where nothing's left that's worth defence,
> They build a magazine.

So this is Dublin.

*H*ush! *C*aution! *E*choland! [The initials, HCE.]

*H*ow *c*harmingly *e*xquisite! It reminds you of the outwashed engravure that we used to be drunkenly studying on the blotchwall of his innkempt house.[12] Look and you will see him. Listen and you will hear the music and laughter of the company, by the Magazine Wall—fimfim fimfim—with a grand funferall—fumfum fumfum.[13] The scene comes to us converted into sound by an optophone.[14] List to the magic lyre. They of the Wake will be tussling forever to the discord of the ollave's harp.[15]

Turn now to this ancient book, the Blue Book of our local Herodotus, Mammon Lujius.[16] "Four things," it says, "f.t. in

[12] I.e., the scene reminds us of a certain picture that used to hang in the tavern of HCE (used to hang, that is to say, in the long ago of a former cycle).

[13] I.e., regard this landscape and you will discern through it symptoms of the Wake, still in progress. "Fimfim," etc., is the jollification motif. Through many transmutations it will recur. It is the sound of a dry leaf "sinsinning" in the winter wind.

[14] An optophone is an instrument that converts images into sounds.

[15] All ollave is an Irish bard.

[16] The Blue Book of our local Herodotus, Mammon Lujius, is finally the dream guidebook, history book, *Finnegans Wake* itself. It is here regarded as any ancient tome that might be at hand. "Blue Book" suggests the well-known "Blue Guide" series of travel books. The name "Herodotus" is modified in the text to "herodotary" ("doting on heroes"). Mammon Lujius is a name based on the initials M. M. L. J. of *M*atthew, *M*ark, *L*uke, and *J*ohn, the four Evangelists whose gospels are the history book of the Living.

Dublin ne'er shall fail,[17] till heathersmoke and cloudweed Eire's isle shall pall." And these four Dublin eternals are: (1) a hump on an old man [HCE], (2) a shoe on a poor old woman [ALP], (3) a maid to be deserted [their daughter Iseult], (4) a pen no mightier than a post [their twin sons, Shem the Penman, Shaun the Post].

The traits of these archetypal figures emerge through every page of the chronicle, as the winds idly turn the pages and we read the entries for various years:

1132 A.D. Men like ants did wander upon the hump of *an old whale* stranded in a runnel. Blubber for Dublin.

566 A.D. *A crone* (14) discovered her basket to be full of little shoes. Blurry works at Dublin.

(Silent)

566 A.D. *A damsel* grieved because her doll was ravished of her by an ogre. Bloody wars in Dublin.

1132 A.D.[18] *Twin sons* were born, Caddy and Primas, to a goodman and his hag. Primas became a sentryman. Caddy got drunk and wrote a farce. Blotty words for Dublin.

[The actual historical events associated with the dates 1132 A.D. and 566 A.D. are of minor moment. Clearly more important than

Word. The four Evangelists coalesce with four Irish annalists, whose chronicle of ancient times is known as *The Book of the Four Masters*. These four again coalesce with four old men, familiars to the tavern of HCE, who forever sit around fatuously rechewing tales of the good old days. These four guardians of ancient tradition are identical with the four "World Guardians" (*Lokapālas*) of the Tibetan Buddhistic mandalas, who protect the four corners of the world—these being finally identical with the four caryatids, giants, dwarfs, or elephants, which hold up the four corners of the heavens.

[17] f.t.: four things. Abbreviation by initialing occurs frequently in the medieval Irish chronicles.

[18] 1132 A.D. St. Malachy became Bishop of Dublin, and Lawrence O'Toole was born. O'Toole and Henry II being representatives of the brother pair, perhaps we are to think of them as the twins, respectively Caddy and Primas, born in 1132. Henry II was born, actually, in 1131, only a few months before O'Toole.

any specific events are the relationships to each other of the numbers themselves.

[Every reader of *Ulysses* will recall the "thirty-two feet per second, per second. Law of falling bodies," which ran through Bloom's thoughts of the entire day. The number is now to run through the entire night of *Finnegans Wake,* usually in combination with eleven, the number of restart after finish. (The old decade having run out with ten, eleven initiates the new. See our discussion of the Cabbalistic decade for Bk. II, chap. 2.) In the present instance the two numbers combine to form a date. This date halved yields another date, 566; there follows a mysterious "Silent" (a world-destroying cataclysm) whereafter the dates appear again, but in inverted sequence—the new world being a kind of Alice-through-the-looking-glass reflection of the old.

[If we add the four dates we arrive at the figure 3396, a play on the number of the Trinity. (The reader will recall Dante's discussion of Beatrice in the first pages of the *Vita Nuova:* "Beatrice is a Nine, because the root of nine is three, and the root of Beatrice is the Trinity." In the *Divine Comedy* the created universe is but a vast amplification of this nine, which is finally a numerical sign for the world-creative fertilization of God by Himself: 3×3: Superfetation!) The sense of Joyce's play stands forth surprisingly when we add the digits 3, 3, 9, 6 and discover the total 21: the Cabbalistic number of the Fall. The Fall is the secret of all history.

[Man rooted in the Trinity yet falling 32 feet per second, falling but ever self-renewing, is symbolized in the old brontoichthyan food-father stranded in the runnel. The rib of All-Father Adam (his "better half") became Eve, and so half of 1132 becomes 566, the Crone of the basket of little shoes. After the world destroying and renewing cataclysm (Silent), the female number reappears in a little rainbow daughter, and the male number in the polarized sons.]

Somewhere, apparently, in the "ginnandgo gap"[19] between

[19] *Ginnunga-gap* ("Yawning Gap") is the name given in the Icelandic *Eddas* to the interval of timeless formlessness between world aeons. An aeon

46

566 A.D. and 566 A.D., the copyist must have fled with his scroll; or the flood rose; or an elk charged him; or the heavens discharged their thunder at him. Killing a scribe in those days was punishable by a fine of six marks or nine pence, whereas only a few years ago a lady's man was hanged for taking that sum covertly from the drawers of his neighbor's safe!

But now let us lift our eyes again from the tome to the idyllic land. The pastor is reposing under the stonepine; the young buck and doe are nibbling at the grasses; the shamrocks are modestly growing among the blades; the sky is ever gray. Thus it has been for donkey's years, since the primeval bouts between he-bear and hairy-man. The cornflowers have been staying at Ballymun; (15) the duskrose has chosen out Goatstown's hedges; twolips have pressed themselves together by sweet Rush; the whitethorn and redthorn have fairy-gayed the May valleys of Knockmaroon; warrior races have come and gone—Fomorans have fought against the Tuatha De Danaan, Firbolgs against Oxmen, pagans against Christians; Little-on-the-Green is childsfather to the City; yet, the blond has sought the brune and the dark dames have talked back to the lightish fellows, and they have fallen upon one another, and themselves have fallen; now-anights even as of yore, the bold pretty floras are inviting their shy lovers to pluck them.

[Thinking on these things, we become aware, guide and tourist, of a fire on yonder hill, and in the flickering light, a figure looms.]

This carl in pelted thongs, like a stone age Parthalonian—who is he? Is he a Mousterian cave man? He is drinking from a kind of skull. (16) What a queer sort of man! Let us cross the heaps of gnawed bones into his firelight. He can, perhaps, post us the way to the Pillars of Hercules. *"Comment vous portez-vous aujourd'hui, mon blond monsieur?* 'Scuse us, Charlie, you talk Danish?"

"N."

"Norwegian?"

"N.N."

endures 432,000 years. Joyce occasionally employs 432, the legendary date of Patrick's arrival in Ireland, as an alternate for 1132.

"English?"

"N.N.N."

"Saxish?"

"N.N.N.N."

Well then, he must be a Jute. Let's have a chat.

[Guide and tourist, now merged into one, have entered the fire-light in the form of a dull, prying, somewhat timorous island-native, Mutt. The lumbering stranger from overseas, with thick and sometimes stuttering tongue, taps his chest and introduces himself, in Germanic accent, as a Jute:]

"Yutah!"

"Pleased to meet you," Mutt replies obscurely.

"Are you deaf? Deaf-mute? What is the matter with you anyhow?"

"Not deaf," answers Mutt; "but I have suffered somewhat damage from a bottle in a local tavern—or rather, from a battle at Clontarf."

Jute stutters, "Hauhauhauhorrible!" Then he gives the blurry native a shake. "Come on! Wise onto yourself! Wake up!"

Mutt, cringing and resentful at the unexpected show of force, disconnectedly belches something about usurpers and the Celtic champion, Brian Boru.

Jute attempts to calm him with a bit of wooden money, a tip. "*Ein Augenblick!* Let bygones be bygones! Business is business. Take this bit of *Trinkgeld* and go buy yourself a drink."

[Perceiving that the money is wooden, the native now definitely identifies the stranger as the perennial invader.] It is he of the billowing greatcoat, Cedric Silkyshag! [20] Obsequiously, now, the native attempts to ingratiate himself by calling attention to the local points of historic and scenic interest: "The spot where Humpty Dumpty fell; (17) by the river, here, the place of the liverish monarch, Mark the First; under the moon, there, Little Mary's Pass; the old stone by the pool." But the great man hardly shares the native's wonder before these things. He has it straight from Taci-

[20] Sihtric, king of the Danes of Dublin, A.D. 1040.

tus simply that a barrow of rubbish was dumped here. Tired of Mutt's half-intelligible patois, he makes to move away.

Mutt stays him a moment. "All right," says Mutt; "but wait a sec. Take a turn around these ancient plains, where the whimbrel once did wail to pewee, and where cities once will rise. From the old inn out there on the Hill of Howth to this Park of the Phoenix the glaciers did spread. Two races have merged here, a sweet and a salt; like tides they have played against each other. Stories have fallen, thick as snowflakes, and they all lie now entombed. *Fuit Ilium.* (18) *Mild und leise.*[21] Here in under they lie —large and small, he and she alike. The ancestral earth has swallowed them. However, this earth of ours is not brickdust but humus. It is fertile. The old figures return. The old round with its four stages will certainly pass again" Then Mutt, abruptly breaking off, with a hush and a whisper begs the fare to Dublin. "Sh!" says he. "Hold your whisht!"

Jute has impatiently listened, with occasional deprecating interjections. Now he sticks on the Irish word "whisht." Mutt resumes: he indicates where the giant lies, and the fay; where lies the Viking grave. "Are you astonished, you stone-aged Jute, you?"

"I am thunderstruck; I am Thor's thunderstroke, I am Thingmote." [22]

[The archaic figures fade. We are following the finger, not of Mutt, but of a learned Courier, conducting a little group of tourists. We are examining the soil for relics of the most distant past.]

"Stoop," says the teacher-guide, "if you are interested in alphabets, to this clay. What signs, please stoop, are here! It is the old story of miscegenations. Neanderthal tales of a Heidelberg heathen

[21] *Fuit Ilium* (Virgil, *Aeneid,* II, 325): the words of the High Priest at the moment of the fall of Troy.

Mild und Leise: first words of the love-death aria of Wagner's *Tristan und Isolde.*

[22] *Thingmote:* the Scandinavian tribal council. Thor, the god of thunder, was patron of the *Thing;* Thor's-day, Thursday, was the opening day of the *Thing.* Jute is at once the invader, the political system of the invader, and the patron god of that system: the thunder pronouncement of the new age.

meandering in the ignorance that breeds the desire that moves the round of existence. Consider these primitive artefacts: a *h*atch, a *c*elt, an *e*arshare. The purpose of the plowshare was to *c*assay [break] *e*arthcrust at all *h*ours [HCE, the plowshare; ALP, the earth]. Here are bellicose little figurines [the Twins]. Here is a naughty little female effigy. Oh, I fay. Ho, you fie! [the Seductress motif]. Up boys, and catch them face to face! [the Three Soldiers]. When a (19) part so *petit* does duty for the whole, we soon grow to use of an allforabit [alphabet]. Here, please to stoop, are pellets such as were used for soldiers' pay. These terrible rocks were for war. Here you behold a midden horde. Here are owlets' eggs. O stoop to please. Snake worms were wriggling everywhere until Patrick came and cotched them all away.

"And now we may study the origins of the earliest books. Axen strokes in ones and twos and threes [the One, the Two Temptresses, the Three Soldiers] they were composed of. They communicated to sons and daughters messages from the ancestors—which will remain with us till doomsday. There was no paper yet; the pen still groaned to give birth to its mouse; but the world is, was, and will be, writing its own runes forever. (20) Begin with a bone or pebble; chip them; leave them to cook in the mothering pot—and Gutenberg with his printing press must one day, once and for all, step forth. Finally, then, you will make the acquaintance of Mr. Typus, Mrs. Tope, and all the little typtopies. So every word in this book of Doublends Jined—till the riverrun that opened it finally brings it to its deltic close at the end of a mahāmanvantara [23]—will be bound over to carry no end of readings.

"For instance, see what you have in your hand. The whole thing is in movement, and with many a tale to tell. The story of One that spied upon Two, was caught by Three, and set the whole town talking. Stories of the old wife and her forty bairn, of old Noah and his mash, of a grave man and a light woman, of golden youths fit for gelding, of what the naughty girlie made the man

[23] A world cycle or aeon (Sanskrit).

50

do. Let us take for example, the tale of Jarl van Hoother [24] and the Prankquean:

(21) "Of a night, late, long time ago, when Adam delved and Eve span, when life and love were wild and free and everyone did as he pleased, Jarl van Hoother, the melancholy widower, was alone. Tristopher and Hilary, his two little jimmies, were kicking their dummy about on the floor of his *h*omerigh,[25] *c*astle, and *e*arthenhouse. And be dermot, who came to the keep of his inn only the prankquean. She asked for a poss of porter. And that was how the skirmishes began. The lord of the castle refused her, in Dutch, and the door was shut in her face. So her grace o' malice kidnaped the little Tristopher and carried him off to her wilderness in the west. Jarl van Hoother bellowed after her, but she carried the boy away. She had the child instructed by her four wise old masters, and he became a blackguard.—Then around she circulated and, be redtom, after a brace of Halloweens, she was back again at Jarl van Hoother's, where Hilary and (22) the dummy were kicking about, like brother and sister, on the floor. She asked for two poss of porter. Van Hoother again refused her. The door was shut in her face. So she set down little Tristopher, picked up little Hilary, and ran off with him to the west. Jarl van Hoother cried after her, but she carried the boy away. She had the child instructed by her four wise old monitors, and she made a Cromwellian out of him.—Then around she circulated, and, be dom ter,

[24] The Earl of Howth and Grace O'Malley (1575). A jarl is a Scandinavian chieftain; the word "jarl" is related to the English "earl." The story goes that Grace O'Malley, returning from a visit to Queen Elizabeth, paused at the door of the Castle of Howth for a night's lodging. The family was at dinner at the time, and the door was rudely slammed in her face. Whereupon she managed to kidnap the little heir of the castle and made off with him to her own castle in Connaught. She refused to return the boy until his father had solemnly promised that the doors of Castle Howth would never again be closed at mealtime. In the present version the events are recounted thrice with modifications, after the manner of the fairy tale, and under the influence of the family pattern of HCE. There is also a play on three historical attempts to reshape the beliefs and institutions of Ireland: the Elizabethan Anglican, the Cromwellian Puritan, the modern socialist.

[25] Vanhomrigh, the father of Dean Swift's Vanessa.

after a pair of transformations, she was back again at Jarl van Hoother's, where the jiminy and the dummy were making love upon the floor. She asked for three poss of porter. And that was how the skirmishes ended. The Jarl himself, the old terror of the dames, came hippety-hop out the portals of his castle, (23) dressed in his ample costume. He ordered the shutter clapped in her face. It was shut. (Perkodhuskurunbarggruauyagokgorlayorgromgremmit-ghundhurthrumathunaradidillifaititillibumullunukkunun!) [26] And they all drank free. For one man in his armor was a fat match always for any girls under skirts. And that was the first piece of alliterative poetry in all the flaming flatuous world: a sweet exposure of the Norwegian Captain.[27] It was resolved that the prankquean should hold to the dummy, the boys keep the peace, and van Hoother let off steam. He is the joke of the entire town."

[This tale concludes the little study of landscape and museum evidences. The prehistoric figures of Mutt and Jute, the medieval notices of the Blue Book of Mammon Lujius, the comparatively recent histories of the Wellington Museum, the entire sweep of the landscape, a certain midden dump (17, 19) and the fantasies of popular tales, all have revealed unmistakable symptoms of a common substratum. We are not surprised to see now, dimly at first, but then gradually more strongly, the Wake scene re-emerging through the traits of the land.]

Oh, happy fault,[28] that drew from heaven the promise of redemption and the descent to man of that precious, unique Son of

[26] The thunder voice (cf. p. 3) resounds now through the anger of the old Jarl. It is his own impotence that has unstrung him.

Note: Unless otherwise specified, page references in the footnotes are to the pages of Finnegans Wake.

[27] The Norwegian Captain we shall meet in Bk. II, chap. 3; he is the Flying Dutchman aspect of HCE. The prankquean is ALP as seductress. The point is, that this folk tale, selected at random, discloses, as does everything else in the world, the traits of our guilty hero and his fall. All conforms to the family pattern of HCE, ALP, their daughter, and the twins.

[28] *"O felix culpa,"* St. Augustine's celebration of the fall which brought the redemption through God's love, "O Phoenix Culprit!" is its usual form in *Finnegans Wake.*

the Father! From the evil action of the devil proceeds the great boon of the Annunciation. Regard again the configurations of this countryside. Behold again the enormous hulk of the fallen sinner, and beside him, the little stream. Cloudcap is on him; his vales are darkling. With lips she lisps to him all the time of such and such and so and so. Impalpable, he reappears, and the waves, the Four Waves of Ireland,[29] are pounding against the promontory of his head. Landlocked by his mistress, perpetuated in his off-spring, the poets could tell him to his face and her to her pudor puff, how but for them, our life-givers, there would not be a spire in the town nor a vessel floating in the dock, nor a single one of us.

(24) He [All-Father Finnegan] gained his bread in the sweat of his brow. He delivered us unto death. And he would again, could he awaken. And he may again. And he will again. Have you whines for my wedding, did you bring bride and bedding, will you whoop for my deading? For my darling is awake! [Someone cries out:] *"Whisky!"*

[The old man stirs to rise. He hollers in his native tongue:] "Soul of the devil, did ye think me dead?"

[Whereupon the twelve gentlemen hasten to hold him down and to soothe him back to sleep. For a new and prosperous world age has been founded on the fact of his demise. It would be nothing short of catastrophic to have the old substratum himself break back into action.]

"Now be easy, good Mr. Finnegan; lie back and take your rest like a god on pension. Things have changed. You wouldn't know the place. You might only be getting into trouble. 'Tis hard to part from old Dublin, sure! But you're better off where you are. You have everything you want. We'll be regularly coming to tend your grave. We'll bring (25) you proper offerings. . . . Your fame is spreading, the fame of the fine things you did for us. . . . They're calling you grand and fancy names. . . . There was never your like in the world. . . . (26) We've left where you dumped it

[29] The Four Master Annalists are known as "The Four Waves of Ireland."

53

that barrow of rubbish. . . .[30] Your form is outlined in the constellations . . . be not uneasy, you've been decently entombed. . . .

"Everything's going on the same old way: coughing all over the sanctuary; three square meals a day; the same shop slop in the window; meat took a drop; coal's short; barley's up again. The boys are attending school. (27) Kevin's a fine little fellow, but the devil gets into Jerry now and then. Hetty Jane is a Child of Mary. Essie Shanahan has let down her skirts and is making a rep, dancing twice nightly at Lanner's. 'Twould delight your heart to see her."

[At this last bit of news the old giant stirs mightily. The men of the company settle him firmly.]

"Easy, easy now, you decent man! Hold him, gentlemen, hold him! It's our warm spirits he's sniffing. Cork up that bottle, O'Flagonan! Fetch here, Pat Koy, give a hand!

"I'm keeping an eye on the household: on Behan, old Kate, and the butter. (28) Your missus is looking like the Queen of Ireland: too bad you're not around to talk to her, as you did when you drove her to the fair. She was flirtsome then, and she's fluttersome yet. She's fond of songs and scandals. Her hair is as brown and as wavy as ever. So rest you! Finn no more!"

[Then they break to him the important news of the arrival of a man who has supplanted him. The heroic, carefree, gigantic times are past. The family man has arrived: HCE.]

"By the hooky salmon, there's already a big lad on the premises, (29) with his Shop Illicit, flourishing like a baytree. A pocked little wife he has, two boys, and a midget of a girl. Round and round he goes; so there's neither beginning nor end to what it was he was seen doing in the Park. But no matter what his scandal may be, he has created for his creatured ones a creation. *H*umme the *C*heapener, *E*squire, has arrived in the twin turban dhow, *The Bey for Dybbling*. And he has been seen reproaching

---

[30] Compare the "wholeborrow of rubbages dumptied on to soil here" (p. 17). This is the midden heap from which the hen, Belinda, is to unearth the letter (p. 110).

54

himself like a fishmummer these sixty-ten years ever since. He is
the big and only One, who will be ultimendly respunchable for
the *h*ubbub *c*aused in Edenborough."

Book I, Chapter 2: HCE—His Agnomen and Reputation

[HCE has supplanted Finnegan. Vico's giant has given place to
Vico's patriarch. An impossible legendary age has been superseded
by the actualities of historic man. Or again, to employ another of
the allegories, the fabulous days of comical granddad have yielded
to the presence of HCE, our living father.

[HCE entered the book mysteriously at the close of Chapter 1.
He arrived from afar and from the ocean, updipdripping from the
depths, "one tide on another, with a bumrush in a hull of a
wherry" (29). This arrival, a vivid birth image, represents the
coming into being of *Homo sapiens* at the close of the Ice Ages,
or of Western Man after the fall of Rome; it represents, too, the
birth of the individual after the night of the womb, and the dawn
of ego-consciousness.

[The following three chapters deal with the stories of the very
earliest days of HCE. Properly, the hero of these chapters is the
infant, half-remembered; the chubby tumbler through whose obscene little deeds and vicissitudes were established the outlines of
character that today appear in the man. Something went wrong
somewhere, but we never quite know what it was. For, as Joyce
declares (51), "in this scherzarade of one's thousand one nighti-
nesses that sword of certainty which would indentifide the body
never falls." Little being known of the facts, gossip, rumor, and
dream memory are at work. The remote events have become thoroughly confused with adventures much more recent.

[Pages 30 to 32 recount the dim legend of how the hero came
by his nickname. The passage may be read as of Adam (HCE)
delving in his garden, who suddenly finds himself playing host to
his Lord and Master. Or it is the story of HCE as an infant in the
nursery, tiny overlord of the tin spade and bucket, visited patroniz-

ingly by his father with a retinue of bemustached cronies. Again, it is the tale of a medieval Irishman visited by the king.

[Through pages 32 to 103 HCE's early biography develops obscurely, in the smoke of half-report. Charged with all the crimes in the calendar, and tried before the double bar of court and populace, he emerges humorously and sympathetically, an epic paradigm of Everyman, bearing his burden of griefs with patience and with only slightly tainted dignity. The present chapter (30–47) treats of the origin of the hero's reputation. Chapter 3 (48–74) describes his trial and incarceration. Chapter 4 (75–103) is the chapter of his disappearance and extraordinary return—the gradual demise of the infant and his reincarnation in the man, the conversion of early into modern times.]

(30) First, then (and postponing for the moment the case of the two girls in the Park), as to the genesis of his agnomen, nickname, or honorary title. There exist many untrustworthy theories. Some would link him back to the first families of Sidlesham. Others would proclaim him an offshoot of Vikings settled in Herrick or Eric. The best-authenticated story is the Dumlat account (read the version of Hofed-ben-Edar [1]). One sultry sabbath afternoon, in pre-Fall paradise peace, while the grand old gardener was plowing in the rear of his house, royalty was announced to have halted itself in the course of a foxhunt on the highroad. Forgetful of all save his vassal's plain fealty, Humphrey, or Harold, stumbled out hotface as he was, in topee, surcingle, sola-scarf and plaid, plus-fours, puttees, and bulldog boots, (31) jingling his turnpike keys and bearing aloft a high perch atop of which was a flowerpot fixed with care. His Majesty, instead of inquiring directly why yon causeway was thus potholed, asked to know what flies were being favored these days for lobster-trapping; whereupon honest blunt Haromphreyld replied: "Naw, yer maggers, aw war jist acotchin' on thon bluggy earwuggers." Our sailor king smiled beneath his walrus mustaches and turned toward two of his retinue—

---

[1] Ben Edair was the earlier, Celtic name of the Hill of Howth. Dumlat, read backwards, is Talmud.

56

Michael, lord of Leix and Offaly, and Elcock, the jubilee mayor' of Drogheda—and remarked dilsydulsily: "Holy bones of St. Hubert, how our red brother of Pouring-rainia would audibly fume did he know that we have for surtrusty bailiwick a turnpiker who is by turn a pikebailer no seldomer than an earwigger!" (One can still hear the laughter in the rustling of the roadside tree, and feel the responding silence in the stone.) But now we must ask the question: Are these the facts? (32) There is a fallacy to be heaved aside, namely, that it was not the king himself, but his inseparable sisters, Shahrazad and Dunyazad,[2] who made this remark. In any case, the great fact emerges, that after that historic date, all the documents so far exhumed, initialed by Haromphrey, bear the *sigla,* HCE. And while he was always good Dook Umphrey to the hungry rascals of Lucalizod, and Chimbers to his cronies, the populace gave him as sense of those letters the nickname Here Comes Everybody. Indeed, an imposing everybody he always looked every time he surveyed, from his viceregal booth, the assemblage gathered in the opera house to see a command performance of the problem passion play, *A Royal Divorce,* with the band playing during intermissions selections from *The Bo' Girl* and *The Lily.* (33) With all his house about him, he was a veritable folksfather, a broad-stretched kerchief cooling his whole neck, nape, and shoulder blades, in a wardrobe paneled tuxedo completely thrown back from the most outstarched shirt in the house.

Foul slanders have been raised against him, and these are to be loftily refuted. For instance, into the very characters, HCE, the man's detractors have read a baser meaning: (*a*) It has been said that he suffered from a vile disease. (*b*) It has been insinuated that he was once reputed to have annoyed Welsh fusiliers in the people's park. But to anyone who knew and loved the christlikeness of the big clean-minded giant, the mere suggestion of him as

---

[2] The sister heroines of the Arabian *Thousand Nights and One Night,* who regaled King Shahryar with their endless story cycle, and thus distracted him from his cruel design to ravish and slay a maid a night. They are comparable to the Two Temptresses in the Park. Their bedside tales correspond to ALP's letter and *Finnegans Wake* itself.

a lust sleuth rings preposterous. (c) Truth, however, compels one to add that there is said to have been, once, some case of the kind —implicating a certain anonymous one, who, about that time, was in the habit of walking (34) around Dublin. It is stated that this anonymous one was posted at Mallon's, at the instance of watch warriors of the vigilance committee, and years afterwards seemingly dropped dead while waiting his dole of a chop somewhere off Hawkins Street. (d) Yet slander has never been able to convict our good man of any graver impropriety than that, advanced by some watchmen who did not dare deny they had that day drunk their share of the corn,[3] of having behaved with ungentlemanly impropriety before a pair of dainty maidservants in the rushy hollow whither the pair had been sent by a call of nature. However, the published testimonies, where not dubiously pure, are visibly divergent on minor points touching the intimate nature of this admittedly incautious but, at its wildest, only partial exposure. It was a first offense with extenuating circumstances.

Such things can't be helped. Guiltless he was of much that has been laid to him; he has said so himself, and hence we have accepted (35) this to be true. (e) They tell the story, how, one happy-go-gusty ides-of-April morning, ages and ages after the alleged misdemeanor, when the tried friend of all creation was billowing across our greatest park in his caoutchouc kepi and rubberized Inverness, he met a Cad with a pipe. The latter accosted him with the drunken demand, could he tell him what o'clock it was? Earwicker, realizing the supreme importance of physical life and unwishful of being hurled into eternity then and there, halted, quick on the draw, and produced from his pocket his watch; but, on the same stroke hearing the ten-ton bell in the speckled church, he told the inquiring kidder it was twelve. And he seized the occasion to stutter thickly—bending to give more weight to the stick he presented—(36) that, whereas the accusation against him had been made by a creature in human form who was quite beneath par and several degrees lower than a snake, he was willing any day to take his stand upon the Wellington Monument, that sign

[3] The Three Soldiers.

of our redemption, and to take his oath upon the Open Bible, in the presence of the Deity Itself, of Bishop and Mrs. Michan of the *H*igh *C*hurch of *E*ngland, and of every living soul which useth the British tongue, that there is not one tittle of truth in that purest of fabrications. In support of his word he tapped his watch and, standing full erect with gauntleted hand chopstuck in the hock of his elbow (gesture meaning: Ǝ!),[4] pointed at an angle of thirty-two degrees toward the Iron Duke's overgrown memorial.

The Cad, swift to make errors, sterne to check himself[5] (realizing that he was here having to do with a (37) type of paleolithic cave-man ethics), bade the man good morrow (a little taken aback all the same that that was all the o'clock it was), and then went about his business (one could have followed him by the scurf and dandruff droppings that blazed his trail), murmuring to himself his reflections on the encounter, and repeating verbatim what he could of the big-timer's words.—Along the quiet darkenings and dark murmurings of the Grand and Royal canals came suppertide. Spitting about the hearthstone, if you please (Irish saliva; but would a respectable fellow who knew the correct thing expectorate after such a callous fashion, when he had his handkerchief in his pocket, pthuck?) and having supped his favorite pottage, this Cad, to celebrate the (38) occasion of his happy escape, sat mixing it with a bottle of Phenice-Bruerie '98, followed by a Piessporter, Grand Cur, of both of which he obdurately sniffed the cobweb-crusted corks.

Our Cad's wife, with a quick ear for spittoons, having overheard her husband repeating the words from his encounter in the Park,

[4] This inverted E is the mark of HCE himself, perhaps referring to the divine essence within, of which his corporal appearance is only the mirror image. (Compare "Dog—God," in *Ulysses!*) Lying on its back (ɯ) the sign represents the Fall (see p. 6). Standing on its legs (m), the sign appears to indicate the prehistoric, megalithic monuments erected by our hero in earliest times, and so, his primordial, gigantic, hairy-man aspect. See Joyce's footnote to p. 299, "The Doodles Family," where each member of the household is given his particular runic sign.
[5] Swift and Sterne form a brother pair in *Finnegans Wake.*

broached the matter, among 111 others, in her usual courteous fashion, the next night but one, over a cup of tea, to her favorite priest, trusting that it would go no further than his Jesuit's cloth. Yet it was this very priest, Mr. Browne, disguised as a Vincentian, who was overheard, in his secondary personality as a Nolan,[6] to whisper a slightly varied version of the confidential words into the ear of one Philly Thurnston, a lay teacher of rural science and orthophonethics, (39) at the racetrack, during a priestly flutter for a tip on the races at Baldoyle, the day after the classic Encourage Hackney Plate was captured by two noses from Bold Boy Cromwell, after a clever getaway, by Captain Chaplain Blount's roe hinny St. Dalough—Drummer Coxon third; thanks to you, great little Winny Widger, you're the greatest jockey ever topped our timber maggies! It was a couple of coves, Treacle Tom, a crook fresh out of jail, and Frisky Shorty, a tipster fresh off the boat, that chanced to overhear the parson as he whispered. Now this Treacle Tom was a habitué of wild and wooly haunts. On a racenight, blotto after divers tots of rum (40), he sought bed in a cheap rooming house, Abide-With-One-Another, in the slums. There he resnored alcoholically the substance of the tale, fragmentarily, during uneasy slumber, within hearing of the three down-and-outers, Peter Cloran, O'Mara (locally known as Mildew Lisa[7]), and Hosty. The last of these, melancholic over everything in general, had been tossing on his cot devising ways and means of going off and putting an end to it all, for he was after having been trying

---

[6] Brown and Nolan, a firm of booksellers in Dublin. It was they who backed the publication of Joyce's youthful paper, *The Day of Rabblement*. Brown and Nolan play a major role in *Finnegans Wake* as representatives of the embattled brother pair.

In Joyce's *The Day of Rabblement,* Giordano Bruno of Nola was referred to as "Bruno the Nolan." Bruno's theory of the final identity of opposites underlies the brother play of *Finnegans Wake*. The words Bruno and Nolan easily combine with Brown and Nolan. Joyce plays with them continually. In the present passage we observe the splitting of a single cleric (Giordano Bruno himself, perhaps) into the brother opposites of "Bruno-Browne" and "Nolan."

[7] *Mild und leise:* the first words of the love-death aria of Wagner's *Tristan und Isolde* (cf. p. 18).

eighteen months to get himself into the bed of a hospital, (41) without success. Lisa O'Deavis and Roche Mongan [note that the names are shifting form] slept, as an understood thing, in the one sweet tumblerbunk with Hosty—and the bustling maid-of-all-works had not been many jiffies furbishing the household, when they were all up and ashuffle across the chilled hamlet of Dublin, to the thrummings of a crude fiddle, caressing with their ballad the ears of the king's subjects, who, in their brick homes and flavory beds, with their priggish mouths all open, were only half past a sleep. After a brisk pause at a pawnbroking establishment to redeem the songster's false teeth, they indulged in a prolonged visit to a house of call, namely, the Old Sot's Hole in the parish of St. Cecily, not far from the site of the statue of Premier Gladstone, and here (42) they were joined by a further fellow, casual and a decent sort, of the had-been variety. They all enjoyed a drink on the damn decent sort, and then, flushed with their fire-stuff-fostered friendship, the rascals came out of the licensed premises, and the world became the richer for a would-be ballad: Hosty's Lay, to wit, of the vilest bogeyer but the most attractionable avatar the world has ever had to explain for. [That is to say, the group came forth with a pasquinade against HCE.]

This ballad ["The Ballad of Persse O'Reilly"] they poured forth by the Liffey, under the Gladstone Monument, to a supercrowd (43) representative of all sections and cross sections of our people. The war arrow went round. Headed by a rough and red woodcut, privately printed by the press of Delville, the ballad soon fluttered its secret on white highway and brown byway from archway to lattice and from black hand to pink ear, village crying to village, throughout every county of Ireland.—To the added strains of a flute, which the Mr. Delaney drew out of his decent-sort hat, (44) "Ductor" Hitchcock hoisted his fezzy fuzz at bludgeon's height for silence, and the canto was chantied there, by the old tollgate.

And around the lawn it ran. And this is the rann [8] that Hosty

---

[8] A rann is an ancient Celtic verse form. There are many stories of Irish poets who revenged themselves against ungenerous or brutal kings by com-

made: "Some call him this, some call him that, but I call him Persse O'Reilly." Come on, Hosty! Leave it to Hosty, boys, for he's the man to rhyme the rann, the rann, the king of all ranns.[9] Have you heard? Do you hear? Here it's coming! It's brimming! This is the end of the old glass-stone deliverer! This is the tumble of the Gladstone Monument. "The (klikkaklakkaklaskaklopatz-klatschabattacreppycrottygraddaghsemmihsammihnouithappluddy-appladdypkonpkot!) Ballad of Persse O'Reilly." [10]

The ballad tells how Humpty Dumpty fell and curled up like Lord Oliver Cromwell by the butt of the Magazine Wall. (45) Once King of the Castle, now he's kicked around like a rotten old parsnip, and he'll be sent to the penal jail of Mountjoy. He was fafafather of all schemes for to bother us: contraceptives for the populace, open-air love, and religious reform. Arrah, says you, I'll go bail for him: all his butter is in his horns. (46) With his bucketshop store, *He*'ll *C*heat *E*'erawan they called him. Soon we'll bonfire all his trash, and Sheriff Clancy'll be winding up his un-limited company. Gall's curse on the day when Eblana Bay saw his Black-and-Tan man-o'-war. He's a Norwegian camel old cod. He made bold a maid to woo, and it was either during some fresh-water garden pumping or while admiring some monkeys in the zoo. (47) He ought to blush for himself. He was jolting by Wel-lington's Monument, when some bugger let down the back trap of the omnibus, and he caught his death of fusiliers. Sore pity for his children and missus. When that frau gets a grip of him there'll be earwigs on the green. Then we'll sod the brave son of

posing satires against them; and frequently (or so they say) the kings literally died of the shame.

[9] "The Wren, the Wren, the King of all Birds, St. Stephen's Day was caught in the furze." A traditional verse sung on St. Stephen's day, when a wren is killed and carried about the town hung on a stick. This Scapegoat Wren is a folk reduction of the crucified god, and as such is an appropriate figure for HCE. The echo of this verse runs through many pages of *Finnegans Wake*.

[10] The thunder noise this time is in the uproar of the ballad, and the fall is that of a reputation. *Perce-oreille* is French for "earwig."

Scandiknavery, we'll bury him in Oxmanstown, with the devil and the Danes. And not all the king's men nor his horses will resurrect him—for there's no spell that's able to resurrect a Cain.

[Thus scholarship, after careful review and evaluation of all the evidence, has reconstructed the earliest history of our hero: his arrival from the deep, the position of trust which he enjoyed as bailiff and bearer of the keys under the eyes of a genial king, the curious origin of his *sigla,* HCE, the bulky dignity of his folk-fatherly presence at the theater. Then come rumors of his fall from grace and a meticulous study of the various stories. There follows an account of his unfortunate encounter in the Park with a tramp-like figure who inquired of him the time, whereupon, in great nervousness, HCE stuttered forth an uncalled-for defense of his entire past. The tramp returned to his poor Irish hearth, where his wife overheard him repeating what he could rehearse of the great man's self-defense. With that, the repressed story sank to the depths of what might be called the social unconscious—that slum world of poverty and failure underlying the presentable spheres of the folk-father's orderly city. From the Cad's wife it went to a questionable priest, who in turn was overheard by a crook and a tipster; the crook resnored the tale in a flophouse, where three down-and-outers picked it up. They, then, with the aid of miscellaneous alehouse acquaintances, sang the whole thing forth to the wide world in the form of a scurrilous ballad. As we shall later learn, HCE thereby lost a popular election.]

Book I, Chapter 3: HCE—His Trial and Incarceration

[The next chapter attempts to follow the history of the trial that resulted from the scandal. Joyce plays with this as a scholar's problem even more difficult than the first. For there have been (it would seem), during the long course of the years, no end of cases of this kind. The features of the parties involved melt confusingly into one another. Yet, through the baffling surface uncertainties emerges an undeniable archetypal configuration, and this, with utmost plausibility, presents itself as the inevitable hero, HCE.

[We begin with a consideration of the effect of the ballad, and a warning of the difficulties to be encountered by the student who would distinguish through mists of time and rumor the precise outlines of the history.]

(48) Talk about unpleasant predicaments! You spoof about visibility in a freak fog, about mixed sex complications, and about the Blackfriars' treacle-plaster outrage! Gentlemen, that ballad [of Persse O'Reilly] released a cloud of poison the like of which this kingsrick has never seen! But it was all so long ago! Those who heard the ballad, together with those who sang it, are today as much no more as though they were yet to be, or had never been at all. Let us consider how they, severally, disappeared from life—the persons in this *Earwigger Saga* (this saga, which, though readable from end to end, is from top to bottom all false tissues, antilibelous, and nonactionable). Of Hosty no one end is known. (49) O'Hara [i.e., O'Mara], crestfallen and down at heels at the time, accepted, they say, the Saxon's pay for service in the Crimean War; he wandered a bit as a wild goose; he enlisted again and soldiered a bit with Wolseley under the assumed name of Blanco Fusilovna Bucklovitch [i.e., Blank, daughter of a gun, son of Buckley]; after which, on the other side of the water, inauspiciously, with his daughter, he perished. Paul Horan [i.e., Moran] ended up in a lunatic asylum. Under the name of Orani he may have been the utility man of the troupe. Sordid Sam passed away painlessly, one Halloween night, propelled from Behind into the great Beyond by foot-blows, after declaring: "Now let the hundredfold selves of my ego-urge, by the coincidence of their contraries, reamalgamate in that identity (50) of undiscernibles where the Baxters and the Fleshmans may they cease to bedevil us." Langley disappeared from the surface of the earth without leaving so much as a trace. His case would lead the speculative to all but opine that the hobo had transferred his habitat to the murk of the earth's interior.—And now we must bend our mind to a more difficult

problem of identity; that, namely, of the priest in the case, of a certain objectionable ass with a raffles ticket in his hat, and of the Cad with the pipe. We are perhaps justified in saying, that, if Father San Browne is Padre Don Bruno,[1] then perhaps both the revered sodality director and the objectionable ass were the same snob with the pipe, encountered by the General on that red-letter morning or May-noon Thursday?

[That is to say—and during the next nine pages (50–58) everything will be done to drive this fact soundly home—the characters of our piece are very hard to fix and distinguish from each other. Here, for instance, the long line of gossiping antagonists enumerated in the last chapter (35–44) threatens to fuse into a single mercurial personality, that of Mr. Browne–Mr. Nolan; and this man, furthermore, is found to have some of the traits of the victim, HCE himself. Still further, HCE has begun to shift shape a little; he is now called "the General." Finally, the hour and day of the encounter are no longer quite as clear as they first appeared to be. Throughout the remainder of *Finnegans Wake,* the reader must watch sharply for incoherent shifts of scene and character; a deluge of gossip has confused the evidence, mixing this story with many another, splitting personalities and recompounding them, mixing centuries, countries, heroes, villains, and tenses, in a great broth.

[And so we read:]
When the deluge of gossip is loosed at a man, 'tis folly to be flaunting fortune; gone to Mix Hotel by the salt say water, he's never again to sea—and there's next to nothing we can do to re-establish the facts of his case. Nevertheless, it is a well-vouched-for fact that the shape of (51) the average human face frequently alters its ego [that is to say, one average person is frequently mistakable for another]. Therefore it is difficult to identify the individual who now appears on the scene. It is very difficult (since in this Arabian Nights Entertainment the sword of certainty which would identify the body never falls), to identify the individual in

[1] See p. 38 for the beginning of this Bruno-Browne complication.

the billowing costume who was asked by three truants to tell them again the story of the Haberdasher, the two Girls, and the three Boys. My, but he has changed since the old days of Thor's streamlet! One, two, three, four, five, six, seven, eight, nine! Look at all those warts, slums, and wrinkles, and the large mungo-park he has grown! [2]

It was the Lord's own day for damp. The request for an explanation was put to this billowing party, as he paused at even-chime for a fragrant calabash. It was during his week-(52)end pastime of executing, with Annie Oakley deadliness, empties which had not very long before contained Reid's Family Stout. Having re-primed his repeater and reset his timepiece, His Revenances rose to his feet, and there, far from Tolkaheim, in a quiet English garden, his simple intensive curolent vocality called up before the truant trio the now mythical habiliments of Our far far-off Father, Author of our days.

[The reader is being asked to see double. A personage very like old HCE himself has been challenged by three truants (who surely remind us of the Three Soldiers) to retell the old story of the Haberdasher (HCE). But the challenge has something the quality of the encounter in the Park, and it will become increasingly difficult, during the course of the next few pages, to keep the more modern alehouse personage distinct from the ancient hero of his tale. In fact, the challenged personage has just been called "His Revenances"; he is a reincarnation of the very man whom he has risen to defend.]

But now let television supplant telehearing, and permit our eyes to behold the man whom the talker is describing: his broad beaver, his four-in-hand bow, his great overcoat, his refaced unmentionables, his gruff woolselywellesly with its buttons, and the gauntlet upon his hand which had struck down the man of whom the nation had seemed almost ready to be about to have need. The talker briefly described the touching scene to our soon-to-be second

[2] Mungo Park (1771–1806), Scottish explorer of the Niger. A reference to the transformation of little England, subjugator of little Ireland, into imperial Britain, subjugator of the planet.

parents. (53) Like a landscape by Wildu Picturescu, or a scene from some dim Arras tapestry, his description comes across the air to us.

Oft thereafter, while joggling in a jaunting car, Jew will tell to Christian, saint to sage, the saga of that fall and rise. Let us try to conjure up the great side show, the scene of that original encounter in the Park: the tree and the stone, the august oaks, the monolith rising stark from the moonlit pine barren, the Angelus hour with ditchers bent upon their farm utensils, the soft belling of the fallow milch deers. And how brightly the great tribal magistrate did out the sharkskin smoke-wallet (imitation!) from his frock, and tip the fellow a topping cheroot, bidding him just suck that brown boyo, my son, and spend a whole half hour in Havana. [Which is a version of the encounter with the Cad rather flattering to HCE.] Then it was told how the Cad had met Master at *Eagle Cock Hostel* on Lawrence O'Toole Street and had wished him a strange wish, namely, had wished His Honor all the pancakes of Gort and Morya and Bray Head and Puddyrick sitting like a starchbox in the pit of his stomach. [Which is still another version of the event.]

Indeed, with all the changes of time, it is very difficult to know what took place. King William's up and Cromwell's (54) down: up boys and at him! Ay, the figures of the past are lost, and yet we can discover many remembrances: Vercingetorix [3] and the Poor Old Woman and the Magistrate's daughter Anne—these figures of history and daily life re-embody the old archetypes anew. Are the old ones dead, or sleeping soundlessly? Lend ears and you shall hear.

Hear, for instance, this babel of tongues, these people of the world who legislate and converse in the very shadow of his tomb. Any day you list you may hear them all, as they pass the bleak and bronze portal of his Palace of Peace; men, boys, and girls, of the Moslem, Bulgarian, Norwegian, and Russian parliaments [4]—

[3] Defender of the Gauls against Caesar. Often identified with HCE.
[4] The *pot au feu* language of the text is difficult but finally decipherable. *Ulema* was the name of a Moslem theological body in the pre-War Turkish

chattering in their sundry tongues. You will recognize his accents in all they say.

Or hear this voice coming over the radio, and again you will recognize the living accent of HCE. Over the microphone, with crocodile tears, he summons attention to himself. Tuck away your nightly novel, girlie; listen to him advertising his credits in oleaginous, foreign English, as he calls the whole universe to witness: "Sure as my Liffey eggs," says he, "is known to our good householders, ever since the ancient centuries of the mammoth, to be that which they commercially are in high British quarters, my tavern and cow-trade credits will immediately stand oh-oh-open, as straight as that neighboring monument's fabrication, before the whole hygienic gllll(55)lobe, before the great schoolmaster's smile!"[5]

The house of Atreus is fallen, but deeds bounds going arise again. "Life," as he himself said once, "is a wake; and on the bunk of our breadwinning lies the cropse of our seed-father." The scene, refreshed, reroused, was never to be forgotten. Later in the century, one of that puny band of fact-ferreters, a popular courier, rehearsed it, while bumping along in a trans-Hibernian jaunting car. The tourists thereupon beheld the seasonal cycle itself as an allegorical restatement of that great one's career, while their convoy wheeled encirculingly about the trunk of a gigantic tree. And all those hearing (56) the popularizer's description could simply imagine themselves transplanted across centuries and listening to an evocation of the doomed but always ventriloquent Agitator, silk-hatted against the dusk, his arm protended toward that overgrown lead pencil which was soon to be his mausoleum, while

government. *Storthing* is the parliament of Norway; *Duma,* of Czarist Russia; *Sobranje,* of Bulgaria. The ten lines of conversation snatches are caught from the lips of a cosmopolitan passing crowd.
[5] Through the sound of the radio advertisements, we hear the voice of HCE calling the whole universe to witness that his wares are as straight and true as the Wellington Monument, and have been so since the beginning of time. "The great schoolmaster's smile" is God's own countenance approving of this universal salesman.

over his features the ghost of resignation diffused its spectral appealingness.[6]

Not otherwise, in primeval days, might some lazy scald or wandering poet have lifted weary-willy eyes to the signs of his zodiac and longingly learned there of a warm hospitality prepared for him, then half begun to smile.

What about that smile? we ask. In pragmatic terms, what formal cause drew a smile from *that* train of thought? Who was that man? To whom smiling? On whose land was he standing?—No matter where he may have been standing (57) time and tide will have transformed all the landmarks. Yet we can discover pointers enough to gauge the compass of the composition: the forefather, the two peaches, the three Chinamen lying low. We'll just sit down here on the hope for a ghost. Hark! The voice of the Four Old Men and their Donkey![7] They answer from their respective Zoa zones: "I," says the one from Ulster, "and a'm proud o'it." "I," says the one from Munster, "God help us!" "I," says the one from Leinster, "and say nothing." "I," says the one from Connaught, "and what about it?" "Hee haw!" brays the Donkey. Then, all together, the four old ghost voices proclaim: "Before he fell he filled the heaven; a streamlet coyly coiled him; we were then but Thermidorian termites. We sensed our ant-heap as a great mountain: and it was a rumbling among the pork troop that thunderstruck us as a wonder, yonder."

Thus, the unfacts, did we possess them, are too imprecisely few to warrant our certitude, and the evidence-givers too untrustworthy.

[6] The drift of this passage is somewhat as follows. No matter where the traveler gazes, at whatever landscape in whatever century, he perceives the shadows and hears the echoes of the life-mover primarily personified in HCE. The "always ventriloquent Agitator" is Joyce's way of suggesting that his hero is the life force everywhere and variously inflected.

[7] This is the first outright appearance of the four old chroniclers. Their voices come to us as we sit musing on the richly historical landscape. Through the present pages, as we try to review the great masses of evidence fragments of every kind, the images race in a swift and confusing sequence before our eyes. These pages demand strict attention and very slow reading. The Four Old Men are counterparts of the Four Zoas of the later visions of William Blake.

Nevertheless, at Madame To-show-us' [Tussaud's] wax museum
he appears completely exposed. There he sits gowned about, in
clerical habit, watching the bland sun slide into the nethermore, a
maudlin tear about to corrugitate his mild-dewed cheek,[8] the farewell note of a tiny victorienne, Alys, pressed by his limp hand.

Yet, one thing is certain: ere the following winter, he was
solemnly tried before a rota of tribunals in manor hall; while in
chit-chat house [the gossip of the commoners] he was likewise
tried, but sentenced. (58) His beneficiaries are legion. They have
waved his green boughs o'er him as they have torn him limb
from limb. With cries and groans and abyssal sighs, the twelve
good citizens have re-enacted over him the traditional feast of
primordial Finnegan's wake. Granny has spread the board. There
have been singing and dancing, food and drink for all. But lo!
By the lamenting gods! The unforgettable tree-shade of the grand
old personage himself looms up behind all the petty jostling of
those malrecapturable days.

[We now consider, one by one, the opinions of the man in the
street:]

Three Tommies of the Coldstream Guards, walking in Mont-
gomery Street, concurred, it was the first woman souped him, Lili
Coninghams, by suggesting they go in a field. A coming young
actress, interviewed in a West End beauty parlor, (59) said, while
adjusting her hat, she hoped he would get a bouquet of orange
and lemon sized orchids, as the world had been unkind. An entychologist remarked, obiter dictum, to his dictaphone, that he is
prehistoric, and his proper name is a properismenon.[9] A dustman

[8] *Mild und leise,* again. We are in the presence of a wax-museum portrait
of Dean Swift, who is represented as musing on the love-death of his
Vanessa.

[9] This sentence is typical of Joyce's tremendous condensation of meaning.
"Entychologist" and "properismenon" do not occur in any dictionary, but
contain roots and overtones which yield a rich harvest of significance.
"Entychologist" suggests the Latin, *ens, entis,* meaning "being." The Greek
entychia means "conversation," and *entychon,* "one met by chance." The
word may be read to mean, "a conversationalist met by chance and skilled

from Glendalough [St. Kevin], asked by the sisterhood the vexed question during his collation in a hash-house, responded impulsively: "All our fellows at O'Dea's say he is a cemented brick, buck it all!" An exceptionally sober cab-driver took a strong view: "Irewaker is just a plain pink-joint reformee in private life, but folks have it that by Brehon Law he has parliamentary honors." A well-known continental chef said: "You wish to have homelette, yes, lady? Your hegg he must break himself." A perspiring old tennis-player panted: "I have no time to collect information, but the frisky troterella, I understand, climbed the wall and pressed the doorbell." A railway barmaid expressed the view: (60) "It would be a scarlet shame to jail him." Brian Lynsky, the cub curser, gave a snappy comeback: "Them two bitches ought to be leashed, canem!" A would-be martyr, when grilled on the point, revealed that so long as Sakyamuni played tricks under the bodhitree with shady nymphs (*apsaras*) sheltering in his leaves, there would be fights all over Cuxhaven. The seventeen-year-old revivalist, Ida Wombwell, said, "That perpendicular person is a brute." "Caligula," the Australian bookmaker, was, as usual, antipodal, with his: "Striving todie, hopening to mellow." El Capitan Boycott sang out: "We have meat two hourly, matadeer." Lord Sniffbox

in the science of being." But the word resembles "entomologist," "one skilled in the science of insects." This resemblance adds an amusing overtone, for is not that earwig, Mr. Earwicker, the *ens, entis,* of all?

But what is this entychologist actually saying about Earwicker? "He is of prehistoric origin and his name is a properismenon." This latter word suggests the Greek *properispomenon,* i.e., "a word having a circumflex accent on the penult." Such a word is "Iris; such a word, too, is *Menis;* these may be concealed in the syllables, "eris-menon." Iris was a Greek rainbow goddess; *Menis* means "wrath of the gods." Cf. Rainbow-Thunder. But *Menis* suggests "Menes," the first Pharaoh. Add the facts that the syllable "ris" means a cereal (rice), that the Egyptian Pharaoh is the incarnation of the god of grain, and the connection with HCE is reinforced. The fusion in one word of a goddess and a king suggests the Hermaphrodite theme: the emergence of the temptress Eve from the very body of her lord. Finally, Greek *smenos* means "beehive," "swarm"; *peri* means "around," and *pro* means "before." Perhaps we may read: "His proper name, a properispomenon, precedes and surrounds [i.e., is the root of and represents] a swarm."

and Lady Flatterfun took sides and crossed and bowed to each other's views and recrossed themselves. "The dirty dubs went too free," declared two dainty drabs. (61) Sylvia Silence, the girl detective, when supplied with information, leaned back in her really truly easy chair to query restfully through her vowel-threaded syllables: "Have you evew thought, wepowtew, that sheew gweatness was his twadgedy?" Jarly Jilke ended with: "He's got the sack that helped him moult, instead of his gladsome rags." Meagher, a naval rating, with whom were Questa and Puella, said, while saddling up his pants: "I lay my finger buttons he was to blame. But I also think, by the siege of his trousers, there was something else behind it."

Now what about all these fablings? Can it be that such diversified outrages were planned and carried out against so stanch a covenanter? Many of the notices, we trow, are given us by some who use the truth but sparingly. One fact, however, comes out clearly, namely, that this city, (62) his citadel of refuge, whither (if accounts be true) beyond the gales of Adriatic he had fled, shipalone, a raven of the wave, to forget, in expiating, manslaughter, and to league his lot with a papist shee, this lotus land, Emerald Ilium, in which his days were to be long by the abundant mercy of Him Which Thundereth From On High, this land would rise against him, do him hurt, as were he a curse. Indeed, he was to be the victim of Ireland's first reign of terror.

[For almost fifteen pages (48–62) the narrative has been bogged in a great confusion of problems, all resulting from the fact that the events in question occurred very long ago. Those who heard and sang the ballad are gone. The personalities of that distant day tend to coalesce; they seem to reappear through the features of men who must have flourished centuries later than themselves. There is the problem, for instance, of that bulky gentleman, challenged by three truants in a pub, who rose ponderously to retell the tale of the Great Man, the Two Girls, and the Three Soldiers. Indeed, the presence of the primordial fathei may be recognized through every trait of history and of the contemporary scene. He lives in the landscapes visited by tourist parties, in the babel of modern parliaments, in the oleaginous radio voice presenting plausible credentials. And when we question the man in the street, we find that everyone, from lord and lady to drab and dustman, knows and is willing to judge the rights and wrongs of the great story.

[Abruptly, now, we are to break out of this tangle of suggestive but not quite clarifying exhibits, and for a while we shall follow a relatively direct narrative: the tale of an encounter, arrest, and incarceration. The encounter comes to us in two versions, and we must judge between them. The entire case resembles that of an American sugar-daddy and his peaches, and so we pause a moment to see a movie version of a love-nest scandal. And the history is complicated by a couple of mysterious episodes: namely, the posting of a certain letter, and the disappearance of a certain coffin. Finally, we shall follow the unhappy later histories of the two women in the case. Nevertheless, through all these complications, the narrative will proceed with relative smoothness, and we shall be able to study, step by step, the progress of the hero.

[The story, curiously enough, will have a strangely intimate meaning. In the depths of our psyche we shall recognize it as our own. Just as in the Egyptian Book of the Dead, where one follows the journey of a soul through a dreamlike landscape to the Throne of the Lord of the Dead, so here, the voyager is not specifically this man or that, but Man, that is to say, ourselves.]

Studying this narrative, we seem to us (the real Us!) to be reading our own Amenti in the sixth sealed chapter of the Going Forth by Black.[10] We read, for instance, that after the show at Wednesbury, this tall man [HCE], humping a suspicious parcel, when returning too late on his way home, had a revolver placed to his face with the words, "You're shot, Major!"—by an unknown assailant (masked) against whom he had been jealous over one

[10] Amenti: the region of the dead. After beating back the demons, the soul reaches the regions described in the "Chapters of the Coming Forth by Day in the Underworld." (Book of the Dead.)

or another of two girls. And when the waylayer (63) pointedly asked what business this tall man had with that fender, it is reported he was answered, that that was for him to find out if he was able. But this account of the incident is transparently untrue, for it does not accord with the facts. One might ask: Why was that heavy-built Ablebody there in a gateway? Was it in connection with a girl? Or was it to explode his twelve-chambered revolver and force a sheriff's entrance? In a butcher-blue blouse and with a bottle in his possession, he was seized after dark, at that very gateway, by the town guard. Whereupon he stated, muttering Irish, that he had had too much to drink; furthermore, that he was falling up against the pillar of the gateway only because he had mistaken it for a caterpillar,[11] and finally that he was a process server and was merely trying to open a bottle of stout by hammering his *magnum bonum* against the bloody gate to call the boots. Maurice Behan, the boots about the Swan, [hastily threw on a pair of old pants, stepped] [12] into his shoes, and came down (64) to the tiltyard from the wastes of sleep, attracted by the noise. Questioned, he declared he was awakened by hearing hammering from the blind pig, and anything like it in the whole history of the Mullingar Inn he never! The battering babel had reminded him of foreign musicians' instruments or the last days of Pompeii. Furthermore, it had brought down the young lady, desperate, and had started the old river woman all over the place, as mud as she could be. . . .

[At which point, suddenly, the American sugar-daddy digression:] Let us turn our eyes to the reel world. Come on, you boys and girls, settle back for a strawberry frolic! First appear the ads. (65) Then comes the following popular feature: Take an old geeser who calls on his skirt. He vows her to be his own honey-

[11] Cf.: "The Caterpillar on the Leaf / Reminds thee of thy Mother's Grief." (William Blake: *The Gates of Paradise,* "The Keys.")

[12] The words bracketed appear in an earlier version of the text published in *transition* (Paris, June, 1927, p. 42); they are missing in the edition of 1939, obviously by printer's error.

lamb, swears they will be papa pals, by Sam, and share good times way down west in a guaranteed happy love nest. She wants to hear from him by return, with cash, so she can buy her Peter Robinson trousseau and cut a dash with Arty, Bert, or possibly Charley Chance (who knows?). But old grum he's not so clean dippy, between sweet you and yum; for, some place on the sly, old grum has his peaches number two, and he would like to canoodle her too some part of the time; so that if he could only canoodle the two, all three would feel genuinely happy; if they were all afloat in a dream-life-boat, hugging two by two in his zoo-doo-you-doo, in his tippy, up-in-down-dippy, tip-top-tippy canoodle, can you?— Finis.

Noise of the film flapping. Applause. Our mutual friends, the fender and the bottle at the gate, would appear to be in the same boat! (66) Moral: There is no use putting a tooth in a thing of that sort. And moral: The amount of all those sort of things which has been going on all over the world has been particularly stupendous.—To be continued.—Presented by Federals' Uniteds' Transports' Unions' for Exultations' of Triumphants' Ecstasies.

Resuming inquiries, we approach the two mysteries of a certain posted letter and a stolen coffin: (1) Will it ever be the postman's strange fate to hand a *h*uge *c*hain *e*nvelope, signed yours *A* Laughable *P*arty, to *H*yde and *C*heek, *E*denberry, Dublin, W.C.? Will whatever will be written in that envelope always seem to have been composed in that Siamese doubletalk used by Sterne, Swift, and jolly Roger? Or will this pouch filled with litterish fragments lurk dormant in the paunch of a pillarbox, till the little old hen pokes her beak into the matter? [13]

(2) A certain coffin, it appears, has been removed from the premises of Oetzmann and Nephew, a noted house which supplies funeral requisites of every needed description.—Why needed? Because of those brides at the Nivynubies' Finery Ball (67) and those grooms that always come right up with you; what else in this

[13] The problem of this letter will be taken up again (pp. 93, 104).

·mortal world, when their hour strikes, would bring these brides and grooms back, thumbs down, to their ashes? [14]

[But to proceed, at last, with the narrative of the arrest of HCE. Having canvassed public opinion of the man (50–62), and having examined and rejected as false a report of his encounter with a masked assailant (62–63), our authority finally accepted as possibly true a strange story of his arrest for thumping at the gate of his own residence (63–64). The study of this story was interrupted, however, by an American analogy (64–66), and then a suspicious notation of the disappearance of an envelope and a coffin (66–67). These latter will reappear during the course of the next chapter and will apparently justify the deduction that even before HCE's official arrest on a trifling charge, an incriminating hen-wife rumor was running wild (the letter), and an outraged public was already preparing to see the great man into his grave (the coffin). The remainder of the present chapter will be devoted to a sketch of the public trial of HCE, in which a surprise witness overturned the policeman's testimony (67), then to a brief review of the later histories of the two temptresses of the Park episode (67–69), finally to an account of how HCE was ultimately incarcerated for his own protection and roundly insulted through the door of his cell (69–73). A concluding passage speaks of the cairns that will stand as evidence of these ancient affairs until the crack of doom (73–74).]

(67) Long Lally Tompkins, the special constable, swore on the stand before the proper functionary, that he had been up against a right queer sort of man [15] in this butcher of the blue shirt. After delivering some *mutt*on chops and meat *jutes* on behalf of Messrs. Otto Sands and Eastman, Limerick, Victualers, this butcher had gone and hic-kicked at the Dun and Dorass Inn against all the rules. And when challenged, he had said simply: "I, upon my

[14] The coffin will be encountered again in the next chapter (p. 76).
[15] Cf. p. 16: "What a queer sort of man!" The Mutt and Jute episode was a greatly distorted dream variant of the archetypal Park encounter between HCE (Jute) and the Native Antagonist (Mutt). This antagonist is, variously, the Cad, the masked assailant, the policeman, and the ballad gentry.

oath, Captain Phyllips!" That is to say, he had been completely drunk. But at this point Constable Long Lally Tompkins was politely interrupted by a certain Marc Partland, who declared him to be knee-deep in error, whereupon Long Lally Tompkins' phizz fell, and his case with it.

Now to the other side of the problem. The heavy Ablebody's excesses are thought to have been instigated by one or either of the causing causes of all; namely, those two rushy hollow heroines in their skirtsleeves. One of these delilahs, Lupita Lorette, shortly after, in a fit of unexpectedness, drank carbolic acid and paled off. The other soiled dove, her sister-in-love, Luperca Latouche, finding (68) one day that she stripped teasily for binocular men, took to necking, partying, and selling her spare favors—offering to mankind precisely that hot delicacy which was dished up to the great MacCool by our own little Annie of the Chili-red Cheeks. For did not little Annie again and again tempt the man from Asia Minor toward his tumble? [16] And did he not misbrand her behavior with iridescent hue and cry down the streets? A queen of the fairy people, a queen of pranks; a kingly man, of royal mien, regally robed: she offered, he hesitated; eyes ravenous, he hears her voice of days gone by, hears but cannot answer. Nor is any memorial required, either to mark the spot, or to expose how blackmailers do cash in on regrets! For if violence (69) has been the typical expression of offended womanhood, has not levy of blackmail always dogged every impressive private reputation?

Now let us turn again to the problem of the wall. Such a wall, and with a hole in it, existed in primeval times, before bronze or wrath ever came to Ireland; before the giants and their midden hordes ever defaced the garden of Woden. The mound is still there

[16] HCE as "the old man from Asia Minor" is a theme founded on two lines of mythological tradition. First: In the Irish cycles the races invading Ireland are represented as having sailed from the lands about Thrace and Phrygia. Second: In the Germanic cycles Woden (with whom HCE is identified) is fabled to have come overland to Scandinavia from Troy. From Scandinavia, then, he descended with the Vikings upon Ireland.

to see, and we'll be coming to the bared facts if you'll be patient.[17] There was a great gate, after the style of Stonehenge. The able-bodied optimist had bought and enlarged here a shack, in which to grow old and happy for the remnants of his years. [At last we are on the track of what would appear to be the most dependable account of the obscure circumstances of the man's incarceration!] He had put a gate on the place to keep out donkeys. And then, just about that time, the iron gate was triple-padlocked on him for his own protection!

Oh, by the by, it ought to be always remembered, that there was an Austrian Herr Betreffender, in number 32 at the Rum and Puncheon, (70) paying 11 shillings a week,[18] mixing business with pleasure, swapping broken Irish for broken German, reporting "The Adam Case" for the *Frankfurter Zeitung,* a continental periodical; and he attested that someone swiped his Melton cloth coat, and that either the same should be returned to him, or he would obtain, with a thousand *Donnerwetters,* a pretty mess of damages. In fact, the entire butchery was a tissue of threats and abuses. For instance, there was an unsolicited American visitor from the Middle West. After having blown some Quaker Oats in through the house king's keyhole to attract attention, this man bleated through the gale, hog-calling and hurling insults, from eleven-thirty to two in the afternoon. Meanwhile, Earwicker long-(71)suffering, in the sit-it-out corner of his conservatory, with his thermos flask, fan, and walrus-whisker-bristle tusk-pick, compiled a long list (now feared in part lost) to be kept on file, of all the abusive names he was called; as, *Firstnighter, Informer, Old Fruit . . . Bogside Beauty . . . Remove that Bible . . . Tight before Teatime . . . Acoustic Disturbance . . . Hatches Cocks' Eggs . . . Luck before Wedlock . . . Peculiar Person . . . Left Boot Sent on*

[17] Again we are digging for evidence into a prehistoric mound. The entire story may be regarded as something drawn out of the subsoil of the soul. This aspect of the theme will become elaborately developed in connection with the discussion of the mystery of the letter which is to be dug up (Bk. I, chap. 5) by a little hen.

[18] 11:32 (see pp. 13–14).

Approval . . . Cumberer of the Lord's Holy Ground . . . Last Past the Post . . . etc., (72) etc., etc., to the number of one hundred and thirteen. But anarchistically respectful of the liberties of the noninvasive individual, Earwicker did not respond a solitary word, because, as he explained when at last shocked into speech, the Dominican mission was in progress at the time and he thought the Romish devotion known as the Holy Rosary might reform him. The unpleasant visitor, before ringing off, drunkishly pegged a few polished stones, all of a size, in support of his words. Then reconnoitering through his semisubconsciousness the seriousness of what he might have done had he really carried out his terrible intentions, he let down the whole cluster of brook pebbles, and then, having sobered up a bit, he (73) quite quit the paleologic scene, after exhorting Earwicker to come outside and be brained. Then, intoning the first couplet of the fugal trope, Opus 1132, *My schemes into abeyance for this time has had to fall,* he proceeded in the direction of the deaf and dumb institutions, about ten or eleven hundred years lurch away, in the moonshiny gorge of Patself on the Bach.

And thus came to close that last stage in the siegings round our archicitadel.

Yet he left souvenirs at many another door of Oxmanswold, as witness his chambered cairns that stand silent, up hill and down coombe, at *H*owth, at *C*oolock, or even at *E*nniskerry. Oliver's Lambs they call them. And they shall be gathered unto him, their shepherd, as little clouds unto great, in that day when (74) he shall wake from earth-sleep to the mighty roll of the horn.

For in those days his God shall call to him; and he shall reply in Latin, "Here I am. Soul of the devil, did ye think me dead?" [19] Silence, O Troy, was in thy festive halls when thy green woods went dry, but there will be sounds of mirth again when our pantry-Patriarch of Constantinople, sitting on the side of his bier, finally gets the pullovers on his boots.

Meanwhile he slumbers. Is his liver poor? Not a *b*it of *i*t. His

[19] Compare the cry of resurrected Finnegan, p. 24.

brain is cool, his pelt humid, his heart is adrone, his blood stream acrawl, and his extremities—located severally at Finglas, Pembroke, Kilmainham, and Baldoyle—are subdued. His puff is but a piff. He slumbers. Words weigh no more to him than raindrops to Rathfarnham. Which we all like: rain: when we sleep: drops. But wait until our sleeping stops.

[Scholarship, through enormous difficulties, having established in Chapter 2 the circumstances of the hero's agnomen and reputation, in Chapter 3 has discovered the main outlines of the history of his arrest and incarceration. The details of a curious night encounter, reminiscent of the earlier encounter with the Cad, are set forth, but they remain obscure. It is even possible that this episode, here presented as following the sorry episode of the ballad, may be simply a reduplication of the earlier encounter. But our scholar has evidently decided that it represents an indipendent event. And, as the first encounter—the encounter with the Cad with the pipe—led directly to the rumor which led to the ballad, so this encounter with an officer of the peace led to a trial and presently to incarceration. It is to be noted that the trial itself (67) went in our hero's favor. But public rumor rose so strongly against him, that he was later incarcerated for his own protection (69).

[A striking feature of this chapter is its tendency to let the figure of the hero and his antagonists become merged. We have already noted the discussion on pages 50–51, where the many characters who had spread the scandal tended to combine in the figure of a certain Mr. Brown[e]–Mr. Nolan; this figure itself then threatening to coalesce with HCE. It must now be noted that the officer of the peace, Long Lally Tompkins (63, 67) has a good deal of HCE about him, and that the unsolicited American (70–73) is simply not distinguished from HCE throughout the last three paragraphs of the chapter. The continental reporter too (69–70) is but a chip from the old tree. In short, the antagonists are the two sides of a one-same power of nature. As we soon shall see, they are "polarised for reunion by the symphysis of their antipathies" (92).]

Book I, Chapter 4: HCE—His Demise and Resurrection

[What can our hero have been thinking during those hours when he was enduring the abuse of that unsolicited American?]

(75) As the lion in our zoo remembers the lotuses of his Nile, so it may be that the besieged bedreamt him still and solely of those two lily-liliths undeveiled who had undone him. At the time of his misdeed he had been gone with age and unaware of the traitors at his wake. Or it may be that he previewed (reviewed) the fields of white-heaped wheat wherein the corn goddess (is her name Ysit?) had shamed and shone. Or, finally, it may be that he prayed, during that three and a hell of hours,[1] that his word-wounder might father a distinguished dynasty of (76) black-faced mongrels; for it was one of his besetting ideas that there should be formed a criminal caste, to eliminate desultory delinquency[2] from the general economy of the state.

[The stolen coffin of page 66 now abruptly reappears:] The teakwood coffin mysteriously removed from the premises of Oetzmann and Nephew was destined presently to reappear, and this is the story:

Any number of conservative public bodies made him, while his body still persisted, their present of a grave of the best Lough Neagh[3] pattern. It was in a fairly fishy condition. It was enriched with ancient woods and dear dirty deeps, an old knoll and a coy troutbeck (may the quilt of her brown ripples adorn lightly his somnolent form!).

This underground heaven, or mole's paradise, (77) first of its kind in the west, was damned and blasted by means of a hydro-

---

[1] One gets the impression that HCE's trial and incarceration are intended to symbolize the crucifixion and entombment of Christ.

[2] The words "much desultory delinquency" appear in the version printed in *transition* (Paris, July, 1927, p. 47). They are omitted from the edition of 1939, obviously by printer's error.

[3] Lough Neagh: a great lake in North Ireland. The name means "Lake of Healing."

mine, which was exploded from a bombing post out of an aerial torpedo, which contacted with the expectant mine field by tins of improved ammonia that were lashed to her shieldplate gunwale and fused into trip-up cables, which latter slipped through tholes and played down from the conning tower into the ground-battery fuse boxes. The ferro-concrete result was then carefully lined with rot-proof brick and mortar. When the job was finished, the engineer who had constructed it, the Master Builder himself, retired to the seven towers of his Castle Villainous; thus encouraging additional councils public to present unto him a stone slab bearing the inscription: "We have done with you, Heer Herewhippet, skidoo!"

Every imaginable gadget of funerary bric-a-brac had then to follow into the prepared grave, enabling that round-the-worlder (78) to live all safe-at-homely, lethe-lulled between explosion and re-explosion, from giant head to giant foot, embalmed, of grand age, rich in death anticipated.

But abide the summons of time! The Rise after the Fall! Buried, but proliferating through all the secret seams of the nether regions, burrowing in Gehenna, propagating there all his popular tinware, the divine one would worm his way back, presently, to the utilitarian surface.

Curiously enough, old Foughtarundser [HCE] permitted himself to be entombed. Breedabrooda had at length persuaded him to be septuply buried in Finntown. But he had not been three monads [three months] in his watery grave, when putrefication began to ramp, ramp, ramp the boys are parching. There was a lightning flash and a flood was loosed. And it is furthermore a problem whether the war which broke out at this time, with its spring offensive on the heights of Abraham,[4] was in any way

[4] The great wars which follow the death of HCE correspond to the noisy brawl at the wake of Finnegan and the brother battles of the sons. With the death of the Master, chaos supervenes.
Throughout this paragraph resound overtones from the American Revolution and Civil War: Heights of Abraham, vigilantes, blessing paper freed the flood (Emancipation Proclamation), bully on the hill (Bull Run). The Irish Americans who carried forward in these wars their ancient struggle

connected with the demise of our hero; or it may have come about all quite by accident. Then there began circulating the rumor that the old patrician had scared some fellows with his grunt, because of all the musketading at the door. There was a battle in progress between New South Ireland and Ancient Ulster, over the question "With the Pope, or On the Pope." Men of all conditions were drawn toward their war goddess's black bottom; from both Celtiberian camps they came, miserables in need of pay, each, of course, on the purely doffensive, since the eternals were owlwise on their side every time. Emancipated from his long fast in the grave, the old specter may have (79) taken advantage of the darkness over the plain to trick the fellow with an illusion of his former corpulence. For it was generally felt among the opposition, that Master Earwicker (who had been known in his days of false plenty—his barmecidal days—to get around his own length of rainbow trout and tarts) must now, like a salmon, be feeding secretly and by suckage on the fat of his own hump.

[This concludes the prehistory of HCE. Like Finnegan of the vaudeville song he suffered a fall, was laid out for dead, and remained in a heavy coma while a noisy quarrel raged among the survivors. He may be expected to revive.

[The remainder of the present chapter deals with the aftermath of the great story. It falls into three distinct sections. The first (79–81) publishes the recollections of an old woman, Kate, who professes to be the widow of the great man.[5] The second (81–96)

against the Anglo-Saxon are for Joyce representatives of the opposition to HCE (cf. England's sympathy with the Confederacy). They add to the theme of the brother battle, a New World theme—a theme of renewal and rebirth of hope. But Joyce is not sentimental about the actualization of this hope. The New World letter from Boston, Mass., which we shall encounter on pages 110–111, reveals all the old motifs, alive as ever, beyond the sea.

[5] Kate, Kathe, Kathleen na Hoolihan, Old Mother Ireland, widow of the ancient Finn MacCool, serves as housekeeper in the establishment of HCE. She had grand old recollections of the grand old days, when it was Finn MacCool, not H. C. Earwicker, who was master man of Ireland. She is

presents the evidence of a posthumous trial, in which there appeared, as witness and accused respectively, two young men betraying the traits not of HCE himself but of his sons, Shem and Shaun. Here, for the first time, appear the patterns which are later to become characteristic of these two. Since the boys enter the stage with a court scene, in which the old history of their father is rehearsed, it is clear that they have inherited not only fractions of the character but even something of the life history and guilt of the fallen patriarch. The final section of this chapter (96–103) deals with the problem of the disappearance of the body from the grave, its possible reappearance anywhere, and the condition of the plucky little widow, ALP.]

(79) Those were the pagan, iron times of the first city, when temptresses giggled everywhere and men erupted with guffaws. Love was free and fickle, morning and afternoon. A lady would woo even a pair of demigods at a time, and anywhere you please.

Kate Strong, the old scavenger-widow who knew the city during those filthy times, paints for us a dreary, glowing, vivid picture. She lived in a homelike cottage of elvan-stone, with rubbish stinking everywhere. She declared that (80) since there were no macadamized sidetracks on those old nekropolitan nights, she let down, as scavengers who will be scavengers must, her filth dump near the Serpentine in Phoenix Park.[6] At her time, the place was called "Finewell's Keepsacre," it was later tautaubapptossed "Pat's Purge."[7] And she chose this place because all over it were the complicated traceries of the past: fossil footprints, boot marks, elbow dints, etc. What subtler time-place could anyone ask for the hiding of a love letter, than then when ructions ended and here where race began? It was precisely then-here that the first

the same who appeared as janitrix of the museum (8–10), and as plunder-pussy-gnarlybird gathering relics of the great days into her nabsack (10–11).

[6] Again the "wholeborrow of rubbages" of p. 17. This time, however, not the old man but his better half is the one responsible. Finally, of course, the heap is composed of Humpty Dumpty fragments, and so it is the old man after all.

[7] Cf. p. 3, "to tauftauf thuartpeatrick." The rubbage dump is Ireland.

babe of reconcilement was laid, by four Promethean hands, in its last cradle of sweet earth.[8]

It was precisely here that All-Highest spake! And His nuptial eagles sharped their beaks for prey: "As it was, let it be!" says He. And it was as though the flood waters withdrew at His rude word. "Posidonius O'Fluctuary, lave that bloody stone as it is! And what are you doing there with that fellow, you dirty minx? Hustle you off to the minister![9] You there, take that barrel back where you got it!" And gish, how they all did scamper! The entire school gushed away with their sashes flying, sish, behind them.

[Thus concludes Kate's brief sketch of the epochal day of the Thunderclap. That was the moment of the inception of the great Viconian *corso,* or road of human destiny. We pause now to consider, for a moment, the lesson of that thunderclap and this road.]

(81) Yes, the invisibles all around us can't be downed. Look at all the slop that this one sent us! [He sent the Deluge.] And we weren't trespassing on his corns either! There is a power, namely, that keeps us to the road. If this road was walked upon by Hannibal, it was built long before his day by Hercules, and a hundred thousand unemancipated performed the dirty work. [Now we consider our present position along this highway:] Behind us lies the mausoleum: before us stand the milestones; world without end, Amen. The past has made us this present of a road. A salute, therefore, to O'Connell, the Liberator. We've reached the church of St. Fiacre! Halt!

[Here we are at the scene of the famous encounter in the Park. And so, it may be possible to gather fresh information. We pause at this point in the highway to consider the ancient story, but the whole adventure has now assumed another cast. HCE is dead and

[8] The midden mound from which a letter is later to be extracted is here located in Phoenix Park. It is the place where All-Father and his woman were making love when the thunder crack was heard.
[9] Here is the voice, with a thick brogue, commanding All-Father and Kate Strong herself to put an end to their recklessness and settle down.

gone. His story comes through the figures of his sons. The following pages (81–93) are a foretaste of the battles of Shem and Shaun which are to dominate the chapters of Book II.

[We begin with a fresh version of the encounter (81–84). We initiate a lame search for further evidence (84–85). We suddenly find ourselves again attending the trial—but it is a trial of Shaun, with Shem as the accuser, not of HCE arraigned by the populace of Erin.]

Hard by the house here, where Liffey and yon tide do merge, the attackler, with truly native pluck, engaged the Adversary, whom he mistook to be Oglethorpe or some ginkus to whom he bore some resemblance. Making use of sacrilegious languages and catching holst of an oblong bar he had, he rose the stick at him. The pair struggled, apparently for some considerable time, (82) around the book-safe, and in the course of their tussle the taller man said to the miner, who was carrying a portable distillery, "Let me go, Pautheen! I hardly knew ye!" Then he asked whether a sum of money had once been pickpocketed from the other, and presently, after some further collision and banter for the best part of an hour, he wanted to know whether his companion might happen to have the change of a ten-pound note on his person, adding that he would like to pay back the sum formerly pickpocketed. To which the other replied, with an obvious stutter, that he had no such thing on his person, but that he could see his way (83) to advance something like four and sevenpence. Whereupon the starving gunman became strangely calm and swore he would go good to him sometime. Then, pleased by the foretaste of all the whisky he would drink at the Red Cow, the Good Woman, Conway's Inn, and Adam and Eve's, he begged leave to depart. The queer mixture having exchanged the kiss of peace and concluded their Treaty of Cognac, the attackler turned fez in the (84) direction of Moscow, emitting a few *horosho's,* [Russian "very well's"] and levanted off with the seven and four to keep some crow-plucking appointment, while the Dane, with a number of plum-sized contusions, reported the occurrence, as best he could, to the nearest watch house.

Now then, worming along gradually in our search for further evidence, we come to the problem of the political leanings and town pursuits of our forebear: (85) (1) As to his Pacific pursuits —(a) he was given to walking or circulating along the public thoroughfares; (b) when mistakenly ambushed, he had been on the brink of taking place upon a public seat by Butt's Bridge, without intent to annoy.

(2) As to his Atlantic pursuits—little headway, if any, was being made toward the solution of this crime conundrum, when, on the calends of March, a certain Festy King [Shaun] was haled into court on an incompatibly framed indictment of both the counts. Soaked in methylated alcohol this Festy King appeared in dry dock, like Kersse's [10] Korduroy Karikature, wearing his fight shirt, straw suspenders, sou'wester, and a policeman's corkscrew trousers, all out of true. (86) The Crown attempted to prove that King, alias Crowbar, impersonating a chimney sweep, having rubbed mud on his face to disguise himself, had gone to the fair in Mudford, on a Thursday, under the assumed names of Tykingfest and Rabworc [i.e., Festy King and Crowbar, twisted about] with a pedigree pig and a hyacinth. The court gathering, convened to help the Irish Muck look his brother Dane in the face and attended by large numbers in spite of the deluge, was distinctly of the scattery kind.

Remarkable evidence was given, anon, by an eye, ear, nose, and throat witness [Shem], who (87) stated that he was pleased to remember the history-making episode. One thing, he declared, which particularly struck him and his two companions [the Three Soldiers], though theirs not to reason why,[11] was how Hyacinth O'Donnell, B.A., with part of a dung-fork, on the fair green, at the hour of twenty-four o'clock, had sought to sack, sock, stab, and slaughter single-handed two of the old kings, Gush MacGale and

[10] The story of Kersse will appear on p. 312. Kersse is Persse O'Reilly. Festy King gives us our first glimpse of Shaun. The witness is to be Shem.
[11] Echoes from "Lawn Tennyson's" "Charge of the Light Brigade" continually break through statements of the Three Soldier theme and culminate in the Crimean War episodes of pp. 338–55.

Roaring O'Crian, Jr., both changelings and of no address; since which time there had been bad blood between the litigants, and no end of petty quarrels. The litigants, he said, had been egged on by their womenfolk. Hereupon there were cries and catcalls from the gallery. But it oozed out in cross-examination, that when and where the three-partied ambush had been laid, (88) it had been quite dark. Accordingly the mixer was bluntly cross-questioned, as follows: "Was the witness one of those for whom the audible-visible-gnosible-edible world existed? Was he sure about the names of the parties involved in this king and blouseman business? How had the green-eyed mister acquired the B.A.? Did the initial letters of all his names add up to HERE COMES EVERYBODY? . . . (89) . . . How account for his condition at the time? Was he a Russian? Intoxicated? What had he said? What was his religion? . . . (90) . . . There had been a fight? A brother battle having to do with the hole in a wall? How had the matter struck him? Like a clap of thunder: Bladyughfoulmoecklenburgwhurawhora-scortastrumpapornanennykocksapastippatappatupperstrippuckputta-nach?" [12] "You have it alright," answered the witness.

But a new complexion was put upon the matter when (91) Pegger Festy himself, as soon as the outer layer of stucco-muck had been removed at the request of a few live jurors, declared in a loud burst of poesy, on his oath, that neither had he stolen, nor had he thrown a stone. Here (while in his excitement he broke into Castilian, shouting in Russian, *"Horosho!"* [Very well!"] and *"Zdrav-stvuyete!"* [Be in good health!]) (92) much yelling and laughter broke out in the hall, in which the testy fighter himself joined.

The hilarious hoot of Pegger's windup contrasted as neatly with the sad tone of the Wet Pinter's [13] as were they, "this one" and "that one," equals of opposites, evolved by a one-same power of nature or of spirit, which we may call "that other." [And here a great law is illustrated; the great law, namely, of Bruno the Nolan; the law underlying the historical polar play of brother opposites

[12] The voice of thunder, this time heard by one of the sons through the noise of his father's tussle in the Park.
[13] The Wet Pinter is the witness, Shem.

generated by a common father. The law is as follows:] (1) Direct opposites, since they are evolved by a common power, are polarized for reunion by the coalescence of their antipathies. (2) As opposites, nevertheless, their respective destinies will remain distinctly diverse. [Regard, for instance, the contrasting experiences, in this court of law, of Pegger and the Wet Pinter:] No sooner had Pegger concluded his statement than the maidies of the bar fluttered and flattered around him, complimenting him, sticking hyacinths through his curls, and bringing busses to his cheeks. And it was not unobserved that of one among them all he seemed blindly, mutely, tastelessly innamorate.[14]

The four judges [the Four Old Men] laid their wigs together and promulgated (93) their standing verdict of *Nolans Brumans*,[15] whereonafter King left the tribunal scot-free. His opposite stank so of alcohol that the twenty-eight advocatresses, pulling up their briefs with the war cry, "Shun the Punman!" safely and soundly soccered that Poser all the way home to Drinkbottle's Dwellings, where (as timid as your true Venus' son, Esau) he shut himself away (like the lion in our zoo) while the girlies shouted insults through the door.[16]

And so it all ended. *Artha kāma dharma moksha.* Ask Kavya for the Kay.[17] And so everybody heard their plaint and all listened to their plause. But now what about that letter! The litter! And the soother the bitter! The letter that would reveal the entire story! Of eyebrow penciled, by lipstipple penned. Borrowing a word and begging the question and stealing tinder and slipping like soap! With greetings and presents from everyone in the book! (94) The

[14] Shaun formula.
[15] *Nolens volens* ("against one's will") transformed by contamination with Nolan Bruno.
[16] Shem formula.
[17] Artha ("success"), *Kāma* ("pleasure"), *dharma* ("duty"), *moksha* ("enlightenment"). This is a traditional Sanskrit formula for the four "ends of life." *Kavya* ("the poet") will give the key; there is a suggestion here of Kathe (the poet's muse!) who supplied the key to the museum, p. 8.

story of the solid man saved by his sillied woman, trackajoking away like a hearse on fire. The elm that whimpers at the top told the stone that moans when stricken. Wind broke it, wave bore it, reed wrote it, Syce ran with it.[18] Hand tore it and wild went war. Hen trieved it and plight pledged peace.[19] It was folded with cunning, sealed with crime, uptied by a harlot, undone by a child. It was life but was it fair? It was free but was it art? It made Ma make merry and Sissie so shy and rubbed some shine off Shem and put some shame on Shaun. Yet there is woe in it. The two girls together spell famine and drought. The king spells tribulation on his throne. Ah, fear fruits, thou timid Danaïdes! [20] Eenie, meenie, miney, moe, one and two and two and three, eenie, meenie, woe is me! A pair of fig-leaf panties with almond eyes, one old lumpy lobster pumpkin, and three meddlers on the sly; Finfin funfun. And that is how from sin from son, a city arose. Now tell me, tell me, tell me then.[21] What was it?

[And the answer runs:] From Alpha to Omega!

So there you are now. And there they were, when all was over, the Four Old Men, sitting around in their judges' chambers, under the auspices of Long Lally Tompkins[22] around their old traditional tables of the law, to talk it all over all the same again. "According to King's evidence . . . So help me God and kiss the book . . ." The four of them and their Donkey. "So pass the push for port's sake. So be it. Amen."[23] "Remember old Dirty Daddy Pantaloons?" one of them asks; "before the Wars of the two Roses? (95) The smell of him! The graces and the rossies playing

[18] Play on the child conundrum: "*A* was apple pie; *B* bought it, *C* caught it, etc., etc. What was it?"
[19] Refers forward to the hen and the manuscript of the next chapter.
[20] Daughters of Danaus; all slew their bridegrooms the night of the wedding.
[21] Leading forward to the "Tell me all about Anna Livia" of Bk. I, chap. 8.
[22] The constable who arrested the hero in Bk. I, chap. 3 (cf. pp. 63, 67).
[23] Here we recognize the accents of the "Grace before Glutton" of p. 7.

him pranks! Old HCE!" "Sure," replies another of them, "I sniffed that lad long before anyone. And I mind the time the red-headed girl and myself were out love-making down Sycamore Lane: 'My perfume of the pampas,' says she (meaning me), putting out her netherlights, 'and I'd sooner one precious sip at your pure mountain dew than enrich my acquaintance with that big brewer's belch.'"

And so they went on, the four-bottle men, the annalists: about that old incident in the bushes—how she was lost in the ferny distance, and how he was like an earwig in an ear, anear, and the rustlings and twitterings and the raspings, and all the scandal-mongers, and the laugh-(96)ing jackass. And then about the old house by Chapelizod; Lillytrilly and Mrs. Niall of the Nine Cor-sages,[24] the old markiss their besterfather, and dear Sir Armoury, and all the goings on, so very wrong, so long ago, while the four were on retreat under Father Whisperer. And then about his bold advances, and the two saucy sisters—peep! [Suddenly the Four break into an argument:] "You're a liar, excuse me," says one. "I will not and you're another," says the second. And Long Lally Tompkins holding their breach of peace for them, bidding them to give and to take, and all will be forgotten. [Whereupon they make up again with a handshake and another drink.] It was too bad to be falling out about her kindness and about the shape of OOOOOOOOOurang's time. "Well, all right, Lally. And shake a hand. And pour us out another. For Christ's sake. Amen."

[That concludes the whole affair of the early life and death of HCE. The queerly infantile stories of his agnomen and reputation, his trial and incarceration, concluded with an absurd burial at the bottom of Lough Neagh. Following this disappearance, a chaos of wars broke out on every hillside. Rumors spread of the old man's reappearances in the thick of twilight battles. Then Widow Kate described the day of the ancient thunderclap, when she and the old pagan were interrupted on their mud mound.

[24] Niall of the Nine Hostages, hero of the Irish cycles.

Shaun and Shem, the sons of the departed, were discovered re-enacting (but with characteristic variations) the well-known history of their afflicted father. Mother Gossip's letter was heard to be at large with all the news. And the Four Old Men were at their driveling, going on and on about the grand old times.

[All might be said to be over. Every theme of *Finnegans Wake* has been sounded. Yet the dream cycle has hardly begun; HCE has hardly opened his career. No sooner have those in his wake become reconciled to his departure, than the news is out that he has disappeared from his grave and is at large and may be anywhere. Innumerable and highly confused reports describe his resurrection.

[This opens to scholarship a new and exceedingly difficult problem: What became of HCE?]

Well?

Such evidence as we have been able to gather may not be dependable. It may not bring the truth to light as fortuitously as an astronomer's calculation might reveal a hitherto unknown planet in the heavens, or as all the languages of the world have evolved from the root of some funner's stotter.[25] Yet soundest sense now holds that by playing 'possum our sacred ancestor saved his brush with his posterity. His escape was like that of a fox. Gun dogs of all breeds were (97) hot on his scent. From his lair he darted across Humphries Chase, from Mullinshob and Peacockstown, then bearing right upon Tankardstown, then through Raystown and Horlockstown and, louping the loup, to Tankardstown again. He was lost upon Ye Hill of Rut in full winter coat with ticker pads, pointing for his rooming house. He was hidden, then, close in covert, miraculously raven fed and sustained by his cud. Hence hounds hied home. Vainly violence, virulence, and vituperation sought to goad him forth.

[25] Vico would have all languages evolve from the attempts of the patriarchs to name the Thunderer. All the rumor and action of *Finnegans Wake* develops from the stuttering of HCE in the park encounter.

But his hesitEncy [sic] will give him away.[26]

Assemblymen murmured, "Reynard is slow!"

There was heard from his hideout an obscure noise. One feared for his days and tried to name what had happened. Was that a yawn? Twas his stomach. Did he eruct? Blame his liver. Was it a gush? From his visuals. Pung? Deliver him, O Lord! In *Fugger's Newsletter* it was declared that he had laid violent hands on himself. His sons were exhibited in the Forum, and a daughter was born to him amidst general acclaim. (98) Big went the bang: then the wide world was quiet: a report: silence. Had he fled again this country of exile? It was said that he escaped via underground as a stowaway in a Dutch bottom and was even now occupying a physical body, Cornelius Magrath's to wit, in Asia Minor, where as Turk of the Theater he was annoying the belly dancers, even while as street arab he was pestering the public for alms. Another rumor had it that he had been recalled and scrapped by the Maker. Others declared he had been claimed by an infamous disease. Or again, he had walked, while inebriate, into a lily pond where first-aiding hands had rescued him. Still again, it was said that on Umbrella Street a kind workman, Mr. Whitlock, had given him a piece of wood. And now everyone wanted to know what those two could have said to each other, and what the piece of wood might have been. (99) Round and round and round he was cycling; he was at large and might be anywhere. It was a time for rumors. A disguised and huge ex-nun, Mother Gigasta, had attracted attention by arbitrary conduct with an omnibus. An overcoat had been found nigh Scaldbrothar's Hole, and people shivered to think what kind of beast had devoured him. The Valkyrie had beckoned to him. The boys had it that on his pink postern, at Whit-weekend, an inked-up had been nailed, inscribed: "Move up,

[26] As noted by Herbert Gorman (*James Joyce,* Farrar and Rinehart, 1939, p. 35), Richard Pigott, who had forged letters implicating Parnell, betrayed himself in the witness box by misspelling the word hesitancy. *Finnegans Wake* is shot through with recollections of the fate of Parnell, but perhaps nowhere more richly than in these episodes of the scandal, trial, death, and resurrection. Parnell and Pigott are amalgamated in the figure of HCE.

Mumpty! Mike room for Rumpty! By order, Nickekellous Plugg'

So it appeared there had been real murder, the MacMahon chaps having done him in. Many went so far as to borrow copies of Dr. Blayney's tri-lingual tri-weekly, *Scatterbrains' Aftening Posht,* so as to make sure of his having become genuinely (100) dead, whether by land or water. Transoceanic cables declared for the latter: he lay under leagues of water in Bartholoman's Deep.

"Attention!" cried out the newsboys. "Read all about the Viceroy and the girlies, and the wrath of his old woman!"

[And he having departed, his successor was elected:] On the morn following the suicidal murder of the unrescued expatriate, there was seen the infallible spike of smoke announcing the election of the new Pope, and the sacred lights of maintenance were lighted within the tower of the temple.

What is the mystical nature of the Pope? Let it not be thought that the Prisoner of the Vatican was at best but a one-stone parable, a rude breathing on the void of to be, or the clue-key to a Reality beyond the space world; for scarce one of his twelve companions cared to doubt the canonicity of his existence as a tesseract.[27]

(101) But what the women wanted to hear was the story of ALP.

Do tell us about her! The war is over. Wimwim wimwim! Who was the girl: was it Unity Moore, or Estella Swifte or Varina Fay or Quarta Quaedam? All the people were asking: Who had been the scourge about Lucalizod and who had struck Buckley? But now it is generally known that it was Buckley himself who struck, and the Russian generals—yes! yes!—who were caddishly struck by him.[28] But finally, with all the gossip everywhere and his name on every tongue, that little woman, nearer him and dearer than all, first warming creature of his early morn, (102) stood forth,

[27] Tesseract: a regular polyhedroid bounded by eight cubes; that is to say, a four-dimensional figure, not to be understood in such simple three-dimensional terms as might popularly be applied to the rock of Peter.
[28] Here the Park adventure is linked forward to the episode of Buckley and the Russian General, pp. 338 ff. *Da* is Russian for "yes."

dragging the countryside in her train, with pawns, prelates, and pookas pelotting in her piece-bag, to crush the slander's head.[29]

[The chapter concludes with a page of praise to this tiny woman, who now must set forth to make live again in glorious memory the guilt-ridden name of her lord.]

Weary weeny wight, plead for Morandmor![30] Notre Dame de la Ville, thanks for thy merciful heart. And let him rest, thou wayfarer: Take no grave-spoil from him. For there's a little lady waiting and her name is ALP. And you'll agree. She must be she. He spent his strength among harem-scarems. And now who but Crippled-with-Children would speak up for Dropping-with-Sweat?

> *Poem:*
> She sold him her lease and he gulped it. Who was the
> C.O.D.?
> > Bum!
> (103) At Island Bridge she met him. There were the soldiers. Up went a hue and cry!
> > Woe!
> By the waters of Babylon, we sat down and wept.

[Pausing now to consider the material of the first four chapters we find that the story of HCE, while resembling that of Finnegan in many aspects, differs from the allegory of the primeval giant in one essential detail. Finnegan once laid away for dead remains prostrate on his bier; HCE though buried in an escape-proof coffin (76–78) works loose and is now everywhere at large. The implication of this contrast reaches down to the root of Joyce's intention. The bier of Finnegan is the stage on which history enacts itself in the goings and comings of HCE. If Finnegan wakes, the

[29] This passage carries forward the theme, introduced on pp. 10–11, of the little woman's bag of battle souvenirs. Later, pp. 205–12, it will be told how she crushed the scandal by distributing among her children the inexhaustible contents of her bag.

[30] *Mor* is Irish for "ancient." *Mort* (pronounced "mōr") is French for "dead." "More," is English for the drive that builds the Empire.

stage is overturned and doomsday arrives. Thus Finnegan must lie quiet, whereas HCE, to perform his function as history itself, must circle endlessly.

[In one essential detail the "afterdeaths" of the two are in consonance. It is characteristic of both stories that no sooner do we see the old man laid out than we behold his little woman taking over the scene, busily cherishing her husband's memory and carrying it forward. Scarcely has Finnegan's dirge begun when the Anna Livia melody is heard (6–7). Similarly, when the world has tucked HCE into his tomb, the cry goes up again for the little woman (101): "Tellus tellas allabouter."

[And so we may expect that during the next four chapters it will be the figure of the mother that holds the foreground. When the standpoint was that of the father's history, the mother presence emerged finally as a warming promise of things to come. Now that the standpoint is to be that of the mother, the father history will appear as something recollected, lost in the deep past, yet brought forward and presented in the souvenir collections of his relict. The dead husband is respected, yet understood in a way which he would not have altogether liked; and his demise, while regretted, is not regarded with a sentiment unfriendly to the irreversible procession of time! Indeed, it is quite as though the little woman, for all of her cherishing of the past, were primarily concerned to foster the best of her old shattered Humpty Dumpty in the lives of her chicks.]

Book I, Chapter 5: The Manifesto of ALP

[Chapters 1 to 4 belonged to the father. Chapters 5 to 8 will be those of his all-embracing consort. The present chapter, 5, is devoted to a study of the letter that she wrote, her "Mamafesta" memorializing the old man. The study opens with a beautiful prayer to her as the Mother of the World, uniting in one personality the traits of the Hindu figure of Māyā ("Bringer of Plurabilities"), the Catholic figure of the Virgin (Bearer of the Word made Flesh), the mother-heroine ALP, the gently flowing waters of the river Liffey, and the wonderful little hen, Belinda, who scratched the letter from the mound. Note the echoes of the "Our Father" in the prayer addressed to her: it is through her that we become partakers of the Father's love.]

(104) In the name of Anna the Allmaziful, the Everliving, the Bringer of Plurabilities, haloed be her eve, her singtime sung, her rill be run, unhemmed as it is uneven!

Her untitled Mamafesta memorializing the Mosthighest has gone by many names at disjointed times.[1]

[Joyce supplies a list three pages long of the names that have been given to ALP's polymorphous Mamafesta (104-7). Ostensibly, they are the names that various peoples of various times and places have proposed for the soiled and almost unreadable letter of lost signature, dug out of a local rubbish heap by a neighbor's hen. The names are presented as collected and edited by a pedantic scholar-guide.[2] The list concludes with an advertisement: "First and Last Only True Account all about the Honorary Mirsu Earwicker, L.S.D.,[3] and the Snake (Nuggets!), by a Woman of the World who only can tell Naked Truths about a Dear Man and all his Conspirators, how they all Tried to Fall him Putting it all around Lucalizod about Privates Earwicker and a Pair of Sloppy Sluts plainly Showing all the Unmentionability falsely Accusing about the Raincoats."[4]

[Having listed its titles, the professor boldly essays the very difficult problem of establishing its date and place of origin, its circumstantiating facts, and its possible meaning or meanings.[5]]

[1] Māyā's memorial to the Absolute is the cosmos; ALP's memorial to HCE is her letter.
[2] This scholar personage affords the author some delicious opportunities for poking fun at the academic manner. He comes fully into his own in the present chapter and the following. His task is to edit and comment upon the letter dug up by the hen.
[3] Pounds, shillings, pence.
[4] Redcoats. The Three Soldiers. The letter, among other things, rehearses the fall of HCE.
[5] Meticulous study of this manuscript will enable us to reconstruct a picture of what must have been the setting and cast of the grand primeval

(107) The exhumed manuscript is protean and polyhedral. Though it seems a mere scribble to the ignorant reader, to the hardy student it reveals the eternal chimera-hunter pursuing his butterfly Vanessas from plant to plant, as well as a multiplicity of coalescing personalities who merge, their contrarieties eliminated, into one stable somebody.

Comes the question: Who wrote the darn thing (108) anyhow, and under what circumstances?

Patience, dear reader, our problem is not simple. A good plan used by worried business folk who have not had time to master Confucius' Doctrine of the Mean is to think of all the sinking fund of patience possessed by the brothers Bruce, their spider, and Elberfeld's Calculating Horses. If, after years of research, there are certain scholars who think they have solved the problem by reducing the whole thing to trivialities, telling us, for instance, that our ancestor was somewhat less than the name he has been given would suggest, that his fabled ear was simply the trade-mark of a radio broadcaster, then, as to this letter with its undeniable nature, where, in heaven's name, is the clever person who will tell us what it means?

We know these learned nay-sayers, and reply to them as follows: (*a*) To conclude from the mere absence of concrete signs that the page cannot have been a product of that period and of those parts is as unjustified as concluding from the mere absence of quotation marks that an author is constitutionally incapable of misappropriating the spoken words of others.

(109) (*b*) To concentrate solely on the literal sense or even the psychological content of any document to the neglect of the enveloping facts circumstantiating it is as hurtful to sound sense as visualizing a lady to whom one has just been introduced, plump

drama. But this is by no means a simple three-dimensional task. The original letter proliferates into a banyan of footnotes, scholarly comments, explanations by a presumed original author, psychological analyses, Marxian commentary, and palimpsest research, until at last we have under our eye, not a scrap of letter, but a magnificent ferment of personages, places, and ideas, which Joyce calls the "Tiberiast duplex."

and plain in her natural altogether, closing one's eyes to the fact that she was, after all, wearing for the space of the time being some definite articles of evolutionary clothing, full of local color and personal perfume, and suggestive, too, of so very much more.

(110) Let a few of the circumstantiating facts, then, speak for themselves. [Firstly, as to its probable place of origin, Lucalizod, "where the wish is father to the event":[6]] Lucalizod, indeed, was the one place in this mad vale of tears where the possible was the improbable and the improbable the inevitable; here the events recounted in our manuscript might well have taken place. Impossible as these events are, they are probably as like those which may have taken place, as any others which never took person at all are ever likely to be.

[Secondly, as to the discovery of the manuscript by that original hen:] Midwinter was in the offing. A certain shivering child observed a cold fowl behaviorizing strangely on that fatal midden heap—the heap that was afterwards, when it one day threw up a few fragments of orange peel, transformed into an orangery.[7] Then another child, keepy little Kevin, appropriated the find and sought approval of his father by passing it off as his own discovery.[8]

(111) The bird in the case was Belinda of the Dorans. At the hour of twelve she was observed scratching at what looked like a good-sized sheet of letter paper. [Thirdly, as to the contents of that letter:] Originating from Boston, Mass., and addressed to Dear somebody, it mentioned Maggy and all-at-home's health, the misfortune of the van Houtens, elections, a wedding cake, and the grand fun about Father Michael. It closed with hugs and kisses. A large tea stain marked it off as a genuine relic of ancient Irish peasant poetry of the Lydia-languishing class.

[Finally, as to the condition of the manuscript:] Any photographer will tell you that if a negative of a horse melts while dry-

[6] I.e., Dreamland. The word "Lucalizod" is compounded of "Lucan" and "Chapelizod," two Dublin suburbs on the river Liffey.

[7] Cf. p. 3: "where oranges have been laid to rust upon the green." A monument is to be erected on this site of battle between Gael and Gall.

[8] Kevin (Shaun) again butt-ends his brother.

ing, what you get is a distorted mass of horse-happy values and melt-while horse. Something of this kind must have occurred to our missive. Heated residence in the heart of the orange-flavored mud mound had, so to speak, partly obliterated the negative, causing features close at hand to become enormously enlarged, while (112) the farther back we manage to wiggle the more we need the loan of a lens to see as much as the hen saw.[9]

Are you feeling lost, reader? Cheer up! The Four Masters may own the approved translation, but even a gypsy-scholar may pick a peck of kindlings yet from the sack of auld hen syne.

So let us optimistically (with the hope that she may guide us to some clue) follow this little hen. Her socio-scientific sense is as sound as a bell, and the gloomy belief that letters have never been quite their own selves again since Biddy Doran looked at literature is not justified; in fact, a golden age of feminism is to come!

She may be a mere bit of cotton quilting, this midget majesty, Mistress of Arts, but her letter is no anomalous bit of hearsay. She is energetic, economical, and has a heart of iron, and will follow the direction of the wind. But how many of her readers (113) realize that she is not out to dazzle with a great show of learned splendor, or to lift a complaint against the man and what he did? Thingcrooklyexineverypasturesixdixlikencehimaroundhersthemaggerbykinkinkankanwithdownmindlookingated.[10] Ladies and gentlemen! Listen please! All she wants (she writes) is to tell the truth about him: He had to see life foully; there were three men in him; his only fault was dancing with disorderly girls. Yours very truthful, Add dapple inn.—Yes, it is an old, old story: the tale of a Treestone with one Ysold; of a mountainman held by tent pegs and his pal waterloosed on the run; of what Cadman could but Badman wouldn't; of any Genoa man against any Venice-Venus; of why Kate takes charge of the waxworks.[11]

[9] Things close to the experience of the reader become enlarged, things unfamiliar to him he misses entirely, must search to find.
[10] Thunder voice now rings through the cozy gossip of the letter.
[11] Cf. pp. 8 and 57. The letter tells the same story as the museum of the janitrix and the waxworks of Madame Tussaud.

But now let us drop this jiggerypokery and talk straight turkey, if you please. Let us be done with hearing what others have said: let us see for ourselves all there may remain to be seen.

I am a worker, anxious to please; you are a pillar of society, unctious to police; (114) we cannot see eye to eye. Yet one cannot help noticing that more than half the lines in this MS run north-south, while the others go west-east. Such crossing is pre-Christian. But the home-grown shillelagh as an aid to calligraphy shows a distinct advance from savagery to barbarism,[12] but with the writing now this way and now back again, now up and now down, it is difficult to discover its sense.

Another point: in addition to the original material used, the document has been soiled by accretions of terricious matter. Finally the tea-time-stained terminal is very important in establishing the identities of the writer complex; for both before and after the Battle of the Boyne, it was a habit not to sign letters (115) always. For why sign anything, when every word, letter, pen stroke, paper space, is a perfect signature of its own!—[Now an abrupt turn to the problem of love:] This is no usual case of spooning, as, for instance, some prostitute in dinky pinks somersaulting off her bisexycle at the entrance of a curate's suite; and he coming out [as Jarl van Hoother to the game of Grace O'Malley] to feel whereupon the virgin was most hurt, and so forth. We old practicing psychoanalysts know, and could tell if we pleased, that there is a deep psychological import even in the slightest superficial symptom: "Father" is not always our zoological relative, and the most innocent appearance may have sexual content, and even a slight statement of fancy may conceal great libido urges. From the Freudian-Jungian point of view, therefore, this is as human a little story as paper could well carry. (116) [But there is also a sociological allegory to be detected:] We have read the pages of *I Was a General,* and have learned to recognize the social content of a work. Therefore, we know that "Father Michael" means "the old regime," "Maggy" means "the social revolution," "cakes" means

[12] The manuscript is thus approximately dated as of druidical times.

"the party funds," and "dear thank you" means "national grati-tude." That is to say, we know a thing or two about revolutions. [Returning, however, to the case of the girl and the curate:] If we interpret 'prostitute" as whoever stands before a door, and "curate" as one who brings strong waters, then we must also re-member (*a*) that there may be many slips somersaulting between the first one at home and the last one abroad, (*b*) that the beautiful presence of wedding cakes will be quite enough to make Mike [Shaun] punch hell's hate into his twin brother Nick [Shem], and (*c*) Maggy's tea is a boost from a born gentleman. That is to say: no matter how complex the possible interpretations, we must not lose sight of the simple, straightforward facts. There is a time and place for everything. For instance, if the language of the bed were preached by our public functionaries, where would their practice be? And on the other hand, if the long words of Pythagorean omniscience were grunted by furtive couples, where would be the human race itself?

Love was, is, and will be. (117) It persists through all stages of the recurrent fourfold cycle. So what are you going to do about it?

If she only knew and he only could: that is the old, old story! That is the story in all history books in every language. For since the naughty little girl first excited him, the man has been ever on the ready to kindle. Though business has been business during thousands of thousands of years, and the peoples have been shout-ing for this cause and that, and the Four Ages have passed along, this ancient story of their weatherings and their marryings and their buryings and their natural selections has come down to us, fresh and made at all hours, like an old cup of tea.

Though we may doubt the sense of the whole, the interpretation of any phrase (118) or of every word, we must vaunt no idle du-biousness as to its authenticity. Somehow and somewhere, some-body wrote it all down, and there you are. Yes, but one who thinks more deeply will bear in mind that this downright "there you are" is a statement conditioned by all the contingencies of phenomenality.

Because every person, place, and thing anyway connected with it was moving and changing every part of the time. It is not a mere mass of blots—it only looks that way. We should realize how lucky we are to possess, at this late hour and considering how much of it we carelessly lost, even a scrap of it. (119) Cling to it, as with drowning hands, and hope that things will begin to clear up a bit, one way or another, within the next quarter of an hour.

[The next four and a half pages (119–23) parody the language of Sir Edward Sullivan's description and analysis of the Book of Kells.[13] The reader of *Finnegans Wake* would do well to study that volume, and particularly its reproduction of the *"Tunc* page." The Book of Kells, a magnificently illuminated 6th or 9th century Irish Psalter, was buried, like our letter, to protect it from the invading Danes, and was dug up again, centuries later, very badly damaged. The meticulously executed, unbelievable intricacy of the profoundly suggestive ornament of this monk work so closely resembles in its essential character the workmanship of *Finnegans Wake* that one is not entirely surprised to find Joyce describing the features of his own masterwork in language originally applied to the very much earlier monument of Celtic art. The *Tunc* page of the Book of Kells is devoted entirely to the words, "Tunc crucifixerant XPI cum eo duos latrones" (Matt. xxvii, 38), i.e., "Then were there two thieves crucified with him." The Greek XPI (Christos) is an interpolation. The illumination is an astonishing comment on this text, strangely suggestive of pre-Christian and oriental symbols. The reader of *Finnegans Wake* will not fail to recognize in this page something like a mute indication that here is the key to the entire puzzle: and he will be the more concerned to search its meaning when he reads Joyce's boast on page 298: "I've read your tunc's dimissage."

[Sir Edward Sullivan begins his study of the Book of Kells with the words: "Its weird and commanding beauty; its subdued and goldless colouring; the baffling intricacy of its fearless designs; the

---

[13] *The Book of Kells,* described by Sir Edward Sullivan, Bart., and illustrated with twenty-four plates in colors, 4th ed., London, 1933.

clean, unwavering sweep of rounded spiral; the creeping undulations of serpentine forms that writhe in artistic profusion throughout the mazes of its decorations; the strong and legible minuscule of its text; the quaintness of its striking portraiture; the unwearied reverence and patient labour that brought it into being; all of which combined go to make up the Book of Kells, have raised this ancient Irish volume to a position of abiding preeminence amongst the illuminated manuscripts of the world . . ." And Joyce describes the little exhumed letter: "those indignant whiplooplashes; those so prudently bolted or blocked rounds; the touching reminiscence of an incompletet trail or dropped final; a round thousand whirligig glorioles, prefaced by (alas!) now illegible airy plumeflights, all tiberiously ambiembellishing the initials majuscule of Earwicker . . ." and so forth, to the top of page 123. Among the features is a curious warning sign "which paleographers call 'a leak in the thatch' or 'the Aranman whispering through the hole of his hat,' indicating that the words which follow may be taken in any order desired." (121) This corresponds to a symbol described by Sir Edward:[14] "The symbol C, known in Irish MSS. as 'head under the wing' or 'turn under the path'—which indicated that the words immediately following it are to be read after the next full line." And toward the bottom of page 122 of *Finnegans Wake* it is even suggested that the form of the postscript of the letter must have inspired "the tenebrous *Tunc* page of the Book of Kells."]

(122) Consider, for instance, the three little boxes which have been painted into the illuminated margin, each box crammed with five human faces. Three when two would have been enough! And why was that "XPI" added to the Latin text? did the scribe have his tongue in his cheek?[15] . . . the fatal slope of the blamed scrawl, the superabundance (123) of four-legged M's, why this, rather than that, letter illuminated? The cut-and-dried form of the semifinal

[14] *The Book of Kells,* p. 10.
[15] These are problems that emerge from the *Tunc* page.

and what patience in that final flourish of 732 strokes! Who, marveling at all this, will not press swiftly on to see the vaulting feminine libido of those interbranching up-and-in sweeps sternly controlled by the matter-of-factness of a meandering male fist? [16]

Professor Duff-Muggli first called this kind of partnership "the ulyssean," or "four-handed," or "duck-and-drakes," or "debts-and-dishes" perplex, following the observation of Tung-Toyd, that the tale of Ulysses was simply a cleverly turned and republished Punic admiralty report, calculated to tickle the gander as game as the goose.

The identity of the persons named in the manuscript (the persons of the Tiberiast [17] duplex, they have been called) came to light in the most devious of ways: The original document showed no signs of punctuation, yet, when held up to the sunlight, it proved (124) to have been gashed and pierced by a pronged instrument. These paper wounds, four in type, were gradually understood to mean: "stop," "please stop," "do please stop," and "O do please stop." [18] Scotland Yard pointed out that they had been "provoked" by the fork of a grave Professor Prenderguest at his breakfast table, piqued to introduce a notion of time into the uninterrupted run of the script by punching holes into space. Against this thesis, however, stands the fact that the professor would not have visited his ire upon the ancestral spirit of one whom he deeply venerated. Then it was detected that the four-leafed shamrock or quadrifoil jab was the more recurrent wherever the script was

[16] Note the Swift-Sterne impulse-restraint antimony. Note that Swift is associated with the feminine, Sterne with the masculine role—Shem-Shaun.
[17] Tiberius, Roman emperor, A.D. 14–37, at the time of the mission and crucifixion of Christ. As the living representative of the classical pantheon he was, so to speak, already superseded by the Christian theology still in microscopic germinal state. Joyce chooses this moment of history as symbolic of the supplanting of the father by the son. One also feels the play between "Oedipus complex" and "Tiberiast duplex."
[18] Cf. "stoop," "please stoop," etc., pp. 18–19. This discussion of punctuation follows again Sir Edward's analysis of the Book of Kells. Meticulous examination of the style of punctuation leads Sir Edward to assign the manuscript to the ninth rather than the sixth century.

clear and the term terse, and that these were the spots naturally selected for her perforations by Dame Partlet on her dung heap. Whereupon, thinkers put two and two together, and a sigh for shame separated modest mouths. Amen. The scribe abruptly signs off, at this point, thus concluding his letter-making of the exploits of Fjorgn Camhelsson, and begging to remain, yours most faithfully.

Small need, after that, you Four Old Men, for quizzing week-end visitors (125) with your obtuse riddles about that fellow; such as: Where has he disappeared to? The name of the scribe is Dire-mood [Dermot] and he is kin to a dearmate [Diarmait].[19] The girls are all out looking for him [i.e., the scribe who penned the letter]. Who is he? Would he be wearing a mustache? Would he be frequenting low-class billiard halls? No! But had he only, only a bit more humor in him he would be! To everyone's relief, at any rate, he is gone, and his room is taken up by that odious note-snatcher, Shem the Penman.

[This concludes the paleographic examination and discussion of the manuscript. The next task is to identify and characterize the persons named in the text, the persons, as they have been called, of the "Tiberiast duplex." Following a suggestion which appeared at the conclusion of the present chapter, this task is to be left to the Four Old Masters. They are in the habit, it seems, of quizzing week-end visitors with silly riddles: let us then listen to what they have to say. The reader will become very soon aware of the fact that the following series of twelve riddles is not only a quiz proposed by four old local codgers, but an examination proposed by a professor to his class. Indeed, our scholar-guide is continually threatening to merge into the collective figure of the four old historians. Finally, the quiz suggests the great riddle-games of the

[19] Diarmait (Dermot) was the name of the young captain who abducted Grainne, the bride of Finn MacCool. Many episodes of the medieval Tristram-Iseult story are modeled after this Celtic love-tale of Diarmait and Grainne. In the present riddle, Diarmait represents both sons—in anticipation of HCE's Tristram dream of Bk. II, chap. 4.

pagan Celtic and Germanic poets. Many stories are told of gods contending against each other not with blows but with riddles.]

Book I, Chapter 6: Riddles—The Personages of the Manifesto

[The professor examines his class on the entire problem of the Tiberiast duplex. This chapter supplies a handy list of the chief characters and themes of *Finnegans Wake*.]

(126) So?

How do you do tonight, ladies and gentlemen?

The answerer is in the back of the wood; call him forth!

(Shaun rated 110 per cent in this nightly quiz.)

1. What myth-erector and bridgemaker was the first to rise taller than the bodhitree or Wellington Monument, went barefoot into Liffey when she was barely in her trickles, wore a cloud cap on the ridge of his skull, sports a Prince Albert over his Hollander's opulence, (127) is escape-master-in-chief from all sorts of hiding places: those were the days and he was their hero . . . (129) . . . real detonation but false report . . . (132) . . . we go into him sleepy children, we come out of him strugglers for life. . . . His three-faced stone head was found on a white-horse hill, and the print of his costellate feet is seen in the goat's grass circle. . . . *H*allucination, *c*auchemar, *e*ctoplasm . . . (134) . . . moves in vicious circles, yet remains the same . . . the king was in (135) his corner wall melking mark so murry, the queen was steep in armbour feeling fain and furry, the mayds was midst the hawthorns shoeing up their hose, out pimps the blackguards (pomp!) and pump guns they goes . . . (138) . . . his troubles may be over, but his doubles have still to come . . . he stands in a lovely park, sea is not far, important towns of X, Y, and Z are easily over-reached . . . (139) stutters 'fore he falls and goes mad entirely when he's waked . . .

Answer: Finn MacCool!

2. [The second question is addressed to Mike (Shaun), a widely traveled son of Anna Livia.] Does your mother know you're out?

Answer [To the rhythm of Father Prout's "The Shandon Bells"]:[1] When I turn my eyes homeward from the cities of the world, my filial bosom beholds with pride the grand old Pontificator, with his dam, night garrulous, by his side.

3. What would be the most appropriate motto for their home (140)?

Answer: Thine obesity, O civilian, hits the felicitude of our orb.

4. What Irish capital city has:

(*a*) the most extensive public park in the world;

(*b*) the most expensive brewing industry in the world;

(*c*) the most expansive peopling thoroughfare in the world;

(*d*) the most horse-loving god-drinking population in the world?

and (*a*), (*b*), (*c*), (*d*): Harmonize your responses.

Answer:

(*a*) Belfast (Ulster)

(*b*) Cork (Munster)

(*c*) Dublin (Leinster)

(*d*) Galway (Connaught) (141)

and (*a*), (*b*), (*c*), (*d*): All melt together and are harmonized in the lilting tonalities of the bells of Shandon. [Note that in reply to Question 2 the bells of Shandon were associated with Anna Livia. She it is who subsumes all differentiations and recompounds them, their contrarieties eliminated, into one great somebody. Then again it will be she as "Bringer of Plurabilities," who sends all forth again, in forms apparently new.]

[1] First stanza of "The Shandon Bells";
"With deep affection and recollection
    I often think of those Shandon bells,
Whose sounds so wild would, in days of childhood,
    Fling round my cradle their magic spells.
On this I ponder where'er I wander,
    And then grow fonder, sweet Cork, of thee;
With thy bells of Shandon that sound so grand on
    The pleasant waters of the river Lee."

5. What lad would be the hired man of all work?

Answer: Pore ole Joe!

6. And what means the saloon slogan: "Summon in the House-sweep Dinah?"

Answer [This reply is given by the old widow house-sweep herself]: Cleaning up after him, and he flattering me; fetching this and that here and there; I hope it pours for their picnic tomorrow! (142) And who ate the last of the gooseberries? and who left that there? and who left this here? and who let the cat steal the chop? . . .

7. What are the twelve component parts of our society? [Who are the twelve good citizens?]

Answer: The Morphios! [The sleepers: those still dreaming the dream that is life, those not yet awake, etc.]

8. And how do the Maggies wage war? [What about the Temptresses?]

Answer: They war loving, they love laughing, they laugh weeping . . . as born to live and wive and wile, (143) Sweet Peck-at-my-Heart picks one man more.

9. If a human being, fatigued, were accorded a view of old Hope-in-Haven, with all the outstanding ingredients to which his recurrent fourfold story would have been recurring; could such a one, while lying beside his woman, behold what is main and why 'tis twain, how the good melts into the bad, the sap rising, the foliage falling, the nimbus round the girlyhead, the twin wrestlers in the womb, and the rainbow with its colors—then what would that stargazer seem to himself to be seeing? [I.e., Could a sleeper envision the whole story of HCE, what would the great view most closely resemble?]

Answer: A collide-or-scape. [The kaleidoscope of *Finnegans Wake*.]

10. [Question addressed, as by a young, rejected lover, to Iseult.] What's bitter love but yearning; what's our love much but a brief burning? It will all end at the end of the cycle!

Answer: [From the leap-year girl herself. Apparently she is

sitting before her mirror-confidante, addressing in her imagination, or through her doll, or in a letter, the awkward, poetical, shy lad, and pretending to know of another "her" in his life. Again, she is Stella, replying to Swift, and through her words run the pet names and pseudoparental tenderness of the Swift-Stella letters.] I know, Pepette, of course, dear, but listen, precious! What exquisite hands you have, you angel, if you didn't gnaw your nails! Isn't it a wonder you're not ashamed of me! I bet you use her best face cream (144) to make them shine so! I know her. Slight me, would she? And when I think of that crude fellow with his fourteen sporting friends parading into the tavern and trying to play up to me! . . . What are you nudging for? Of course, it was too kind of you to remember my size in stockings . . . (146) . . . Someday I'm to marry an engineer, a regular Tristram . . . Move your mouth toward mine, more, preciousest, more on more! Don't be a . . . I'm not going to! Sh! nothing! A cry somewhere! (147) Let them, the four of them, and the twelve boozers too, and my twenty-eight class-birds too. When the bride is married they'll all begin to sing: then everyone will hear of it. Bright pigeons all over the world will fly. . . . Close; you mustn't look. Now open, pet, your lips, Pepette. . . . Are you enjoying this same little me, my life, my love? (148) Shshsh! Don't start like that, you wretch! It's only another queer fish in the damned old river again. Excuse me for swearing, my love, I swear I didn't mean to . . .

11. [Question addressed to Professor Jones (Shaun type). The question is set to the rhythm of Thomas Campbell's "The Exile of Erin."[2]] If a poor drunken exile with his aching eyes [Joyce

[2] First stanza of Thomas Campbell's "The Exile of Erin":

"There came to the beach a poor exile of Erin,
   The dew on his robes was heavy and chill;
For his country he sighed when at twilight repairing,
   To wander alone by the wind-beaten kill.
But the day-star attracted his eye's sad devotion,
For it rose on its own native isle of the ocean,
Where once, in the flow of his youthful emotion,
   He sang the bold anthem of Erin go bragh."

himself, as Shem] were piteously (149) to beg the professor for the wherewithal with which to save his soul, would the respectable gentleman care to today?

[The answer is simply, "No!" But the professor feels it necessary to spin out an elaborate justification of his refusal. The result is a very scholarly discussion of the so-called "Dime-Cash Problem," with careful attention to the writings of other scholars on this matter, and with anecdotes to illustrate, for the less learned members of the audience, the principle involved. The argument is obscured by the professor's parenthetical remarks. He is a man who has taken all learning for his province, and who seizes occasion to baffle his classroom with demonstrations of his scope. As a result, his audience is everywhere going to sleep on him, and he is frequently compelled to scold and insult them back to at least the appearance of alert interest. Elaborately presenting an academic restatement of the meeting with the tramp in the evening twilight of the Park, the professor leads us, step by step, from this Encounter theme to a new view of the Seduction; furthermore, he is at pains to demonstrate, point by point, the relationship of the second seduction pattern (that of the Shem-Shaun-Iseult configuration) to the first (that of HCE and ALP). His thesis thus prepares the way for the emergence of the forms of Book II from those of Book I.

[The lecture may be reduced to three great phases: (1) a discussion in abstract terms of the general principles involved; (2) a fable, "The Mookse and The Gripes," translated from the Javanese and quoted by the professor to illustrate the main drift of his argument; (3) a more complex classroom illustration, the story of Burrus, Caseous, and the cowrymaid Margareen, to clarify the more abstruse of the professor's implications and to carry the argument forward to its final point.

[The lecture opens with an indignant negative, and a reference to the earlier works of the professor on this theme. He has already refuted a certain scholar, Bitchson, whose thesis is precisely the thesis of the begging tramp,[3] and he has discredited the man by demonstrating both the sources of his faults and the true gist of the argument which he and his ilk speciously misrender. The lecture proceeds to a discussion of the writings of Lévy-Brühl[4] and finds in the work of that eminent sociologist support for the great theme of Professor Jones, namely, that the life form of the space-oriented man is not only more practical than that of the time-oriented, but no less just in its relationship to the finally unknown and unknowable transcendentals.[5] The professor then calls his pupils to order and regales them with his translation of the fable of "The Mookse and The Gripes." The passage is extraordinarily difficult to grasp and rerender; the following must serve as the roughest outline.]

Answer: No; do you take me for a sentimentalist, fool or pervert? You should consult my earlier disposal of this dime-cash problem elsewhere. There I remarked: (a) that the sophisticated argument of Bitchson, while apparently motivated by a purely dime-dime urge is not without his cash-cash characteristics; (b) that these characteristics have been borrowed from his fairy godmother, Miss Fortune; (c) that the argument is in reality only a ridiculous parody of the Whose Who and Where's Here theories of Einstein. That is to say, the speech form is a mere surrogate,

[3] See pp. 81–84. Bitchson and the poor exile are further examples of the Cad-Assailant-Beggar figure; at the same time they are Shem. Similarly, Professor Jones is a compound of HCE and Shaun.

[4] Professor Lucien Lévy-Brühl's discussions of "mystical space," "mystical participation," "collective representations," "polysynthetic perceptions," "bipresence," etc., etc., etc., whatever their value may be to the anthropologist, can be immensely helpful to the reader of *Finnegans Wake*. See, for instance, his volumes, *Les fonctions mentales dans les sociétés inférieures* (8th edition, Paris, 1928) and *La mentalité primitive* (8th edition, Paris, 1933); they are translated under the titles *How Natives Think* (London, 1926) and *Primitive Mentality* (London, 1923).

[5] This is precisely the argument with which St. Patrick will refute the dream logic of the Archdruid in Book IV, thereby discrediting the Night World of *Finnegans Wake* itself, and preparing the way for the opening of the eyes to the Facts of Day. It is the "daylight refutation" of Joyce's "night work." Joyce knows, as well as any, the case against his own book.

while the *quality* and *tality* are alternately harrogate and arrogate, as the gates may be.

But *talis,* a word frequently misused, (150) originally meant the same thing as *qualis,* and this fact is proven by many examples.[6]

But the problem can be approached from another angle. Professor Lévy-Brühl has discussed the nature of the relation of the accidental to the proper, and has drawn certain conclusions for the history of religions. He declares that "by Allswill" the inception and the descent and the endswell of Man is *temporarily* wrapped in obscurity. Yet, he continues, looking through the accidents of this phenomenal existence, I can easily believe in my own most spacious immensity (151) as my proper and most intimate sphere. And so he finds that the number of queer faiths in the world is not to be appreciably augmented by the one-another-slugging of a couple of clods. Following this discussion of Professor Lévy-Brühl's, we may draw certain conclusions anent the All in its relation to the When and the Where, and these conclusions may be applied directly to the problems at hand: (*a*) What the romantic fellow in rags pines after and what he demands our sympathy for is the purest waste of time. He and his ilk are always with us, looking back to a time *when;* (*b*) But on the professor's showings, one man's when is no other man's when; meanwhile, the All is not when, but where, in love as in war; (*c*) (152) on the plane where my arts soar, you would encounter thunder: I shall flourish in the place fit for me, and he meanwhile is in the place fit for him.[7]

But since my explanation is probably above your understanding, I shall resort to a method which I frequently use when I have to do with muddlecrass pupils. Imagine that you are a squad of sniffly urchins. And you, Bruno Nolan, take your tongue out of the ink-

---

[6] A layman might be excused for rendering the argument as follows: The pleading manner of speech of the beggar is only a veneer; what is really taking place is alternately outright violence or downright intimidation, as the case may be—and these amount to the same thing.

[7] Shem is here associated with time, Shaun with space.

pot! As none of you knows Javanese, I will give you a free translation of the old fabulist's parable, "The Mookse and The Gripes."[8]

Ladies and gentlemen:

Once within a space there lived a Mookse. Feeling lonely, he went walking. Having spruced himself he left his fine estate, to see how badness was badness in the worst of all possible worlds. With his father's sword he was girded.

He had walked not far, when (153) he came upon a boggy-looking stream. As it ran it dribbled, like any lively purliteasy.

And on the opposite bank, hanging from a tree, was the Gripes. The Gripes, completely desiccated, had never looked so badly.

Adrian (that was the Mookse's name now)[9] sat down across from the Gripes, on a stone,[10] as pontifically as possible.

Whereupon the Gripes greeted him in a whining voice, (154) and asked to know the news.

The bull bellowed at him threateningly to remember to whom he was speaking.

The Gripes asked to know the time.[11]

"This," replied the Mookse, "is what I, with my Bull, *Laudabiliter,* have come to settle with *you.* Will you give up?"

You should have heard the voice that answered him! What a little voice!

"I was just thinking of that, sweet Mookse; I can never give up to you. My temple is my own. Nor shall I ever be able to tell you (155) whose cloak you are wearing."

[8] "The Fox and the Grapes" (Aesop); "The Mock Turtle and the Griffon" (*Alice in Wonderland*). The Mookse is a combination of King Henry II and Nicholas Breakspeare (Pope Adrian IV). Pope Adrian, an Englishman by birth, is said to have sent to the king a bull, opening with the word *Laudabiliter,* suggesting he take over Ireland and thus fulfill God's will that the Irish church should be co-ordinated with the Roman. (This bull figures in a lively passage in *Ulysses,* Random House ed., pp. 393 ff.; Paris ed., pp. 381 ff.) The Gripes (Gryphus, Griffon) is Lawrence O'Toole, bishop of Dublin at the time of Henry's invasion, 1171 A.D.

[9] Pope Adrian IV.

[10] Stone of Peter's church.

[11] Cf. request of the Cad with the pipe, p. 35.

"*Your* temple, you pig in a poke! Mine is always open to men of stout heart. Whereas, I regret to proclaim that I cannot help you from being killed by inches. My side is as safe as houses; I can prove that against you, I bet you this dozen of tomes."

The Mookse elevated, to give point to his remark, his jeweled staff to the star vault. And he proved it to the extinction of the Gripes altogether; proved it by Neuclidius, and Inexagoras, and Mommsen, and Thompsen . . . and after that he re-proved it (156) by the binominal theorem and every other authority in the book.

While the Mookse was promulgating his *ipso-factos* and *sed-contras,* this rascally Gripes had all but succeeded in making monophysites of his subordinates. But though the Gripes had, time and time again, sought to teach his own flock how to trumpet forth the double meanings of his doctrines,[12] his pastors were found to be at loggerheads and at variance with the constitutions of his provincial creed, and so he got the hoof; he having wished to follow the Eastern rather than the Roman interpretation of the relation of the Father and the Son to the Holy Ghost.[13]

"In a thousand years, O Gripes, you will be blind to the world," said the Mookse.

"In a thousand years," answered the Gripes, "you may be still more bothered."

"I shall be chosen as the first of the last by the electress of Vale Hollow," said the Mookse, proud of his fine English cut.

"I shall not even be the last of the first, I hope, when we are visited by the veiled horror," confessed the Gripes limply, miserable foe of the social order.

(157) And like dog and serpent they went at each other viciously.

Meanwhile, the Little Cloud Girl, in her light dress, was leaning over the banistars, listening all she childishly could. She was

[12] This colloquy between the Mookse and the Gripes sets forth obscurely the theological differences between the Roman (Mookse) and Irish (Gripes) churches. The Irish church was pre-Gothic in character, mystical in spirit, and resembled the Greek Orthodox.

[13] Filioque Controversy.

alone. She tried to make the Mookse look up at her and to make the Gripes hear how coy she could be, but it was all mild's vapor moist. Their minds were beset with their learned quotations. And she tried the winsome wonsome ways her four winds had taught her. (158) But she might just as well have carried her daisy's worth to Florida! For the Mookse was not amused, and the Gripes was lost in obliviscence.

"I see," she sighed. "They are stupids!"

The shades began to glidder along the banks, dusk unto dusk. The Mookse could no longer hear, the Gripes no longer see. The Mookse thought of the deeps he would profound on the morrow, the Gripes of the scrapes he would escape if he had luck enough.

And the dew began to fall.

Then there came down to the thither bank a woman of no appearance, and she gathered up the Mookse where he lay. There came down to the hither bank a woman too all-important, and she plucked down the Gripes from his limb.[14] (159) There were left now only an elmtree and a stone. And Nuvoletta, the Little Cloud Girl, a lass.

Then Nuvoletta reflected for the last time and made up her drifting minds. She climbed over the banistars, gave a childy cloudy cry, a light-dress fluttered, she was gone. And into the river that had been a stream there fell a tear—it was a leap tear.[15] But the river tripped on her way.

No applause, please, ladies and gentlemen!

Nolan Brown, you may leave the room.

[Having concluded his fable, the professor resumes the argument. He is unfolding, though perhaps in rather complicated

[14] In terms of fable, these women are the Banshees, Celtic Valkyries, carrying the dead heroes from the battlefield. In terms of a context to be developed in Chapter 8, they are two washerwomen, come to carry away a butcher's apron hanging from the branches of a tree and a hotel sheet held down by a stone (cf. p. 213).

[15] The leap-year girl (twenty-ninth of the little school group) is the sign of Iseult.

fashion, a case against the man who fails to develop a life style essentially practical. His first point was, that though the beggar may appear to be a pathetic figure, he is actually an undeserving and even dangerous one, and may be properly resisted. His second point was that the man's entire world outlook is of an inferior type, being rather of an inward than of an outward orientation. Kant has called Time the form of the inner sense, and Space the form of the outer. The beggar in question is a man who lives, so to speak, under the sign of Time (Shem), indrawn from the contemporary scene and absorbed in a regressive brooding on times past; this sort of introversion inevitably confining him in a sphere of only personal validity. But the professor lives under the sign of Space (Shaun), realistically measuring his capacities against the actualities of the world and making the best of himself and of things: he asserts that a healthy effective relationship to the actualities of space is the way to come to terms not only with oneself but with all.

[In the fable, the hard-headed and enormously successful style of the Roman Mookse was contrasted with the more mystical, relatively quiescent and politically ineffectual style of the Celtic Gripes, and though the fable itself dealt somewhat ironically with the Mookse's achievement, the professor clearly intended his talent for survival to stand as an argument in favor of his metaphysics and as a testimonial to his own virtue.

[Toward the conclusion of the fable there emerged the cloud girl, Nuvoletta. From her standpoint, neither of the contending males represents an adequate reply to the cry of her nature. Her problem is to be developed during the next pages, in the professor's discussion of the relationship of the cowrymaid Margareen to the embattled brothers, Burrus and Caseous (Butter and Cheese, Brutus and Cassius, Shaun and Shem). The professor returns to his argument with a fling against a colleague who is, no doubt, rather of the Shem than of the Shaun type.]

I am a greater man, declares the professor, than my friend, Gnaccus Gnoccovitch. I am a much more deserving genius than he is. Nevertheless, I feel a sympathy for him; he is so bally clever.

while I must slave to methodiousness. He should go and live on Tristan da Cunha, where he would be the 106th inhabitant,[16] and be near Inaccessible. (Which reminds me, by the way, that this exposed site (160) with its luxurious trees should be classified under the genus *Inexhaustible*. It is as though hawthorns should grow on Mount Curraghchosaly [in Ulster], which looks plane as a lodgepole until one sees the painting of Verney Rubeus, where the East Indian cedar is depicted there in a pure stand, but without such self-sown seedlings as occur on *East Conna Hillock*, where the tree mixes with acacias and sallows and is tender: the seedlings on this latter place are a species of proof that the largest individual *can* occur at such an elevation.) [17] Alderman Whitebeaver, indeed, should go away for a change of ideas. If I weren't the man I am, I'd elect myself to give him his sendoff. He is a barefaced robber, plagiarizing my publications!

Come, let us murmur quietly. I am being overheard by the Four Old Annalists, Bill Faust, Walsh, Philip Dublinite, and Mr. West. From the point of fun where I am trying to arrive you at, they are all four as feeble-minded as you can feel they are fable-bodied.

But now to the problem of Burrus and Caseous. My reader will recall how (161) I proved that the object of Professor Ciondolone's hypothecated beggar is nothing more than a mere cash-dime, for to him dime *is* cash. But, under the conditions of the actual cash system, unless Burrus and Caseous are not yet disentangled from each other, I cannot have or not have the coin in your pocket quite as you can not half or half the matter I've in mind.[18]

[16] According to the Encyclopædia Britannica, the population of the little South Atlantic island of Tristan da Cunha was in 1800, 109 and in 1925, 130. Twenty miles from Tristan is Inaccessible Island.

[17] Great trees growing on mountaintops, whether in Ulster or on Tristan da Cunha, are representatives of HCE. The professor is rambling inexcusably, but will return presently to the point.

[18] This curious statement seems to make the point that, though men may be, from the pseudomystical standpoint of Shem's time philosophy, finally one, yet insofar as they exist in a space world, they are separate from each other. The twins, Burrus and Caseous, before the egg split in the womb, were indeed identical, but they are now disentangled from each other; and

What about these two, Burrus and Caseous? Burrus is a prime [Shaun]; Caseous is the reverse of him [Shem]. It is the old, old story we used to be reading till Daddy would shut up shop—our Old Party, united around the salad bowl at Commons: the Parson, Pedersill and his sprig of thyme, the twelve citizens, the twenty-eight little girlies, pretty Lettucia, you and me. (Stop screwing that cork, Schott!) To help you understand this complicated matter I have made the following arrangement:

(162) Old Caesar being outworn with age, the twins are billed for reappearance. One of them, Caseous, bethinks himself a kind of Cavalier and sees the mote in Ireland's eye. The other, Burrus, is a Roundhead of soft-thinking fideism [19] and has the lac of wisdom under every dent in his lofter. When he was a youth, he was a very king off duty and a joy forever. He had a cheery ripe outlook. (163) He ate only butter and honey, that he might know how to reprove evil and elect good. This explains why we were taught to play in childhood: *Der Haensli ist ein Butterbrot—und Koebi iss dein Schtinkenkot!* [20] *Ja! Ja! Ja!*

Here, just to show you, is Caseous himself, the brother scutch, a pure tyro. "Cheese, ugh!" you complain; and I must say you are not wholly wrong.

So you see, we cannot escape our likes and mislikes. The philanthropists, I know, advance, at this point, the temporal plea. I, however, would conclude simply that we should be tolerant of antipathies. Now I must turn aside for a moment to declare that I am not to be understood as hereby endorsing: (*a*) the tavern-keeper's Cusanus philosophism, to wit, that the smarter the spin of the top, the sounder the span of the bottom; or (*b*) the god-

under present circumstances, though Burrus may share the thought wealth of Caseous and the latter become thereby no whit the poorer, it is absurd for Caseous to expect to share, in the same way, the hard space nuggets of Burrus's cash.

[19] If the Mookse represented the Anglo-Norman invasion of the twelfth century, Burrus, his later incarnation, represents the Cromwellian Roundhead of the seventeenth.

[20] *Schinkenbrot:* ham sandwich; *stinkend' Kot:* stinking filth.

lover's Nolanus theory, to wit, that while eggs will fall cheapened all over the walled, the Bure will be dear on the Brie; or (c) the Silkebjorg tyron-dynamon machine for the more economical electrolysis of these two adipates.[21] I must first find space to look into this latter problem a little more closely myself. Meanwhile I shall go on with my discussion, after having shown you how these two products of our social stomachs (164) are mutually polarized. Positing as above, two male poles and looking wantingly around our undistributed middle between males, we feel we must waistfully want a female to focus. And at this stage there pleasantly appears the cowrymaid, M.,[22] who introduces herself upon us at some precise hour which we shall agree to call absolute zero.[23] And so, like Saul who went forth to find his father's asses, we come down home gently on our own turned-about asses to meet Margareen.

Now comes a period of purest lyricism: a song of distress sung by Caseous, and a song of hope by Burrus. And, by the way, talking about music: the science of criniculture can explain to us quite precisely about the appearance of this silver thread among the gold; I am offering this bit of information to Signorina Cuticura and intend to bring it to the notice of Herr Harlene. And, by the way again, another piece of advice: unskilled singers still afflict our ears by subordinating the space factor—that is to say, the aria— to the time factor—the tempo. I should advise any unborn singer who may still be among my heeders to forget her temporal diaphragm at home (165) and attack the roulade with a swift *colpo di glottide* and then to close her eyes and open her mouth and see what I may send thee.

I shall later have a word to say about the acoustic and archi-

---

[21] This machine for splitting butter and cheese out of a single emulsion, milk, represents allegorically the world process itself, which brings thesis and antithesis out of synthesis.

[22] Magnetism.

[23] She appears before the beginning of time; in fact, her presence is a precondition to the beginning of the world process.

rectural management of the town hall, but it will be convenient for me, for the moment, to pursue Burrus and Caseous for a rung or two up their isocelating biangle. Now every admirer of my painting style has seen my gouache of Marge (she is so like her sister, you don't know, and they both dress ALIKE) [24] which I titled "The Very Picture of a Needlesswoman." This genre of portraiture of changes of mind should evoke the bush soul of females, and so I leave it to the experienced victim to complete the general suggestion by the mental addition of a kangaroo hop or Congo teal. But the point to be made is this: the hatboxes which composed the rhomboid or trapezoid cubist portrait of Marge in her excelsis, also comprise the above-mentioned isocelating biangle, which we shall now call the B-C climactogram,[25] and they suggest men's spring modes—which carry us back to Cenozoic times and to the *boîte à surprises* of political evolution. Boxes of this kind are worth about fourpence apiece, but I am inventing a new process, after which they can be produced at a fraction of their (166) present cost by even the youngest of Margees.

I have now quite got the size of that young female, Marge. Her types may be met with in any public garden, or at the movies, or holding a baby out over the gutter at arm's length, teaching his Infant Majesty how to make bad waters worse. (The Smythe-Smythes now keep TWO domestics and aspire to THREE male ones, that is to say, to a chauffeur, a butler, and a secretary.)

(As for the baby out over the gutter, I am closely watching Master Pules, for I have a reason to suspect that the "little man" is a secondary school teacher, who is being utilized thus publicly by the young woman to conceal her own more mascular personality. But my solutions for the proper parturience of mothers and

[24] Development of relationship of Iseult to the Maggies.
[25] Perhaps the following diagram resembles the isocelating biangle of Burrus and Caseous, now called "the B-C climactogram" and identified with Marge (compare the diagram in which ALP appears as a completed triangle, on p. 293).

the education of micturious mites must stand over for the moment, till I tackle this hussy.)

[And so now, on with the story:] Margareen is very fond of Burrus, but she is also very fond of cheese. And while Burrus and Caseous are contending for her mastery, she complicates the position by implicating herself (167) with an elusive Antonius—a wop who would appear to hug a personal interest in refined cheese of all shades, at the same time pretending to be rude like a boor [*beurre*]. [And now comes the grand conclusion to the entire argument:] This Antonius-Burrus-Caseous group-triad may be said to equate the *qualis* equivalent with the older so-called *talis* on *talis* one.[26] This is why any fool you like to dress may be awfully green to one side of him and fruitfully blue on the other, which will not screen him from appearing to my searching eyes as a blasted idiot.

No! Twelve times now I have said it. My unchanging word is sacred: the word is my wife, and may the curlews crown our nuptials! Where the tongue hath named, *there* is Justice! Against the foreigner always draw the line! That man who hath no lawgiver in his soul and is not awed by the conquests (168) of word's law, who never to himself hath said, "This is my own, my native land," if he came to my beach, a proud purse-broken ranger, to beg for a bite, would myself and MacJeffet together foot him out? Ay! were he my own breast brother and though it broke my heart to do it, still I'd fear I'd hate to say. . . .

[Thus ends the great humanists *apologia pro vita sua*. And now only one question remains to be solved. We have heard from nearly everyone in the room. But there is a shabby fellow cringing in the

[26] Antonius appears to represent the addition of a synthesizing male figure to the thesis-antithesis polarity of Burrus and Caseous. This compounding factor completes the restatement of the traits of HCE, in whom Burrus's and Caseous' characteristics were organically combined. In terms of the geometrical parable, Antonius completes the triangle and establishes the equivalence of this pattern of the children to that of the older figure from which it was derived.

corner. The final question of the series, Number 12, is addressed by the righteous one toward that other.]

12. *Sacer esto?*—Shalt be accursed?
Answer: *Semus sumus!*—We are Shem!

Book I, Chapter 7: Shem the Penman

[The riddles of the Tiberiast duplex led inexorably to the miserable personage named in the last of the questions. But why should an entire chapter in a section of the work devoted to the mother be assigned to Shem the Penman? The answer is not far to seek: of the two sons, Shem is the mother's pet and Shaun the father's. Shem, indeed, as the Penman, is the scribe responsible for the actual writing of the mother's letter. He is, in fact, as the reader will immediately perceive, James Joyce himself. ALP in one of her manifestations is the Muse invoked by the poet: the poet does not invent his verses but discovers their materials in those deep layers of the psyche where lurk the infantile, buried reminiscences of the mother. She is the Muse; the poet her favorite child. But the language of the missive which he pens under her dreamlike enigmatic inspiration is not wholly clear to the waking eye, though deeply familiar to the soul. Feared and resented, consequently, by his fellows, this child of the mother is doomed to seek his joys where his brother Shaun sees only misery and sin.]

(169) There are a few who still maintain that Shem was of respectable stock; but every honest man today knows that his past will not bear description. Putting truth and untruth together, a shot may be made at what he looked like.

His bodily getup included an adze of a skull, one numb arm up a sleeve, a few stray hairs to his lip and chin, the wrong shoulder higher than the right, not a foot to stand on, a handful of thumbs, a blind stomach, a loose liver, eel's-blood in his cold toes, etc. On first seeing himself, while playing in the nursery, (170) he dictated to all his little brothers and sisters the first riddle of the universe, to wit: "When is a man not a man?" All tried to guess the answer but failed. Then he gave them his own solution: "When he is a Sham."

Shem was a low sham, and his lowness first was evident in the things he chose to eat. He preferred salmon tinned to the plumpest ever gaffed in River Liffey, and he often said that no jungle pine-apple ever equaled those you shook out of cans. None of your thick juicy steaks or legs of mutton (171) for that Greek-hearted Jew! He ran off to the lentil hash of the Continent sooner than meddle with Ireland's split little pea. Once, when drunk, he hiccuped that he could live forever on the smell of a citron peel. He preferred windigut applejack to first-rate whisky, gin, or beer.

Talk about lowness! His lowness oozed out all over him, and to such a degree that when a camera girl once shot his snap and this gun-and-camera-shy coward tried to escape her by taking a short cut (172) into the shop of Patatapapaveri's, fruiterers and musical florists, she could tell he was a bad fast man by his walk.

(Advertisement: John's is a different butcher's. Ex! Exex! Exexex! COMMUNICATED.) [1]

One generally suspected he would turn out badly, develop hereditary pulmonary T.B. and do for himself one dandy time. But he wasn't even true enough to type to commit suicide. Once he wired his brother for help, and was abruptly spurned.[2]

You see, chaps, he was low. Meanwhile he was gathering up every crumb of his neighbor's talk. If, during a conversation, a hint touching his evil courses were given, (173) he would root with thoughtful pencil in his ear and then would begin to tell the intelligentsia the whole story of his low existence, abusing his deceased ancestors—one moment celebrating his fine Poppamore, Mr. Humhum, next moment jeering his rotten little Peppybeg, Mr. Himmyshimmy—(174) avoiding the issue of the original reproval, and thus betraying himself at every turn.

He disliked anything like a plain straightforward fight. When

[1] Cf. p. 67.
[2] Cf. p. 149 ff.

124

called upon to umpire, he would agree to every word uttered, and then at once focus his attention on the next antagonist.

One stormy night, therefore, he was soccered through Dublin, from Mr. Vanhomrigh's house,[3] by rival teams, who instead of ruggering him back, decided they had better be streaking for home. There was once a hope that people, (175) after first giving him a roll in the dirt, might pity and forgive him. But he was born low, and sank till out of sight.

Headlines! Headlines! All Saints beat Belial! Mick beats Nick![4] All ready? Sing:

[The victory song is a combination and modification of the *recorso* paragraph of page 3 and the "Ballad of Persse O'Reilly." It reviews, with cheers for the way of the world, the now familiar themes: the world parents and the thunderclap, Napoleon and Wellington, the mound and the invader, the voice from a fire and the baptizer, Satan's fall, Adam's fall, Humpty Dumpty's fall from the wall, the mountain and the stream, the Wake scene, the Temptresses, the Four, and the Twelve:] "Hirp! Hirp! for their Missed Understandings! chirps the Ballat of Perce-Oreille."

O fate! Darkies never played games with that poor coon; those old games we used to play with Dina and old Joe; (176) games like: *Hat in the Ring, Nickel in the Slot, Two's and Three's, Fox come out of your Den, Broken Bottles, Postman's Knock, Battle of Waterloo, Hops of Fun at Millikin's Make.* . . .

Now it is known how on that bloody Unity Sunday, when the all-star bout was the rage and Irish eyes of welcome were sinking daggers down their backs, this scut in a bad fit of pajamas fled like a leveret for his bare lives, pursued by the scented curses of

---

[3] Vanessa's father's house.

[4] Belial: a Semitic god of the underworld, identified in the Jewish Testaments of the Patriarchs with Satan. Balliol: an Oxford college in which are enrolled numerous Hindus and other outlanders. "Mick beats Nick" carries on this Light vs. Darkness theme, Mick representing the Archangel Michael, Nick representing the devil.

the village belles and without having struck one blow. He corked himself tight in his inkbottle house where he collapsed under a bedtick, (177) moaning feebly (Hail, Mary, full of grace! Holy Mary, Mother of God!) his cheeks and trousers changing color every time a gat croaked.

How is that for low? Girlies, revolting at the bare mention of the scaly ribald, exclaimed: "The Fish!"

But would anyone believe it! No one ever nursed a higher opinion of himself than did this mental and moral defective. He was known to have grunted on one occasion, while drinking heavily of spirits, to that interlocutor he used to pal around with, one Davy Browne-Nolan, in the porchway of a gypsy's bar, that he was aware of no other Shakhisbeard to match himself, and that, though he was foxed, with all the teashop (178) lions up against him, he would, if his lifeline lasted, wipe any English spooker off the face of the earth.[5]

After the thorough fright he got that bloody St. Swithin's day, though every doorpost in the land was smeared with the blood of Irish heroes and every gutter gushing with tears of joy, our low waster never had the pluck to stir out and about the compound. While everyone else waded around chanting a chorus from the *Book of Patriotic Poetry,* and members of the fairer sex went stone-stepping across the sevenspan bridge set over the slop after the war to end war,[6] he went peeping through a three-draw eighteen hawk's-power telescope, through his westernmost keyhole, with a hope of finding out whether true conciliation was forging ahead or falling back after the celestial intemperance. And (179) he got the charm of his optical life when he found himself at point-blank range blinking down the barrel of an irregular revolver, of the bulldog-with-a-purpose pattern, handled by an unknown quarreler, told off to shade and shoot him should he show his snout.[7]

[5] Cf. Stephen's conversations with Lynch, in *Portrait of the Artist as a Young Man* and *Ulysses.*
[6] Rainbow Maids after the Flood.
[7] Cf. situation of p. 62. Here is a corresponding episode, but in Shem style.

What in the name of all the heroes and gods was this low fellow really up to?

He had become a drug and drink addict, with a growing megalomania and a loose past. This explains the line of honorific letters which he so loved to inscribe behind his name. And it would have been diverting to have seen him in his greenish den making believe to read his unreadable book, *Ulysses,* turning over three sheets at a wind and telling himself that every splurge on the vellum he blundered over was a vision more gorgeous than the one before—the splurges conjuring up before his mind images of morbid delight; (180) or to have seen him when he squealed the top squall in "The Dear Little Shamrock of Ireland," singing infinitely better than that baritone McGluckin with the scrumptious cocked hat and three green plumes on the side of his yellow head.[8] But what with the murky light, the botchy print, and his body full of ills, he was hard-set to memorize more than a word a week. Can you beat it?

He used to boast aloud alone to himself (181) how he had been toed out of all the more chic families who had settled and stratified in the capital city, ordered off the premises in most cases on account of his smell. Then what did he do but study how to copy all their various styles of signatures so as one day to utter an epical forged check on the public for his own profit, until the Scullerymaid's and Househelp's Sorority turned him down and shoed him out.

(Advertisement: Jymes wishes to hear from wearers of abandoned female costumes. To start city life together.[9])

One cannot even begin to figure out how low he was. Who can say (182) how many shams and forgeries may have slipped from his plagiarist pen.

Be that as it may, but for his gnose's [10] glow, as it slid luciferously within an inch of its page, he never would have quilled a line to sheepskin. By that rosy lampoon's effluvious burning, however, and

[8] An account of Joyce's experience at the singing contest is given in Herbert Gorman's *James Joyce,* Farrar and Rinehart, 1939, pp. 121–22.
[9] Contrast advertisement on p. 172. Compare Bloom's interests in *Ulysses.*
[10] Nose's plus gnosis.

with the help of the flash in his pan, he scribbled nameless shame-lessnesses about everybody ever he met, while he stippled idealized portraits of himself in the margins.

His house, known as the Haunted Inkbottle, no number, Brim-stone Walk, Asia in Ireland, with his pen name, SHUT, on the doorplate, in which he groped through life at the expense of the taxpayers, (183) was a stinksome inkstink, godforsakenly littered, (184) wherein the whirling dervish, Tumult son of Thunder, self-exiled, would be shaking, noonday-terrorized to skin and bone by an ineluctable phantom,[11] writing the mystery of himself in furni-ture.

Of course he was his own valet, so he cooked eggs for himself with cinnamon and locusts and wild beeswax and star dust and sinner's tears, while chanting fermented words.[12] (185) And when the pulpit dictators, on the nudgment of their legal advisors, boy-cotted him of all mutton-suet candles and rome-ruled stationery for any purpose, he winged away and made synthetic ink and sensitive paper for his own end out of his wit's waste. How? Let the answer to this question be cloaked in the Latin of Rome, so that an Anglican, not reading it in his own rude tongue, may behold the brand of scarlet on the brow of Babylon and feel not the pink one in his own damned cheek.

[The Latin passage describes the alchemistical operation by which the isolated one transmuted his own waste matter into indelible ink. The matter was placed in a retort and there mixed to the incantation of a psalm.]

Then pious Aeneas wrote over every square inch of the only foolscap available, his own body, till by its corrosive sublimation one (186) continuous present-tense integument slowly unfolded all cycle-wheeling history.[13] So perhaps the blond cop who thought

[11] Cf. Stephen's fright at the thunderclap, *Ulysses,* Random House ed., pp. 388 f.; Paris ed., pp. 376 f.
[12] Fermented words—the language of *Finnegans Wake.*
[13] A statement of the nature and aim of the art of *Finnegans Wake.*

Shem's encaustic was ink was out of his depth but right in the main.

The cop was Petty Constable Sistersen. Detailed to save him from the effects of foul play and mob-mauling, the officer encountered him, an evening near Knockmaree, on his way from a protoprostitute (he would always have a little pigeoness somewhere, along with his archgirl, Arcoiris, smock name of Mergyt), just as he came round a corner to the door of a brothel (187) and skittled in. The guardian was astonished over the painful case the whole afternoon, got drunk on it, and marveled the more when he was told things about the fellow which he could not understand.

Neither can we understand them! But enough of such black lowness; we cannot, in mercy or justice, stay here the rest of our existence discussing Tamstar Ham.

[And now become manifest, through the persons, respectively, of the Shaunlike cop and his Shemlike prisoner, the two qualities of Justice and Mercy:]

JUSTICE (to him-other): Brawn[14] is my name and broad my nature and I'll do this bird up brown or my gun's gone bandy. Stand forth, Nayman of Noland, move me, twin though I be, to laughter, ere you be put back forever; till I give you your talking to! Shem, son of Adam, you know me and I know you in all your Shemmeries. Where have you been (188) since your last confession? I advise you to put yourself in my hands and have a nice long homely little confession. Let me see. It is looking pretty black against you.

Let us pry. You were brought up in piety in this blessed island and now, forsooth, you have become of two minds forenenst the gods. You have reared your disunited kingdom on the vacuum of your own most intensely doubtful soul. Do you hold yourself then for some god in the manger, Shehohem, that you will neither serve nor let serve, pray nor let pray? And here I must fear for my own purity, while scrutinizing your shame. God gave you the means

[14] Of Brown and Nolan, cf. p. 38.

with which to repopulate the land of your birth, but you thwarted (189) the pious wish, and added to the malice of your transgression by even writing down your apologia—thereby adding to the troubles of this our pop-eyed world—with countless educated women, the mannish as many as the minneful, gathered around you for acres, struggling to possess themselves of your boosh, one son of Care for all daughters of Anguish; they mutely eying for that natural bond which it would have been so simple to have, with a wedding ring, achieved.

Sniffer of carrion, you who sleep at our vigil and fast at our feast, you have foretold death and every disaster, (190) but it has never struck your mudhead's obtundity that the more you hack up and the harder you work at it, the merrier fumes your new Irish stew.

You shirked the duties of life and beat it, to sing us a song of alibi, (191) you unfrillfrocked quack friar, you discoverer of surprises, you Europeasianized Affer-yank!

There grew up beside you that other, that pure one, a chum of the angels, that good-looker without a flaw, whose spiritual toilettes were the talk of the town; but him you laid low with one hand one fine May morning, to find out how his innards worked! [15]

Ever read of the great-grand-land-father of our vision-builders, Baaboo, the bourgeoismeister, who thought to touch the heavens with his tower and was humbled? [16] (192) Ever hear of that heretical mason and the two sissymaidies?

What has Your Lowness done, meantime, with all the goods that you've borrowed and begged, pretending to be so badly off? Where is that little alimony nest egg against our predictable rainy day? Is it not a fact that (193) you squandered among underlings the overload of your extravagance?

Come here, Herr Studiosus, till I tell you a wig in your ear. It's secret! I had it from Lamppost Shawe, who had it from Mullah, who took it from a bluecoat scholar: Sh! Shem, you are mad!

[15] Shem as Cain, Shaun as Abel.
[16] Finnegan, HCE, Ibsen's Master Builder. The last pages of Ibsen's play throw light on the Fall theme.

He points the death bone and the quick are still.

MERCY (of his-self): The Lord be with you! My fault, his fault! I who forswore the womb that bore you and the paps I sometimes sucked, you who ever since have been one black mass of jigs and jimjams, haunted by a sense of not being all that I might have been or you meant to becoming, (194) lo you there, in the innermost depths of my still imperfectly contrite heart the days of your youth are ever mixed with mine, and now, at this final hour (when all is precisely as it was even before the beginning) it is to you, first-born and first-fruit of woe, but to me also, i randed sheep, pick of the wastepaper basket, to you alone, wind-blasted tree of the knowledge of beautiful and evil, and to me, unseen blusher in an obscene coal hole, because ye left from me, because ye laughed on me, that our turf-brown mummy is acoming, Anna Livia Plurabelle, running with her tidings, all the news of the great big world —little old-fashioned mummy, little wonderful mummy, ducking under bridges, bell-hopping the weirs, dodging by a bit of bog, rapid-shooting round the bends (195) giddy-gaddy, grannyma, gossipacious Anna Livia.

He lifts the life wand and the dumb speak.

"Quoiquoiquoiquoiquoiquoiquoi!"

[Through four hypothetical transformations the Shem-Shaun sequence has been developed: firstly, Professor Jones was to imagine himself encountered by the Exile of Erin, asking him for assistance of some kind; secondly, the Mookse confronted the Gripes across a stream, the Gripes asking to know the time, and while the two were engaged in conflict, Nuvoletta, unable to draw attention to herself, dissolved in tears; thirdly, Burrus being at odds with Caseous, Margareen discovered her ideal fulfilled not in either of the brothers, but in an elusive, momentarily glimpsed Antonius, who combined, or at least appeared to combine, the characteristics of the two; finally, Justice challenges Mercy and with righteous self-complacency judges; but the little turf-brown mother will come, and, without distinction, bring her blessings to the two.

[The Shem-Shaun conflict suggests that each of the brother op-posites has developed only one half of his man's nature. Shem, acutely aware of his need for assistance from the other half, has begged for help, but Shaun, unable to admit his need for the other, yet compelled to protest very elaborately his independence, has refused to collaborate and has insisted on his own unique power and right to occupy the seat of dictation. From the lower seat of Mercy, Shem forgives his brother even while castigating him with the lash of accusation. The female power clearly supports Shem's belief that neither of the male powers is adequate by himself. In her younger, sisterly, and idealizing form, she dreams past the two brothers to an ideal which would synthesize the qualities of the two—a hero to come who would be as all-inclusive as was her father; but in her mature, motherly, and realistic form, she simply comes forward and embraces both of her quarreling sons, effecting through her unquestioning and no longer forward-looking love, not an ideal but an actual reconciliation of the brother battle—a reconciliation which does not require even that the antagonism should be dissolved.

[Two of the four transformations through which the story passed are explicitly identified with epochs of Irish history: the Mookse episode with the Anglo-Norman conquest, the Burrus episode with the arrival of the Roundheads. Thus it is suggested that great cultural epochs manifest, and by stages develop, those same polar tensions which are first discoverable in the little forms of the family.

[The passage ended with the arrival of the mother. The next chapter, one of the most charming in the book, brings forward in strongest statement the all-dissolving, all-refreshing, all-recreat-ing theme of the mother. Two of her representatives (in the form of washerwomen scrubbing and airing dirty linen, one on either bank of the Liffey) chatter on about HCE and ALP, their children and their neighbors—the twilight meanwhile descending. One of the washerwomen is old and of the Kate type, the other is some-thing of the young temptress. The life wand of Mercy has just evoked them, like spirits, from the countryside, the elder from a stone, the younger from a whispering elm, and as the dusk thickens they will melt back again into their elemental forms. Thus, they may be thought of as Banshees, or, as the popular speech of Ireland would put it, the Washers at the Ford. In Eleanor Hull's valuable little book, *Folklore of the British Isles,* appears an excellent discussion of these shadowy Celtic sisters of the Germanic Norns and Valkyries and the classical Fates. "They are found before a battle washing the bloody garments of those about to fall in the fight. . . . Sometimes the Washer appears as a fair young maiden, at others as a withered crone. . . . She appears in nearly all stories of the death of heroes." [17]]

Book I, Chapter 8: The Washers at the Ford

[The Washers are at the Ford.[1] The flowing of the river is to carry us forward to a new book and a new age. The chattering voices begin with an echo of the "tell us, tell us, tell us all," first sounded on page 101.]

(196) O tell me all about Anna Livia! Well, you know when the old chap went futt and did what you know, or whatever it was they tried to make out he tried to do in Phoenix Park? He's an awful old rep! Look at the shirt of him! Look at the dirt of him! And how long was he under lock and key? [2] The old rep, mixing marriage and love-making! (197) And the strut of him! How he used to hold his head as high as Howth, with a bump of grandeur on him like a walking rat. Ask the four old readers, they know. What is it they call him? *H*uges *C*aput *E*arlyfouler.[3] Or where

---

[17] Eleanor Hull, *Folklore of the British Isles,* London, 1928, pp. 59–60.
[1] The Irish name of Dublin, Bailé átha Cliath, means "Town of the Hurdle Ford."
[2] Lough Neagh; see p. 76.
[3] Hugh Capet (938?–96), founder of the French Capetian dynasty; Henry the Fowler (876?–936), father of the German Otto the Great. France and Germany, as representatives of the brother pair, are united in the father, HCE. *Kaput* is German for "broken."

was he born or how was he found? Were their marriage banns ever announced in Adam and Eve's, or were him and her only captain-spliced? I heard he raped her home in a parakeet's cage. In a gabbard he sailed from the harborless ocean till he spied his landfall. And he sailed right up into Liffey mouth. (198) And he earned what he got; he worked hard for it. He was called a child of the deep. But sure she's nearly as bad as him herself. Do you know she was calling girls from all around to go into him, her erring chief, letting on she didn't care—the proxenete! [4] And is that what she is? But little I thought she'd act that low. Didn't you see her in her window, rocking on a chair, pretending to read music on her fiddle, which she can't fiddle a dee? [5]—Well, Old Humber, he was a glum one, his whole place littered up, and he sitting somber on his seat asking queasy questions of his rueful countenance,[6] (199) hunger-striking all alone and holding judgment over himself. You'd think all was dead belonging to him, the way he sat in durance vile. He had been belching for several years. And there she was, Anna Livia; she daren't catch a wink of sleep, purling around like a chit of a child, to wish him good day and to please him. And she'd cook him up fish and lay her eggs at his feet and bacon and toast and a cup of Greenland's tea or black coffee or sugary Sikiang or his ale and a slice of bread, for to please him; but Hek, he'd cast them from him with scorn, and if he didn't peg the tray at her toe she was lucky. Then she would offer a hymn; but not a peep out of him. Then she would flick at him, sparkling, her fan and her tresses, (200) in a period gown of changeable jade, and call him pet names, cheep little love songs, letting on she was daft about the warbly songs from back home, but he, in his sandy cloak, was as deaf as a yawn. And so didn't she up and trot down to her door, puffing her old pipe, and every silly servant girl or winsome farmerette walking the roads usedn't she make her a sign to slip inside and up to him? Calling them in one by one, and legging a jig or so on the sill to show

[4] Proxenete: negotiator, marriage-broker, procurer, procuress.
[5] The names of many rivers are woven into the gossip of the washerwomen.
[6] Don Quixote, knight of the Rueful Countenance.

them how to shake their benders and all the way of a maid with a man.

And what was the rhyme she made? Anna Livia's cushingloo, (201) that was writ by one and rede by two and found by a hen in the Park.[7]

It ran as follows: "What I want is a brand new bankside, for the one I have is worn out, waiting for my old Dane hodder dodderer. Is there a lord or knight would pay me to wash his socks? We're run out of horsemeat and milk! Only my bed's so snug, I'd be off to the beach to feel the gay air of my salt Dublin bay!"

O tell me more! How many young fishies[8] had she at all? I can't rightly tell you that. Some say it was 111.[9] She can't remember half the names she gave them. They did well to rechristen her Plurabelle. (202) She must have been a gadabout in her day. She had a few men of her own. Tell me, how could she come through all her fellows? Who was the first? When was it? She says herself she hardly knows who he was or what he did or how. She was just a pale soft shy thin slip of a thing then, sauntering by silver moon lake, and he was a heavy trudging lurching lie-abroad of a Curraghman, making his hay for the sun to shine on, as tough as the oaktrees. No, you're wrong there, it was ages behind that, in County (203) Wickenlow, garden of Erin. Are you certain? Tell me where, the very first time. I will if you will listen. You know the dingle dale of Luggala?[10] Well, there once dwelt a local

[7] Cf. the promise of the letter, pp. 93–94. Here the letter and the ballad are understood to have been a poem by ALP herself.

[8] The word "aleveen" in the text means "young fish," especially a newly hatched salmon. The strong play on the salmon theme throughout *Finnegans Wake* corresponds to the importance of the salmon in Irish myth and folklore. It was from the taste of the flesh of the great, wise salmon that Finn MacCool, according to the ancient tale, acquired his "Tooth of Knowledge."

[9] The number 111 for the children of Anna finds its parallel in the popular Russian attribution of 111 children to the Old Man of the Waters. The mythological number of plenitude is also 111.

[10] We are proceeding up the course of Liffey to its springs in the hills of Wicklow. This gentle, wooded and watered country is celebrated as the place of St. Kevin's hermitage.

hermit, Michael Arklow, and one Friday in June or July, O so sweet and so cool and so limber she looked, Nance the Nixie, Nanon l'Escaut, in the silence of the sycamores he plunged both his newly anointed hands into her singing saffron streams of hair. He could not help himself, thirst was that hot on him, so he lowered his lips in smiling mood, kiss akiss after kiss, on Anna-na-Poghue's of (204) the freckled forehead. But two lads in breeches went through her before that, Barefoot Burn and Wallowme Wade, Lugnaquilla's [11] noble Picts. And ere that again, too faint to buoy the fairest rider, too frail to flirt with a cygnet's plume, she was licked by a hound, Chirripa-Chirruta, on the spur of the hill of old Kippure.[12] But first of all, worst of all, she side-slipped out by a gap in the Devil's Glen, while Sally [13] her nurse was sound asleep, and fell over a spillway before she found her stride and lay and wriggled in all the stagnant black pools of rain under a fallow cow. And she laughed, innocent and free, with her limbs aloft, and a whole drove of maiden hawthorns blushing and looking askance upon her.

Tell me, why was she freckled? Was she marcelle-waved or was it merely a wig she wore? And what am I rinsing now? Mrs. Magrath's! You ought to have aired them. Baptize me, Father, for she has sinned! [14] (205) The only pair with frills in all the plain. And here are her maiden initials with an exe after them to show they're not Laura Keogh's. Now who has been tearing the leg of her drawers on her?

Well, after it was put in the papers, even the snow that snowed on his hair had it against him. Everywhere you went or every tavern you went into, you found his picture upside down or the cor-

[11] Lugnaquilla: loftiest summit of the Wicklow Mountains.
[12] Kippure: headwaters of the Liffey.
[13] Sally Gap: near another source of the Liffey.
[14] Mrs. Magrath and Laura Keogh here appear as variant incarnations of ALP.

ner boys mocking his effigy and a fellow taking him off. (206) And the rabble around him in judgment, making a great fracas. She swore she'd be level with them yet. So she said to herself she'd frame a plan to fake a shine, the mischief-maker, the like of which you never heard.

[The following is the chief episode of this chapter. It tells the story of how ALP crushed the scandal's head, by distributing presents to all her children from her bag of after-battle knickknacks. Each gift was a token of the recipient's own destiny.]

What plan? Tell me quick! Well, she borrowed a sac-bag, a mailsack, off one of her swapsons, Shaun the Post; and then she went and consulted her chapbooks, old Mot Moore, Casey's *Euclid,* and the *Fashion Display,* and made herself up to join in the masquerade. O it's too screaming! I can't go on! O but you must, you must really. Make me hear it. Tell me more!

First she let her hair fall down and it flowed to her feet. Then, mother-naked, she shampooed herself with water and fragrant mud. (207) And after that she wove a garland for her hair. Then she made bracelets, anklets, armlets, and a necklace of clicking cobbles and pattering pebbles and rumbledown rubble of Irish rhinestones. That done, she sent her boudoir maids to His Affluence, with respects from his missus and a request might she step out for a minnikin to pay a call. She said she wouldn't be half her length away. Then as soon as the hump of his back was turned, her bag slung over her shoulder, forth she came.

Describe her! Hustle along! Here she is, Amnisty Ann!

Old Moppa Necessity, mother of injuns. It might have been ten or twenty to one, the Night of All Souls or the last of April, when the flip of her igloo flappered, and out tiptoed a bushman woman, the dearest little mamma ever you saw, nodding around her, all smiles between two ages,[15] a judyqueen, not up to your (208) elbow. She wore a plowboy's nail-studded clods, a pair of plowfields in themselves; a sugar-loaf hat with a gaudyquivery peak; owl-

---

[15] Between two ages; cf. the figure on p. 293. ALP is the link between generations. In her cosmic aspect she is the link between aeons.

glassy bicycles boggled her eyes; a fishnet veil; potato rings in her lobes; salmonspot-speckled nude cuba stockings; a fourpenny bit in each pocket-side weighed her safe from the blow-away wind-rush.

Hellsbells, I'm sorry I missed her. And they crowned her Queen of the May. There was a chorus of drought-dropping sur-(209)face-men, boomslanging and plug-chewing, fruit-eying and flower-feeding, the twelve solid citizens, lolling on North Lazer's Wall; and as soon as they saw her meander by and twigged who it was under her bonnet, they declared: "Either her face has been lifted or Alp has been doped!"

But what was in her bag? And where did she get her plunder? Well, gyrating around in a wavery line she pattered and swung and sidled, with a Christmas box apiece for each and every one of her children. And they all about her, chipping her and raising a bit of a jeer or a (210) cheer every time she'd nab into her sack and reach out her merchandise, her sons and daughters, a thousand and one of them, and wicker-pot-luck for each of them. A tinker's damn and a barrel to boil his billy for Gypsy Lee; a cartridge of cockaleekie soup for Chummy the Guardsman; for sulky Pender's acid nephew, deltoid drops curiously strong; a cough and a rattle and wild-rose cheeks for poor Piccolina Petite MacFarlane; a jigsaw puzzle of needles and pins and blankets and shins between them for Isabel, Jezebel, and Llewelyn Mmarriage; a brazen nose and pig-iron mittens for Johnny Walker Beg; (211) for Seumas, though little, a crown he feels big; a stiff steadied rake and good varians muck for Kate the Cleaner; a hole in the ballad for Hosty; a letter to last a lifetime for Maggi beyond the ashpit; a change of naves and joys of ills for Armoricus Tristram Amoor St. Lawrence; an oaken knee for Conditor Sawyer; a sunless map of the month, including the sword and stamps, for Shemus O'Shaun the Post; whatever you like to swilly to drink, (212) Guinness or Hennesy or Lager or Niger, for Festy King and Roaring Peter and Frisky Shorty and Treacle Tom and O. B. Behan and Sully the Thug and Master Magrath and Peter Cloran and O'Delawarr Rossa and Nerone MacPacem and whoever you chance to meet knocking around. . . .[16]

My, what a bagful! That's what you call a tale of a tub.[17] Here throw us your soap. You've all the swirls on your side the current. Only the little paper cones for selling snuff drift my way, that the old clergyman[18] chucks out of his cassock, with the notes from Esther to make him recant his vanity fair, and bits from his Bible marked with tittles drawn on the tattle page. (213) Where's the soap? But go on! Tell me more!

Well,[19] don't you know or haven't I told you—every story has an ending. Look, the dusk is growing. My branches lofty are taking root. What age is it? Oh, my back! There's the Angelus bell! Wring out the old, wring in the new! And grant thy grace. Amen. Will ye spread them here now? Spread on your bank and I'll spread mine on mine. It's turning chill. The wind is rising. I'll lay a few stones on the hotel sheets. A man and his bride embraced between them. And I'll tie the butcher's apron here.[20] Where now are all her children? Some here, more no more. I've heard tell of one married into a family in Spain. Some in America, (214) one in the gutter, some broke. Do you tell me that now? And didn't you hear it a deluge of times? It's that wadding I've stuck in my ears, it hushes the least sound. [In the gathering dusk one of the women thinks she sees a shape; the other rebukes her:] Is that the great Finn himself in his kimono, on his statue, riding the high horse? You're thinking of Astley's Amphitheater, where the bobby restrained you making your sugar-stuck pouts to the

[16] In this last cluster of names appear the balladmongers, together with Festy King and with Sully, who is to appear later; all are variants of a single role.

[17] Swift's *Tale of a Tub* is frequently compared to *Finnegans Wake,* throughout the text.

[18] Swift in his later years.

[19] This is the point at which begins Joyce's phonograph recording, "Anna Livia Plurabelle."

[20] Cf. The Mookse and the Gripes, p. 158. Sheet and apron, respectively, are the Mookse (Shaun) and the Gripes (Shem).

ghost-white horse of the Peppers. Throw the cobwebs from your eyes, woman, and spread your washing proper. Were you lifting your elbow in Conway's Carrigacurra canteen? Amn't I up since the damp of dawn soaking and bleaching boiler rags, and sweating cold, a widow like me, for to deck my tennis-champion son, the laundryman with the lavandier flannels?—Holy Scamander, I saw it again! Near the golden falls. Subdue your noise. What is it but a blackberry growth, or the gray ass them four old codgers owns? (215) Is that the Poolbeg lighthouse flashing, or a fireboat coasting nigh the Kish, or a glow in a hedge, or my Garry come back from the Indies? We'll meet again, we'll part once more. The spot I'll seek if the hour you'll find. I'm going.

Ah, but she was the queer old skeowsha anyhow, Anna Livia trinket-toes! And sure he was the queer old buntz too, Dear Dirty Dumpling. Gammer and Gaffer, we're all their gangsters. Hadn't he seven dams to wive him each with her different hue and cry? He married his markets. But at Michaelmas who was the spouse? Anna was, Livia is, Plurabelle's to be. He had twins of his bosom and tittering daughters. . . .

Can't hear the waters of. The chittering waters of. Flittering bats, fieldmice, bawk talk. Ho! Are you not gone ahome? What Thom Malone?²¹ Can't hear with the bawk of the bats. Ho, my feet can't move. I feel as old as yonder elm. A tale told of Shaun or Shem? All Livia's daughter-sons. Dark hawks hear us. Night! Night! My ho head halls. I feel (216) as heavy as yonder stone. Tell me of John or Shaun? Who were Shem and Shaun the living sons or daughters of? Tell me a tale of stem or stone.²² Beside the rivering waters of, hither-and-thithering waters of. Night!

[Thus conclude the chapters of Anna Livia's Mamafesta, of the book of HCE and ALP. The gossips, asking for a tale of Shem and Shaun, point forward to the chapters of Book II.]

²¹ Night is falling, the banks of the river growing wider apart as we approach the mouth of Anna Liffey; the washerwomen are having difficulty in hearing each other.
²² Elmtree and stone: change and permanence, Shem and Shaun, Mercy and Justice, time and space. Tree and stone undergo many metamorphoses throughout the book.

BOOK II

THE BOOK OF THE SONS

[The Book of the Father and Mother, Book I, belongs to the deeps, where history becomes transmuted to legend, and legend takes on the aura of myth, and myth leads the mind to the mysteries of the Form of forms. The Book of the Sons, Book II, will belong in the present. Its figures will show a plasticity and solidity very different from the queer fluidities of Book I. There will be complications, indeed, and difficulties even greater than those characteristic of the father and mother problems; this book will seem even darker than the first—as the sense of the present is darker than the sense of the past; it will be harder to see around the figures and to envisage the field of their action, not because they will be lost in shadow, but because of the opaqueness of physical circumstance. Let us turn, then, prepared for a new experience, and yet an experience carrying all the familiar features of the past, to the story of the sons.

[Book II is divided into four chapters. The first (219–59) deals with a troop of children playing, about sunset, on the road before the tavern. The second (260–308) tells of the studies of the children, after supper, in their nursery upstairs. The third (309–82) describes the revelry of the tavern gentry, chattering and drinking through the night; the keeper himself, when they have all gone home, guzzles the dregs and collapses in a stupor. The fourth (383–99) projects the dream of the tavernkeeper, a rumpled hulk on the floor.]

Book II, Chapter 1: The Children's Hour

[Chapter 1 is presented as a play given by the children before their parents. The outline is simple enough. Glugg is thrice tempted to adventures which he cannot accomplish, first by a game of charades, next by a coy little note, and finally by a sign that carries his mind to "the house of breathings." Each of his failures results in a dance of triumph of the girls around Chuff, and in an excess of black bile within his own unhappy soul. First he swears to himself the three oaths of Exile, Silence, and Cunning; next he shows repentance, but confesses his father's and mother's sins instead of his own; finally, he indulges in sinful lustful thoughts. Whereupon the valiant Chuff makes at him, and they wrestle until the voice of the father summons them home.

[The little game is an image of the endless round of the aeons: the children tramp along Vico Road re-enacting the old story of their parents. The awakening of the father from his nap is analogous to that awakening of Finnegan which is to come at the end of the cycle. Then will take place the reconciliation of Mick and Nick: all contrarieties will have found their resolution in the eternal.]

(219) The chapter begins as an announcement of a play, which is presented every evening, just at lighting-up o'clock, in Phoenix Playhouse. The name of the piece is *The Mime of Mick* [*St. Michael*], *Nick* [*the devil*], *and the Maggies* [*the tempting girls*]. Entrance fee: for little vagabonds, one crab apple; for the quality, one shilling. The play is produced with the benediction of the Holy Genesius Archimimus [God Himself], under the patronage of the Four Old Men, while the Caesar-in-Chief [father] looks on. As played, after humpteen dumpteen revivals, before all the King's Hoarsers and all the Queen's Mum. Broadcast over seven seas in teuto-slavo-zend-latin sound-script. In four tabloids.

The caste:

GLUGG (Shem), the bold, bad, bleak boy of the storybooks, who (220) has been divorced into disgrace-court by:

142

THE FLORAS (Girl Scouts from St. Bride's Finishing Establishment[1]), a month's bunch of pretty maidens, twenty-eight in all, who form the guard for:

IZOD (Miss Beautyspot), a bewitching blonde approached in loveliness only by her sister reflection in the mirror. Having jilted Glugg, she is being fatally fascinated by:

CHUFF (Shaun), the fine frank fair-haired fellow of the fairytales, who wrestles with Glugg, geminally, until they adumbrate the pattern of somebody else or other, after which they are carried off the set and brought home to be well soaped, sponged, and scrubbed again by:

ANN (Miss Corrie Corriendo), their poor little old mother-in-lieu,[2] woman of the house, playing opposite to:

HUMP (Mr. Make-all-Gone), with watch and topper, the cause of all our grievances, who, having partially recovered from a recent impeachment due to egg everlasting,[3] is engaged in entertaining in his customhouse those statutory persons:

(221) THE CUSTOMERS (Components of the Afterhour Courses at St. Patricius' Academy for Grownup Gentlemen[4]), a bundle of a dozen representative citizens, each in quest of outings, sloppishly served by:

SAUNDERSON (Mr. Knut Oelsvinger), spoil-curate and butt of:

KATE (Miss Rachel Leah Varian: tells fortunes during intermissions), cook and dish-drudge.

TIME: the present.

PROP DESIGNERS, ETC.: Pageant of Past History by Messrs. Thudd and Blunder; Shadows by the Film Folk; Promptings by Elan Vitale; Shots by Hexenschuss, Coachmaher, Incubone, and Rocknarrag.[5] Tree taken for grafted; Rock rent; the Crack by a smoker

---

[1] St. Bride is St. Bridget, cf. "mishe mishe," p. 3.
[2] Anna is frequently described as being not the mother but the stepmother of the children of HCE.
[3] Hump is HCE himself, long after the affair of the trial.
[4] St. Bride and St. Patrick are associated, respectively, with the Twenty-eight and the Twelve.
[5] Ragnarök: Doom or "Weird" of the Gods (cf. *Poetic Edda*).

from the gods; the Interjection (Buckley!) by the fire-(222)ment in the pit. To start with, a community prayer, everyone for himself. To conclude with, a chorale in canon. The whole to be wound up for an afterenactment by a Magnificent Transformation Scene showing the Radium Wedding of Night and Morning and the Dawn of Peace, Pure, Perfect, and Perpetual, Waking the Weary of the World.

ARGUMENT:

Chuffy was an angel then; his sword flashed like lightning. Holy St. Michael defend us in battle.[6] Make the sign of the cross, Amen.

But the devil himself was in Glugger. He was puffing and spitting and cursing like anything. Depart from me, ye cursed, into everlasting fire.[7] Acts of feet, hoof, and jarrety.[8]

The girls were flittering teasingly. How pierceful in their suggestiveness were those first girly stirs. (223) Marylamb, she was suffering all the dis-easiness of the unheard of. For all her help, Glugg could not catch her; nor could he catch the others, Rose, Sevilla, Citronelle, Esmeralde, Pervinca, Indra, Viola; nor these seven four times over.[9] Then they pantomimed before him the color heliotrope, as follows: up tightly in the front, down again on the loose, drim and drumming on her back, and a pop from her whistle.[10] What is that, O holytroopers? Is it given you to guess?

Up he stumbled with a fling. They confronted him.

Napoleon was never more fated for a fall.

[6] From the prayers at conclusion of Holy Mass.
[7] God's words on doomsday to the damned.
[8] Faith, hope, and charity, here transformed to suggest the animal foot of the devil.
[9] The seven rainbow girls who tempt the father and the twenty-eight who tempt the sons are here identified with each other.
[10] Eugene Jolas (*transition,* February, 1933, p. 103) has described this sentence as "an attempt to sound-describe the word heliotropes from the viewpoint of Sir Richard Paget's idea of gesture" ... "a picaresque illustration of the theory expressed by Sir Richard Paget in his 'The Nature of Human Speech' (at the Clarendon Press, S.P.E. Tract No. XXII)."

They bid him arrest himself. *Il s'arrêtait,* and he sought to prof-ter to his favorite a trifle plucked from the grass.

"Who are you?" he asks. "The cat's mother," one replies. "What do you lack?" he asks after a pause. "The look of a queen."

But what is the answer to the riddle? The fiend buzzles his brains.

He sought advice and help from the four elements [the Four Old Men]. He asked help from the fire of the sun [Matthew]. He sought help from the air about him [Mark]. He looked upon the earth beneath his feet [Luke]. He listed back to the water of the stream [John].

And he received not a word from the wordless ether either.

He was hard set then. He wanted to go somewhere, while he was waiting, and make wee-wee. He wished to grieve on the (224) four gentlemen. He was at his thinker to give the Four the present of a curse.

And thereby hangs our tale.

Poor Glugg! Truly deplurabel! So sad of him about his old font-mother and all the freightfulness he inhebited from his col-line-born janitor of a father. He thought of their scoldings and spankings; and of their quarrels; when in his subconscious he would scarce not know whether his mother had burst a blabber, or if the bird tones that hit his ear meant that merely his excuses had not convinced her.[11] He was entirely stumped and they were mocking him.

The girlies are drawn up in a row. The boy-fiend thinks how he must find for himself, by guesswork, what color they are showing. Meanwhile, he is trying to hold nature back with his hand. The girls mock him (225) and break into hilarious laughter. Holding their noses, they insinuate he has made pee in his breeches and is playing with himself.

"Werewolf! Off! Taboo!"

[11] Throughout this chapter Glugg's moments of anxiety and defeat are extraordinarily difficult to decipher: they contrast strikingly with the blithe and simple moments of Chuff's joy and triumph. The present fairly thin approximations to their sense only indicate the trend of his emotions.

So off he ran as fast as legs would run, and he squatted on his hunkers, making believe to have a belly ache.

The little girl of girls found him terribly dumb. If he'd only talk instead of gawk like that! as though someone had stuck a stick through his spokes; and if he would not worry so!

[He makes, now, his three guesses:]

"Moonstone?"—No.

"Ruby?"—No.

"Van Diemen's [12] coral pearl?"—No.

He has lost.

Whereupon he is immediately rejected, and Chuff is acclaimed: "Off to clutch, Glugg! Farewell!" "Ring we round Chuff! Farewell!"

But little Izod is in tears. Who can her mater be? She'd been promised he'd eye her; but now he's away and fled.

Drooping and wilting (226) poor Isa sits aglooming in the gloaming. Why? Because her beau, Glugg, has gone. But we know she'll meet a new fancy, and she'll be married and helping her husband one day, with a little girl of her own. Mammy was, Mimmy is, Minuscoline's to be. The same renew. So, though she's sad, she'll step up and teach that troop of other girlies how to hop. And up she steps.

Toe by toe, to and fro, they go dancing around Chuff; for they are an angel's garland. And they look so lovely. They romp-ride round in rout. They circle clockwise: R-A-I-N-B-O-W; and they sing their lilting play song: "Miss Oodles of Years before the Flood does-like. So. And Miss Endlessness of Aeons after the Day (227) of Wrath does-like. So. And then again does-like. So. The merry wives of winsure."

[Their clockwise dance revolves forward through the years, and reveals them as they will appear some decades later:] A grocer's bawd, a lady in waiting, Mrs. Wildhare Quickdoctor, a widow Magrievy, a bountiful actress, a girl telling a priest she's pot on a chap, a lady of great wealth. But then they reverse the direction of

[12] Van Diemen's Land: Tasmania, rich in pearls.

their dance: W-O-B-N-I-A-R; and bound counterclockwise back
again to become again the florals: while there's leaf there's hope.

Glugg, meanwhile, was green with shame, rocked from head to
tummy with rage. If only so much as a smile were granted him!
But they were all against him. He flew into a tantrum.

He ran amuck against seven good little boys [the seven sacra-
ments] who were playing with the company: dove his head into
Wat Murrey [baptism], gave Stewart Ryall a puck on the plexus
[confirmation], wrestled a hurry-come-union with the Gillie Beg
[eucharist], wiped all his senses, martial and menial, out of Shrove
Sundy MacFearsome [penance], excremuncted as freely as any
froth-blower into MacIsaac [extreme unction], had a belting bout,
chaste to chaste, with McAdoo about nothing [matrimony], and
inbraced himself (228) with what hung over from the MacSic-
caries of the Breeks [holy orders].

Then he swore in his mind an oath. He would take ship and
ride into exile—like Coriolanus, the exiled Roman. He would hide
in silence—like the Bruce in his cave protected by the spider. He
would save himself by cunning—like a Jesuit of Ignatius Loyola.[13]
He would wander from city to city, far away, where every monk
is his own wall and council. And then he would write, firing off
his First Epistle to the Hebrews. Free loves for everybody! (229)
Ham and eggs till the end of the world! Wild primates wouldn't
stop him from his Handy Andy writing. For he is General Jin-
glesome.

He would go in for writing, in the language of Small-Profits-
and-Quick-Returns and would expose the entire lot of them.

He would write, for instance, the chapters of *Ulysses*.

He would bare to the entire world the secrets of his pa and ma.
He would just set it all down in a Jeremiad for all people: about
who stole his innocence, about the gruesome head's (230) discovery
of his spectroscope, about why he was off color, about how he was
thumped by the very spit of himself, about why he was spilled out

---

[13] Cf. the three oaths of Stephen Dedalus: "Exile, Silence, Cunning," *Portrait
of the Artist as a Young Man,* Modern Library ed., p. 291.

of his humpty-dumpty home, about how he could not join the flood of socialism, and about how to black out the sorrows of sex until the day of tryst in paradise. He would sit through several centuries, so as somewhere to meet payment in go-to-sleep music and personal company, following which, *ipse secum,* when he began to foil the fluter, she could have all the *go-to-sleep Music* she cared for, while he would have recourse of course to poetry. Was life worth leaving? Nej.[14]

He thinks of the fallen estate of his family,[15] reminiscent, dreaming largess of life-sighs over expired ancestors. They had all been old sowers of the sow-scepter, a highly cultivated historic family, beginning with Avus and Avia [grandfather and grandmother], that simple pair, and descending to Nurus and Noverca [daughter-in-law and stepmother], those notorious nepotists, all pictured in their sober senses, all of them taking after their forefather; and, judging by the look of their faces and their so-serene eyes, like transparent glass, they were patriots to a man, all pillars of this moneyed world; once on easy street, now stone broke. "And," says he, "I'll paint you a poem if you'll trace (231) me the title to the riddle, Where was a Hovel not a Hovel" (the first riddle of his universe).[16] (Give up?) When it is home.

Then he traced a little poem about God who is our Home, the consolation and protection of our youth.

[Whereupon he underwent that black moment of disillusionment with respect to the value of his own writing, which every young writer one day knows:] His mouthful of ecstasy shot up through the error-roof of his wisdom (he had thought himself feast-king of Shelleys and Lovelaces, regal and plumed, and was but a John Boyle O'Reilly, a Thomas D'Arcy McGee),[17] and he flushed and looked like an ass. Joshua Croesus, son of Nunn!

---

[14] Cf. the question put to Iseult on p. 143. It now becomes clear that Shem was the melancholy questioner, and Shaun the coarse other fellow. Iseult is playing the two of them.

[15] A reference to the fate of the family of Stephen Dedalus.

[16] Cf. Shem's first riddle, "When is a Man not a Man," p. 170.

[17] Second-rate Irish-American journalist poets of the nineteenth century.

Though he live a million years, he will never forget it. Hell's bells and bloody acres! Like nothing on earth!

But, by Jove Chronides, Seed of Summ, after he had beat his wings, forgetting his birthplace, he soon had himself again under control. By a prayer? No, that comes later. By contrite attrition? No, that we passed.[18] Mid asceticism? Right.

And it was so. He sang a scurrilous song at them all, and did a jig. Look at him! (232) Is he having a belly ache? The worst is over. He was about to be getting himself under control, when—a message, a little sign, a butterfly from her handbag, a wounded dove from her temple cotes (call her Vanessa! call her Stella!) escaped to him from the girl: a letter—suggesting that she was through with her other love affair and would love to have her melancholy boy back again, calling him Pepette,[19] and teasingly tempting him, as the prankquean tempted van Hoother. Her letter invited inspection (Please stoop, O to please);[20] mind the step![21]

And so, like a coastguard cutter answering an S.O.S., in less time than it takes a glacier to submerge an Atlantis, he was standing again before the trembly ones, shaking the storm out of his hiccups. A pigtail tar, back from the sea! (233) And he'd like to be showing off a bit.

Angel girlies! Hide from light those rainbow hues that your sin beau may bring to light! Find the French for frocks and translate it into shocks of such and touch and so and show.

He is guessing for all he is worth. Hark to his wild guesses and play fair, lady.

Making a balderdash for liberty of speech, letting pun plays pass for earnest, he asks:

"Are you speckled Fergusons?"—No.

[18] Cf. p. 194, "my . . . attrite heart."

[19] The reply of pp. 143 ff. is an amplification of the present moment.

[20] Cf. pp. 18 and 124, punctuation marks introduced into the ever-flowing letters of Mother Earth and the mud mound, respectively.

[21] Cf. p. 8, warning at entrance to museum. Mother Earth, mud mound, museum, and the present situation are now all equated.

"Are you yellow May flies?"—No.

"Are you perchance pretty little nun-moths?"[22]—No.

Get!

And he did a get, slinking his hook away, hotfooting it to the hoots of "Beat it!" For he could chew up your pure undefiled English as rashly rascally and as badly Basquely as your Spanish cow.[23] (234) He had his spirits all fallen on him; he was giddy, triste, and looked like bloody hell. A cock-shy? A donkey shot at [Don Quijote]? A Spanish dollar sent to join the armada?

But Holy Showbread [Sancho Panza]! Could any brother have looked more twinlike than the one Glugg left behind him? Candidate, blooming, gold-gleaming, and without fault! How he stood there, most saintly, favored son of sire Sixtusks, surrounded by vestals, sweetly smiling, flattered, admired.

The girlies lift a hymn and prayer in his honor: hymn number twenty-nine. Happy little girlicums to have adolphted such an Adelphus! They've come to chant in choir. They say (235) their salute, prostrating themselves severally and ensemble. "For the sake of the Färbung [coloring] and of the Scent and of the Holiodrops [Father, Son, and Holy Ghost]. Amen."

A pause. Then their orison arises, mosque-white; as Ottoman glory, ebbing westward, leaves to the soul of light the fading silence of the muezzin sounding in a turquoise sky.

"*Sanctus! Sanctus! Sanctus!* We thank thee, mighty innocent, that didst bring it off *tout de suite*. In after years, when, after desk-job-duty, you come up in the business world, we and I shall reside with obeisant servants in a fashionable neighborhood. We'll save up and nab what's finest. We'll buy a beautiful plot of land with beautiful trees, a pale peach letter-box fixed to the railings. Tea will be waiting for us. Percy, the pup, will watch the door, and Tabitha, the cat, will warm the hearth. Lady Marmela Shortbred will visit us for supper in her Sundae dress and with her

---

[22] Glugg appears to be guessing in terms of colored insects and fishing flies, lures of the love-angler.

[23] From the French expression, *"Il parle français comme une vache espagnole."*

sucking stick of peppermint (236). And Prince Le Monade will be graciously pleased, with six chocolate pages before him and a coco-cream behind. We'll be a pair alone, and we'll sing a song of sixpence. So come on, everyone, for all the fun."

Indeed, though times have changed and the hours have danced their changes through the years, the dance of the little girls is as gay today as ever.

They are very pretty little flowers (237) as they turn toward him in their sun worship [heliotropism], and he can see right through them, as, dutifully, all are alisten to his elixir.

And they say to him:

"Dear young confessor, we who are about to blossom salute thee. Pattern of our innocence, pageant master, deliverer of soft missives, write to us—now that you know our names—while you are traveling around the world [like the sun]. You are clean and do not defile. You have been touched by the gods.[24] Return, sainted youth, and walk among us. We await you. (238) We will be constant, and bless the day you befell us. Now promise to keep our secrets. Let bashfulness be tupped. *Mea culpa, mea culpa, mea maxima culpa.*[25] Kicky Lacey, the pervert, and Bianca Mutantini, her converse, drew their favorite, Duke Wellington; but me and my cosine, we have our three good chances to get Bonaparte. She's practically my twin, and I love her as myself. Eire's wrath for old Sour Rind, dumdum bullets for the Irish riflers, queen's wealth of seductive power for the jinnies.[26] Dearest, you have excited us all. (239) Please communicate with us, for we are yearning to burgeon. We can respond in the wink of an eye to the requirements of your moods. *Sursum corda!* Behold the handmaids of the Lord! [27] We hope for the heavenly day beyond marriage. Vanity, vanity, all is vanity.

[24] An echo from the Egyptian Book of the Dead.
[25] From the "Confiteor": "Through my fault, through my fault, through my most grievous fault."
[26] Cf. Wellington and the jinnies, p. 8.
[27] Parody of a phrase from the "Angelus," celebrating Mary's conception of Jesus.

"When that day comes, there will be enough for all, and every scullery maid will have as many rights as every yard scullion. All of us romantic Kathleens will be emancipated. But meanwhile, it's only Mary knows! Mary's the only one who knows where the dickens he dwellest amongst us;[27] so the rest of us go ring-around-a-rosy, hand in hand."

While the girlies thus danced around angelic Chuff, Glugg sprawled in a foul, unsightly, miry place, with oaths, screams, and groans, breech end up. (240) No honorable guest, he, on our social list. He was dazed and laid in his grave.

But lo! he rises! confessing! Shivering to be shriven, with pitiful eyes and woebegone voice. First: examination of conscience. Next: resolution never to sin again; he duly recants his Albigensian heresy, performs penance, promises to behave as he ought. Finally: a chip off the old block, even if he goes to jail for it he will tell his story. (a) He is a relative of the remarkable builder, Anaks Andrum, pure-blood Jebusite, proprietor of a hospitable tavern, who though gaining flesh can still look mighty fine; one of the Lord's sheep; togged out in silk hat and peachskin pongee. The report that his portmanteau is crammed full of potato wards [wards won by bribery] is not true. (241) Ditch-diggers have accused him of trying to seduce little girls with sugar candies; but obviously this is a colossal lie.[28] He is true to his pipe-wife, Mistress Meerschaum.[29] He is a good man, and his story is well known. Others accuse him of having been sunk in Lough Neagh—or of having lock knees [from gonorrhea] but this is tommyrot. Curse these lying rascals: the two Whales of the Sea of Deceit and the three Dromedaries of the Sands of Calumdonia![30] Bishop Babwith proves, in his *Just a Fication of* (242) *Villainies,* that this Mr. Nelson has many dependable business qualities, and has, at

[27] Parody of a phrase from the "Angelus," celebrating Mary's conception of Jesus.
[28] Note that instead of confessing his own sins, the young scamp is reciting the story of his father's.
[29] *Meerschaum:* sea-foam—Venus.
[30] The Two Temptresses and the Three Soldiers.

eighty-one, a darling baby-boy bucktooth coming on. That's why everybody's excited. That's why he was brought up before a female jury, in celestial sun-hat, with two young things agitating.

(*b*) And now Glugg will tell on his old lady, the woman who did. She's just as finny as he is fulgent, as funny as he is vulgar. Never taught by him to be independent, she would not swap her little mountain home for the finest castle in Britain. Who does not know her as she appeared when first (243) she came into the picture more than 111 years ago, factory fresh and foaming at the mouth, wronged by him and thenceforth easily terrified? Yet she boasts all around about his poorliness before he harbored her and led her into ancient consort-room and bound her so as she could not steal from him. And it was in their contract that he was to foot her funeral expenses, whereas she would feed and tend him. And if he would reform and keep his tavern proper, she would prepare the dinners and would give up her flirtings and would behave with all due propriety toward the papal legate from the Vatican, and would donate her half dollar to be offered up in masses.

(244) Hear, O world! A tiny tot is tattling! Be wary everybody!

But who now appears alight over the horizon? 'Tis the moon! This is neomenia [the time and feast of the new moon]. The feast of taverners is at hand. Shut up shop, Ireland, Isle of Destiny! Toll the bells. The curfew rings. Hurry up, 'tis time for children to go home. Come home, wee child-chicks, when the wild werewolf's abroad. Ah, let's away to where the log fire's burning.

It grows dark in our fun-animal phenomenal world. Yon marsh pond with its dry sea wrack is visited by the tide. *Ave Maria*. We are circumveloped by obscurity. Man and beast are acold. Lay on coal and keep us warm. Where is our honorable spouse? Within. And he? At home—with Nancy Hands.[31] Hound has fled through the maize. Isengrim the wolf is abroad. Farewel!. The wind has subsided. The Milky Way has not yet appeared. Nothing stirs in the little thicket. In deer haven the birds are silent. The watches

[31] Cf. p. 382, "the stout ship *Nansy Hans*."

of the night have begun their solemn round. Panther monster, *pater noster* in the zoo, send us love and brightness tomorrow. The big tusker has said his elephant prayers (245) and is ready now for sleep. All the animals are still. Light now the lights of Hanukkah [the feast of Dedication]. Otter leaps and the poppy land allures, while the lighthouses punctuate the coast. And now with our bedtime story listened out, the little fishes in the Liffey have stopped their wriggling, and an ear laid to the river would not hear a flip-flap in all Finneyland. Watchman, how goes the night? The park is acoo with lovers. Rosamund's by her wishing well. Soon tempt-in-twos' will stroll at venture and hunt-by-threes' strut musketeering. Where the tide of the bay meets the waters of the stream.[32] But meetings meet not as planned. And if you wend to Liffey, wanderer, a welcome awaits you at the tavern. Pull the bell—it bongs like thunderation! You with the colic, and we lacking honeyed wine? No siree! And were you Mary Queen of Scots herself, here's mugs and rooms strewn with sawdust; and Mr. Knight, tun-tapster, with his tiny wife, and Watsy Lyke who sees after the rinsings; and don't miss Kate, homeswab homely, put in with the bricks. A's the sign and One's the number: the old house by (246) the churchyard. So whoever comes over for the holiday must put up at the Jug and Chambers.

But heed! Our half-hour war has subsided. All's quiet on the field of gore. Father calls like a crack of thunder. Mother stirs the pot for her children, and you can hear all the bubbles prophesying: the coming man, the future woman, the food that is to build, what he will do when he's fifteen, and she with her ring; a plague for her, a saucy for her, ladlelike spoons for the winner. But they're going to have it out—Glugg and Chuff are going to have a fight; and poor little Leonie is to have the choice of her life between Josephinus and Mario-Louis. Ready. Now for Iseult la Belle!

[32] At Island Bridge. See, for instance, p. 103. Here the brackish tidewaters of the Bay meet and mingle with the sweet waters of the Liffey. This is the place of the love embrace of HCE and ALP. Island Bridge is across the stream from Phoenix Park; near by are barracks.

The battlefield calls them, and vamp, vamp, vamp, the girls are marching; tramping along Vico Road. They are ready for the fray. Glugg and Chuff are not on terms since their last battle, nor will they be atoned in any fight to a finish, that dark-deed doer and this well-willed wooer. The girls are competing for Chuff; and *she* must have him; or else she will be alone.

Returning to Glugg and his Jeremiad, the tale (247) goes on to say, how, suddenly possessed and running amuck, the wicked little fellow was set for getting the better of the young worthy. Grimacing and quite vicious, he threw the entire circle into turmoil with his mad rush.

Once more, then, he began to weep. He could see what lay ahead of him, and he wept for it. What a sight he was! And they bore false witness against him. He didn't like it at all, that the girls, sympathetic with that other fellow, should be looking scornfully at his own bruises. His disreputable predicament was a great pain to him. He was looked upon as an untouchable. But he is having his secret mental revenge. He knows something about girls! He has seen it in black and white! The twenty-eight may scintillate (248) and she, the fairy-girl Iseult, among them!

Advice to one about to be seduced:[33] if you would not fall victim to the predatory evil of her insentiate mirror-eye, you must make sure to discover her complementary, i.e., her lack, her sister-opposite, her shadow! Look! She's signaling to you from among the stars. Arise, fallen one! do your best, now; this is your chance.

[And now we hear, as in a dream of the beauty of Helen of Troy, the seductive voice of Iseult.] She vaunts the overpowering architecture of her own person, vaunts the effectiveness of her perspicacity, vaunts the facile variety of her techniques. She offers a few tempting titbits. She brags of her (future) husband: "a twelve-walrus-power hulker, but he knows as much about manning a wife as a congenitally color-blind person about matching

---

[33] Glugg is about to be provoked to a third attempt to solve the riddle of the little girls. This threefold motif of impotence is a childhood version of the Prankquean and van Hoother episodes.

colored yarns." She invites him to the kissing woods. She rehearses the story of the saintly man at Glendalough.[34] She offers
her favors (249) with a hint that her old man never will know.

The mind is assailed with a vision of the house of breathings:
where the walls are of precious stones and the gates of ivory. All
that house is filled with the breathings of her fairness. There lies
her word—there it vibrates. The way is open: but keep your other
eye out for the paypaypay! There you have it, old Shem, pat as
ABC. But the fair-haired boy is coming to land her, the boy she
now adores. Make way! Make way! Here he comes!

The girls curtsy to Chuff and point with revulsion at Glugg.[35]
Twenty-nine of bloomers against one man (250) arose. They
play with Glugg a teasing game to celebrate the occasion:

"Would you like to be tamed by some little horse-breakers?"
He pretends to be tight in ribbons round his rump.

"Are you Blackhands, the chimneysweep?"
He pretends to be sweeping their chimneys.

"Can you tell the difference between good-by and divorce?"
He pretends to be cutting with a scissors [cutting up with a pair
of sisters], biting at them and spitting.

You've had your say, little girlies.

So now be quiet, little birds. (*Seid da ruhig, kleine Vögel!*) Return to your places, for you've dawdled all the day. Now's the
time for the big event.

For Birnam Wood is come to Dunsinane.[36] Glamis hath murdered sleep and therefore Cawdor shall sleep no more. Macbeth
shall sleep no more.[37]

L is for libelman Libeling his lord. Lo! Loverman, you loved to be
living libidinously! Lift your right hand to your liege lord; link

---

[34] Cf. pp. 203 and 604–6.
[35] The style of this passage is reminiscent of that of the "Walpurgisnight"
or "Brothels" chapter of *Ulysses.*
[36] *Macbeth,* Act V, scene v, ll. 44–45.
[37] *Ibid.,* II, ii, 43–44. Macbeth is about to suffer for the sin to which he
was seduced by the Three Weird Sisters.

your left to your goddess of liberty. La! leaperman, your leap's but a loop to lee.[38]

The vervaine virgins draw a sacred line and warn him that he must stay on his own wicked side.

The floral troop deploys before him. Twice he has followed her beck; now she is at him a third time—with her entire flock behind her, like Mary with her little lamb. And just as the eyes of the schoolhouse widened to see a lamb at school, so now the faun flares of the boys are excited to see a floral's school.

Led by Chuff, the sainted standard-bearer, in four happy hops they flay the outcast, marrer of the crowned realm.[39] They taunt him (251). They bid the Hun stand up and confront the visitation now in his cistern.

He stands there, natural man, oblivious of his very *proprium,* thrust from the light. He spoors loves from her heats. He blinkth. Almost anything might happen. He is set about by the most dangerous conditions. The heat of his desire is mounting and his heavenly wisdom is going into shadow. He betrays the signs of sinful thoughts.

He thinks, for instance, what a good tutor to her he might be in his big chair of learning, turning and fingering the most tantalizing Dantean picture-pages in the lingerous longerous book of the dark—as Paolo with Francesca fingered the pages of the love story of Lancelot. "Consider," he might say, "this difficult passage about Galileo. Turn now to this page of Machiavelli." *Zut alors,* he'd be sure to make his point. Thus it has been since Adam taught-touched Eve, in all times and fashions, with man's mischief in his mind, while her eyes were filled with exaltation.

Which is why deceivers become mixed up in duels [why trumps lead to duels: why ones become twos]. So here they are, the two of them: B. Rohan [Brown] about to meet N. Ohlan [Nolan] for the prize.

Listen to the mocking temptress. Listen to the mocking hero

[38] Cf. p. 5, "Hohohoho, Mr. Finn, etc."
[39] The Crowned Realm: a Cabalistic theme, to be developed in the next chapter.

157

baring his arms against the bard. This is a story we've heard since the beginning of time. As he was (252) squaring his shoulders, so was I. And as I was clenching my fists, so was he. And as we were puffing our cheeks, so were you.

Come, twin brethren, thrust! parry! dare! The mad long rearing and the warlike threatening postures of mankind's parliaments! the learned lack-learning, merciless as wonderful.

"Now may St. Mowry of the Pleasant Grin give you a smooth lawn on which to hop." Many thanks.

"And may St. Jerome of the Harlot's Curse make a family man of you, which is much better." Thanks, I lead.

And each was wrought with his other. The twin yolks of the one egg, split-apart bickerers, superfetated,[40] while their girls are in confusion, striving to know which of the two be orthodox, which heterodox; for nice girls can strike exceedingly bad times unless they choose rightly the one who is to make their great moments greater. So they attend to Charles Darwin's problem of Natural Selection; they sing the Ascent of Man. They go ring-a-round-a-rosy before Humpty Dumpty's fall.

Glugg is licked. Without creed or crown now hangs the haughty head. There ain't no more red devil in the white of his eye. He dares not think what is to become of his progeny, exiled (253) to Peru; for, in Erse, "I have done it," means, "I shall certainly do it again." And he dares not think about the Russian past of his ancestors; for, in Slavic, "Look at me now," means, "I once was otherwise." He dares not consider the manner in which the map of the world has been changing pattern while the youth of the world has been playing its unchanging games—since the beginning of time and races; since wise ants have hoarded and careless grasshoppers been improvident.[41] He dares not think of the ways of empire: how the drivel of a London's alderman is ladled out to the inhabitants of subjugated continents and islands. If he were to follow the dictates of honor, he would swear, with the help of

---

[40] See "natural man," p. 251; then cf. p. 308: "Naturality" followed by "Superfetation." Superfetation is the history-making principle.
[41] Cf. Ondt and Gracehoper, pp. 414 ff.

Matthew, Mark, Luke, and John, to cherish her till death do them part, no matter what. But actually his way was that of "come into the garden, Maud." [42]

Evidently he has failed this third time as badly as he failed the two times before; and quite as patently, there would be no chances more. Tonight's game, however, was not to conclude with the usual shifting about of the lassies, the tug of love of their lads, all ending with great merriment, hoots, screams, scarf drill, cap fecking, ejaculations of urine, and general thumb-to-nosery. (Miami's a young country!) For one must reckon with the sudden and gigantesque appearance, among the brawling middle of this village kindergarten, of the long-suffering lord of Court Lucan. [43]

But honestly, now, how account for him [the father] at all? by analysis or by synthesis? god of all machineries, and tombstones of Barnstable! compound of Isaac, Jacob, General Jacqueminot, Moor, Mormon, and Milesian!

(254) Was he really pitched, for example, as some have claimed, against our sea wall, as might occur to anyone, to Layamon's *Brut* or to the princeliest champion of our archdeaconry? Or was he merely named from history's clippings, past being linked with present as the human chain extends? [I.e., which interpretation of the Human Universal (HCE) is correct, the Realist or the Nominalist?]

Like a rumor about some uncharted rock or evasive weed, so comes the murmur of the story to the mind's ear. Only the child born with the caul [44] knows his thousand-first name: *Hocus Crocus, Esquilocus; Finnfinn the Fainéant;* he is the old fellow we are recurrently meeting, by Mohammed himself! in cycloannalism, from space to space, time after time, in various phases of scripture as in various poses of sepulture. For now, at last, they are going to

[42] That is to say, he writes sentimental poetry, like Tennyson's "Maud."
[43] The geminal battle has at last adumbrated the pattern of the father, as foretold, p. 220.
[44] Among the pagan Irish and Germans the caul was supposed to bring to the child born with it good luck and, frequently, heroic powers.

be going to him, to Long-abed, that more than man, the herb lord whom the gillyflowerets are so fain to flutter about. (255) Kapila-vastu,[45] destroyer of the shadow of our lives.

Attach him! Hold!

Why wilt thou wake him from his earth, O someone or other, O summoner? He is weatherbitten from the dusts of ages. The hour of his closing hies to hand; the alarm that shall sound its klaxon at him, wherever he may be. [He sleeps like Finnegan, the Giant. The hour of his awakening is at hand.]

Jehoshaphat, what doom is here! Angels and saints protect him! Lord, rain mercy on them and do not stint. Though old Punch may be a proud one, his Judy's his better for her wife's bit of wit; and here she comes:

The producer (Mr. Giambattista Vico) caused a deep sleep to fall upon Father Adam, and He took one of his ribs: a cutlet-sized consort, weighing ten pebble ten, scaling five footsy five, and spin-ning thirty-seven inchettes round the good companions [bust], twenty-nine ditties round the wishful waistress [waist], thirty-seven alsos round the answer to everything [hips], twenty-three of the same round each of the quis-separabits [thighs], fourteen round the beginning of happiness [calf], and nicely nine round her shoed for slender.[46]

(256) And ere you could pray mercy to goodness, Chanticleer's hen has collared her pullets. Their bone of contention makes off in a twinkling (and every blessed little hen came aclucking) and each is called by her proper hue.

Home all go. And no more noise now. Your show's nearly over. And prayer time's soon to come.

'Tis good.

Too soon are coming task books, and good hominy bread, and Bible bee: French grammar, history by the Four Masters about

[45] The Buddha was born in Kapilavastu; his teaching reveals Universal Truth and destroys the life-illusion.
[46] ALP, at her matronly prime, is described as the rib drawn from HCE's side. Her appearance is the gage of God's mercy.

what happened to Ireland 1132, catechism, physics, Latin, geography, chemistry, geometry.

That little cloud still hangs in the sky: little Iseult still dallies before getting into bed. Singabed sulks before slumber. The little fellow who must have a light on at night has a nightmare in his expression. (257) Izzy is most unhappy.

While scampering around, they jeerilied along, rehearsing the timeless story—while the old clock, a bit on the tinny side, ticked on—about Old Father Barley how he got up of a morning early and met with a couple of platinum blondes named Hips and Haws; and about how he fell in with a fellow of Trinity, like Auld Daddy Deacon who could stow well his piece of bacon, but who never could hold a candle to bold Farmer Burleigh who begged Diddiddy Achin for the price of a piece of bacon for Wold Forrester Farley who was fond of the round of the sound of the lound of the Lukkedoerendunandurraskewdylooshoofermoyportertooryzooysphalnabortansporthaokansakroidverjkapakkapuk.[47]

Curtain. Success. Applause.

The play thou didst present here endeth. This is the end of the game. The curtain drops by deep request.

Applause amain.

The tumult, smoke, and sudden rains of Ragnarok:[48] Gunnar sends his gusts; Arbiter answers; (258) the rocks are rent; this is the day of doom. Götterdämmerung. The timid quake and break in fear. Go to! let us extol the angel of death with our cries, our brews, our jigs.[49] He is awake! "Soul of the divil, did ye think me dead!"[50] Hip, hip, hurrah! And great is he who is over Ishmael. Let Nick at this time extol Michael, and let him say to him, in pig Latin: "I am Sem. And shall not Babel be with Lebab?" And

[47] The noise of the children is suddenly silenced by a door slammed by the father; through this slam resounds for them the thunder voice. It comes precisely at the moment when their little sing-song is remembering Old Forrester Farley who was fond of the sound of the thunder.

[48] Cf. p. 221. Following are echoes of the Eddic *Völuspá*, ll. 44 ff.

[49] The play of the children was like the dancing at the Wake.

[50] The rousing of their father was like the resurrection of Finnegan.

161

he shall answer: "I hear, O Ishmael, how thy Lord is only as my Lord is one. Though you have wallowed in filth, my excellency is over Ishmael." [51]

Applause amain again.

For the Clearer of the Air has spoken, and the inhabitants of the earth have trembled from top to toe.

Lord hear us! Lord graciously hear us!

Now have thy children entered into their habitations. Thou hast closed the doors of the habitations and hast set guards thereby, that they may read in the book of the opening of the mind to light [52] and err not in the darkness of the postphenomenal void. They are under the vigilant eyes of your watchmen, Pray-your-Prayers Timothy and Back-to-Bunk Tom.

(259) Till tree become stone forever.

O Lord, hear, we beseech of thee, the prayers of each of these, thy unlighted little ones. Grant sleep in hour's time.

Do care for them.

Lord, heap miseries upon us yet entwine our arts with laughters low!

And now you may hear the distant sounds of the animals in the zoo.

And now all is mum in mother dark.

Book II, Chapter 2: The Study Period—Triv and Quad [1]

[This chapter, perhaps the most difficult in the book, describes the course of events during the study hour of the children. It amplifies the moment into an image of studenthood in general, and enlarges the little tasks into representations of the great scholar tasks that have occupied mankind from the beginning. The

---

[51] Whereupon the pairs of opposites become reconciled in the Eternal.
[52] Egyptian Book of the Dead.
[1] In this chapter we cannot adhere strictly to our system of bracketing. Text and comment are so intermingled that it is frequently impossible to draw the bracket.

principal references are to the medieval studies of the Trivium (Grammar, Logic, Rhetoric) and Quadrivium (Arithmetic, Music, Geometry, Astronomy), and to the esoteric doctrines of the Cabala. The marginal notations are of two kinds, those in the right-hand margin (in small capitals) being solemn (Shaun type), those in the left (in italics), smart-aleck (Shem type): the first, no doubt, introduced by the professor and the second by the youngsters. From page 293, however, the left-hand margin is the solemn one. The footnotes are generally of the Shem type.

[The narrative outline of this chapter is fairly simple, but obscured by the intricacies of the student problems. The chapter opens with a review, in allegorical terms, of the process of creation; twenty-six pages (260–86) are devoted to the description of the descent of spirit into time and space. First, the will to create moves the world father to beget the universe; then the world becomes possible, takes form, actually appears. Man comes into being with his primitive lusts and taboos, and becomes localized in the tavern of HCE. There, in the nursery of the children, the entire human comedy presents itself in miniature.

[The last pages of the chapter (286–308) are centered in the nursery. The boys are at their tasks, and their sister is musing over letters. The good little boy, named Kev in this chapter, is having trouble with his geometry; bad little Dolph assists him, and in doing so teaches him something which elicits a blow from the indignant hero. Dolph recovers from the knockout and the two are reconciled. Then comes supper, and time for bed.

[The opening discussion of the process of creation is provoked by the enigma of existence:] (260) Here we are; whence have we come, and where, after all, are we? UNDE ET UBI [whence and where?]. For whether we be mere tomtit-tots or the sum total of existence, here it is we are! And here too is the motherly cup of tea.[2]

[2] As the tea plant adds to water a delicious stain, so does the goddess of life add the stain of nature to the abstract purity of the waters of heaven. The cup of tea has already played a large part in *Finnegans Wake,* and

With his broad and hairy face, to Ireland a disgrace. This note in the left-hand margin refers to the face of the Father.[3] "Ireland" can be read "Land of the Peace": it was something of a disgrace to the realm of eternal peace when the Great One inclined to the very questionable adventure of Creation. SIC: "Let his deed stand, though it is clearly a mistake."

The will to create having come over the world father, there began, so to speak, a fermentation in the transcendental realm; which ended in a materialization of the female principle, the only possible reply to the yearning of the father. Her he covered, and thus the world was begotten. How else might our life adventure have begun? He knew the pang of love, and he begot us, and she was glad to mother and bring forth his world.

IMAGINABLE ITINERARY THROUGH THE PARTICULAR UNIVERSAL: *Mainly about people:* From that mother womb is to proceed the round of the world aeons, the way of destiny. Certain great men may be taken to represent the stages of this universal way. The road will wheel from Livius Lane [Titus Livius, 59 B.C.–A.D. 17; Roman *Historian,*] through Mezzofanti Mall [Giuseppe Caspar Mezzofanti, 1774–1849; *Linguist*—spoke fluently fifty or sixty languages; cardinal; keeper of Vatican library], diagonally crossing Lavater Square [Johann Kaspar Lavater, 1741–1801; *Physiogno-*

here it is again. It is the brew of life. "Tea tea" suggests "titty": the source of the infant's brew of life and primary image of motherly nourishment. "Tea" may be read *thea*—goddess.

[3] Makroprosopos, "the Great Face," God the Father in his aspect of Creator, the Concealed Ancient One from the Strands of Whose Beard the entire world proceeds. "That beard, the truth of all truths, proceedeth from the place of the ears, and descendeth around the mouth of the Holy One; and descendeth and ascendeth, covering the cheeks which are called the places of copious fragrance; it is white with ornament: and it descendeth in the equilibrium of balanced power, and furnisheth a covering even unto the midst of the breast. That is the beard of adornment, true and perfect, from the which flow down thirteen fountains, scattering the most precious balm of splendor. This is disposed in thirteen forms.... And certain dispositions are found in the universe, according to those thirteen dispositions which depend from that venerable beard, and they are opened out into the thirteen gates of mercies." (*Ha idra rabba qadisha,* chap. x, vss. 212–14, 233.)

164

mist], up Tycho Brache Crescent [Tycho Brache, flourished *ca.*
1590; Arabian *Mathematician,* formulated the cosine theorem for
oblique triangles; perhaps also, Tycho Brahe, 1546–1601; Danish
Astronomer], shouldering Berkeley Alley [George Berkeley, 1685–
1753, Irish *Metaphysician;* "Idealist"], crossing Gainsborough Car-
tracks [Thomas Gainsborough, 1727–88; English *Painter*], under
Guido d'Arezzo's Gateway [Guido d'Arezzo, *ca.* 990–1050; "Father
of modern *Music*"], to New Livius Lane [back again to Livy].
Thus it will be the old story again of Vico Roundpoint.—But bear
in mind that behind all this, sustaining it, will ever remain the
eternal marriage of the god with the goddess whom he produced
from his own substance, (261) the couple whom we recognize in
the old hill and its neighboring stream, and of whom the humming winds are telling us. His earth home is the place of all origins, where maker mates with made; hence, taking tides, we haply
return. Our names for him are many: *Swiney Tod, ye Daimon
Barber* [4] (*Dig him in the rubbish!*), *Ungodly old Ardrey, Cromwell beeswaxing the convulsion box.* He is a manyfeast munificent,
more mob than man.

CONSTITUTION OF THE CONSTITUTIONABLE AS CONSTITUTIONAL: [Phi-
losophers trying to discuss the mystery of creation are reduced to
what Joyce calls "broken heaventalk," i.e., paradoxical, metaphori-
cal, half-statements, which rather point toward than define the
problem. In the cabalistic texts, the Creator is spoken of as "Ainsoph." He is represented by the number One. The movement of this
Power toward Queen Zero, his bride, generates the numbers from

---

[4] The Demon Barber is the hangman of *Ulysses* (Random House ed., p.
298; Paris ed., p. 291), who is a symbol of the destroying aspect of God—
the Hangman-God. The actual model for this role was Sir Horace Rumbold,
who was the British minister in Berne while Joyce was in Switzerland.
Gorman tells us (*James Joyce,* Farrar and Rinehart, 1939, pp. 262–74) that
when this man was transferred to Warsaw, Joyce dashed off a little verse,
beginning, "The pig's in the barley . . ." and ending, "Rumbold's in Warsaw,—
All's right with the world." Note: Swiney Tod—piggish death. Later,
when Rumbold was sent to Ireland, Joyce wrote another version of the
verse, comparing Rumbold and the Mayor of Cork to the Mookse and the
Gripes.

two to nine, and his ultimate union with her, in the number ten, 1–0, initiates a new decade. Joyce plays with this idea in the following paragraph. Ainsoph is described in a footnote as "Groupname for grapejuice"; for it is he who is present in the consecrated wine.] Ainsoph, this upright One, with that noughty besighed him Zeroine! He is the Mercury of the alchemist, and to see his metabases in the mystical retort is a thing of horror. He is the terror of the noonstruck by day; the secret bridegroom of each nightly bridable. But, to speak broken heaventalk: Who is he? Whose? Why? How much? Which? When? Where? How? And what is there about him (262) anyway?—that decent, decade-forming man!—Reply: "*E*asy; *c*alm your *h*aste! *A*pproach to *l*ead our *p*assage."

PROBAPOSSIBLE PROLEGOMENA TO IDEAREAL HISTORY: [Before the process of history can have actually begun, there must have taken place the world-begetting union of the One with Lady Zero. He descended to her—fell down the ladder of the mystical decade. The event may be represented as a fall, or as the progress of a decade, as an infusion of spirit into matter, as a passage down River Liffey, as a night of marriage, or as the shattering of a Humpty Dumpty. Joyce's present description suggests the entrance of a night voyager into a guarded castle.] The bridge is approached and crossed (X); thus the castle is reached, and he knocks (Castle Knock); the password is given (Persse O'Reilly) and the door is opened with a Yes,[5] whereupon the thundercrack is heard—the old boy is hooked and the noise of the joyous multitude goes up. *The sight near left my eyes when I saw her put the tea in the pot.* O governess of repose, wake them! This then is the house of eating.[6]

[5] Molly's final monologue in *Ulysses* was described by Joyce to Mr. Frank Budgen as "the indispensable countersign to Bloom's passport to eternity." (Budgen: *James Joyce and the Making of Ulysses,* London, 1934, p. 270.) Molly's "Yes" is the mother-affirmation. Here we have them again, the countersign and the yes.

[6] The realm of matter is the realm of food. In Vedāntic doctrine the body is called "the sheath of food" (*Annamayakosha*).—N.B., *Anna* in Sanskrit means "food."

GNOSIS OF PRECREATE DETERMINATION. AGNOSIS OF POSTCREATE DE-
TERMINISM. [The nature of the demiurgic determination that
launched the universe on its thenceforth predestined course may
be known, at least to the angels; but the accidents of history that
are to determine the precise circumstances through which Inevitable Destiny is to become *actualized,* no one, not even the Creator
himself, can wholly know! Having treated of the transcendental,
intelligible problem (the union of Lord One and Lady Zero) the
author now invites us to consider the countryside (Lucalizod)
where the results of the world-engendering union are about to be
made evident.] First is perceived the tavern of HCE, that well-
known resting place, with its staple-ring to tether to, and its step-
pingstone to mount by: The Boots, at Pickardstown. A great press
of celebrating folk fills the den. *Tickets for the Tailwaggers Ter-
rierpuppy Raffle.* (263) And among the rare ones that most fre-
quent him are the Four Old Men: Ignatius Loyola, Egyptus, Major
A. Shaw, and old Whitman.—But it was all so long ago; one cannot know precisely. The old man has disappeared, but is refeatured;
so let bygones restate themselves here at Gunne's. [I.e., The original
tavernkeeper and tavern company have long since disappeared. We
must content ourselves with their modern representatives. Fortunately, however, everything that happens today carries the impress
of those primordial times.]—There is a mystical correspondence
between Heaven and Earth; the apparent confusion of our multi-
farious world is actually systematized under one original sun—one
original sin. O felicitous culpability! [7] Sweet bad cess to you, Father
Adam, for an archetype!

[We must try to understand that original family man and his
sin.] (264) ARCHAIC RIVALRY: *H*onor *c*ommercio's *e*nergy, yet *a*id the
*l*inkless *p*roud. Horn of Heathen! Brook of Life! The old man,
the two girls, and the Three. THE TELEOLOGICAL ODIUM: We seek
the blessed One, *E*ven *C*anaan the *H*ateful, ever agoing, ever
acoming.

[His setting: between Lucan and Chapelizod.] LOCALIZATION

[7] *"O felix culpa!"* "O Phoenix Culprit!" See our footnote to p. 23.

*Move up, Mackinerny, make room for
Muckinerny.*[8] Here where Liffey winds her way; this is the lovely
river bank. Regard the pretty surroundings, the beautiful town,
the May field, the orchard, laurels, etc., the glen, the hill,
the Norman court at the boundary of the ville, the ivy-covered
church, the king's house (265) of stone, the mill, the cloister, the
elm—all for the retrospectioner. Skole! Note the strawberry-bed
fragrance, the phoenix pyre still flaming, the nest of wren. There
is the cottage for the cobbler and the bungalow for the middle-
aged parvenu. Here are garland gardens for Iseult . . . *in snow-
drop, trou-de-dentelle, flesh, and heliotrope* . . . and all for her;
lilypads, hedges, etc. The tavern is conveniently located, far away.
And here's our dozen cousins from the stars and stripes. (266)
Treetown Castle under Lynn. And if you would enter you would
see the bridge of dreams leading up to the sleeping rooms where
he reclines—his puff is but a piff [9]—and where the children are at
their studies.

[Having begun with a theological consideration of the vast problem of creation itself, and having proceeded to a specific microcosmic example of the creation, and having been led thus, inevitably,
to the tavern and up the stairs of the tavern to the sleeping rooms,
we now center our attentions upon the nursery, where we may become aware of the great powers of nature at work.

[In the boys' room is a picture of two boxers face to face, counterparts of the boys themselves. They have been studying about the
Battle of Châlons (A.D. 451) fought on the Catalaunian Plains,
where Attila was turned back by the combined armies of the
Romans under Aetius and the Visigoths under Theodoric. The
picture of the boxers becomes associated with the story of the Hun

[8] Move up, you great Archetypal Man, and make room for our local
example. Reference to cabalistic *Makro-* and *Mikro-*prosopos, "The Great
Face of the White Beard" (see footnote 3, *supra*) and "The Little Face of
the Black Beard," his inferior emanation.

[9] Cf. passage on p. 74, "his puff but a piff, etc."

and the Roman, at the time of the collapse of a civilization; thus it suggests that age of furious, barbaric strife which, in the Viconian cycle, is represented as the age of the pagan giants. We are following a fourply allegory: boxers on the wall, boys in the nursery, historical Huns and Romans, mythological Viconian giants of the days of the Deluge. Not only battle, but unrestrained pursuit of women is characteristic of this stage of preculture chaos; so we read in the right-hand margin:] PREAUSTERIC MAN AND HIS PURSUIT OF PANHYSTERIC WOMAN. In the left-hand margin is the daring atheistical boy-suggestion: *Bet you fippence there's no purgatory, are you game?* (267) Civilized James Joyce and his readers at this point resolve to follow the example of the giant of that age: *There was a sweet hopeful culled cis;* [10] Pluto culled Persephone, the blond giant culled cis-Alpine Gaul; and now we ourselves shall pursue, with intent to cull, the Meaning of Meaning.

URGES AND COUNTERURGES IN A PRIMITIVE SEPT: [The study has advanced from the field of theological to that of sociological problems. We now study, through examples supplied by the nursery, the nature of primitive lusts and the origin of primitive taboos. Joyce here is burlesquing Freud's *Totem and Tabu,* but at the same time coordinating the psychologist's view with the mythological vision of Vico.] May the heavenly rainbow-goddess enmesh us in her toils! [This is the prayer of the primitive urge.] Flash becomes word: the flood of wrath pours down! [This is the Viconian thunderclap, the Freudian fear of the Father's revenge (Castration complex). It immediately follows the deed of lust and gives rise to a resolution to sin no more (taboo).] *The Big Bear bit the Sailor's Only: Trouble, trouble, trouble. Forening young Christlike Kevin.* Whereupon the old era gives way to the new, the old temptress to a young one—with a more complicated and subtle style but the same old meaning. [Saintliness and virginal innocence will supervene, but the old throb of nature will be there, just the same:] As ever, the Only Only Little Girl will wend her innocent way of honey and myrrh, while the May bee still mantles the May flowers. And before her (268) coyness has faded from the

[10] A limerick sticks out its tongue!

flower, you will find all of them, the little flowers, arms enlocked in ring-a-ring, thinking of It . . . *Tell me all about Anna Livia* . . . i.e., thinking of the pleasure she will find in someone's arms.

EARLY NOTIONS OF ACQUIRED RIGHTS: Soon the twins will be battling over some problem; while she, object of their tussle, will sit on a sofa and knit, having invited her hero . . . *Will you carry my can and fight the fairies* . . . to help her.

THE INFLUENCE OF COLLECTIVE TRADITION UPON THE INDIVIDUAL: [The older age will teach its lessons to the new. This is a sociological law. We find this law exemplified in the spectacle of grandma teaching her old and tried "love-grammar" to Iseult:] *Alma Mater, Auctioneer:* Iseult has been taught by Grandma Grammar the arts of conjugating and declining young men; viz., if there is a third person, mascarine, phelinine, or nuder, being spoken about, the mood proceeds from the person speaking to the person spoken to, and it is she herself (the person spoken to) who is the direct object of all the remarks. Take the dative with the ablative, only mind you're genderous toward his reflexives, as I was to your grandpapa . . . *Old Gavelkind the Gamper* . . . when he was my joy and I his lovable pygmy doll. There is comfort in the (269) knowledge that often hate on first hearing comes of love by second sight. Have your little sin talks in the dark of subway junctions, two by two. But even the airiest chap around may, perhaps, chance to be about to become a pale Peter Wright, while you are wall-flowered for the butter half of a yearn or sob. For you may be as practical as is predicable, but you must have the proper sort of accident to meet that kind of a being with a difference. The game goes on like a song, coo-coo. *Andante umoroso. M. 50-50.* (270) But remember it's men have the easier time: a brat, my child, can choose from so many—while it's many a fine woman is left sitting. Note, for instance, the Respectable Irish Distressed Ladies and compare with them the Merry Mustard Frothblowers of Humphreystown Associations! So don't you let him get away!

[Having observed the nursery scene, we now turn to a long and very difficult analysis of its metaphysical and sociological implications (270–78). The nursery scene exhibits a double play of polar principles: war and sex. These principles have been at work throughout the course of history.] We have just been reading in the history books about the Punic Wars, Caesar, Cleopatra, and the triumvirate, and though you may fail to see the import of it all, the implications and the principles which they illustrate are nevertheless at hand.

It all adds up to C.O.D., Cash on Delivery, which is the fundamental law of history. Each of the mystical letters, C.O.D., may be thought of as generating three qualities, and each of the nine resultant qualities is to be found illustrated in history, fact, or legend.[11] From C, for instance, are derived the principles of COURAGE, COUNSEL, AND CONSTANCY. These are illustrated, COURAGE by Hireling's Punic Wars; COUNSEL by the Four Master Historians—O'Brien of *Ulster,* (271) O'Connor of *Munster,* MacLoughlin of *Leinster,* and MacNamara of *Connaught*—together with their Donkey; CONSTANCY by Caesar and his two druidesses . . . *Cleopatra, thy nose makes history* . . . and by the triumvirate of Octavian, Lepidus, and Mark Antony. From O are derived OMEN, ONUS, AND OBIT, and these are illustrated, OMEN by the fact that though you may fail to see the import of all this, Suetonia, and need not care whether the three cuddle his coddle or no, she'll confess it by her figure and deny it to your face, and if you're not ruined by that one, she won't do you any whim; ONUS by the split between "to have been" and "will be"; OBIT by the mortal fact that because they warred in their beginnings, ease now we'll never know. From D are derived DANGER, DUTY, AND DESTINY, and these are illustrated, DANGER by the share of each in the guilt of Original Sin (*E*at early earthapples: *C*oax Cobra: *H*ail, Heva: This is the glider that gladdened the girl); DUTY by our response to heaven's call: we're listen-(272)ing! we're believing; DESTINY by the result of it all: Leda, Leda, so does your girdle grow: willed without witting, world without end. [These nine principles having been reviewed, we come next to the number ten—Queen Zero joined to

[11] This derivation of nine qualities and of all creation from a Trinity of letters, parodies the cabala.

the original One. Herewith is sounded anew the great and basic theme of sex polarity and its consequences:] POLAR PRINCIPLES: Papa-Mamma: war wets wit—who wits why: tails for toughs, titties for totties.[12]

The analysis continues with what the professor calls a PANOPTICAL PURVIEW OF POLITICAL PROGRESS AND THE FUTURE PRESENTATION OF THE PAST. Dark ages feed the roots of the present; so stop, you modern miss, if you are interested in B.C. or A.D.[13] [The musical notes in the left-hand margin are B C A D.]—Here, you boys, take your heads out of that Tale of a Tub! Stop doting on the dung pile of the past. The new has shunted the old, and this has happened since you shrimps stuck your heads in that dead wash of Lake Sleep. The brew has done its work: the battles have been waged of Bull against Bear; gringrin gringrin. *Up boys and at 'em.* (273) The old fellow has tumbled from his wall. But, hail the sevenfold rainbow-bridge of peace—of the people, by the people, and for the people. So hang up the shubble and the hoe!—Anna Livia, shrewd shoplifter, trots about with her basket, distributing her presents to all . . . *All we suffered under them Cowdung Forks and how we enjoyed our pick of her basket. Old Kine's* [14] *Meat Meal* . . . her basket's as good as the museum that we visited, with a wink for Wellington and a nod for Napoleon.—And this is the poor bold horse with its tricuspidal (274) helm emblem on—for the man that broke the ranks at Mount St. John. What means the riddle? It means that that is already with us, ahead of schedule, which already is plan-accomplished from of old. *Pas d'action, peu de sauce.* For example, Daft Dathy is still on the Matterhorn, daring Dunderhead to shiver his timbers;[15] Hannibal

[12] We do not promise that we have correctly related the passages in the body of the text to the principles named in the margin; every reader will have to do this job himself! The present rendering is put forward only as a suggestion.

[13] Cf. pp. 18 ff.

[14] "Silk of the Kine" is a pet name for Mother Ireland.

[15] I.e., the Master Builder is aloft on his tower even today, as he was in the beginning; Moses is this moment on Sinai; the mysteries symbolized in the decades of the past are effective *here* and *now*.

MacHamiltan the Hegerite is building churches up in St. Barma-brac's; 32 West 11th Street still looks onto that datetree of sorrows which more than ever leafeth, wondering what the devil, in that house that Jerry built for Massa, Missus, and Hijo de Puta [Son of Harlot], they are (1) sliding, (2) sleeting, (3) scouting, (4) shooting about. And Dagobert is in Clane's home town learning how to put a broad face bronzily out through a broken breached material (275) bought from Brian Awlining, Erin's *h*ircohaired *c*uloteer [Ireland's goat-haired tailor].

[So much for the great historical inevitables and timeless arche-types. The question now arises: what is the relation of the peculiar idiosyncrasies of the individual to this vast and general scheme? The professor has his reply. There are processes in the develop-ment of the individual which do not strictly recapitulate the de-velopment of the race. Through these an element of novelty is in-troduced into the great picture. But the resultant dichotomy of individual versus species is resolved through the formation of a new species capable of procreation, or—if the individual variation be only a slight one—through the formation of a new family or variety. So there proceeds a process of "superfetation." This matter is discussed under the learned heading:] FROM CENOGENETIC DICHOTOMY THROUGH DIAGNOSTIC CONCILIANCE TO DYNASTIC CON-TINUITY. It is a pattern of one world burrowing on another: *Two makes a wing at the telluspeep.* Yet there is a persistence of the old: *From the Buffalo times of bysone days.* Consider, therefore, the archetypal couple, even today, in their palace of quicken boughs, called "The Goat and Compasses." They have discussed their tales of the past. They have survived all the little innovations and sur-prises. Yet who knows what the morrow will bring? (276) Each has made mistakes and is willing to do penance: the gladhander, that dolorous dirger, and she who tears up lettereens she never apposed a pen upon.

THE MONGREL UNDER THE DUNG MOUND. With the coming of night all the surface innovations will become obscured and we shall realize anew the persistent and unchanging SIGNIFICANCE OF THE

INFRALIMINAL INTELLIGENCE. This is a power to be appeased with offerings: OFFRANDES. Already the night is approaching. Vespers are ending. It is the hour of good warm supper. Hush. It will be a long time before dawn. Are those bats there peeping? At Tim Finnegan's wake all is still going strong [16] . . . *Saving the public's health.* His impressive figure dominates our meal. *Superlative Absolute of Porterstown.* (277) His seven-colored garment is now soot (Ochone! Ochonal!). His imponence is one heap of lumpblack. *He is the reason so many spick bridges span our River-road.* Rivers of drink have been released for the Fenians at his funeral.—*The throne is an umbrella stand, the scepter's a stick. Lady jewel is present, our daktar deer:* [17] ever-flowing Anna. As Anna was at the beginning, lives yet, and will return, so we dream our dreams till Pappy returns; existence renewing itself. We will not say it shall not be.[18] Some may seek to dodge the (278) gobbet, but who wants to cheat the choker's got to learn to chew the cud—with a pansy [*offrandes*] for puss in the corner.[19]

INCIPIT INTERMISSIO: [The professor has finished his analysis and it is time for recess. We are permitted to relax. And our minds

[16] Here is the most important appearance of the Finnegan figure since Bk. I, chap. 1. Out of the deepest past, out of the deepest dark of the unconscious, emerges the prehistoric form of Finnegan. And the threat of his memory is to be propitiated with offerings. The domestic foreground, set with supper dishes and umbrella stands, clashes like an upper cymbal against the lower cymbal of the sleeping giant, and the concussion gives off echoes of both.

The Dog theme suggests an association of the Finnegan figure with the forces of man's lower, animal nature,—the "Id" of Sigmund Freud. Yet divinity dwells here too: "dog" spelt backwards is "God"—see *Ulysses,* Random House ed., p. 584; Paris ed., p. 561.

[17] With Finnegan comes Anna, here compared to an oriental deer. Also *dak,* Hindustani for "mail"—the letter writer.

[18] Here is Joyce's world affirmation, for those who require to see it in so many words.

[19] Puss in the Corner, a frightful animal-demon in Irish fairy tale, here suggestive of the Finnegan fear.

turn, of course, to Iseult. As the little woman between cycles, so now the little girl between periods of study!] Behold the handmaid of the Lord! [20] Witness the little girl's heart: how easily she sighs! Her mind is entirely on letters. *Uncle Flabbius Muximus to Niecia Flappia Minimiss.* All the world's in want and is writing a letters. (To be slipt on, slept on, conned to, and kept up; and when you're done push the chain.) And all the world's on wish to be carrying letters.—And when political plans are afoot . . . *Dear Brutus, land me arrears* . . . men then want to be writing a letters.—So—are there any letters today, postman? Try! A little assortment, please.

[(Footnote, p. 279) A note from Izzy to her teacher:] "Frequently I have been melancholy enough to commit suicide, but have been saved by recalling your libidinous erringnesses. You may rue your severities, for I am now engaged: I shall appear in the movies and thus taunt my silly classmates.—Old Norse nurse Asa [21] taught me the rules—and all about the two girls, the man, and the peepers.—Wasn't it divine that day I was sitting astride the druids' altar?—Don't blush! I know the rules! God is merciful. Truth is stronger than fiction." [22]

[During this moment of intermission, between two periods of strictest study concentration, a thick compost of reminiscences flows in disordered sequence through the relaxed mind. In the period past we dealt with the nature of reality; in the period coming we shall see the action of the brothers probing the mysteries of sex. The intermission, devoted largely to the languorous erotic mood of Iseult's letter writing, swims between the two, touches both banks, and brings to mind half-formulated reminiscences. The mood is that of a nocturne.]

(278) MAJOR AND MINOR MODES COALESCING PROLIFERATE HOMOGEN-UINE HOMOGENEITY: We have wended our way, until now the force in the stream is faint afarred (279) and the face in the tree bark

[20] Opening words of the "Angelus."
[21] The mother of Ibsen's Peer Gynt. Cf. Grandma Grammar, pp. 268–70.
[22] Compare Iseult's letter, pp. 143–48.

feigns a fear.[23] This is rainstones ringing [rhinestones singing].[24] Strangely cold for this time of year. But the daisy blooms ever. Since all's war that ends war, let's take things easy and play the game fair. Let us pause and listen. (280) A scene at night: branches sing dark wisdom of future and past, as the moon shines on memories of a year ago And if the forest could write, it would be a letter much like that of che little hen. It would run something like this: "Dear ——, well, and I go on to— (She licks her pencil.) . . . I and we—tender condolences for happy funeral—so sorry to— mention person suppressed for the moment, F[ather] M[ichael].— Well—inquiries after all healths—how are you, maggy?—A lovely Persian cat. (She rubs her.) (Those pothooks mostly she hawks from Poppa Vere Foster, but these curlimequeues are of Mippa's molding.) [25] (She rubs her other: wave gently in air, turning it over.) Well, mabby, consolation; with best from cinderella—if prince charming . . . (She licks her other.) From Auburnchen le magne."—Pious and pure fair one! All has come to this: that she shall tread the very way of life which has shone in silence through the aeons; and that the Bandusian spring shall play liquid music and sigh of musk.—Sleep, drink, dance, and dream, until (281) harvest, blithe as this flowing wild.

THE PART PLAYED BY BELLETRISTICKS IN THE BELLUM-PAX-BELLUM. MUTUO-MORPHO-MUTATION: Today, as in the times of Pliny and Columella, the hyacinth thrives in Gaul, the periwinkle in Illyria, the marguerite on the ruins of Numantia; and while around them cities have changed masters and names, or have entered into annihilation, and while civilizations have been smitten and broken, the peaceful generations of these little flowers have traversed the ages and have come down to us, fresh and smiling as in the days of battles.[26] *Thus spake Zarathustra.*

[23] The human race, having come far from its original source, has lost much of its primal sap; and a premonition of the end is apparent in the thickening and desiccation of skin and senses.

[24] Compare the opening lines of ALP's final soliloquy: "I am leafy speaking" (p. 619). Echoes of the "raindrops when we sleep" passage of p. 74.

[25] Cf. the analysis of the letter, pp. 119–23.

[26] Briefly: "Art survives the city, and nature survives both."

SORTES VIRGINIANAE: The love-language of flowers! The little hanging cloud [Iseult]! But Brutus and Cassius are interested only in thrice-complicated ideas, whispered willfulness, and shadows multiplying shadows: they tackle their quarrel. *A saxon shilling for the sexton, but nothing for that parish priest.* Ancient is the anger, and each claims the glory.—What if she love Victor less though she leave Glory moan? And that's how our occident has gotten hold of half their world. [Life favors the victor, whether lovable or not.] Moving about in the free of the air and mixing with the ruck. Either-or.

INTERROGATION: And?

EXCLAMATION: Nay, rather!

[This returns us to the battle problem of the two boys, and the major action of the chapter. Their names are Dolph (Shem) and Kev (Shaun), and they are back again at their lessons. The little outcast brother will be asked by the other to help him with his tasks; and so we read in the marginal heading:] (282) ANTITHESIS OF AMBIDUAL ANTICIPATION: THE MIND FACTORY, ITS GIVE AND TAKE: Lo, the boor plieth as the laird hireth him.

AUSPICIUM: A blessing on knowledge of the female. [They are going to investigate the mystery of Mother.]

AUGURIA: Ad Majorem Dei Gloriam.[27]

[They begin with a series of arithmetic and algebra problems; and since mathematics has always gone hand in hand with the most profound studies of theology and metaphysics, the sums and problems will reveal quietly the personality of HCE, and the sexual secrets of ALP. In the margin appears a theological formula for the final implication of all mathematical conclusions from the known to the unknown:] DIVINITY (NOT DEITY) IS THE UNCERTAINTY JUSTIFIED BY OUR CERTITUDE.

[Let us now regard the boys. First we look at Kev (Shaun):]

[27] Motto of the Jesuit order. The initials A.M.D.G. are placed by students at Jesuit institutions at the head of their task sheets. The words occurring here indicate that the twins have settled down to do their sums.

This one was good at manual arithmetic, for he knew from his cradle why his fingers were given him. He had names for his ten fingers: first there came boko, then wigworms, then tittlies, then cheekadeekchimple, then pickpocket, with pickpocketpumb, pickpocketpoint, pickpocketprod, pickpocketpromise, and upwithem. And he had names for his four love-tried cardinals: (1) his element curdinal numen, (2) his enement curdinal marrying, (3) his epulent curdinal weisswasch, and (4) his eminent curdinal Kay O'Kay.[28] Always would he be reciting of them by rote, from first to last, going over them in various ways, to the rhythm of pin puff pive piff: piff puff pive poo: poo puff pive pree: pree puff pive pfoor: pfoor puff pive pippive; poopive;—Niall Dhu, (283) Foughty Unn, Enoch Thortig, etc.—like pitching your cap onto ten tall spilikins. Or again: Boreas [North wind], notus [South wind], eurus [East wind], zipher [West wind: cipher]. Still again: Ace [1], deuce [2], tricks [3], quarts [4], quims [5]—multiply. of course and carry to their whole number: while on the other hand, reduced by their common denominator to the lowest terms for their aliquant parts: sexes [6], suppers [7], oglers [8], novels [9], and dice [10].[29] He could find by practice the value of thirtynine articles,[30] and, with the helpings from his tables, he could reduce fulminants to tumblers, links into chains, Norfolk weys [40-bushel weight] to York tods [28-pound units], ounces to pounds, thousands to hundreds, imperious gallants to Irish gells; bringing a living-stone all laughing down to grave cloth-nails, and a league of archers, fools, and lurchers, under the rude rule of

[28] Here the four fingers, called cardinals and reminiscent of the Four Old Men, are named in terms of the four Viconian ages: (1) age of the thunderclap, when God's name (nomen) was heard; (2) age of the patriarchal family (marrying); (3) age of disintegration, theme of burial (weisswasch, white winding sheets); (4) age of the return (K, eleventh letter of the alphabet, i.e., beginning of the new mystical decade, see p. 261; O, the circle of return; then K repeated; also, Kay, key of knowledge, see p. 93; key of knowledge now in our possession, hence, O.K.). One senses puns on actual names of cardinals, viz., Newman.
[29] A round of plays of four against ten. Parodies on cabalistic computations.
[30] Perhaps a reference to the Thirty-nine Articles of the Anglican church.

thumb.[31]—But, 'tis strange to relate, though he was unequaled in reading, writing, and reckoning, he always received low marks for his geometry and algebra.—EXAMPLES: (1) Show that the (284) median, hce, che, ech . . . *A stodge Angleshman has been worked by eccentricity* . . . intersecting the legs of a given obtuse one, biscuts both the arcs that are in curvicord behind. (2) A telegraph pole on the Height of County Furmanagh (Ulster) has a certain inclination, and the graph for all the functions in Lower County Monaghan (Ulster) may be involted into the zeroic couplet: "all's well in his heaventh like noughty times infinity" [may be inverted into the heroic couple who signify infinity]. Given these facts, find how many combinaisies and permutandies can be played on the international surd, pthwndxrclzp! [thunderclap], its cubic root being extracted by a series of hypothetical assumptions.—Answers (for teachers only): 10, 20, 30, C, X, and the Three. Imagine the twelve differentiated infinities explained above to be the continuation through regeneration of the original utterances of the Work in Progress. It follows that, if the Two Temptresses are on bicycles and the three wenchers trundle tricycles, the answer presents to us an automatic turko-indian rainbow illusion, as long as summer lasts; (285) but, if the cycling reader be outraged by all this Merlin magic—with harem girls running here and there, while the ex-archon, HCE, frantically pedals around the Park apparently in the lead but at the same time pursuing—then MPM [the old man between the two magnetic fields] brings us a cloudier pandemonium in Finnish. In other words: one from five [HCE, of the family of five], two to five's one's [the two girls with HCE's Libido], one from fives two millamills with a mill and a half a mill [the millimanting[32] in the Park], and the twos fives fives of bully-

---

[31] The name of Livingstone, associated with British imperialism in Africa, leads to the thought that these mathematical calculations are means by which Englishmen have brought primitive races to heel via commercial manipulations. Compare also Jeremy Bentham's attempts to reduce moral values to mechanical units, thus turning living-stone to coffin-nails. Little Kev is going to grow up to police the world.

[32] See Congreve, *The Way of the World.*

clavers [the multiplying gossip stories].[33]—By no means to be com
prehended. Inaccessible as God's ways. The axioms and their pos-
tulates (286) explain his earthly woes.—It all adds up to Alpha,
Omega and the Fall.[34]

HEPTAGRAMMATON: P.t.l.o.a.t.o.[35]

HYPOTHESIS OF COMMONEST EXPERIENCES BEFORE APOTHEOSIS OF THE
LUSTRAL PRINCIPLE: So, after those initial falls and that primary
taint, as I know and you know and the Arab in the ghetto knows
and any Mede or Persian knows—comic cuts and serious exercises
always were to be enjoyed in Casey's First Book, page 230 (to be
bought at Hickey's huckster, Wellington's Iron Bridge)—and so
now at long last, he must trump and wave adieu to those card-in-
hands which he missed: hearts, diamonds, spades, and clubs. The
time being no help for it, *please to lick one and turn over.*[36]

[We come directly to the study desk of the two brothers. It is
for his geometry problem that ingenuous Kev desires help of the
libertine Dolph. Thus we read the heading:] INGENIOUS LABOR-
TENACITY AS BETWEEN INGENUOUS AND LIBERTINE. [The problem in
question has to do with triangles. The triangle, Delta, is the sign
of ALP (see diagram on p. 293) and also appears on the label of
Bass's Ale. So we read:] *The boss's best bass is the pride of Mullingar* [HCE's tavern]. Problem ye first: construct an equilateral
triangle. In the name of the Father and of the Son and of the Holy
Ghost, Amen.

[Dolph and Kev query each other:] NEARNESS AND FARNESS IN
THE CONVERGENCE OF THEIR CONTRAPULSIVENESS:

[33] Mr. Edmund Wilson very kindly sent us a copy of Joyce's corrections
of misprints in *Finnegans Wake.* We have rendered the present passage in
conformity with these corrections.

[34] These last two pages are intentionally very obscure. Our rendering is
necessarily a long shot.

[35] "Please to lick one and turn over." Wet your finger; turn a new page
of life; it is time to move on.—Cf. "Tetragrammaton," p. 194, *infra.*

[36] Radmachrees: red hearts. Rossecullinans: rough diamonds (Cullinan Diamond, discovered 1905 at the Premier Mine, Transvaal). Blagpɪkes: joke-
piques—joke-spades. Suitclover: clubs. No time now for regrets, we must
push on.

"Can you do her, numb?" asks Dolph (the Trouveller), suspecting the answer, know. "I can't, can you, ninny?" asks Kev (of the Disordered Visage), expecting the answer, guess.—Nor was the noer long disappointed, for he was told. *The aliments of Geomantry:* "O, tell it to us! do! Sem!"—"Well, 'tis thusly: First, mull a mugful of mud—so." "Oh, glory!" (287) prays the more virtuous one, "O Lord, what the devil would I do that for? That's a goosey's answer you're giving me. What the devil would you do that for?" ("Will you walk into my wave trap?" said the spiter to the shy.) "Now there's no royal road to Puddlin; take your courage—take this mud for a first beginning. *Washerwomen at their weirdest.* Anny liffle mud which cometh out of Mam will do, I guess. And to find a locus for an ALP get a Howth [hold] of her bayrings [bearings] as a first O; and for a second O unbox your compasses. —I cain but are you able?" "No!" "Good! So let's set off between us.—Take a point of the coast map to be called *a* but pronounced alpha. There's the Isle of Man, ah! O! Good.—Now all's in apple-pie order."

[Dolph is leading Kev along the path of illicit knowledge. Abruptly, at this point, the explanation is interrupted. It will be continued on page 293, where the figure will be found which Dolph is constructing. Already it is clear that his explanation is not entirely innocent of geographical, obscene, and metaphysical overtones. What he is doing is introducing his brother to the secrets of the mother. Joyce, in the guise of our old professor friend, breaks the narrative with a parenthesis of five and a half pages.

[In Latin he invites the spirits of the ancients to sit in on the interesting lesson:] Come, O past ones, while, in the Latin tongue of the dead, a little bit of paper liviana is exposed to view; seated over pots of meat, let us revolve in our minds the ancient wisdom of Bruno and Vico, to wit, that all flows as a river, and that every river is embraced by rival banks.

The professor discusses Dolph, dean of idlers, describing how.

though barely a stuttering boy, he often coached rebellious Mikes at Backlane University (288) for a dillar a dollar, changing letters for them, and blending schemes for them, and double-crossing twofold truths, and devising tail-words; meanwhile, counting that another would finish his sentence for him, he would smile a bit eggwise and pick his ten dirty nails, retelling himself by the hour a reel of funnish facts about the girl from the fairy hill, the charm-him-girl-of-love. In fact, he would review in his mind the whole damning letter, how, first of all and on second thought and third, and furthermore, and fifthly. . . . That is to say, he would review to himself the Patrick-Tristram story of his old man and woman, as recounted in the books he had read. For instance, when the voyager [St. Patrick; Sir Tristram] landed in Leinster for the second time, leaving Lipton's Strongbow launch, the *Little Eva*,[37] he converted its natives, showed them the celestine way, and the cult he introduced is still prevalent in this land—for our people still hold (289) to their healing and believe in the old ways innovated by him, and nothing would induce them to change back to their earlier flash and crash habits of Pales' time, which they let drop, presto.—But, to return to the coxswain on the first landing,[38] if pretty abbess and beauty dare discuss such a matter: where now (290) is she that was the belle of La Chapelle, who, after the first compliments, gave him a cuddlebath with her own hands; that is to say, if she then, the then that matters. . . .

[The professor, at this point, unable to follow any longer with-

[37] Patrick first came to Ireland as a captive. It was his second landing, as a bishop, that began his mission. Strongbow was the leader of the invasion of Henry II. Eva was the daughter of the dissatisfied King of Leinster. She was offered to Strongbow for his aid.

[38] Tristram, of Tristram and Iseult, came twice to Chapelizod. First he was ill of a wound received from the sword of Iseult's brother. She, not knowing the cause of his wound, and not knowing who he was, nursed and bathed him. Then she discovered, while he was in the tub, that he was the man who had slain her brother, and she threatened him with his own sword. It was on his second visit to Ireland that Tristram came to fetch Iseult to King Mark.

out protest the thoughts of this scurrilous little boy, breaks off his own discussion to put forward an indignant defence of the lady Iseult:] But, *seigneur!* She never could have foreseen such a cold douche as him doubling back under that shirt of iron [a suit of armor] and under a waterproof name, with a peaceful white cheek, and with his wash tub and his diagnoser's lamp-look, to buy her in, and two other mavourneens ("Come, mesdames, name your price!") on behalf of old-established (291) King Mark of Cornwall.[39] It must have been terrible, making up to that old Adam-he used-to [King Mark]—the poor isolated girl! And short wonder so many Tom, Dick, and Harrys came to console her at her window. But to think of Tristram then fondling an Iseult the second [Iseult of Brittany, whom he married]! Where and when he did escapes my forgetfulness, for many a false word he whispered to many a lying ear. And to try to analyze that pair's pair of arms [the two Iseults] trying to embrace all of that sneak's virility [Tristram's] in their delightful Sexsex home, as though he were a regular newborn babe! Well, Diarmait and (292) Grainne,[40] if that is what lamoor seems to be circling toward out yondest [if that is the problem that this black Dolph is describing with his compasses], heaven help his hindmost! And it begins to look like it, indeed, if we are to judge from the remarks [against Joyce] of Wyndham Lewis in his book, *Time and Western Man.* There's no use your preaching Dolph to cheese it, or praying young Catholics to take warning by the past! Could you peep into the brain of this good-for-nobody, you would see a great litter of times lost, lands strayed, and tongues lagging. Also, could you look far into the future, your brain would reel just to fancy the endless repetition of what stale words have already described. But the crime of it is that just when the swift eyes of the young are letting you know that no mouth has the might to set bounds to the march of a lan-

[39] I.e., Iseult did not know that Tristram would return to procure her for his uncle, King Mark.
[40] Diarmait and Grainne, Gaelic counterparts of Tristram and Iseult. Cf. p. 125.

guage, the beast of boredom is going to remind you sternly how you must draw the line somewhere.[41]

[That ends the professor's interruption. When we return to the story of the two boys at their problem, we discover that the marginal comments have exchanged places; the pedantic forms are now at the left hand and in italic type.[42]

[Kev, instead of listening attentively to the instructions of his brother, has been dozing. The parenthesis of the professor, in a sense, was but an amplification of the content of the good little boy's lapse from attention. Kev comes to with a start:]

(293) WHY MY, AS LIKEWISE WHY HIS: "Coss? [43] Coss ist? Pardon! You make what name?" he asks. (And in truth he had all but lost himself, so had he gazed in the lazy eye of his *Lapis in Via von Dublin*,[44] the Turnpike under the great Elm with Mearing-stone in Foreground.) (Drumcondra's dream country where the butterflies blow.)

[With that, we are ready to see the brother battle resumed:] *Uteralterance, or the Interplay of Bones in the Womb:* Kev continues: "Given now ann linch you take in all. Allow me; and heaving the jaw-breaking expressions of Sir Isaac Newton aside, let us proceed. *The Vortex:* given the line AL, A is for Anna, like L is for Liv. This we may call the *Spring of Sprung Verse.* Aha, haha, Ante Ann you're apt to ape aunty annalive! Dawn gives rise. Eve takes fall. Aiaiaiai, Antiann, we're last to the lost, Loulou! Perfect.

[41] This is a paraphrase of Parnell's famous statement regarding the English repression of Ireland's natural development. One can read in it a rebuke to critics (viz., Wyndham Lewis) who censured Joyce for his creative experiments with the English language.

[42] Compare the mathematical change from + to − in the passage through the Cartesian co-ordinate.

[43] Coss:—"Algebra," from *cosa*—"the unknown." Coss ist?: *Was ist?*

[44] *Lapis in Via:* stone in the street—the philosophers' stone. *Lapis in Via von Dublin*—philosophers' stone of Dublin. The philosophers' stone is androgynous: it is HCE and ALP. The figure the boys are drawing is the geometrical counterpart of the philosophers' stone. Kev has been dreaming out the window: the landscape holds the same secret as the geometry figure.

Now (294) we see the straight line AL (in Fig., the forest [45]) stops
at lambda, which we shall call *The Vertex.* Now then, take this in.
Sarga, or the path of outgoing: [46] with Olaf as centrum (A) and
Olaf's lambtail (L) for his spokesman [i.e., with the line A-L as
radius] circumscript a cyclone [circumscribe a circle] as round as
the calf of an egg!" Kev exclaims: "O, dear me! Another grand
discovery, after the fashion of MacPherson's Ossian! You've hit
upon something! Remember though the proverb, 'Early clever,
surely doomed.' You will be doomed: *Docetism and Didicism:* [47]
like your Bigdud dadder in the vaudeville song with the two girls—
Maya-Thaya [48]—and the Three—*Tamas, Rajas, Sattva:* [49] Papacoco-
potl by his magazine fall." Dolph, nothing daunted, proceeds: "But
it's not all over yet. The mystery repeats itself, as our mother Gaud-
yanna used to sing, now and then, over her posset pot, (295) yesterday and forever, and for a night and a day. *The Vegetable Cell and
its Private Properties.* Poor little mother of mine; so she used, indeed. May her soul and all the souls of the faithful departed, rest
in peace.—When I'm dreaming back like that I begin to see we're
all only telescopes!—But to return: We now draw another circle,
as follows: Beginning with the letter L as center and with A as
radius, turn a somersault, as round as your bottom! O, dear me,
that was very nice indeed. It makes us a daintical pair of accom-

[45] Forest of the pubic hair bounded by the line just drawn (line AL in
figure on p. 293). Dolph is drawing a picture of his mother's genitals.
[46] *Sarga* (Sanskrit): "process of world creation or emanation."
[47] Opposition of two theories as to the nature of Christ's body. Docetism
holds that Christ's fleshly body was illusory, *didn't* really suffer. The pun
following says it did, *Didicism.*
[48] Maya-Thaya: continuation of the docetism-didicism contrast. *Māyā* (Sanskrit) is "illusion" as mother of the world. *Thaya* suggests corporeal existence
(see footnote 2, *supra*); *Thāya* (Sanskrit, dative): "to the thump of a fall."
[49] *Tamas, Rajas, Sattva* (Sanskrit): the three gunas, or qualities of Māyā,
which constitute the nature of the world. They are, respectively, inertia,
activity, and harmony. They are here associated with the Three Soldiers
responsible for HCE's misfortune. Thus, all the figures of the Park adventure
are allegorized as factors of the world process. The cosmic background of
Dolph's misbehavior is delineated.

plasses.[50] Now the next point! *The haves and have-nots: a distinction.* Now, there's a pair of tricklesome points where our twain of doubling bicirculars dunloop into each other: Lucihere![51] (296) *Zweispaltung as Fundemaintalish of Wiederherstellung:* [52] Now, I'd like to make a capital Pee for Pride down there—where Hoddum-and-Heave, our monster bilker, balked his bawd of parodies. And let *you* go and mick your modest mock Pie out of Humbles up your end.—Are you right there, Michael?" Dolph calls up to him. "Ay, Nickel," replies Kev, "and I'll write!" "Now," says Dolph, "join *a*lpha-*p*ee and *p*ull-*l*oose by dotties, and join *a*-*p*ie and *p*ale-*a*le by trunkles,[53] and I'll make you see figuratively the womb of your eternal (297) geomater. (1) *Destiny, influence of design upon:* [54] If you flung her clothes over her head, you'd wheeze why Solomon set his seal sixfold[55] on the gown of a witch." "Arrah, go on!" exclaims the excited and impatient Kev. "Fin for fun! Let's have at it!" Dolph proceeds to the final act: "Subtend me now," says he. "Pisk! We carefully, if she pleats, lift by her hem (like thousands done before) the maidsapron of our ALP, till its nether nadir is vortically where its navel's napex

---

[50] As shown in the figure on p. 293, Dolph has drawn two interlocking circles of radius A-L, the one with A as center, the other with L. These may be thought of as two cosmic cycles, or as a pair of lassies' arm in arm, or again, as the two hips of ALP. Joyce's text also plays with the image of HCE circling about the entire figure.

[51] The circles intersect at two points; these are to be called *p* and *π*, and are to be identified respectively with the vagina and the navel of the mother. Dolph claims *p* for himself and assigns virginal *π* to Kev.

[52] Splitting-in-two as a precondition to reassembly. The phrase suggests Hegel's dialectic of world history, also the words of Giordano Bruno (Brown-Nolan): "Everything can come to a knowledge of itself only through contrast with its opposite."

[53] The triangle A-L-P is indicated by dots; the triangle *a*-λ-*π*, by lines.

[54] Dolph is about to use this figure by way of illustrating the secrets of the earth mother (geo-mater). Step 1: he will lift her apron, A-L-P, by lifting P to *π*. Step 2: he will light a match to help Kev see in the mother dark.

[55] Solomon's Seal, the six-pointed Jewish Star, is composed of two counterimposed triangles.

will have to be. (2) *Prometheus, or the Promise of Provision.*[56]
You must come near, for it is dark. And light your match. And
this is what you'll say: 'Waaaaaa! Tch! Sluice! Pla!' And there,
Redneck, is the living spit of dead waters, the firm fastness of
Hurdlebury Fenn, distinct and isoplural in its sixuous parts.—
Midden wedge of the stream is your muddy old triagonal delta Δ
plain for you now, first of all usquiluteral threeingles, the constant
of fluxion, Mahamewetma, pride of the province. And when the
old man, that tidled boare, rutches up from the Afrantic, ALP's
body is his bett and bier. (298) *Double meanings and their role:*
Which is whom you see; it is her. So post that to your pape and
smarket: and you can haul up that languil pennant, mate. I've
read your *Tunc's* dimissage." [57]—Now we come to the general
conclusions: (1) *Ecclesiastical and celestial hierarchies: the Ascen-
ing, the Descending:* (*a*) Let ALP be represented by zero and
HCE by one. Then any quantity you like, X, to the power of
zero (X^0) will be either greater than or less than 1. (*b*) Let Doll-
the-laziest [Dolph] be dissimulant from Doll-the-fiercest [Kev]:
then, the victorious ready-eyes of ever-two circumflicksrent
searclhers never film, in the elipsities of their gyribouts, those
fickers which are returnally reproductive of themselves.[58] Which
is unpassable. (2) Corollary: *The peripatetic periphery. Its Allothe-
sis:* The locus of 1 to that base anything (X) when most char-
acteristically mantissa minus [1 minus a decimal part] comes to
nullism in the endth. And vice versa, the infinisissimals of her facets

[56] Compare Freud: Prometheus' fire-bringing as an Oedipus adventure.
Also Freudian: science as a sublimation of infantile sex curiosity. Here the
entire system of scholarly and scientific curiosity is reduced to its infantile
base.
[57] Joyce here seems to suggest that the *Tunc*-page illuminations of the Book
of Kells carry the message revealed in the present chapter. See our discussion
of pp. 119–123.
[58] These two propositions sum up the cosmogonic implications of what has
just taken place. The first speaks of all things as functions of the relationship
between HCE and ALP. The second says that the children or products
of this relationship, for all their research, never wholly perceive the full
secret of this world-begetting parental embrace.

become manier-and-manier, as the calicolum of her undescribable shrinks from shurtiness (299) to sherts.[59] (3) Scholium: There are trist sides to everysing, but ichs on the freed brings euchs to the feared.[60]—Q.E.D. [Kev fails to follow the entire drift of the lesson he has received from his brother:] Kev: "Mother of us all! Oh, dear me, look at that now! The beatenest lay I ever see. And a superbposition coincidence!—as Oliver Cromwell said, when he slepped over his grandmother." Dolph: "But you're gaping up the wrong place! as if you were seeing a ghost. You must lap the reflection below. Here!" Kev: "Oh, dear, that's very lovely. It will be a lesson to me all my life."—Suddenly understanding, Kev turns indignantly on his instructor, and assails him with rebukes and high-minded admonitions: "Ever thought about Guinness's? And Parson Rome's advice?[61] (300) Want to join the police?" (Picking on Nick again.) "You know you always were one of the bright ones," he continues; "one of the fakes, you hoax! You'll be damned one of these days!"

[The brother battle is now fully under way again. The marginal notes state for us the theme:] SICK US A SOCK WITH SOME SEDIMENT IN IT FOR THE SAKE OF OUR DARNING WIVES: *Primanouriture and Ultimogeniture:* Our Shaun, with the help of food, sought to liberate the mess from his corrective mouth; while that Other, by the help of his creative mind, offered to liberate the masses from the booty of fight. And since he would ever have the last word, candy-kissing P. Kevin [Shaun], was wont to mumble to me in

[59] The drift of this very complex passage seems to be: HCE when dismembered or otherwise suffering loss always returns to ALP. Whether they are faithful to each other or not, their private relationships become more numerous and binding as the frillier aspects of ALP's marriage role give way to the more domestic apronly ones.
[60] There are three sides to everything and the all-father knows them all; but in the limited world of the sons, I, happy, make you fearsome.
[61] Probably a hint of the Roman Catholic advice to avoid the occasions of sin. Next: "Want to join the police?" warns Dolph that unless he mends his ways he will never be a big strapping roundsman of the law, as Kev is to be.

bewonderment of his chipper brother. Dolph, according to Kev, was unconsciously grafficking after trigamies and godolphing in fairlove, trying to see around the waste of noland's brown jesus. Kev would mumble thus about his brother till the jugular veins in his neck stood out like tightropes.[62] *No Sturm; No Drang. Illustration:* (301) Call a bloodletter! Pray for blaablaablacksheep! And to calm Kev down one should say to him: "Sure you could write as fine as that lousy Erewhig yourself, Mick, if you but would!" Kev's writing, for instance . . . *Ascription of the Active* . . . would be a fine letter to Milady, as follows: "Dear . . . he would pine for her . . . how he would pun fun for all. And how are you, Waggy? My spirit is sorrowful."—Nick too was sorrowful. Oh, jerry, he was sad. Look at his twitches! *Proscription of the Passive.* Lesson: Sink deep, or touch not the Cartesian spring!—He was lying low on his raw-side laying siege to goblin castle. But on the other hand he was lying long on his laugh-side too. (302) Any letter he would write would be a dreary begging letter, as, for instance: "And hope soon to hear! If you could lend me till my resurrection, sahib, the price of a plate of poultice. Period. With best apologies and many many thanks to self for all the clericals and again begs pardon for trespassing again on your beneficence." And a typical reply, such as might come from the woman . . . *Ensouling Female Sustains Agonizing Overman* . . . would be something like this: "Well, wiggywiggywagtail, and how are you yaggy? With a capital Tea for Thirst. From here Buvard to dear Picuchet. Blott."

Now watch him signing away in happiness complete: WHEN THE ANSWERER IS A LEMAN: *Sesama to the Rescues. The Key Signature:* "And I hope you've been a good girl. (Lisp year sends you all and more, souvenirs soft as summer snow, sweet williams, and forget-

[62] This passage may be read: Shaun (Kev) eats some food to take the bad taste of illicit knowledge out of his mouth, while Shem (Dolph) seeks to clear the atmosphere by rational discussion; whereupon Kev belittles Dolph's aims and deplores his resemblance to those aspects of HCE which find vent in licentiousness and metaphysics. Kev becomes so angry that his neck veins swell in rage. He is on the point of striking his brother.

us-knots) To fall there at bare feet. To be continued. Anon." [63]

ALL SQUARE AND ACCORDING TO COCKER: All the characters in the drama: This is how they do it (303).—Pose the pen the way I do, the way I was taught. Bold strokes for your life. Tip. *Force Centers of the Serpentine: Sacral*—Wilde; *Spleen*—Swift; *Navel*—Sterne; *Heart*—Steele; *Throat*—Burke; *Intertemporal Eye*—Yeats; *Fontanelle*—Shaw. *Conception of the Compromise and Finding a Formula:* Charles Stewart Parnell going between grave Danny boy and cool Connolly. Upanishadem [Up boys and at 'em]! Tip. Erin go Bragh.

TROTHBLOWERS: And Kev was wreathed with his pother. [He is about to deliver his knockout blow.]

FIG AND THISTLE PLOT A PIG AND WHISTLE: But, after all Dolph's autocratic writings and meddlied muddlingisms, his brother sent a blow right through his pergamon—hit him where he lived . . . *Ideal present alone produces real future* . . . and it did for him, like it done for many another unpious one of the hairy firstlings, till at length he measured his earth: our frankson who was misocain. Once (304) one's one! Rip! And his countinghands rose counting him out.

WITH EBONISER: How simple! [He now has a beautiful ebony-black eye.]

IN PIX: Slutningsbane! [MOVIE TABLEAU: Twilight of the Gods!]

[But now, in the most surprising fashion, Dolph, all graciousness, instead of resenting and retaliating the blow, simply recovers his feet and moves toward reconciliation. This moment corresponds exactly to the moment in *Ulysses* (Random House ed., p. 585; Paris

---

[63] This page contains two hypothetical letters contrasting the temperaments of the two boys, and a third in the manner of the eternal female, echoing the letter of the mud mound.

Immediately following, the theme of creative writing will blossom into a classification of Irish writers according to the "force centers" of Yoga; these are enumerated in the left-hand margin and the corresponding Irish writers (their order shuffled) appear in the text.

Dolph understands writing, both as an art and as a mystical process. This is the cause of Kev's resentment of him. Suddenly, Kev's rage becomes converted into action. He strikes his brother.

ed, p. 562) where Stephen is struck down by the Redcoat, Private Carr. This is the stroke of the lance, delivered by the Roman soldier at the Crucifixion.[64]]

EUCHARIST. MERCI BEAUCOUP. AND MIND WHO YOU'RE PUCKING, FLEBBY: *Service superseding self:* "Thanks ever so much. Point carried! I can't say whether it's the way you strike me or that red mass I was looking at, but at present, potential as I am, I'm seeing rainbows all around me. Returning good for evil, I'd love to take you for a buggy ride. If my maily was bag enough I'd send you a toxis. By Saxo Grammaticus, you done that lovely for me!— Didn't he now, Nubilina?" [The speaker has turned from his opponent to "Little Cloud," the dream girl, Iseult.] Tiny mite! She is studying something? With her listening-in coiffure [her ears are showing], her dream of England's last day, and the glory of being presainted maid to majesty. A pity! for she isn't the lollipops she easily might be if she had, for example, Virginia's air of achievement.—*Catastrophe and Anabasis:* "As I was saying, while returning thanks, you have given me new life."—*The rotary process and its re-establishment of reciprocities:* "We're awful offal-boys both. I've picked up all the crumbs from your table, singing Glory Hallelujah! Accordingly, (305) we read in the good book: 'He prophets most who bilks the best.'"

The reconciliation takes place through the operation of *The Twofold Truth and the Conjunctive Appetites of Oppositional Orexes.* Says Dolph: "That salubrious sock in the jaw has upset all my hazeydency. Forge away, Sunny Sam, shipshape. I'm only out to bridge over the gap in your hesitency-tendency.[65] I could

[64] Is Dolph's acquiescence strength or weakness? Joyce does not conceive the problem in moral terms; the whole course of the book shows that an indisposition to stand up even for his own rights is Shem's norm of action. He enjoys his revenge, however, in the knowledge that he controls spiritual power not accessible to his self-righteous brother. Shaun, half-aware of this superiority, and fearing it, can retaliate only by increasing violence.

[65] This refers to HCE's hesitancy (i.e., stutter), a psychological symptom traceable to a sense of guilt. This guilt is inherited by both the brothers. In Shaun's case it takes the form of secret knowledge of his own unworthiness to dominate the world; in Shem's it is a recognition of inability to

try to psychoanalyze you till you would be blue in the face. If you're not your brother's keeper, may I never curse again. Where is the twin who does not know that you, who are my popular antithesis, have a secret defect?" HOW DO YOU SPELL CUNCTITITITI- LATIO?[66] TWO AT A TIME. THREE ON A TRICKY. [The passage ends with a Trisagion of peace:] *"Shanti, shanti, shanti."*[67] *Ave!* Evocation of maiding waters. OHIO IOIO MISS.—Rewards from the Four Masters will be distributed tomorrow [Graduation Day], (306) when Daddy, parent who offers sweetmeats, will give us his Nobel Prize. *Abnegation is Adaptation.* With his praiseworthy praising purpose let us be satisfied. Between me and thee and St. John. —Item: mizpah ends.[68]

The day has come for action. The student life is done. Commencement Day is at hand. Why the devil are they dawdling over the mugs and the grubs? We have studied steadily: now we shall guide the multitudes. ENTER THE COP. HE SECURES GOVERNMENT OF THE ENTIRE GLOBE. We've had our day at triv and quad (trivium and quadrivium), and have written our bit as intermidgets. We have completed our courses in art, literature, politics, economics, chemistry, humanity, etc.

[The next two pages sum up, in the style of college theme titles and examination questions, the characters that have been studied

meet life's challenge. The constant effort of the two brothers to supplement each other leads only to collisions and recoil.

The word "hesitency," which belongs to HCE (for the misspelling, see our note on p. 97) is transformed in the present passage to fit the two sons: for Shaun it becomes "his-citendency" and for Shem "hazeydency."
[66] Shem taunts Shaun by challenging him to spell out a name of the all-father obscenely transformed by his fault (Cunctitititilatio). "Two at a time. Three on a tricky" recalls the girls and the soldiers. The spelling test refers again to the Parnell trial, where Pigott, the accuser, was unmasked by his misspelling of the word "hesitancy."
[67] *Shanti* (Sanskrit): peace—intoned thrice at close of prayers. *Sanctus:* Roman Catholic Trisagion.
[68] Mizpah, meaning "watchtower," is the patent name of a contraceptive device. The sense here is that the time for youth has ended; the students must go forth and be fruitful.

in the great school of *Finnegans Wake;* for example:] *Ovid:* The
Voice of Nature in the Forest (Where Lily-is-a-Lady found the
nettle rash). *Adam, Eve:* Your Favorite Hero and Heroine. *Homer:*
Describe in Homely Anglian Monosyllables the Wreck of the
Hesperus (Able Seaman's Caution). *Marcus Aurelius:* What
Morals, if any, can be drawn from Diarmait and Grainne? (307)
Noah: A visit to Guinness's Brewery. *Isaac:* When is a Pun not a
Pun? *Tiresias:* Is the Co-education of Animus and Anima wholly
desirable? *Nestor:* Hengler's Circus Entertainment. *Joseph:* The
Strangest Dream that ever was half-dreamt (Something happened
that time I was asleep, torn letters or was there snow?). *Esop:*
Tell a friend in a chatty letter the Fable of the Grasshopper and
the Ant. *Lot:* The Shame of Slumdom. *Castor, Pollux:* Compare
the Fistic Styles of Jimmy Wilde and Jack Sharkey. *Moses:* Glory
be to St. Patrick! *Job:* What is to be found in a Dustheap? (308)
Xenophon: Delays are dangerous.—Hurry, hurry! Then says Gob-
ble Anne: "Tea's set; C's enough! Soon Mox will be through the
chancellery of his exchequer."

[Study hour is over. It is time for supper. Mother calls. Their
feed begins. And what they will be eating, of course (in terms of
the imagery of the sacramental meal) will be the substance of their
father.] [69]

Now comes a list of ten monosyllables which gear the circling
wheels of *Finnegans Wake* into the cabalistic decade of the
sephiroth.[70] This is the powerhouse of the book, with energy currents going to every page. The syllables, each representing a number, fall into three groups of three, with one remaining. They

[69] The marginal note at this point, MAWMAW, LOOK, YOUR BEEFTAY'S FIZZIN'
OVER, is perhaps the only phrase in *Finnegans Wake* that reproduces, word
for word, a phrase in *Ulysses* (Random House ed., p. 554; Paris ed., p.
532): "Mamma, the beeftea is fizzing over!"
[70] The numbers from one to ten represent, for the cabalists, the stages of
the descent (or fall) of Eternal Spirit into phenomenal manifestation. Each
connotes a mystical quality (Beatitude, Wisdom, Intelligence, Mercy, Justice,
Beauty, Honor, Glory, Generation, and Dominion), and is attended by a
choir of angels.

represent the descent of all-highest One (Aun) down the ladder of the decade to union with Zero in order to form the number ten (Geg). Each rung of the descent is matched by a marginal word corresponding to a phase of cosmic evolution.

The highest aspect of the Godhead is the *unmanifest*. No sign or word can encompass it. The highest *manifestation* is the Person of the Father, called Ainsoph (cf. p. 261), or Makroprosopos. But such a manifestation immediately implies a knower of the manifestation, and this Knower is the Son. A known and its knower implies a relationship, and this Relationship is the third member of the *heavenly* trinity, the Holy Ghost. Joyce indicates the three personalities of this heavenly trinity in the first three terms of his mystical decade:

Pantocracy:	Aun
Bimutualism:	Do
Interchangeability:	Tri

As the Father generated the *heavenly* trinity, so the Son generates the trinity of man. He himself is the all-inclusive, androgynous image of man, subsuming both HCE and ALP. The first term in the *human* series is Tetragrammaton, the Logos, the word that is to be made flesh, the vehicle of God's descent into the world. The second term, Superfetation, stands for this image fallen into the condition of multiplicity. At this stage the pairs of opposites stand against each other (brother battle). But this opposition implies a relationship between the opposites, and this relationship is represented by the third term of the human three. Joyce indicates this trinity as follows:

Naturality:	Car
Superfetation:	Cush [71]
Stabimobilism:	Shay

[71] Joyce's footnote on Cush (p. 308) is highly important, indicating as it does that the descending power splits at the fifth rung into two opposing forces, Cush and Kish (brother battle again). The diagram thumbs the nose at Kish, Antichrist, Shem. The five fingers of the hand represent rung five, and symbolize the incarnate Son. There are two sides to the hand,

From the Holy Ghost proceeds the trinity of the *physical* world; respectively, Time, Space, and Causality. Joyce lists them as follows:

Periodicity:	Shockt
Consummation:	Ockt
Interpenetrativeness:	Ni

This entire series of nine terms is an extension of the *masculine* aspect of the Godhead. None of these principles becomes effective in living forms until the *female* aspect has received them, as it were, into her womb. The ninth term of the masculine series is the male member of the divine body, to be united with its negative counterpart. The feminine principle is represented by zero, 0, and through its addition to the now-exhausted series, the decade refreshed in Geg is fitted for continuation in another series. The theme of the new series is announced in the phrase "Their feed begins." Having gathered the broken fragments of the exhausted decade (the fallen Humpty Dumpty, the prostrate hod carrier Finnegan), Mother Zero serves them up again to the new generation: "Grampupus is fallen down but Grinny sprids the boord" (p. 7).

"Geg" indeed actually suggests the eggs to be served.[72] At this point procreation as well as feeding begins anew, and the brother pair, Box and Cox, alternate in the marriage bed.

The chapter concludes with a NIGHTLETTER from the chil-

front and back. The word "Antichrist" is transformed into "anticheirst" (contra-hand); and the comment is a contemptuous "back of my hand to him."

[72] The schoolboy illumination in the lower left-hand corner of the page yields several secrets. The topmost element is the profile of Makroprosopos, who is always represented in profile. It is through the nose that his sacred breath (Spirit, Expiration) is sent forth to become the creating force of all the worlds. The second element is the hand in profile, thumbing the nose (Cush vs. Kish). The third element is a pair of crossbones, suggesting death, which is associated traditionally with love (in Hinduism, the God of Love is also the God of Death): The kingdom (Ten, Geg) is the place of love and death. X represents kisses, but also crucifixion. Had God not loved man he would not have been crucified.—This juvenile illumination also carries a suggestion of the *Tunc* page of the Book of Kells.

dren, who are to be thought of as having gone forth into their world adventure. They cable back from their new world,[73] sending greetings to Pep and Memmy and the old folks in the realm of the ancestors.

Book II, Chapter 3: Tavernry in Feast

[The theme of eating is always associated in *Finnegans Wake* with the eating of the god: the consuming of the life substance of the father by his sons and retainers. This chapter, then, will show the denizens of HCE's tavern consuming the life substance of their host—and not only eating and drinking him out of house and home, but tearing apart with their talk the garment of his reputation. It might have been called "Tavernry in Feast." Overtones of the Last Supper are certainly present.

[The setting is the tavern of HCE. The radio is blaring and the customers are pushing each other about, swapping yarns, and drunkenly joking. HCE is at the till. It becomes gradually apparent that all the yarns and radio broadcasts taken together add up to something like the ancient story of the shame of HCE. The yarns cut across each other, and yet carry forward the inevitable tale.

[The thread of this chapter is composed of some nine interwoven strands. There is (*A*) a Tavern Brawl underlying the entire action. Next in importance is (*B*) the story of a Norwegian Captain and his inquiries concerning a Tailor in the town. There is (*C*) a radio skit of the brothers Butt and Taff. Butt tells a col-

[73] Throughout *Finnegans Wake* the new world is symbolized as America. Joyce here consciously follows the precedent of William Blake, in whose symbology *The Boston Tea Party* represents the first upturn of Man from his long Fall—that cosmogonic Fall which began in Paradise and attained its nadir in the "diseases and mildews" of the brutal merchant-empire of the Giant Albion. Blake's imagery combines easily with Vico's. It furnishes many of the strongest themes of *Finnegans Wake*. The tea-stained letter from Boston, for instance, unfolds new secrets when regarded in the light of Blake. Blake's image of a fundamental sleeping individuality, Albion, around whom revolve the figures of the Four Zoas, and whose emanation is the symbolic Jerusalem, and who will not awake from his Universal Dream until the Last Judgment—is precisely HCE.

lateral tale (*D*) of his shooting the Russian General at the Battle of Sevastopol. During intermissions are presented brief news reports and short-shorts: (*E*) the Steeplechase, (*F*) a televisioning of four interesting Mullingar Events, (*G*) an account of the Annihilation of the Atom, (*H*) a radio review of the Dismemberment of a Hero, and, besides, an endless Tale of a Tub recounted by the host himself. Through all this smoke and spilth emerges the all-flavoring, self-justifying presence of the Tavernkeeper, HCE.

[The chapter opens with a view of the tavern company and a summary of the themes of their talk.]

(309) It may or may not be of concern to the Guinnesses, but—if there be four themes, which, in Etheria Deserta as well as in Grander Suburbia, are, amongst Finnfannfawners, in dispute, they are the following: (1) back in the doom of the balk of the deaf lies the fright of a man's life; (2) the height of his life, from a bride's eye standpoint, is when a man wades a lymph; (3) the pride which undoes him begs the glory of a wake; (4) the circular scheme is like your rumba round me garden.[1]

Therefore they had chipped in and bought for their proprietor a handsome twelve-tube radio, as modern as tomorrow afternoon, equipped with umbrella antennas for distance-getting, and connected with a vital-tone speaker capable of catching everything, key clickings, vaticum cleaners, etc., and of boiling the whole thing down in a sounds-pound so as to serve him up a mulligatawny mary-go-round, electrically filtered for all Irish hearths and (310) homes. This engine they caused to be worked from a magazine battery. And they connected it to an auricular arrangement, a mighty conch, capable of conducting all broadcasts, so as to lull the Big One till the end of his earish life.

This tavern is the "House of Call," where the host unbulges an O'Connell's ale, while his eyes watch carefully the till. The house's *c*artomance[2] *h*allucinates like an *e*rection in the night. This ale is

[1] Compare these with the themes of the four Viconian ages: Harry me, Marry me, Bury me, Bind me.

[2] HCE's tavern holds the phantasmagoric secret of destiny, as cards do.

just a tug and a fistful for him—as it would have been for Coolson MacCool, the old Patagoreyan giant of the former dispensation,³ who might have swallowed down Lough Neagh. There is quite a pop when he pulls the cork, and a foam slides (311) down the sloppery side of the bottle; and then the mugs are filled.

This was a long time after the days of yore: long after the day when he put into port with his ship, and not so long after the day he was asked was there a tailor shop in the town? Not before the day he threw out Kerrse [Persse O'Reilly]; and not before the day, when, athwartships, he buttonholed the Norwegian Captain.⁴

The host sought, meanwhile, with guilty conscience and open ear, a clue to the popular judgment on him. [In his head ticked phrases reminiscent of the "Negative Confession" of the Book of the Dead:] "I have not mislaid the key of Efas-Taem. I have not left temptation in the path of the sweeper of the threshold."

[Then the customers lifted, with half-threatening implication, their glasses to a Sinn Fein toast:] "Ourselves, ourselves, alone!" And the drinks were tossed off in the very manner of an "Up boys and at 'em." ⁵

[Whereupon there began to be unwound and resnarled the endless yarns: (A) A Tavern Brawl, confused with (B) A Tailor in the Town. Apparently, a blustering mariner, known as the Norwegian Captain and very like the figure of HCE, was in the habit of putting into port and then sailing away to roam the deep again for years. He was something of a Flying Dutchman. On one of his visits he encountered the Ship's Husband—another bulky fellow very like the figure of HCE. The Captain asked where he might order himself a suit of clothes, and the Ship's Husband recommended a shop, successor to Ashe and Whitehead. In the wild disorder of the tavern tellings and retellings of the tale the Ship's

³ Finn MacCool, hero of the primeval, as HCE is of historical times.
⁴ These episodes will appear in the coming yarns.
⁵ The attitude of the drinkers in the tavern is hostile, essentially that of the soldiers who bore witness against HCE.

Husband becomes confused, or amalgamated, with the obscure personality of the tailor.[6] The Norwegian Captain is fitted, but then, instead of decently paying his bill, sets out to sea. And the Ship's Husband bellows after him in vain.[7]

[The reader is reminded by many rhythmical echoes of the story of Jarl van Hoother and the Prankquean, the Norwegian Captain playing in this case the role of prankster. One is not surprised to see the Norwegian Captain circle past twice again. On his second visit he enters the tavern and orders a great meal, but instead of paying, simply departs, leaving the Ship's Husband whistling for the bill.]

—Then said the Norwegian Captain to the Ship's Husband, "Where can I get myself a suit?" "Suit?" said the Ship's Housebound,[8] "There is a tailor, successor to Ashe and Whitehead." And

[6] The whole tailor complex suggests immediately Carlyle's *Sartor Resartus* and the transcendental philosophy symbolized in that work on clothes. Clothes represent the material sheaths, which cover the core of being. In the world of appearance these are considered more important than the body of truth which they cover. Also, there is more than a hint in HCE's spiritual agony of the problem of Carlyle's Everlasting Nay and Yea.

A traditional mythologic image known to East and West is that of God as Tailor. Sitting cross-legged He sews the thread of spirit into the world of matter. Thus He fashions for the entire universe a cloak of appearance. The problem of the Everlasting Yea is precisely that of affirming God's own delusive handiwork.

In Swift's *Tale of a Tub* an allegorical costume is the subject of endless theological squabbling. The three antagonists, Peter (Church of Rome), Martin (Church of England), and Jack (The Puritan), who seek to justify their several prejudices with divergent misreadings of their father's will, roughly correspond to the Three Soldiers of *Finnegans Wake*.

[7] This Theft and Flight motif resounds through all mythology. Prometheus, Jason, and Jacob are classical examples of the hero who wrests symbols of life substance from an older dispensation. Often, as in the case of Prometheus (and HCE), atonement is exacted.

[8] The "Ship's Housebound" is HCE as tavernkeeper. The Norwegian Captain who approaches him corresponds to HCE in his earlier aspect of searover. The progress of the story will show how the sea captian defrauds the landspeople in various ways, running off with a tailored suit, cadging huge meals, and making love to their collective daughter. This story, which runs with interruptions through the entire chapter, is a paradigm of HCE's

then: "O'Hara," said he, turning to that best of his friends, "sell a suit of clothes to this gentleman." So he was measured and fitted out. A bargain was struck, and he made to go. But the Ship's Husband cried after him: (312) "Stop thief! Come back to my Erin!" And the Norwegian Captain answered: "All likelihood!" And aweigh he yankered on the Norgean run, so that he was breast-bare to the briny-bath seven years. And the tides made, veer and haul, and holey bucket, dinned he raign!

Hump! Hump! laughed the tavern company, with knowing glances at the tavernkeeper.

[After this first visit of the Norwegian Captain, a young hero called Kersse goes out after him. Now "Kersse" is a Gaelic mispronunciation of Persse, and Persse was the character given HCE in the scurrilous ballad of Book I. In a sense, Kersse is the reverse side of HCE himself; in other words, the other man in him, who is to undo him. But again, Kersse is the son of Ashe, of the tailoring establishment, who may be taken to personify those powers which are to prove the "curse" of the rover.]

"I will do that!" said Kersse, meaning staying out the rigging for the Ship's Husband.

"Not so?" the company hunched back at the earpicker.

But old sporty, reigner in rye-house, did not fear these short sharks plotting to get something on him. There was gossip of the Earl of Howth and his prankquean lady; there was speech exchange by three blend customers, to wit, the Gill gob, the Burklley bump, and the Wallisey wanderlook.[9] Group drinkers make great thinkers, and 'tis they constitute the twelve of the jury: saddlers, leather-sellers, skinners, salters, pewterers, paper stainers, parish clerks, bow and arrow makers, (313) girdlers, dealers in textiles,

early history, accounts for part of his unsavory reputation, and coalesces finally into the barroom brawl.

[9] Three theologians, John Gill (1697–1771), George Berkeley (1684–1753), and John Wesley (1703–91), all contemporaries of Dean Swift; they represent various shadings of metaphysical belief, comparable to those satirized in the *Tale of a Tub*.

shoemakers, and weavers.[10] They all encourage the speaker: "Go to it!" they urge. "Say ahead, agitator."

"I will do that, please God!" said Kersse; and in the flip of a jiffy the speaker belched: "As sober as the Ship's Husband he was, my godfather, when he told me the story, and so I am satisfied that this is how it goes: the widower, so help me God, is consistently blown to Adams!" [to atoms! back to Adam and Eve's].

Whereafter Jarl, still passing the change, pushed their whisper in his hearing, and threw a cast: "A few pennies," said he, "and here you are, and no cheating. Take your copper token with this good sixpence from my run-bag of jewels." And in his lewd brogue he counted out the money.

Thus the Dutch coins plunked in his hold.[11] (314) "Who caused the scaffolding to be first removed?" someone asked. "You gave orders," they readily replied. On the Q.T. the correspondent in the conflict drew a kick at the witness, but missed. "And for whom in the devil did Kate remove the planks?" somebody asked. "They were wanted, boob!" came the quick reply.

Bump!

Bothallchoractorschumminaroundgansumuminarumdrumstrum-truminahumptadumpwaultopoofoolooderamaunsturnup! [12]

"Did do a dive," said one of the tavern company, aping a diver.

"He was the cause of it," said a second, in a bass voice.

[10] The twelve of the jury and their simple trades here take on the coloring of the Twelve Apostles at the Last Supper.

[11] Echoes of the fall of Finnegan begin to ring in here, and become combined with the already bewildering doubletalk. One can count at least three threads of narrative: HCE stands at his till making change; a schooner on the high seas is being overhauled by a pursuing vessel; Finnegan on his wall is teetering toward his fall. A new hint of HCE's perfidy is introduced with the suggestion that he himself had removed the planks which caused the collapse of Finnegan's scaffold. A bribe is involved. The sound of Finnegan's fall and God's thunder voice is mingled with the hubbub of the tavern. For the present it will be impossible to convey Joyce's meaning in one-dimensional narrative. Until the barroom atmosphere of murk and confusion clears on p. 324, our text will be blurry with a double focus.

[12] The thunder voice is heard through the din of the tavern. The theme of the fall is under discussion. HCE's reputation is going to pieces.

"That was the fall of Finnegan," said the third. "By the Magazine Wall. Bimbim bimbim. And the maidies seen all. Himhim himhim."

For the rest, let legend tell of the scene—that scene so humpty dumpty.—What a dust it raised aboriginally! Luck's leap to the lad at the top of the ladder: so long as Sartor's Resorted, why the sooner the better. (Advertisement—The Safest Road in the World.) Here in the Dalkey tavern—where their Dutch uncle plays host and serves them damn well right—will be presented to us in the near future a cast of characters from the past, with subtitles in Norse-made-Irish. And when you are watching the show, mind the narrator, but give the devil his due.

"That's all mighty pretty, but what about the Ship's Husband's daughter?" hissed they (the four of them) who were one time young chaps themselves. Answer: "She was the apple of his eye. She was on her way to school in slippers. There were no peanuts in her family, so no wonder she tumbled for the Norwegian Captain's (315) *Royal Divorce*.[13] He was a botcher butcher bachelor of arts arsed out of Trinity College. Wasn't he out sporting, the night of Finnegan's wake?"

Second Round [14]

[The drinkers—and three among them are most prominent—demand another round of drinks. The yarn-spinning continues. The remarks of the brawlers are slanted to emphasize the return of the Norwegian Captain on his second visit. During their story HCE re-enters his own tavern after an excursion to the outhouse. His re-entry as "Burniface" coalesces with the coming of the Norwegian Captain.]

Shufflebotham suggested: "An inlay of a little more lining might be licensed all at once."[15]

13 Cf. p. 32, the favorite play of HCE at the theater.
14 Another round of drinks; another round—hazier and noisier—of the story.
15 Let's have another drink; you might put more lining in the garment. I.e., We are still carrying the two stories.

Burniface [16] at an angle of lag, heavily breathing, overhauled them and cheek by jowl shot a glance at the three tailors, butting back then to Moyle herring, and he threw the sheets in the wind, exclaiming, "Howe *c*ools Eavybrolly!"

"Good morrow," said he breezily, as he put into bier-haven. His ear was to the lee of their voices. And he asked concerning the course of the yarn.

Whereupon another of the company, Shinshanks, said: "Skibbereen has common inn, and sadder raven evermore," meanwhile whispering to his companion to tell again (316) the anecdotes of Pukkelson concerning the low tricks of the invaders. A toast to Brian Boru!

"Good morrow, gentlemen!" persisted good mothers gossip, bobbing and bowing both ways—when they were all in the old walled city of Kinkincaraborg, hibernating after seven oak ages.[17] He, fearsome where they might be, had gone dump in the twilight—where the pixies would pickle him.[18] And they laying low for his homecoming. He made the sign of the hammer.[19] "God's truth," said the Ship's Husband, beholding the Norwegian Captain back again in port, "how life pauses! Here you are back in Dublin, a slave to trade, vassal to spices, and a drug-on-the-market, just when methought you were soused out of the mackerel." "So sell me a drink," said the Norwegian Captain; "where's that waiter? A bite of cheese," he said, (317) "or a whisky and soda," he said, "time deposit on a thoroughbred Kennedy's; and when I'm soured to the tipple, you can sink me lead." "O.K.," said the Ship's Husband. He made the sign of the feaster. Cloth be laid! And a dish of oysters for the swanker! He was the carelessest man I ever see, but

[16] St. Boniface is the patron of innkeepers.
[17] The phrase conjures up the mythological image of the heroic dead in their magic hill carousing on the beer of immortality.
[18] It is very difficult to keep separate the two threads: (1) Someone very like the tavernkeeper himself has entered the tavern after relieving himself in the twilight (this episode is probably closely linked to the celebrated episode in the Park); and (2) the Norwegian Captain has circled back again to port.
[19] Sign of the hammer: a sign of blessing in honor of the thunder-god Thor.

he sure had the most sand. "One fish ball with fixings, for a son of a gun of a gambler. Quickly," said he, "sonny mine, Shackleton Sulten [the waiter]! Up and at him, or this ogry Osler will maul us all," said he; "Say when!"

Three drinkers at the tavern (three tailors) [20] hereupon introduced remarks:

The first breeches-maker reminded, "He didn't curse or hoot at the suit!"

The second cutter snipped curtly, "Humpsea, dumpsea, the munchantman."

The three of them then together: "An eye for an eye. Take my worth from it. And no mistake! Everyman for himself."

The Norwegian Captain apologized: "Put it on the bill!" And he was himself such a hulk that he was oblivious to the head of the host, which rose before him out the shadows, like a dolomite, with its plastered hairs (do you ken yon peak with its coast so green?) [21] still sorrowfully in mourning for his Annie: (318) him her first lap; her his fast pal.[22]—Oh, listeneth to me, Veils of Mina! I always did wash and prink up before we sat down to soup and fish. Now the vintner eats over these contents oft, with his sad slow munch. I have performed the law in truth for the lord of the law, Taif Alif. I have held out my hand for the holder of my heart

[20] The Tailor Shop theme and Tavern theme have run together. The three tailors are represented as the Fates weaving the cloth of man's destiny.

[21] This is the first appearance of a John Peel motif ("D'ye ken John Peel at the break of day?") which rises in a crescendo through this chapter. John Peel, archetype of the fox-hunting English squire, is HCE. Every one of the following lines from the popular ballad carries a theme of *Finnegans Wake*.

> "For the sound of his horn brought me from my bed,
> And the cry of his hounds which he oft times led,
> Peel's 'View halloo!' would awaken the dead,
> And the fox from his lair, in the morning."

[22] The Norwegian Captain suddenly blends into the figure of HCE approaching the head of Howth for the first time. The Egyptian phraseology (borrowed from the Book of the Dead) in which he couches his invocation to the eternal Anna looks both backward to his love sins of the past and forward to those he is still to commit.

in Annapolis, the city of Anna, my youthrib city. Be ye then my protection unto Mesopotamia, before the guards of the city.

(319) The drinker, Pukkelson, was continuing with his story. "I should be shot for bringing briars to Bembracken, but Time is for tailorman testing his tape (talerman tasting his tap)."

He drank down his three swallows in one gulp.

The two others followed suit.

Pukkelson said: "I put him behind the outhouse, that double-dyed dealer, and he's wallowing awash of the Tara water. The curse of Olaf on him! I'm telling no lie."

The loafers laughed till the tear trickled down—all but the Ship's Husband and the starer to whom this story was told.

(320) "Curse him," said he, "and the shines he cuts, boasting to be among the most elite; the free of my hand to him." Muttering Irish, if he didn't call him all the schimpf-names in the gutter! "He is the worst West End shirt-maker that ever poked needle in a cloth!" [23]

Thus, for the second time the whole company had the story: how he sailed from his dream-a-dream-true, back to Brighton-on-the-Baltic and thirty hours a week. "Come back to Erin!" shouted the Ship's Husband. "Ill luck to it," blasphemed the scamp-tail, faring out to sea. And near he nighed till Blawland Bearring; and the sea shoaled and the saw squalled. And, soaking scupper, didn't he drain. . . .

Third Round

[The third round presents another baffling variation. The rover enters very much as he entered on his second visit, and is soon followed by the figure of Ashe, Junior—or Kersse. Kersse has been to the races. His description of the event (and it appears to be itself a variant of his own pursuit of the Norwegian Captain) is lost in a drunken uproar, which culminates in a loud, boastful and

[23] Here the Tailor Shop theme takes over entirely, and the second round of the tale becomes clearly a variant of the first.

probably impotent Fenian threat against the buccaneering Flying Dutchman. All concludes with a toast to Sinn Fein.]

Liquor having gone the rounds, the baffling yarn went in circles. It was now high time for the remaining pair of snipers to drink till they, (321) like the first, should have literally no more powers to their elbows.—Ignorance is bliss; and in total ignorance of what had been going on, their rifle-butt target, HCE, upholding a lampthorne as wand of welcome to all men of goodwill, coasted along to the point of Dublin Bar, breaking there and entering, from the outback's dead heart. A well-known tall hat and a kiber galler [24] were signaling Gaelic warnings toward Wazwollenzee Haven (*was wollen sie haben?*) to give them their bearings.—*Hir*cups Emptybelly! [25] Music. And old lotts have funn at Flammagen's ball.

Business is business.

Counter-scene: HCE on the alert at his till.

He cupped his ears to catch the drift of the conversation, and attended to his business, blending rum, milk, and toddy, scooping in the pounds, shillings, and pence.

And with the gusto of a spring wind, the trouble-makers and swagglers piked forth desert roses in that Mullingar pub.

Re-enter Ashe, Junior. "Fine day! Cheerio." [26]

(322) "Take off that white hat!" [27] (Lo, Kersse come back from

[24] "The age is grown so picked that the toe of the peasant comes so near the heel of the courtier, he galls his kibe." (Hamlet, Act V, scene I, ll. 151–153.) A "kiber galler" is a peasant's toe.

[25] The old man went out into the yard to relieve himself, and there became involved in a practical joke, an ambush set to reduplicate the situation which had brought about his disgrace some time in the past. And when he returned the stories that were going the rounds sounded very much like rehearsals of the old scandal.

[26] Ashe, Jr.: Cf. Ashe and Whitehead of the first round. Ashe, Jr. is apparently Kersse. Ashe-Kersse-Persse: the self-destructive side of HCE. Whitehead: his "misunderstood citizen" aspect; cf. p. 535.

[27] "White hat" refers to the Finn MacCool theme, and specifically to Finn as the young hero about to overthrow the old.—The story is told of Finn, brought as a boy of fifteen to a hurling match. The King was present and when he saw the boy he cried, "Who is that *fin cumhal* ('white cap')?" The boy's grandmother, who had brought him, then shouted, "Fin mac

the Baldoyle Steeplechase, dangling his old coat over his top-gallant shoulder, looking very like a novice in the navy.)

"Take off that white hat," they cry at him. (Kersse, as it turned out, had been making a great hullabaloo—a sample of the custom of the country.)

"Take off that so foul and so wrong, welsher, you son of a bitch, and confess yourself." (For, be-Kersse, he had cut up and misfit such an armful of clothes that his own father wouldn't know him. [He is wearing an outlandish costume.])

Chorus: "With his coat so gray! And his pounds that he pawned from the burning!" [28]

"And how did you do at the Baldoyle racetrack today, my dark-horse gentleman?" he was asked. "Search me!" said he. And when he had said this, he stood them the whole course of training, told them how the whole blazy race had gone, from spark to phoenish.

There developed a considerable uproar: the three newcomers asked questions in pidgin: they had been malt-treating themselves to their health's contempt.

Others, on the point of obsoletion, responded.

Then one of the drinkers broke forth in a tirade of wrath: "And so help me God!" said he. (323) "That buccaneering Flying Dutchman!" he said. "That highsay-dighsayman corsair, creeping into our navy through the small of a hawsehole! God confound him! Voyaging after maidens! Curses on him, till I spit in his face, the lands-lewder. Reefer was a wenchman. One can smell it on his clothes how he is coming from a breach of promise—a beach of promiscuity. Where is that old mutinous spirit, may I ask? Free kicks he would have from me, turncoats, if I was a few years younger. He'll feel the weight of my fist. The gory-bellied Pukkel-son, with his bellows pockets full of potatoes; [29] there was never a tailorman in the five-fifths of Ireland or in the whole length of

Cumhal will be his name." (MacCulloch, *Celtic Mythology,* Marshall, Jones, 1918, p. 167.)—The white hat here is probably that of an English tar. Kersse has joined the English navy.

[28] "John Peel" again.

[29] Potato wards.

Scandinavia, from Drumadunderry to the remnants of Muckross could milk a colt in thrushes with that hole in his tale!"

With all this noise and static from the radio, the lord of the saloon listed his hump and turned, eyes to all sides, to this bunch of palers on their rounds, his beforetime guests, who were bound to loose a laugh when they felt their joke was coming home to them, like the dead spit (324) of his first prototype, the filibustered, the fully-bellied. With the old sit in his shoulders, earning his bread in the sweat of his brow, his tail toiled of spume and spawn, and the bulk of him! They hailed him cheeringly, the merman, ye seal that lubs you lassers.

"Heave, coves, empty-bloddy!"

And ere he could stir to suit them, the conspirators were shouting.

"Sit down!" cried the tailors opposite the talkers. "Change all that whole set. Sit down and shut up. Our set, Sinn Fein, alone!"

And they poured oil on the fire. Skaald!

(B) *A tailor in the Town. Next episode: The caging of the rover.*

[The atmosphere of the text suddenly clears. A radio broadcast breaks through all interference. The story to be told is that of the catching and the caging of the rover. This high-flying rogue is collared and married with all ceremony to the daughter of the Landsman, a character who is both the tavernkeeper and the tailor. Amid general festivities the newlyweds are bedded down in a broadly humorous episode. As later developments reveal, this marital capture of the wanderer corresponds to the incarceration of HCE in Book I.

[The story sequence opens with a radio program, apparently devoted to weather announcements and news broadcasting, strangely broken by interference from a spiritualistic séance. The radio begins with a general hallooing (Waterlooing) and announcement.]

A séance message for all good and true sirs, begging any bereaved, passing person to bring back or reimpart Finnegan to the

polity-master, *H*oved, *C*lontarf 1-0-1-4, *E*llers,[30] for the greater
glory of God. (A.M.D.G.)

[Next follows a weather forecast, which forebodes the coming
event:]

Outlook for to-marry [tomorrow]: Wind from the north.
Warmer towards muffin-bell. Lull.—As our columnist predicted
in last month's chatty sermon, the expected depression over Scandinavia, having filtered through the middle half of the kennel on
its way wealthwards and incursioned a sudden rush of low pressure, missed in some parts, but with local drizzles, the outlook for
to-marry being brider; his ability good.

What happens today?—Giant crash in Eden. Bird flights con-
firm approaching nuptials. (325) Burial of Lifetenant-Groevener
Hatchett, R.I.D.

Laus Deo.

[General announcement:] I wish an auspicious day for the stork
derby. It will be a thousand to one; and soon to bed. After which,
from midnight onwards, the four-poster harp quartetto.

[The actual capture of the rover:] "Come hither, Horace, thou
mighty man of valor, till I find thee a father-in-law to become
your son-to-be, shaun-shem-sons both," said the head marine's tale-
bearer. Then said the Ship's Gospfather to the Husband's capture:[31] "And either *you* does or *he* must this very moment. So
peace be between ye! Let a pact, a brothers' oath, be sworn between you, Aestmand Addmundson and Paddley MacNamara; for
the two breasts of Banba [32] are her soilers and her toilers." Turning directly to the Nowedding Captain, he said: "Come hither, my

---

[30] Battle of Clontarf, A.D. 1014. Here the invading Norsemen under Sigtrygg
were defeated by the Irish under Brian Boru. The battle took place on Good
Friday. In the present chapter Adam, Sigtrygg, Christ, and HCE are
amalgamated.

[31] The Husband's capture is the Ship's Husband's captive, the Norwegian
Captain. The Ship's Gospfather is a clergyman who is to marry the rover
to the daughter of the Ship's Husband. He is a bit of Dean Swift.

[32] Banba: goddess of the land of Ireland and pet name for Ireland. Her
two sons are the invader and the native, the Gall and the Gael.

merry-time sea wolf, into the folds of our quadruped island;[33] and no more of your maimed acts after this, (326) or I'll rehearse the commandments for you and first-martyr you entirely. A Trinity judge will crux your boom." With that he baptized him: "I baptize thee, Ocean, Oscarvaughther, and Erievikkingr, in the name of the Father, Son, and Holy Ghost, unconditionally Count of Galls and chief hero of the Clans a-Keltic; and let this do for you and for all the pukkaleens to the wakes of you, and be damned to you. . . ."

"Nonsense, you snorsted!" protested the victim. He was considerably set against all religions. Wherefore was he to be sold out and duped by Priest Goodfather of the sacred-haunt suit in Dublin-Dalkey at St. Patrick's Cathedral? But hear this:

"And here, my rear admiral Peter-Paulson," said the tamer to the second-named suitor, "come stand round that wine and lift your horn to show you're a scholar, for whether you like it or not your summer has come.[34] And, taking your leave, to let you in on some Christian doctrine, here is the nicest pork of a man swimming in Dublin waters," said he (while the heart of Lucky Swain slaughed in his icebox, to think of all the ways [327] he would behave toward her); "just consider him, our godsend Brandonius, *filius* of a Cara, spouse to Fynlogue. And he has the nicest pert of a little woman in the house, that he dotes upon of anny livving plusquebelle, to child and foster, the leap year's wonder of Totty-go, gritty yet soft; and never a Hyde-row Jenny the like of her lightness; and when that mallaura's over till next time and all the trim horsies are out dress-parading and the horns are tooting to the glory of God, making every Dinny dingle after her down the Dargul Dale, and when it's somewhere calling and she can hear the piano tuner beyond the beyonds, and she's leaning out through her dreamer window for her Flying Dutchman, she can work miracles, and she can give Norgeyborgey good Irish times, while her turf is kindling up the flue; and she'll be cooing to him sweetly,

---

[33] Cf. the Donkey. Ireland's four provinces, the four legs of the Donkey.
[34] Cf. *Ulysses,* chap. 3, Random House ed., p. 51; Paris ed., pp. 49–50, where Stephen sees the summer solstice as foredooming him to marriage.

for (328) there's no fool like an old fool; and she'll beat his barge into a pram." Then said he, the marriage-mixer, to Kersse, son of Joe Ashe, her coaxfonder: "By my fairy fee, I will turn my thoughts to thinks of love and I will speak about three as one, poles apart and zones asunder, tie up in hates and repeat at luxure; you can bet your true-blue protestant arson, though the clock in his tower strikes one, and were he laid out on the counter there, when it comes to the right honorable who is to make plain Nanny nee Sheeres into a full Doña Marquesa in the privacy of the first night, at that meet hour of night, while daylight is yet slipping under their pillow and before St. Martin's in the Fields, ringsend ringsend, brings *H*eri the *C*oncorant *E*rho, and the Referinn Fuchs Gutmann gives us 'I'll Bell the Welled' or 'The Steeple-boy's Revenge,' 'tis no timbertar she'll have then in her arms-brace, our fiery queen, upon the night of the things of the night of the making to stand up the double tet of the overseer of the seas who cometh from the mighty deep, and on the night of the making of *H*orus to *c*riumph over his *E*nemy,[35] with St. Elizabeth blessing the bed pain. (329) She will make a Siamese pair and a singlette,[36] for my old comrade saltymar here, Brigadier General A.1, Magnus, master of the good lifebark *Ulivengrene,* of On-slought, who is the best bluffy blond blubber of an olewidgeon what overspat a skettle in a skib."

Caught. Caged. [The marriage ceremony has been completed.]

And Dublin did glow that night. All sang together. The soul of every-elses-body rolled into its ole-sole-self. A double-month's li-cence of mirth, while honeymoon and her flame went honey-suckling. What boom of bells! Even the ghosts were walking that night. Even Tombs drew on the dour-nailed clogs that Morty Manning left him and legged in by Ghosttown Gate; and some say they seen old dummydeaf with a leaf of bronze on his cloak so gray, trooping his color a pace to the rear. It was a day of jubilee. You could hear them swearing threats on the Himalaya

[35] Echoes from the Book of the Dead. Marriage-death parallel. The Fall.
[36] She will bear him the twins and a daughter.

Mountain. The grandest seen or heard since Skin (330) the Goat [37] ate the Suenders Bible. Every lane had its lively spark and every spark had its several spurtles and each spitfire spurtle had some trick of her trade—a tease for Ned, nook's nestle for Fred, and a peep-at-me-mow for Peer Pol. So that Father Matt Hughes looked totally troubled. But Danno the Dane grinned. And it was dim upon the floods only, and there was day on all the ground.

But some fine old families felt a nick in their name. Old Victorians sat down on their airs and straightened the points of their lace. Red Rowleys popped out of their lairs and asked what was wrong with the race. Mick na Murrogh used dripping in layers to shave all the furze off his face. The Burke-Lees and Coyle-Finns paid full fines for their sins—when the Cap and Miss Coolie were roped.

Advertisement—See the Motion Pictures of the Marriage.

He got a berth; she got a man; all of God's chillun gonna wed.

And there were to be begotten Twins of War and a Daughter to be Wooed.

Children gathered, a hundred and one of them, and they barn-danced around. They played children's games (331) such as: *He knows he's thrilling and she's sure she'd scream; The three-legged man and the tulip-eyed dewydress.* Tell us all about them; we're brimming to hear. Here, children, stop your roughhousing!

So, whoops-about a plebiscite on this mountain of Delude, you Twelve, with toroidal coil, trader arm slung around beauty belt. And was it the twilight, the month of the year, or the feint of her smell, made the seamen assault her (whimwhim whimwhim)? To the laetification of disgeneration by newhumorization of our kristianization. As the last liar in the earth gaily waylaid the first lady of the forest. For the wild main from Borneholm has jest come to crown.[38]

[37] Skin the Goat figured in the Phoenix Park murders (May 6, 1882). These murders cast a great cloud over Parnell's public career. In *Finnegans Wake* they are associated with the scandal in the Park.

[38] The Wild Man from Borneo has just come to town: a motif to be heard many times hereafter.

(332) Now hear the end of the story—of a little trip-trap and a big tree-schooner. For he put off the ketyl and they made three (for fie!). And if hec don't love alpy, then, lad, you annoy me. For hanigen with hunigen still haunt ahunt to find their hinnigen where Pappappapparrassannuaragheallachnatullaghmonganmacmacmacwhackfalltherdebblenonthedubblandaddydoodled,[39] and an unruly person creeked a jest. Fine again MacCool! Peace, O wiley!

Such was the act of Goth: his loudship converted to a landshop: when that boy and his girl roamed over Erin, sea-lump becoming dump to bump slump a lifflebed. Him, that scolding old man, to be that hard of hearing; and her, the petty tondur with the fix in her changeable eye. Bluebeard and Lady Precious Stream. . . .

But before that there was a certain Encounter: [40]

A little theogamyjig incident, that January morn, when he collided with the Cad out on the Beg . . . [This marine version of the Encounter is most difficult to render. It is flooded with suggestions of postdiluvian times when the human hero was still struggling to put down the giants, and conquer the watery terrain with bridges, causeways, dams and river control. Note the words bridge, piers, pontine, assuan. The human hero himself has barely risen from his leviathan deep and has the harpoons of his captor still sticking out of him. Phoenix Park suffers a sea change and becomes the entire Balto-Mediterranean world.

[The next five pages present a series of three short flashes which obliquely summon the past and suggest the future. In order of

[39] Thunderclap at the moment of intercourse. Radio static?
[40] It is now clear that we are following again the whole story of HCE. The three rounds of the Norwegian Captain correspond to the impropriety in the Park. Now comes the encounter with the Cad (Kersse). Which encounter was followed by his incarceration and disappearance (just represented as his marriage). The two episodes, in the present retelling, appear in inverted order: first the marriage-incarceration, then the encouter when the Rover was overhauled on the high seas. Through the crisscrossing of the tavern and radio yarns, the old tale re-emerges.

their occurrence they are: (1) Kate the Housesweep's arrival from the bedroom of ALP with a message for HCE at his till; (2) a glance at a mezzotint on the wall depicting the charge of the Light Brigade at Sevastopol, yet somehow suggesting a tallyho about to set off on a journey; (3) an attempt on the part of HCE to satisfy a popular request for a story often told by him and strongly suggestive of the material in Book I, chapters 2 and 3. His long-winded exordium bores the listeners who turn impatiently back to the radio for this night's installment of a popular serial, entitled "Butt and Taff."

[Here in strong concentration appear themes from all parts of the book. This short interlude is a kind of transforming station refreshing and redirecting the thematic currents of *Finnegans Wake*.]

Interruption 1: Czechoslovakian Diversion

(333) Why, what is the meaning of this opening door? And who is coming in? Softly, anni slavey.

The aged, mummified confusionary, Kate Kattershin, clopped back along the Danzig corridor between the two allied divisions. Mind your hats going in! Mind your boots going out! [41] And remarked to herself in her slavic drawl: "Now you are in the Museyroom . . and the Willingdone git the band up. . . . Tip."

And she bragged about the message which she brought below from the Missus—she that had her stays outside her chemise, to keep up the fashion since the king kissed her hand. The message was to tell him how, now that his sons were winking and waking, and his daughter lulled to sleep, if he wished to lecture her, (334) 'twas her hour for the chamber's lycopodium; [42] with love to my

[41] Kate comes down with a message from the madam, inviting HCE up to bed. But he will remain at the till. This scene points backward to the museum (p. 8) and forward to Sevastopol (pp. 338 ff.), both of which are developments out of the Battle theme. This scene reminds us of Grinny grannybird's battle role; also of the Seduction theme.—Kiss Cross!

[42] Lycopodium powder, "A fine yellowish, highly inflammable powder composed of the spores of various species of *lycopodium* . . . used in the manufacture of fireworks and in medicine as an absorbent in excoriations of the skin." (Webster's New International Dictionary.) *Lyco* = wolf; *podium* = a small foot, a footlike part.

lost Panny Kostello, from X.Y.Z. And she was a wanton for De Valera to take her genial glow to bed.

"This is time for my trubble," reflected Mr. Gladstone Browne.

"This is my vulcanite smoking," profused Mr. Bonaparte Nolan.

"And this is the defender of the defeater of the funst man in Danelagh," willingtoned the panellite pair's common denominator. "And this is his big whide harse. Tip."

"A prosit to her midgetsy."

Interruption 2: The Mezzotint on the Wall [43]

Oh, rum is the most comical thing, how it pickles up the Punch and his Judy. He banged the scoop and Kate held the sugar bag, while the whole pub's population stared at the mezzotint on the wall, which showed the Charge of the Light Brigade—or perhaps, a tallyho ready to go.

So the Katey's came and the Katey's gone—and the henchwench that opened it there shuts the door.

(Silents)

Yes, we've conned yon print in its gloss so gay,/How it came from Finndlader's, Yule to the day,/And it's Hey Tallaght Hoe on the king's highway/With his hounds on the home at a turning.[44]

(Advertisement—When visiting at Chapelizod taste the waters from Carlowman's Cup.)

(335) The mezzotint tells its tallyho story of the twelve-eyed man for whom majesty drew rein.

It is like a stage set for the Grimm tale of how Holispolis went to Parkland to find the right place for it—when the hunt called a halt at that lightning love-maker's tender appeal, and Buckley shot the Russian General.[45]

Let us prepare ourselves for the fray.

---

[43] Cf. pp. 13, etc. The mezzotint on the wall is to form the frame for the Sevastopol adventure, and refers it back to the adventure of Bk. I, chap. 2: how HCE received his agnomen.

[44] "John Peel" rhythm.

[45] Leading event of the Sevastopol episode, pp. 352 ff.

The Wellington storm is breaking. The sound is murmuring. The Wellington storm waxes fiercer. The strength of the Russian General is known throughout the world. Let us see what a wee ambassador can do.

Interruption 3: The Host's endless Tale of a Tub

All of them, each in his different way, were calling for the Hibernian Nights Entertainer, who was having another endless tale of a tub wished on him. And so he began: "It was before Aimee stood in the nude for Arthur Duke and fell from grace so madly [Grace O'Malley]. And it was in the green of the wood, where obelisk rises when odalisks fall. (336) And it was cycles after he had made the sign of the cross. And he applied his whole bold soldier boy's shoulder-width for fullness. . . . " (They were calling again and again, the lousy measlers, six to one.)

They plead with him to hurry his story.

When a tale tarries, shove on.

Of this man and these washerwomen nothing more is told, till now, their autumnal hour. We are again as babes wandering in a wood-made-fresh [word made flesh], where, with the hen in the storybook, we start from scratch.

Well then, nothing but the truth.

"It was of the grand old gardener, Publius Manlius, my wife and I thinks; his feel for younging fruits; and though the peccadilloes of his meetings be ever so lightly soiled, the candidacy of his soft-boiled bosom should be apparent even to our illiterate null-latin-enties."

To all of which one of the listeners snapped: "But what of it, if it was (337) only a pigeon shoot in which the old man of the centuries was bowled out by judge, jury, and umpire?"

What matter what all his Freudian friends say? [I.e., let the baser nature of HCE be lost to sight.] Let Hutch just keep on being a vanished consonant, and let Annapal Livibel prettily prattle a play all her own, and let that subliminal salmon be solemnly angled in gate and out. A truce to love calls. Leave the letter that never begins to go find the latter that ever comes to end—written in smoke and blurred by mist and signed of solitude, sealed at night.

Simply imagine two wood nymphs and a stutterer, big master Omnibil. Then imagine three lurking lobstarts [Redcoats]. Pet her, pink him, play pranks with them. She will nod and smile. He may seem to appreciate it. They, as practical jokers, are sure to participate. Say to yourselves slowly: "So this is Budlim! How do you do, dainty daublimbs? So pleased to pick on you in this way."

(C) Butt and Taff: (D) Sevastopol

[The tavern company breaks into a general cry for the radio skit of "Butt and Taff." These vaudeville comedians are due to present the story of how Buckley [Butt] killed the Russian General at Sevastopol.

[This episode is turbulent with alarums and excursions, dark with wild surmise, yet a powerfully integrated keystone in the arch of Joyce's narrative. Obviously Butt and Taff are the two brothers; Butt is associated loosely with Shem, Taff with Shaun. They first appeared in Book I as Mutt and Jute, respectively the native and the invader.

[In the present version the leading role is played by Butt; and his discourse, though extremely enigmatic, resolves itself into recognizable elements. He is obviously one of the Three Soldiers who witnessed HCE's misdeed in the Park, and his lines are largely a rehearsal of that primal sin, now amplified with bizarre and perverse detail. Butt's ambiguities and innuendoes fan out into a veritable Krafft-Ebing report of sexual depravity, implicating even Butt and his soldier companions in a mish-mash of homo-hetero-anal-voyeur misconduct. Through this smeared lens HCE is seen, metamorphosed into a Russian General. Simultaneously, Butt becomes Buckley, and Phoenix Park is transformed into the Crimean battlefield of Balaklava. Thus the brother battle becomes magnified to gigantic terms of imperial conflict.[46]

[46] The Crimean War (1853–56), stripped of its accidental features, was a struggle between Russia and England for ascendancy in the Near East. (See Kinglake: *The Invasion of the Crimea,* Edinburgh, 1863.) The original

[It is not surprising that the protean HCE, the representative of English imperialism, should now take on the lineaments and costumery of Slavic imperialism. Obbligatos on the Imperialism theme are sounded in the Kipling and Tennyson echoes throughout this passage. Reverberations of Blake extend the significance of the problem to cosmic proportions. According to Blake, Albion (Industrialist-imperialist England) personifies the nadir of the human fall. The diseases, mildews, and enslavements which Albion inflicts upon the bodies of men provoke the victimized to revolutionary explosion. Butt as the symbol of man degraded in the service of empire (Danny Deever, Tommy Atkins; also, the slum-dwellers of the world) participates in the obscene orgy, but driven to the limit of endurance abruptly turns and destroys the oppressor (353).[47]

[Amusing variations on the Defecation theme should not be overlooked, particularly as the whole passage reeks of it. Defecation as a creative act is a well-established infantile idea. What the witnesses in the Park have seen may be interpreted, in part, as the moment of creation. It is conjoined with the moment of the fall and of Vico's thunderclap. It is at the same time the moment of

dispute started with a controversy over the key to the church of Bethlehem: should it be held by monks of the Orthodox church or by those of the Roman? Russia supported the Eastern, while England and France became champions of the Western Catholic cause. This historical setup enables Joyce to elaborate a threeply allegory: (1) brother battle, (2) Oriental church vs. Roman, (3) the clash of commercial imperialism (England vs. Russia).

Up to his old tricks, HCE plays on both sides of the line. Attired in all the regalia of famous English generals, he fuses into the figure of the antagonist, the Russian General, who is shot by the volunteer Redcoat Buckley. I Bk. I, chap. 3, the ballad-singer O'Mara was identified with Buckley (p. 49) and HCE was termed "the General" (p. 50).

James Joyce wrote to his friend, Eugene Jolas, when Russia invaded Finland in 1940: "The most curious comment I have received on the book is a symbolical one from Helsinki, where, as foretold by the prophet, the Finn again wakes, and volunteer Buckleys are hurrying from all sides to shoot that Russian General." (Eugene Jolas, "My Friend James Joyce," *Partisan Review*, VIII (1941), II, p. 93.)

[47] The text contains more than one suggestion that HCE made improper advances to the soldiers and was "killed" for thus insulting them (p. 353).

Noah's shame: Shem, Japheth, and Ham, witnessing the nakedness of their father, are counterparts of the Three Soldiers.

[Much of Butt's testimony describes his military education and the history of arms from earliest times. This blends into the tumult of the Battle of Balaklava, which in turn resolves itself into the crash of Humpty Dumpty's fall from the wall and the roll of the Viconian thunderclap.]

"We want Bud Budderly bodily," the tavern gentry cry. "There he is in his Borri saloon," they cry. "The man that won the Battle of the Boyne. Order! We call on *T*ancred *A*rtaxerxes *F*lavin [Taf] to compeer with *B*arnabas *U*lick *D*unne [Bud].[48] (338) Order! We've heard it sung a thousand times: How Buckley shot the Russian General. Erin go bragh! For honor go brawll!"

A public house. Citizen soldiers.

TAFF (*a smart boy of the peat friars, looking for a revolution of the Carmelite–Karma-life order, previous to hoisting an emergency umbrella by way of solution to the riddle in his head*). Was everything flashing bloody red? What say, bloody watch? Tell us the story, ever so often!

BUTT (*motley youth, clerical appearance, supposed to describe the sorry disaster or be disgraced for ever and a day*). But da.[49] But dada. Ever so often. Sevastopol.

TAFF (*helping himself out with a yell; puts up his furry hair*). Describe him to us, the groundsapper, with his Sunday-side out and his Monday-side in. The governor-general and lord-leftenant of the Baltic! Describe his resemblance to Bruyant the Bref, when the Mollies mistook his leg for his thumb. And may he be an Interpretation of our Dreams[50] which we forget at waking. Let's hear."

[48] Tancred: Norman leader of first crusade. Artaxerxes: Persian kings, I 465–425 B.C., II 405–361 B.C. Flavin: "Blond." Cf. also "*Taf*fy was a Welshman" (Welsh lead Norman invasion of Ireland).—Barnabas: Apostle, "son of exhortation." *Uleeka* (Russian): evidence (of a crime). Dunne: brown. Cf. "the buddies behide in the byre." p. 340.

[49] *Da* (Russian): yes.

[50] Cf. Freud: *The Interpretation of Dreams.*

[By subtle transposition Joyce uses the three Redcoats as links to the Crimean Battle episode. The dream atmosphere is very thick here; the text will be crammed with references to world-flung British wars.]

BUTT (*switches on his highland fling, his laugh neighs back,* (339) *his Nipponese language wambles*). He was like old Daddy Icon when he cooked up his eggs and bacon.[51] He got a fit, we got a fit, all of God's chillun got a fit! Poor old piss-abed! Limbers afront of him, limbers behind.[52] He was enveloped by the enemy. Crimean bastion. With his cannon-ball insignia. In his Raglan [53] coat and his big Malakoff [54] bulb and his varnished Russians and his Cardigan [55] blouse-jacket and his scarlet mancho-cuffs [56] and his tri-colored cami-flag and his perikopendolous gaelstorms. (Tailors' advertisement—From Karrs and Polikoffs, the men's confessioners. Pleasant time payments. Mademoiselles would turn back to look at you.)

TAFF (*all starry eyed and eared at the narration*). Grossartig! *Tod-lebens!* [57] Some garment guy! *C'est magnifique; mais c'est né pour la guerre!*

BUTT (*if he hides, forgotten, his night of glory amid the floras of the fields, his spendthrift's livid smile gives all the benefit of the doubt*). A bear he was, reigning among the stars in his consecra-

---

[51] Cf. p. 257.

[52] Cf. Tennyson: "The Charge of the Light Brigade."

[53] Lord Raglan, trained under Wellington, commander at Sevastopol.

[54] Malakoff fortification near Sevastopol; taken by French, 1855.

[55] Earl of Cardigan, commander of Light Brigade at Battle of Balaklava, Oct. 25, 1854.

[56] Prince Menshikov was the Czar's special ambassador to Turkey and later a commanding general in the Crimean War. He was at the same time Russian governor of Finland (the Finn!). His blundering violence in diplomacy was overmatched by the consummate skill of the British ambassador to Turkey, Lord Stratford Canning. The lineaments of Prince Menshikov mingled with the traits of the Czar himself loom large in the composite figure of Joyce's Russian General.

[57] Name of a Russian lieutenant colonel.

tion robes! Erminia's *c*apecloaked *h*oodood man! First he steps, then he stoops.[58]

TAFF (*trying, like a loyal Dubliner, to remember the sign of the cross, who strangled Attila, what poisoned Montezuma, and failing to remember that he had been a child of the Kremlin before baptized a Roman, makes the masonic sign of the holy polygon of the Ant and the Grasshopper*).[59] (340) Scatterer of gold! He is notorious in every Rotary Circle. With his Welsh brush up? And his bogus brags?

BUTT (*tongue in his cheek. Pink forefinger pointing to impossible objects beyond the mist, such as, the Dublin Alps and the Howth Riviera, where he and his true love may ever made a game*[60]). There you see the blasted heath of the Weird Sisters. Here fairy glen. There fairy pass. Thanks! With the old ape-man at the ready to prink the pranks of the temptresses. And the soldiers hiding in the byre.

TAFF (*striving to recollect all the struggles for wife in the rut of the past*). Oh, day of rath! Ah, murder of mines![61] Ah, my Russian palace! MacMahon from Oslo, eager for sweet prolettas on his prowl!

BUTT (*back to his petrol pump, "Swee Gee's Wee Rest"*). Bruinoboroff[62] the Honeymooner, and the grizzliest man in Meideveide! Whose annal lives the highest! For he defiled the lilies of the field, and he confounded the Three Soldiers.

TAFF (*ill-certain whether he sees Bishop Ribboncake's prized thumb going forth on his visitations of marriage, or Miss Horizon unsheathing a shoe-laced limb aloft to the stars*). Guess this riddle: How do you do, kettles, and how do you do, pan? The Riss, the Ross, the sur of all Russers. My first is near to hear, my second is

[58] Czar Nicholas was a highly respected figure in Europe, until he stepped into the Turkish affair and stooped to gross deceits in diplomacy.

[59] See pp. 414–19.

[60] Butt is pointing out the landmarks of the battlefield to Taff, as Mutt the landmarks to Jute, pp. 17 ff.

[61] Rathmines: Dublin suburb; Irish battlefield.

[62] Brian Boru combined with Russian Bear.

meet to sit on, while my whole's a Persse (341) O'Reilly.[63]—You certainly beat up that pole-cad, bang on the mouth, gurg in the gorge, rap on the roof, and your fly is unbu . . .

BUTT (*doing a vaudeville dance to "The Little Brown Jug" and "Whang goes the Miller"*). Bim-bam-bom-bumb. His snapshot appeared in the *Rumjar Journal,* while the girls he loved be-eyed him.

TAFF (*obliges with a two-step yoga-coga symphony on the bones, for ivory girl and ebony boy*).[64] Balaklava! Tovarish! I tremble!

BUTT (*making the sign of the sickle and the hammer, parodies something through his anger*). Water! The aged monarch venturing to protect his investments by war. I saw his influence rising in Turkey. By these signs shalt thou defeat him! Tit for tat, and my pipe for his cigar![65]

Interruption: (E) News Report of a Steeplechase
Presentation by *The Irish Racing World* of the *C*aerholm *E*vent:
Up to this corkscrew bend an admirable presentation of the world-renowned Caerholm Event has been given by *The Irish Race and World*. Everyone has been alive with excitement while the news has been going round. A helioscope flashes news of the placers, for the gates to see. "My God!" That was Mr. Thomas Nolan telling the Very Reverend Father Epiphanes of St. Dhorough's how Backlegs shirked the Racing Calendar.[66] The saintly scholar's roistering guffaw at this tells of the chestnut's absolutely romping success. A lot of lasses and lads without mothers or dads, but with collecting boxes: one ought to spare one's trifles; it is coppers for the children. Slippery Sam, hard by them, physically present but (342) morally absent, was slooching about, asking Mick, Nick, and the Maggies, to deck the ace of duds. Tomtinker Tim, his unremitting retainer, is in Boozer's gloom, sulking in his

[63] Taff bids Butt divulge the meaning of these HCE riddles, as the professor in Bk. I, chap. 6; cf. pp. 126–39.
[64] All through the scene the vaudeville pair are carrying on their song-and-dance act. This is presented in the stage-directions.
[65] Cf. Cad with pipe, p. 35, and HCE tipping the boy a cigar, p. 53.
[66] Compare the priest, Mr. Browne, at the racetrack, p. 38. Also a play on "how Buckley shot the Russian General."

222

tents. And the chic summer frocks are shimmering. You see the following distinguished personages: a chief smith, several scandalmongers, a *midinette* from the Casabianca, and Mr. Fry. It is De Valera's Dominical Brayers. And, incognito under that weird hood, the lost Governor-General from the Punjab, Jagganath.—Great Jupiter, what was that? Seven-times luck! It is the Thousand-to-one-Guinea Gooseberry's Liverpool Silver Cup. Hold hard—they are at the turn of the ford of the hurdles.[67] Emancipator, the Creman hunter (Major Hermyn C. Entwhistle), with dramatic effect reproducing the form of several sires on the scene of the formers' triumphs, is showing the way to Mr. Whaytehayte's three geldings, Homo Made Ink, Bailey Beacon, and Ratatuohy, while Princess Il and The Other Girl (Mrs. Boss Waters, Leavybrink) are showing a clean pair of hides to Immensipater.—(This eeriedreme has been offered to you by Bett and Tipp, our slapstick quack-chasers, in "From Topp-hole to Bottom" of *The Irish Racing World*.)

(*C*) *Butt and Taff*: (*D*) *Sevastopol* (Resumed): *The Provocation*

TAFF (*aware that the first sports report has now been corroborated by a second, shifts direction and* (343) *points to the symbolic constellation of the Dragon*). You called the turn on the Old Pirate, you and the Three Soldiers; I'll bet you did; I'll bet by Strongbow's Tomb. You had just been planning an advance on the Holy Sepulcher, aided by the retreating French and followed along the rout by the stench of the corpses [references to Crimean War]. Tell the gospel truth; come, my lad! Perfidious Albion! Think again. Get on with the story.[68]

BUTT (*slipping his coat over his shoulder, so as to look more like a gentleman, as he scents the anger mounting behind the noise. He is in a state, however, because an erection on the susceptible side of him spoils his proportions*). Great Jupiter! Of all the queer asses

[67] Bailé átha Cliath ("Ford of the Hurdles"): Irish name for Dublin.
[68] At least three elements mingle in this passage. Taff is telling Butt that he knows how he came to shoot the Russian General. In doing so he plays with historical themes and rings changes on the old story of HCE.

and all the queer men in the tragedies of the Ant and the Grasshopper, that son of a gun, with his Sabbath epaulettes, smoking
his candle at both ends, takes the prize! He was legging it bodily
from some powder sparks and looking for a stool-easy; and when
I heard his lewd brogue reciting his cheat-gospels to all and sundry, I thought he was only after having his breakfast; but I no
sooner seen the gist of his frightfulness than I was bibbering with
fear.

(344) TAFF (*with a pique in his cue and a tear in his eye and a
bend of his back and a croak in his cry, as though harm were
leaning over him*). Weep on, Song of Sorrow-man whom Goethe,
Shakespeare, and Dante well know! Papist! Take the coward's
blow! [69]

BUTT (*giving his simulated twinge in acknowledgment of his
humiliation, suddenly drops to his heels; he changes uniforms as
he is lifting the gat out of the holster: his face glows green, his
hair grays white, his blue eyes become brown to suit his Celtic
Twilight. [He talks like Synge]*). But when I seen him in his one-
ship fetch along within hail, that terrible tall, and like a brandy-
logged Roman Catholic, lugging up and letting down his livepelts,
and exposing his old sinful self by manuring in open ordure [ma-
neuvering in open order], I thought he was only recovering breath
from some headquarters beyond the Caucasus. But when I got a
full view of him through the storm and caught the fierce smell of
his aurals, I was blubbering. *Mea culpa,* I confess, when I looked
upon the Czar of the Russians, with the weight of his age full
upon him, there was fear on me, and it was heavy he was for me
(345) then, so that I mingled my Irish Hail-Mary's with his Russian Lord-have-Mercy's, till I hadn't the heart to.[70]

[69] The Butt-and-Taff exchange predominates, for a moment, over the
Sevastopol adventure. The coward's blow: cf. *Ulysses* (Random House ed.,
p. 585; Paris ed., p. 562), where Carr, the Redcoat, strikes Stephen down
with "the coward's blow": "He rushes towards Stephen, fists outstretched,
and strikes him in the face." Compare the Glugg-and-Chuff, Dolph-and-
Kev brother battles.

[70] *Hospodee pomeelooie* (Russian): Lord have mercy.

Against a seeming backdrop of military exploit, Butt describes how he
saw HCE (the Russian General) defecating in the Park. This is the event
referred to on pp. 316 and 321.

TAFF (*premeditating how such a wild man from Borneo seduced country clowns: proposing to see him pluggy well murdered, sleepy though he be*). Great Scot! You hadn't the heart! What fun!

BUTT (*hearing someone or other give three snores, he waits to see might he stir,*[71] *and then goes on*). Merde! I met with whom it was too late! My fate! O hate! Farewell! And think of that when you turn smugly to read Bagehot.[72]

TAFF (*who, meanwhile, at arm's length, has been upon the speaker's innkeeping right*). Drink off this cup and be a bloody offering!

BUTT (*he whips off his chimney pot, his lips love-curling to the tongue-opener. He takes up the cup of communion and forgiveness from the hands of the forgiver of trespassers, and then reciprocates the hospitality by offering some salt bacon*). There are cares enough in this old world, so send us delights for the improvement of our forces of nature by reacting upon me like a bosom fiend.

Interruption: (F) Televisioning of four interesting Mullingar Events

(1) How the fashionable fictionable world (346) is afeebling themselves with rich pastry. (2) How Spanish gold is being played up by the Anti-Greenback party. (3) How Albion [England] professes to maintain the holy crypt against the devil dances of the East. (4) How successful American businessmen are making resolutions never to grow old or raise salaries or become spiritually complicated or donate money to encourage philosophy.

(C) Butt and Taff: (D) Sevastopol (Resumed): *Autobiography*
TAFF (*has been given a shillelagh by a Peter Piper who wants him to join the Irish. They all are beating pots to raise a din for old Daddam Dombston to tomb and womb again, glimpse a leg and glance again*). Since you are set to say your piece about Vercingetorix, go ahead with it. Tell us how Buckley shot the Russian.

---

[71] Snores of the Dreamer of *Finnegans Wake!* He nearly wakes himself!
[72] An English journalist who reported the Crimean War.

Generals, how Buccleuch [73] shocked the rosing girls! The four-score seculars are watching to call the old scapegoat's bluff. The counselor placed here his head while someone somewhere tinkle-dinkle-delled. In the myrtle of the bog two Sinn Fein men stood up to slog; and three bondmen lay lurking. Tell us all about Dick Whittington! 'Twill be a nice change. Can you come it?

BUTT (*who, in the depths of his God-forsaken heart is a nihilist: the bell in his guts goes off, all at once, lest he should challenge himself*).[74] *Horosho,*[75] Taff! My days under Corporal Phailinx (the Macedonian Phalanx) came first. Hittit (the wars of the ancient Hittites in the twelfth century B.C., also the rise of the Khwarizm-shahs in the twelfth century A.D., and again, the campaign at present under discussion) was (347) of another time, on the plain of Khorasan, 1132 years ago. After a power of skirmishes we sighted the beast. And I was in the Royal Irish Militia, a Sandhurst cadet under Sir Arthur Woolwichleagues. I was still weeping over the whoredom and poverty of my London suburbs which are duplicated all over the map; but when again through disease and wars the great day comes, the excellent fine splendorous long agreeable toastworthy cylindrical day foretold by the prophets and in the Book of Kells, Ireland will be free. We were not doing so well until we liquidated the loafers. I studied the problem and soon showed them how to give the cold shake to those blighty perishers. How I was applauded!

TAFF (*though a perfect gentleman, still smoking his favorite Turkish in the presence of* (348) *ladies*). Whom battles joined, no bottles sever! Weren't you aide-de-camp?

[73] "Buc," *cf.* Latin *bucca,* cheek. "Cleuch" is a Scotch word meaning "clough," a cleft in a hill, a ravine. The reference is to the backside of HCE. In one name HCE and his enemy, Buccleuch and Buckley, are combined.

[74] Butt hears the call of nature, as Glugg, p. 225. This paragraph will review the history of armaments and battle formations under the guise of recounting Butt's military career.

[75] Russian, "Very well!" This links Butt to the gunman of pp. 81–84. Butt being now partly in the Russian role, we shall see Taff next playing the Turk.

BUTT (*He feels about like a bottle full of stout, but falls about like a barrel full of beer*). Between my associations in the past and my disconnections with a future, I've a bottleful of memories in my bosom, and my tears run slow as I recall them old Russian knights now rollicking in Valhalla, my Alma Martyrs. I yearn for them with the nostalgia of absence. A toast to them! We were all barracksers in Clongowes Wood together: [76] three Turkomen with the two girls in their toileries! Up Lancasters and at 'em!

TAFF (*who still remembers the heaven-sent heroines who entertained him. They were rivals, new arrivals from sunny Spain, and they played wopsy with his wallets in the thick of the battle of Waterloo, consoling him for his broken teeth with truth-bosh about international amity*). The rib, the rib, the quean of all birds [Mother Eve]: hurrah for your whores that are ready to take on any soldier in the world, till they're (349) riddled with disease. What are you afraid of, Mr. Pencho? Drumhead court-martial, or gonorrhea? Mind your P's and Q's, Mister!

Closeups of (C) Butt and Taff and (D) Sevastopol—at zero hour
In the heliotropical noughttime, following a fade of transformed *Tuff* and, pending its vice-versa-version, a metenergic reglow of beaming *Batt;* [77] the television screen of tastefully taut geranium satin, tends to frame and step up to "The Charge of the Light Brigade." Down the slope, with the bits between their teeth, the misled hopes glitter-clatter. Cannons rake from right and left and the fire of the gunners traverses the sundered lines. Amid the fluorescence there coagulates stealthily a still: the figure of a fellow-chap in the Holy Ghost, Popey O'Donoshough, the Russian General. He exhibits the seals of his orders. He shuts his eyes because he confesses to peeping at the girls. He blocks his nose because he confesses that he is always smelling his guilty fingers. He wipes his

---

[76] Cf. *Portrait of the Artist as a Young Man.* Stephen's schooldays.
[77] Note that the names have become confused with each other. After the coward's blow Butt and Taff become amalgamated: this will effect the annihilation of the atom (p. 353). Compare the transfer of marginal comments in Bk. I, chap. 2, p. 293.

mouth with a sort of cloth, because he confesses how often he used to be over-and-undering her. He bundles together his hands with his feet, as he confesses their accomplishments and crimes. And (350) he touches upon the tree of livings in the middle of the garden, because he confesses to its having been jolly well generously used.[78] Poor old Pumpey O'Dungaschiff! There will be a hen collection of him,[79] after evensong, on the field of honor. Tumble down, ladies and gangstermen! Dtin, dtin, dtin, dtin!

(C) Butt and Taff: (D) Sevastopol (Resumed): *Self-defence*
BUTT (*with an expansive gesture and sunflowered buttonhole, pulled up point-blank by Shaun-the-Post at Old Bailey Court. He tells—through the hesitancy of his melo-velance—how, when he was first making his first lord of creation, the wife of his bosom was the very last thing to enter his mind*).[80] I plead self-defence against every kind of debauchery. Be at pains, please, not to forget, or else betake yourself to some other place. Correct me, please. if I am wrong.—No more card games for this poor sun-basker.—I had my bellyful of duckish delights, my ramsbutter in their Anglo-Saxon ribs, when the Assyrian came down like the wolf on the fold. And we borrowing cigarettes, Tommy Atkinses all, for Father Patrick Spence to go leave us and dawn to shed a light on the document—feeding on the Huguenots and raining revelations over the Albigensians. Yet I was a game fellow will-mate. Oh, send (351) us victories for Victoria. We were Tom, Dick, and Harry. And all the fun I had at Finnegan's wake.[81] He was a strange man, wearing a barrel: Iron Fitz, the farmer boy, the Rainbow!—

[78] This is a burlesque of the sacrament of Extreme Unction, in which the eyes, nose, mouth, hands, and feet are anointed to invoke God's forgiveness for the sins committed by them. These are commonly called the Last Rites of the Church; the Russian General is about to die.
[79] The hen will unearth the letter.
[80] Compare Festy King's trial and self-defence, pp. 85 ff., esp. p. 91.
[81] Briefly: "I was one of the Three Soldiers; we were all Tommy Atkinses together and having a good time." Also: "We Roman priests had a free field."

Those were the halcyon days for our fellows, and we were the raw recruits, laddies three and British too. We had a wheeze, we English-Irish, about Dark Rosaleen, while Woodbine Willie, so popular with the cigarette girls was bluing the air.—And we all jined in with the shoutmost joviality: Paddy Bonhomme, he lives *encore!*[82]—It was buckoo bonzer [first rate], believe me. I was a bare private, but I did not give one humpty dump touching those Russian Generals. I could always take good care of myself. I knew the right people, and so had pull.—And I never let a chap down, till, at the head of the wake, up comes stumblebum, (352) the Russian General; and I seen his offensive breecher-shirt vis-à-vis to those scarlet runners, and I seen how they gave love to him and he took the ward from us. My kingdom for a revolver! Bung goes the enemy. Persse O'Reilly got me to blow the grand off his ace-upper. We insurrected, and I shot him, Hump to dump! Tumbleheaver!

TAFF (*sensing that the Volga Boatsong is heading to Sea Red, but too well bred not to ignore the unseemliness of his rival's rifle's proceedings, in an effort toward self-salvation effaces himself in favor of the ideology of homosodalism*). Oho! Bully clever of you, Brigadier-General! A race of fierce merchants against a nation of Irish sharpshooters!

BUTT (*breaking into the Danny Deever warcry*). He'll rob no more graves, nor horn and hound for gay gazelles in dead men's hills. Captain *H*is *C*umbulent *E*mbulence!

TAFF (*who has been suffering all the purgatories* (353) *of sin-practice*[83] *in failing to follow the agonies of the damned*). The man-goat! In sober truth?

BUTT (*He scoffs, but is disturbed by the thought that bleaching bones give but little assurance to the pious doctrine of death followed by resurrection*). Yes, sir! He dared me do it, and I did it. For when I seen him rolling over our land, heaving up that sod

[82] Echoes of the Wake scene, p. 6.
[83] Purgatory of St. Patrick, cf. pp. 3, 80.

to claim his share, and undoing his *culottes,* at that instant I let
fly my arrow and cockshot rock robin! Sparrow!

Interruption: (G) Annihilation of the Atom

The annihilation of the atom by the grinder of the first lord
of Hurdleford detonates through all Persse-O'Reillia with a rumble.
Amidst the general confusion there are perceivable male-atoms
escaping with female-molecules, while well-fed Coventry bumpkins
smother themselves in the London elegance of Piccadilly. Similar
scenes are projected from Honolulu, Borneo, imperial Rome, and
modern Athens. Twelve o'clock, no minutes, no seconds.

(C) Butt and Taff—Concluded

TAFF (*skimperskamper, his wool-gatherings all over the Kremlin
cromlin, what with the crackery of the firearms and their* (354)
dumdum bullets). Where are all the bulbs up there? What's all the
hubbub upstairs? Shadow-movie?

BUTT (*Taking a final swig, becomes faint*). Sure enough! Shear-
ing off! Like Finn MacCool!

BUTT and TAFF [They merge into one] (*desperate slave-wager
and feudal foeman unshackled, now one and the same person,
overcast by the shadow of Old Ireland's mythical Finn MacCool
whose sway had been reviled by craven minions. The mythical
figure falls by Goll's gillie.*[84] *But he is heartened by the insistent
Persse O'Reilly keen of a Sicilian hurdy-gurdy. Shaking everybody's hands, while enemies become reconciled, and, pledging the
pledge of Fiannaship, he palms it off*). Of old, when all the world
was a garden and Aphrodite first unfoiled her limbs, there where
lived the warrior twins, they had their mothering Eves, and their
murdering ideas, and deadly wraths, in that winey grove. But
there'll be bright flowers in the cool bowers when the maggy-gossip
screeches about the raven and dove.[85] Though *you* love the sex

[84] Finn MacCool's greatest feud was with Goll of Clan Morna. Finn slew
Goll but was killed by Goll's followers and the followers of his other
victims. A "gillie" is a young attendant on a Celtic chieftain.
[85] "Raven and dove," throughout *Finnegans Wake,* refers to the two girls
in the Park.

of his head and *we* hate the set of his trousers, yet he's dancing attention on the ladies and waving his sword. And he'll be buying boys, and he'll go gulling girls, with his flotsam and jetsam of wind, silk, and honey, while the rest of us will be playing ever our game of angels and devils; and what's pudding for us makes our coy cousin's mouth water. So till Butt again shoots the Russian General, let Shaun thrive on his righteous indignation and Shem stick to his Swiftian scrivening.

(355) *Grand Finale: Moment of Ideal Rest*

The cosmic actors are reassembled in ideal formation. The battle noise is over. The relationship of present to past and future is made known to all the senses. General formulas are shown for all values. Fadeout, gradually. . . .

[So the great radio program concludes.

[After attending the television broadcast, the customers of Earwicker's tavern break into an uproar of comment.] "Shut off the machine," they cry. "Butt did right," says someone. Speech lit face to face on all around while they argued as to whom the major guilt pertained to. Meanwhile the Hersy Hunt harrowed the hill for outlaws, them rollicking rogues, those racketeer romps.

Night. Battle pause. Fair bosom.

(*A*) *Tavern Brawl* (Resumed): *Tavernkeeper's Comment*

[After the audience has generally approved Butt's action, the tavernkeeper steps forward with a short apologia for the self-assertive vitality of the Russian General. He exhorts the company to regard this man charitably, and gives examples from his own life to show that the guilt of the High Personage is shared by mankind at large. This places him in direct opposition to the tavern company and leads swiftly to his humiliation and collapse.]

"Too true," asserts the tavernkeeper. "It is true of every country and it has been true since the days of the Egyptians," he declares, one well-nourished one, overlord of suns and satellites, heavy on shirts, lucky with shifts, Misto Teewiley Spillitshops, who keepeth watch in Khummer-Phett, whose spouse is An-Lyph, warmer of his couch. "For we are all lepers and wanderers; and such have we been since the Fall. (356) That piece represented the overthrow of us each.

"It invites all to consider, whether there be a Primum Mobile, and to reconsider the first riddle of the universe, to wit: why is man, that old offender, not man? And it gave examples of the points in question.

"Once, when I was a kid, the darkies held a great fish-fry and they soaked good red bread with sweet meat in the kettledrum.[86] But now to come to the point. I have just been reading a suppressed book—a scarcely yet appreciated book—embellished with expurgative plates which I have been enjoying with warmest venerections before the wordcraft of this early woodcutter (357) (so splunderdly English) Mr. Aubrey Beardsley. Cheap and well worth the trial. There is, among other pictures which I love and which are favorites of mine, one which I have pushed my finger in for the moment, and there is another which I have fondly fingered frequently. What ravening shadow! What dovely line![87] Not the king of this age could feast his eye more richly.—And whilst I have been idly turning the pages, while sitting on the toilet, often, so far as I can chance to recollect from some far nights ago, when I—if you will excuse me for this leading down of ill-expressibles—am entrenched up contemplating myself with my naked I, I sometimes with some shock (358) have a notion that I am catching snapshots of distant relations from ficsimilar phases in the behindscenes of our earthwork, at no special time precisely with regard to concrete chronology. And I am then highly pleased to see—by the loudest reports from my three-spawn botterv parts (shsh!)—that, when I have remassed me after my contractual expenditures, I am big altogether."

He beached the bark of his tale and set to till and cultivate the

[86] Cf. Marc Connelly, *The Green Pastures,* Part I, scene II.
[87] Raven and Dove theme.

vine—and the harbor master told all the living conservancy how Win-a-gain was in again. Flying the Persse O'Royal,[88] with all aboard: the whole cast of Finnegan's wake. Loud cheers for his lucky hump. And they waxed and winxed till they woke the alderman.

(H) Dismemberment and Dissolution of the Hero

[The perspective suddenly shifts and we are again listening to the radio, which is now broadcasting a program of short pieces. It soon becomes apparent that these are canvassing the theme of dismemberment and dissolution. The tavernkeeper, having betrayed his sympathy for the master-type individual, is now about to suffer the consequences of popular disapprobation. More specifically, he is about to be torn to pieces and flung to the winds.]

The twenty-nine heroines are taking him apart: with discrimination for his Maypole and a rub over his hump. And they are pleased to say, in respect to the matter of Document Number One: (a) he had to die, the beetle; (b) he did it himself; (359) (c) the best of him had already been transferred to his children; (d) bad before flood, he had been not much better after; (e) no better than he should have been before, he could have been better than what he wasn't after; (f) reduced even to ashes, he is the same old rep— whether fitting tires onto Dunlop boys, or fluttering flaus for laurettas—no matter what they say about him in the romances. What we want to hear, Jeff, is the woods chirping to "Swing Low, Sweet Chariot," and "Knock 'em in the Old Kent Road."

Radio announcement:
You have just been listening to an excerpt from John Whiston's production: *The Coach with the Six Insides* [a coffin?], from the

---

[88] Unmistakable allusions to the Norwegian Captain remind us here that that old wanderer and the keeper of the tavern are one and the same person.

Tales of Yore; to be continued in *Fear-son's Nightly*. With a tirra lirra rondinelles, ahunting we will go.

Attention! Stand at!! Ease!!! [the Three Soldiers.]

We are now broadcasting, to our lovers of this sequence, the twofold song of the nightingales [the Two Girls], from their sheltered positions, hiding in rose-scenery on the hither side of the alluring grove. (360) Silence all! Let every sound keep still; and when we press the pedal pick out and vowelize your own name. We are happy in being so fortunate that—bark-and-bay duet, with Man Goodfox's in-chimings, having ceased for the moment—night's sweet Mozart will entertain us.—Secret hookup.

The listeners claim to recognize the ventriloquence of old Roguenaar Loudbrags[89] in the voice of the announcer.

Meanwhile there runs rippling the twinfold song of the nightingale and the leaves:

"I will shally. Thou shalt willy. You wouldn't should as you'd remesmer. I hypnot. 'Tis golden sickle's hour.[90] Holy moon priestess, we'd love our grappas of mistletoes. Tabarins comes, to fell our fairest. I soared from the peach and Miss Molly showed her pear to—one, two, three, and away!—Did you ever see such an eerie Whig? The enormous his; our littlest little! Let (361) him peep up our combinations. We'll pose him a piece and teach him twisters in Irish tongue, till Arthur comes against us and St. Patrick is reformed.—We are the seven seductive trees. Taunt me threateningly! Whose nose is out of joint with jealousy now? Why, heavilybody's. Somebody put it in, will anybody pull it out? Call Kitty Kelly! Kissykitty Killykelly!"

Here all the leaves lifted aloft and fell alaughing over Ombrellone and his parasollieras with their black strong guards from

[89] Ragnarr Lodbrók, 9th century Danish sea-rover. Cf. also, pp. 221, 257.
[90] With a golden sickle the Druids cut the sacred mistletoe (the Golden Bough) from the oak. This castration ritual is about to be re-enacted on the grand oak, HCE.

County Shillelagh. Ignorant invincibles.[91] A lark of limon ladies; a lurk of orange-tawny men!

And they leaf-laughed most foolishly, to the coming of the destroyer of mirth, Jack the Ripper, and then they ceased to be. But may we laugh in our lifetime as much as they.

Interruption. (A) Tavern Brawl (Resumed): *Protest after Tavernkeeper's Comment*

Cease please storywandering around with these Gesta Romanorum, and let us get back to old Droughty. The water of the face has flowed.

All the sorry-jowled blotty-eyed boys in that (362) smoke then came off and agreed in condemnation upon the old man, since, as someone tried to explain to someone, seeing that he had resigned from empire over the island, he might just as well have answered to roll call and rolled out of the kettle auction altogether, till the sea got him. He, that hun of a horde, is a Finn; his tent-wife is a Lapp. Look at their house: dirty bedding all over the place; a broken ceiling; three vacuum cleaners at the back gate; a pair of chairs used alternately by husband, when writing for Druids' Friendly and other societies; horsehair sofa with a modicum of cloth; hired piano used by the youngsters for churning out old strums; three bedrooms upstairs, of which one with a fireplace; greenhouse in prospect.

[The entire company begins to heckle him:] "And you, when you kept a pub in Dublin, were you always (363) what we knew how when we were you know where?" "Why, he was caught redhanded and a noise went up!" (The rann, the rann, that keen of old bards.) Detective Almayne Rogers disguises his voice, shelters behind a hoarse chest-note. Heat waves are rising; they jest keeps rising; he jumps leaps rising: howlong![92]

[91] Among the leaves, singing of the coming dismemberment of HCE, we hear a faint murmur of ancient Irish battles against the invader.
[92] "Ol' Man River."

"Do you know that tom?" someone asks. "I certainly do," some-one replies. "Is they been baptized?" "Has they been redeemed?" [93]

[Now ensues one of the most moving moments of the book. HCE, his back to the wall, delivers with dignity and noble resig-nation an apologia for his life. Acknowledging his crimes, and even confessing to one hitherto unknown (apparently he drowned someone long ago, and the corpse has been discovered floating in the surf), this patriarchal sinner points out that the good he has done for his people heavily outweighs the evil. Almost Christlike in forgiveness he turns to the young soldier who has been the chief witness against him, and admits that incestuous dreams of beauty have indeed possessed his mind and tempted him into wrongdoing. Yet somehow in this process the very soldier who has spied upon him has become endeared as a sharer in his dream. HCE concludes by saying that some people see only the pig in human beings, but that for himself, he is ready to die like Caesar rather than truckle to such base constituents.]

The tavernkeeper could stand it no longer. He spit in his fist, he rose to their cries of encore, tickled her palm, and sought their friends' leave:

"Guilty! Yes, I am guilty. But, fellow culprits! Indeed, I felt that the submerged face had betrayed the case to waterside laborers. But since we have changed all that, and for the good of all at home have chanced so much, it's a great pity which spoke through the tangled hair of the head buffeted in the surf, as it spoke of unheard-of trespass. Though I may have done one thing and might have done another, still I am incapable of unlifting upfallen girls —and so I have been misunderstood. (364) They have borne false witness against me. Twenty-odd females are hurrying to the post office with presents for my valued favor. The true Irish approve the raid. It is all clean fun and may the devil rape the handsomest. And if my legitimate went cackling it about, scattering all the

[93] *The Green Pastures* again, Part I, scene II.

riflings of her vacuum [giving to all her life presents], (365) I am, nevertheless, I like to think, a gentleman to the manner born. I confess the worst, as love rescuer of these missies who acquiesced in it. Now cold, I used to be a warm one. You may be three abreast, nosing at the wall hoarding, and you would damn me, damn you! But no mum has the rod to pud a stub to the lurch of a motion.[94] My little love apprentices! It was merely a feel with these—for my hand was already given to the curliest wee woman in the world. (366) I appeal against the light! A nonexistence of evidence!—I have wanted to thank you such a long time so much now, my dear beautiful young soldier, who have watched your share at our love tennis squash rackets, when only the bold did deserve the fair—and while I reveal thus my deep-sea daughter which was borne up proudly out of my dreams, unclothed, when I was pillowed in my prime, I declare that I am indeed the asthmatic old ruffian supposedly seducing little girls. And if brutal louts or cautious fellows only see the pig in the human, then I want to say that if it's people like this that I've undertaken to govern, I'm willing to be shot at, any Ides of March."

His rod was in air.

And down went McGinty to the bottom of the sea, dressed in his old suit of clothes.

The desire of Miriam is the despair of Marian, as Joseph's beauty is Jacob's grief. (367) Look at Lokman! And he drew back into his grocery baseness, and there you are!

Here Endeth Cincinnatus!

(A) Tavern Brawl: Verdict of the Quorum

[The next four pages offer a potpourri of tavern personalities and gossip. The four old judges give their verdict and lay down "Thou shalt not's." In this passage the ecclesiastical aspect of the Four Old Men is stressed. Next the tavern jury rehash the old stories of the Park episode and the letter, both of which by now

[94] Cf. p. 292, Parnell dictum again, but now coming from the opposite party.

have become completely distorted by misrememberings and dislocations, yet preserve withal their essential flavor.]

The Four Old Men: Mask One, Mask Two, Mask Three, Mask Four. They open their eyes and look around. Three-story sorrow-telling was too much for them. They maddened and jowled: they matthewed, marked, luked, and johned.

Like Deucalion or Noah, the old seagoer had sent his prime pullets, the twins, one by one, to fare forth; he had beheld the last remains of a deluge delusion: the foggy doze still going strong, the four old maskers facing this way and that. The Four had now come from their respective dream mansions, (1) where lightning leaps from cloud, (2) where MacCool by his cauled bride lieth languid, (3) the bounds wherein our bodies atombed attain rest, (4) appoint, that's all.[95]—But see what follows: the circus of the ages cycles incomprehensibly around an undiscoverable point, and the wind of the Word blows over the deeps.

(368) Guns:

[The sharp commands now of the Four:] "Keep back! Never interrupt authorities! On no account do the following: not to frighten people; not to shoot Russian Generals; not to be wandering at small hours playing piggy games or pederasty; not to be unfaithful to the marriage vow, or carry on clandestinely with a dozen; never to wake in brothels, to sleep drunkenly, or to hate the clergy for their self-complacency; and never to cease till the ending."[96]

> And thus within the tavern's secret booth
> The wisehight ones who sip the tested sooth
>   Bestir them, as the Just has bid, to jab
> The punch of quoram on the mug of truth.

[95] The mansions of the Four Old Men are the four ages of the Viconian cycle: Age of Thunderclap, Age of Marriage, Age of Disintegration, Age of Return.
[96] This paragraph consists of interdictions representing the Tables of the Law. Certain things must not be done. As it turns out, most of them are things of which HCE is already guilty.

K.C. jowls, they're sodden in the secret.
K.C. jowls, they sure are wise.
K.C. jowls, the justicest jobbers,
    For they'll find another faller if their ruse won't rise.

                        —Whooley the Whooper

[Description of the Four Old Men:] Squarish Matthew, bright brown-eyed Mark, peaky-nosed Luke, ruddy-haired John: Moscow, Athens, Rome, and Dublin: staring all four, snuggled and cozied in bed, (369) while their soft couch causes gossip and begging supplies all their demands.

Six of the jury were there, too, passing judgment on HCE from various religious standpoints, to whom add the tout that pumped the stout in the tavern that jack built [Jesus in the church].
They had heard: (1) that a king Roderick had come to inn court; (2) that the great sight there was a yardstick with a love glove on it; (3) that manners make the man, while worship wins the woman; (4) and so how would you like it if someone were to start to tell the story?
And everybody there was gossiping about the letter: (*a*) that the secretary had made believe to write to correspondents, with autosuggestions from Shem the Penman; (*b*) that Madges Tighe, the postulated listener, is hoping for the old man to turn up before her funeral comes—it being likewise true that the end of the whole thing may twaddle out with a "hopes soon (370) to hear"; (*c*) the old man didn't have time to write because his secret amours had exhausted his strength; (*d*) "it's so long since I thanked you . . . I thank you . . . as you introduced me to the secrets of love"; (*e*) will these remind the sane of anything? (*f*) Fool step.
You were in the same boat yourselves, gentlemen—meaning the twelve of you.

(A) Tavern Brawl: The Rann [97]

[The tavern man-of-all-work hears from afar the sound of an approaching multitude singing a song. It is another ballad promis-

[97] Cf. pp. 44–47.

rng an end to HCE. The tavernkeeper himself gets wind of it
and tries to hasten closing time. It is already near midnight. The
shutters come down, the drinkers stumble out. Subtly Joyce's
imagery transforms the tavern into a departing schooner with the
farewell visitors stumbling down the gangplank. They mingle with
the approaching multitude and join their voices to the crescendo
of the ballad.

[Still on board are HCE and his family, as well as the Four
Old Men who lie asleep in their bunks below, swinging to the
rhythm of the waves.]

And now what is this Saracen head uprising thus out of the
rumpump like an oak? It is the head of Noggins, who dusts the
both sides of the seats of the big chaps of the parlor bar of the
Mullingar of the Lochlann foreigner of the fief of far-famed
Chapelizod.

It is the Sockerson boy, ready to pump the fire of the lord into
those souls of debauchees. Meantime he is rinsing their smutty
bottles and bouncing the obstreperous ones. (371) And as he went
about his duties, he heard from afar a piping. As? Of?

It was the approaching sound of the rann that Hosty made

> Dour douchy was a sieguldson.
> He cooed that loud nor he was young.
> He cud bad caw nor he was gray
> Like wather parted from the say.

Ostia! Lift it, Hosty!
Himhim, himhim.

The Saxon, hearing it, remembered all the things he had mis-
tributed in the past. It was closing time. The customers were try·
ing to capture the last drops before the Saxon locked up the door.

> For be all rules of sport 'tis right
> That youth be dower'd to charm the night
> Whilst age is dumped to mind the day
> When wather parted from the say.

The humming, it's coming.

Old Fingool MacKishgmard was bowing and scraping in recal-citrant right-about-face, and these fellows crying for an extension of his hostillery. He bombing their ears: "Time, gentlemen, please!"

> From Dancingtree till Suttonstone
> There's lads—no lie!—would filch a crown
> To mull their sack and brew their tay
> With wather parted from the say.

Along the streets those Mullingar minstrelsers are marshaling—by turnpike road, under where, perched on a hollowy hill, Duke Wellington, h.c.e., (372) had bowed to the belles and been trapped by the mausers. The church bell rings out—as frolicsome as the prankquean herself. While the houseboy shoots down the shutters, and they all pour forth. But without Tuppeter Sowyer [HCE], the Russian General, a battler of the Boyne, still our favorite Ben-jamin, once Franklin of this city. And there they went, all the taverners.

Because they wanted to get out by the gangway before the ship was loosed, in order to wish the Welshers well and to make their way to Brownhazelwood on the banks of the So-and-So. They turned again, westing homeward, to Danesbury Common, having drained their forty buckets, till they caught the wind abroad (*a*loafers *p*assing-jeering), all the boats crowding the ways.

Oh, there! Ahoy!

Come on, Hosty! for an inundation of merrification!

> His bludgeon's bruk, his drum is tore.
> For spuds we'll keep the hat he wore
> And roll in clover on his clay
> By wather parted from the say.

Hurray! All ready for a lynching party. The Shaun van voght, the whistling thief . . .

But it was impossible to bring the Four from their berths. They were at their wetsend in the mailing waters, trying to Hide! Seek! Hide! Seek! Number One lived at Bothersby North; (373)

Number Two digged up Poors Court; Number Three slept with Lilly Tekkles at The Eats; Number Four was berthed to the west with the celluloid Donkey. And they were all trying to and baffling with the walters of, hoompsy-doompsy walters of, High! Sink! High! Sink! Highohigh! Sinkasink! Waves.

> The gangstairs strain and anger's up
> As Hoisty rares the can and cup
> To speed the bogre's bark away
> O'er wather parted from the say.

Hark! Most important general announcement!

[Inside his tavern, HCE hears the throng assembled. Their turbulence develops into a gigantic proclamation of his guilt, together with diverse suggestions for exterminating him. In prospect the mob enjoys the various deaths to which they will put him; in anticipation they drown him, bludgeon him, burn him, and thrash him in every conceivable kind of athletic contest. To these violences they add warnings that the police are framing him, that his sons are in revolt, and that his wife is on the point of marrying the man of their choice. They gloat over the fact that his whole miserable life story will appear in the morning papers, and that the new sun will rise on a world freed at last of his encumbering presence.]

He should be ashamed of himself for hiding that shape in his coat, that sheep in his goat, and for resembling so barefaced the magreedy prince of Roger—the pirate! The hunk in his trunk would be an insult to a pig's trough! Hunting the Park on an inebriated mission whenever there's imberillas, and calling Rina Roner Reinette Ronayne.—He was heard by orderlies, beadles, and postbillers.—Begetting a wife which became his niece; that was when he had dizzy spells. (Advertisement—Glad-stool's pills made him ride as them all.)—Stop his nonsense! Ink him! Run him down the lane! Penalty, please! This is not the end of this by no manner of means! (374) It's all being taken down for the morning papers. You'll read it at breakfast. Streamer headlines. Wait till we hear the Bishop reeling around your pastoral letter! Epistlemade-themology for Dear Dirty Dublin!—Our Island, Rome, and Duty! Good try, Buckstiff! Bat in, boot! Sell him a breach of contract, the buy-lawyer! Finnish MacCool!—First you were Nomad, next you were Namar, now you're Numah, and it's soon you'll be Nomon. The Foreign Office is on the move to lay you out a dossier. Darby's in the yard, planning it on you, the whispering policeman, the find of his kind, an artist. Look to your reputation. You're in for it now!—Do you know who was written about in the Orange Book of Estchapel? Basil and the other two men from King's Avenue. Now just try to recall. Just press this cold brand against your brow for a moment, carefully; that's it.—*H*ung *C*hung *E*gglyfella now speak. How you fell from story to story (375) to lie. Enfilming infirmity.—And here's witnesses! Glue on him, Greevy! Bottom anker, Noordeece! Wait till they send you to sleep, scowpow!—You'll have loss of fame from Wimmegame's fake. There'll be a youthful herald, then, who'd be our choice in romance. And it's all us rangers you'll be facing in the jury box, between all the Misses Mountsackvilles gasping to die for shame. Just hold hard till the one we let out gets her hearing. *H*ired in *c*ameras, *e*xtra! You thought as how your sons would never wake up, did you? One bully son growing the goff, and his twin read out by the Nazi priers. When the court collects, 'tis the child which gives the father away.—Good for you, Richmond Rover, let him have another! A grand game! Dalymount's decisive!—It'll make quite a story, you and she! Don Governor Buckley's in the Tara Tribune, sporting the insides of a Russian General and little Mrs. Ex-Skaerer-Sissers is bribing the half-pricers to pray for her widower in his gravest embezzlement. You in your stolen mace and anvil, and she in her borrowed circus clothes; Finn MacCool with a veiled Grainne—much as she was when the fancy cutter spied her seesawing on a fern, she the smiling ever (Tailor's Advertisement—A tailor would adapt his caulking trudgers on to any shape at see.) and the lovablest (376) Lima since Queen MacCormick, only a little wider. Tip. Scapulars, beads, and a stump of candle—all the trimmings from the tree, picked up at Clontarf. Waterloo.[98]—The doom of the oracle is on you. The Real Hibernians are going strong at knocker-knocker. You ought to take a dose of fruit, you're getting heavier and it serves you right, damn ye! Niece, whom you bound not to loose, is gone on Nephew, ever since she clapped eye on him at the Gunting Munting Hunting Punting. He'll pick the lock of her fancy.—Good jump, Powell. Clean over their heads! We could kiss him for that one!—Sparkes is the one to win the girls. Better get after him, Scaldhead, before you bunkledoodle down upon your birchentop again—after them three blows from time, drink, and hurry, the same three that nursed you: Skerry, Badbols, and the Gray One. All of your own club, too!—Clan Ruckland forever! The Fenn, the Fenn, the kinn of all Fenns!—The fistful of berry-berries were for the masses to be said for your soul. (Buy bran biscuits and you'll never say die. —Advertisement.) If they never ate fried sole peace, they're eating it now: with Easter (377) greeding: Angus! Angus! Angus!—The keykeeper of the keys of the seven doors of the dreamadoory in the household of Hecech saith: "Give it up, Magraw! Never mind your gibbet hump. Slip on your ropen collar. No one will know or heed you, Postumus, if you skip round by the back and come front to beg, in one of the little boys' sailor suits."—Well spat, witty wagtail! Now, pawn to bishop's fourth: move!—There's Mendelssohn's "March" cranking up to the honeymoon couple. Drag us out "Ivy Eve in the Hall of Alum." Feeling the jitters? You'll be tight when the knot is knotted. It's now or never! Peena and Queena are duetting a giggle-for-giggle and the little bride, Alannah, is lost in her do-you-mind waiting [diamond wedding]. What a magnificent gesture you will show us this gallus day. And here's the hearse and four horses, with the interprovincial crucifixioners casting lots inside to know who is to be their gossoon, and who is to break the news to mother.—Our masterbuilder has fallen asleep, the flesh-lump-fleeter from Poshtapengha; he bares sobsconcious inklings shadowed on his soulskin; it's signed: "Yours, the stroke

[98] Cf. pp. 10–11 and 205–13.

of a hen."—Laying the cloth to fore of them; and thanking the fish, in core of them, to pass the grace for Gard sake! Ahmohn. Matthew, Mark, Luke, and John, and the ass-cart behind! They've got a date with a swimminpull trolley!—Isn't it great, he's swaying above us, for his good (378) and ours! Fly your balloons, boys and girls! He's doorknob dead; and Annie Delap is free once more! We could eat you, by Bacchus, and imbabe through you: one fledge, one brood, till *h*ulm *c*ulms *e*vurdyburdy. He heard his name and seen it written up in the flashmarket, Persse O'Reilly of the Royal Irish Artillery. The lewd-lightning-dream-tram-conductor! The unnamed non-Irish-blooder that becomes Green-islander over-night. (We're melting statuettes out of his guts.—Advertisement.) He's alight there still, by Mike, the plague will soon be over! [99]— We didn't understand what you said about thirteen to a loaf, sir, kindly repeat.[100] Or let us alone with your language, profound personifier of our idle words. Shaw and Shea are teaching Ibsen to hurry up. You can't impose on *Freischütze* like us. Every tub [Butt] here spits his own fat [Taff]. *H*ang *c*oercion *e*veryhow! And to smithereens with Grimm's law! [101]—In the beginning is the void, in the muddle is the sound-dance, and thereinafter you're in the unknown again, and vice versa.—You talk a dunsker's brogue, man, we our soul's speech. Silence in thought. And wear an artful of outer nocense.[102]—So it will be quite material what may be un-enveloped for you, old Mighty, when it's oped in Philadelphia in the morning. Ha! ha! (379) Knick nuck, Knockcastle! Muck! And you'll nose it without one word from we. We don't know the sender or to whom it was sent, but you'll find that Chickenchugger is taking the Treacly-shortcake with Bugle; and the Bitch is pairs-a-drawsing; and Horssmayres Procession is tighting up under the trees. Stop. Press stop. To press stop. All to press stop.—Anyone

[99] Tarred, feathered, and burned, he is still in flames.
[100] Last Supper hint.
[101] Grimm's law describes the sound shifts of the mute consonants from Pre-Germanic to the historical Teutonic tongues.
[102] Soul's speech wearing an artful of outer nocense—a maxim for Joyce's literary style.

can see you're the son of a gun. Woe to the worm quashed, and wor to the winner. Give him another, his lights aren't all out yet! —With seven whores always in the home of his thoughts—two Idas, two Evas, two Nessies, and Rubyjuby: no wonder he stinks like a goat. One night he had a nightmare and thought all seven queens were mobbing him. Abdicate yourself! It just gets our goat. He'll be the death of us, Popocatepetl. Yes sir, faith, you will. —What are we after? Why do we come? None of your business. You keep that hen of yours and her forty candle-power glim look, but of all your wanings send us out your peppy ales and you'll not be such a bad lot. . . . We sincerely trust that the missus and the kiddies of sweet Gorteen has not been to their very last tittles deranged if in bunk, and we graciously augur for your Majesty a BENK BANK BONK [103] to sleep in.—It's your last fight, Megantic, fare you well! [104] The referee's took to hailing to pass the time. There go the Valkyries all in white to carry off the slain.—But we're being carried away beyond all bounds, so we'll leave it to Keyhoe, Danelly, and Pykemhyme, the three muske-(380)teers at the end of this age, to tell of all that befell after that to Mocked Majesty in Mullingar.

(A) Tavern Brawl: How the night at the tavern ended

[We are astounded to find that the preceding events are part of a story being told in the tavern by drunken narrators. Yet no sooner is this fact noted than Joyce's bifocal method lets us see that the action is at the same time the action of the present night in HCE's bar. The company having left, the tavernkeeper, drunk and terribly depressed, stumbles around his barroom drinking the dregs left by the company, and to the consternation of the servants (and

[103] These capitalized syllables represent the fall of Finnegan, the rocking of a boat at the bottom of the sea of sleep, also a series of stiff punches that the prizefighters are throwing at each other; in sum, a combination suggesting the ultimate collapse and doom of HCE.
[104] "It's your last trip, Titanic." Cf. p. 480, footnote 4.

also of the ancestral pictures on the wall) falls drunk and Humpty-Dumpty-wise to the floor.]

So you were saying, boys? Anyhow, he what?

So anyhow, after that, to wind up that long-to-be-cherished get-together at Glenfinnisk-en-la-Valle, after the feast was over, poor old *h*ospitable *c*orn and *e*ggfactor, King Roderick O'Conor [105] the last king of Ireland, between fifty-odd and fifty-even years of age at the time—or, at least, he wasn't actually the then last king of all Ireland, he was the eminent king of all Ireland after the last pre-eminent king of all Ireland, the joky old top that went before him in the Taharan dynasty, King Art MacMurrough of the feathered leggings, now of parts unknown (God guard his generous comic-song-book soul!) [106]—nevertheless, the year the sugar was scarce, and himself down to three cows, wait till I tell you, what did he do when he found himself alone after all of them had gone off with themselves to their castles of (381) mud, as best they could? Well, sir, faith, he just went hell-tapping through the winespilth and weevily popcorks that were knee-deep round his own table, with his hat at a leary [107] cant on him, overwhelmed as he was with black ruin, like a sponge out of water, singing through his tears and his belches that Clare air, the blackbird's ballad, "I've a terrible errible lot todue todie todue tootorrible day," and, arrah be damn, but he finished by lowering his woolly throat with the wonderful midnight thirst was on him, and wishawishawish if he didn't go round and suck up, in some particular cases with the assistance of his venerated tongue, whatever surplus rotgut was left by the lazy lousers in the different bottoms of the various drinking utensils left there behind them, (382) such as it was, no matter what the brew, till the rising of the morn, till that hen of

[105] Cf. p. 3, Rory O'Connor and Henry II.
[106] High King Art, of the legendary times of Finn MacCool. Joyce here identifies him with the vaudeville-song hero Finnegan.
[107] King Leary (Lughaire), High King of Ireland at the time of the arrival of St. Patrick. Cf. p. 610.

Kevin's shows her beaconegg,[108] and the chapel windows stain our history told,[109] and Father MacMichael stamps for eight o'clock mass, and the *Litvian Newspaper* is seen, sold, and delivered,[110] and all's set for restart after silence [111]—like his ancestors to this day after him, and under the very gaze of the two servants and of the ancestral pictures, he came acrash acrupper. Whereupon, heave ho! one to do and one to dare, par by par, a peerless pair, our wineman from Barleyhome he just slumped to throne.[112]

So sailed the stout ship *Nansy Hans* [113] from Liff away, for Nattenlaender. As who has come returns. Farewell! Good bark, good-by.

Now follow we out by Starloe.

Book II, Chapter 4: Bride-Ship and Gulls

[HCE's mind now sails forth, like a sea-wanderer returning to the bounding deep, on a ship of dream. What he is to dream will form the matter of the present chapter. It will be a dream of the honeymoon voyage of Tristram and Iseult. His body, helpless on the floor, will be the King Mark of the story; but his spirit, rejuvenated in the sonlike image of the successful lover, will know again the joys of youthful love. The honeymoon ship is surrounded by waves and gulls, and these become the presences of the Four Old Men asleep. They had failed to quit the tavern with the departing company, and now bear witness to the dream of the broken master.

[The chapter opens with the song of the gulls as they mock the helpless King Mark with a promise of what his bride will be doing in her nuptial ship with Tristram.]

[108] Hen as dawn, mother of the sun-egg.
[109] Sunlight will illuminate the history of St. Kevin in the stained glass of chapel windows. Cf. pp. 604–6.
[110] Morning paper as Hen's letter, carrying the story of HCE.
[111] *Recorso* theme.
[112] HCE, dead drunk, slumps to the floor.
[113] Cf. p. 244, HCE with Nancy Hands.

{383} Three quarks for Muster Mark, he hasn't got much of a bark. It will be fun to see him hunting for his shirt in the dark—for his trousers in the Park. He's the rummest old rooster ever flopped out of a Noah's ark.—And Tristy's the spry young spark, that'll tread her, wed her, bed her, and red her without winking the tail of a feather; and that's how that chap's going to make his money and mark.

The seaswans sang that song when they smacked the kiss of Tristram and Iseult.

There, with the wheeling birds of the sea, were the four of them, listening in as hard as they could, (384) all sighing and sobbing and listening.

They were the big four, the four master waves of Erin, spraining their ears, listening to the oceans of kissing—when he was cuddling his Colleen Bawn on the fifteen-inch loveseat behind the chief-stewardess's cabin, the hero, the Gaelic champion, the onlyest one of her choice, her blue-eyed ideal; cuddling her and kissing her in her ensemble of blue, Isola; and whispering to her about their being one—Trisolanisans. And they, all four, remembered the old days, remembered who made the world and how they used to be at that time (385) cuddling and kiddling her after an oyster supper in Cullen's barn, in the good old bygone days of Dion Boucicault, in the other world, in one of the far-back centuries when who made the world—when they knew the doorman, O'Clery. They were, all four, collegians at that time, with their slates and satchels, playing conic sections, etc., in the Queen's Ultonian Colleges, along with another fellow, a prime number, Totius Quotius, and paying tribute to the butler of Clumpthump to see the mad Dane eating his vitals and throwing his tongue in the snakepit. It brought the dear prehistoric scenes all back again to watch that pair of lovers. And after that now there he was, vowed to pure beauty and his Arrah-na-poghue. When she, murmurously, after she let a cough, gave her firm order for a song from the dozen favorite national blooms in Love-illicit. Before the four or them the couple reveled scandalously. And there they were, like a four-master [four-poster bed; four-masted schooner; four masters] listening to "Roll on, thou deep and dark blue Ocean—roll," (386) as tired as they were, all wishing for a bit of the bygone days—all four listening and spraining their ears for the millennium and all their mouths making water.

[And now first we have the recollections of Johnny MacDougal:] Ah, well sure, and that's the way. And it so happened there was poor Matt Gregory, their paterfamilias, and the others. And they were indeed four old he-ladies with their half a tall hat—just like the old despot himself, only for the extrusion of the salt water; or like the auctioneer in front of the place near O'Clery's—at the Document Number One—who arranges the auctions at the colleges—auctioneer James H. Tickell, J.P., going to the horseshow (387) in his gray half a tall hat to find out all the improper colleges. And there they were now listening right enough, the four salt-water widowers, and they could remember the days when my heart knew no care, when Fair Margrate waited Swede Villem—and Lally [1] in the rain; the landing of Lady Jales Casemate in the year of the flood, 1132 S.O.S., the christening of Queen Baltersby, the drowning of Pharaoh in the Red Sea, and the drowning of Martin Cunningham [2] whose widow is writing her memoirs for the *Grocery Trader's Monthly*. Where the (388) old conk cruised now croons the Yank. Exit Mark of Cornwall through a door. Enter Nephew with lifted revolver, fire-escaping in his nightshirt. Iseult tumbles. And *mild und leise* is as loose as her knees. Embrace without end. Like new actors in the old play, *A Royal Divorce*.[3]

[And now next we have the recollections of Marcus Lyons:] He too could recall the days when my heart knew no care. The Flemish Armada, scattered and drowned one morning about 11:32, and St. Patrick and St. Kevin and Lapoleon, then the Frankish

[1] Lally Tompkins, the policeman of Bk. I, cf. pp. 67, 96.
[2] Martin Cunningham is an important figure in *Ulysses*. No mention is made of his death, but he is associated with the theme of the "drowned father."
[3] Cf. p. 32.

fleet about the year of Notre Dame 1132 P.P.O., disembarking under General Bonaboche in his half a gray traditional hat, and then there he was poghuing her scandalously under the sycamores in 1132 Brian or Bride Street, and then again they used to give the grandest lectures in history to oceanfuls of collegians (389) round their twelve tables in the four Trinity colleges of Ulster, Munster, Leinster, and Connaught, in the Janes-danes Lady Andersdaughter University, showing the spirit of nature as divinely developed in time,[4] past, present, and future tenses—*arma virumque romanorum.*—How it all came back to them as they watched him kiddling her.

Ah, dearo dearo dear! And Lally, when he lost part of his half a hat and all his belongings, in his old futile manner repeating himself and telling him how (390) to forget the past—when the burglar shoved the wretch in churner oil, and contradicted all about Lally and his old fellow in the lighthouse, and the turner, and Skelly, and the bold drakes up the lane; and he couldn't stop laughing over the four widowers in their half a Roman hat, all divorced four years before, which had been foretold in song and proverb.

[Lucas Tarpey's recollections:] And, oh, so well they could remember at that time, when Carpery of the Golden Hand was King of Poolland,[5] Mrs. Dowager Justice Squalchman, in full-bottom wig (391) and beard, about 1132, 1169, or 1768 Y.W.C.A., at the auctioneer court in Arrahnacuddle. And poor Johnny, frightened because of her full bottom; and the four chorusing because he was so slow to brush her shoes for her when he was grooming her ladyship; and poor Marcus persecuted because he forgot himself; and then poor Dion Cassius Poosycomb, drowned before everybody because he, well, he confessed on his two bare marrow-bones to Her Worship his Mother and Sister Evangelist Sweainey and now . . . (392) well . . . forget and forgive . . . old age com-

[4] Hegelian formula—history as manifestation of the Absolute.
[5] Pool-land: Ireland. Cairpre was the name of several legendary Irish kings. Nuada of the Golden Hand, too, was a king of the legendary cycles.

ing over him he was tempted to familiarities with the nurse-ten-
dered hand but went off to sleep. . . . Ah, dearo dearo dear!

[Finally:] And where is Matt Emeritus, laychief of Abbotabishop?
Achoch. they were all so sorry for pourboire Matt, in his salt-water
hat and overalls, too big for him, the old matriarch: a queenly
man, sitting there, the sole of the settlement, below ground, in
expiatory rite, in her beaver bonnet, the king of the Caucasus, a
family all to himself, on his multilingual tombstone; and she due
to kid, her face to the wall, ready to blow his brains out—till the
heights of New Ireland heard the Bristol Tavern waiting for the
end to come. Ah ho! It was too bad entirely! All devoured by Act
of Parliament, and all on account of the (393) smell of Shakeletin,
and his mouth watering, acid and alcoholic. And so now pass the
loaf for Christ sake. Amen.
And it can't be helped. Ah, God be good to us! Poor Martin
Cunningham!

And still and all, at that time of the dynast days, the days of
old King Cedric Silkenbeard and Burgomaster Bart, in Hunger-
ford-on-Mudway,[6] where first I met thee—and how William poled
him up his bucket of water and made a name for himself—they
were always counting and contradicting every night, thinking of
auld lang syne, and their four hosenbands now happily married
to old Gallstonebelly, and they used to be getting up from under,
with all the worries awake in their hair, at cockcrow, to see was
the Boston *Transcript* come, all puddled and mythified, the way
the wind wheeled the schooner round, crossing their sleep when
they were in dreams of yore. (394) And they were always putting
on their half a hat and repeating themselves, like the time they
were dodging the turkey cock that chased them, and they were
kids at school. And there they used to be, flapping and cycling
round the wakes of ships, in the wake of their good old Foehn
again, the clipper-built and the five four-masters and Lally of the

[6] Hurdleford (Dublin)-on-Liffey.

cleftoft bagoderts and Roe of the fair cheats, exchanging fleas from host to host, and telling him, before he forgot, the old anecdotes: the subjects being their passion grand. That one fresh from the cow about Aithne Meithne married a mailde; that one from the Engrvakon Saga about a goth who gave a goth an egg; and the parkside pranks of quality queens, etc., etc., etc. Or telling him about when theeuponthus Eysolt of binnoculises sabcunsciously senses (upers the deprofundity of multimathematical immaterialities where the all-immanence of that which Itself is Itself Alone exteriorizes on this our-here-now plane in disunited solid) [7] likeward and gushious bodies, with intuitions of reunited (395) selfdom: and telling Jolly MacGolly and all the other analists, their eyes peering through windows into the honeymoon cabins, there to see the first-class ladies in lovely morning toilet for the thrill driver; all four forgetting to say their grace and quaking, and all, he he he, quaking, so fright-, and, shee shee, shaking.

For it was then a pretty thing happened—when his hand at the just-right moment. . . . the vivid girl, deaf with love. With a cry of joyous crisis, she reunited their disunited, when, as quick as greased pigskin, Amoricus Champius with one thrust drove past the (396) both lines of forwards into the goal of her gullet.

And now, up and at 'em, and keep it to yourself, as one man or woman to another. There was this modern old Irish princess, nothing under her hat but red hair and solid ivory and a first-class pair of bedroom eyes of blue.—"Could you blame her," we're asking, "for one psychological moment? What would Ewe do? With her so tiresome old milkless ram, the tiresome old hairy beaver!" If the whole tale must be told, they two-oned together, and it was a frightful moment for the poor old timekeepers. Till he gripped the spark that plugged spared the chokee and they could hear the thong plipping out of her chapellledeosy.

It was totally terrific.—And after that they used to be so forgetful, trying to remember her beautiful (397) maiden name.

[7] A week end with Schopenhauer's *World as Will and Idea* will clarify for the reader this parenthetical remark.

But, sure, that reminds me now, how they used to be in lethargy's love, at the end of it all, always tired and all, after doing the housework, squatting round two by two, the four confederates, in Old Man's House, Millennium Road, in gala attire, lapping their portion of peace, reading a letter or two every night on their old one-page codex book of old year's eve 1132 M.M.L.J., old style, their Senchus Mor, final buff noon-meal edition, in the regatta covers, obtainable from the author, for to regul their reves by incubation, and Lally with them, through their gangrene spectacles. And all the good they did in their time, the rigorists, for Roe and O'Mulcnory a (398) Conry ap Mul, or Lap ap Morion, and for Buffler ap Matty MacGregory, for Marcus on Podex by Daddy de Wyer, beeves and scullogues, churls and vassals. And so they sing a mamalujo to the heroest champion of Erin.

And now, going on from that embrace and union, let us run on to say a prayer for all:

Hear, oh hear, Iseult la Belle! Tristram, sad hero, hear! The drum, the clarinet, the fife, the trumpet:

Hymn for Iseult la Belle:

You'll be loved by a Sunday child,
(399) And not by some damned lout.
Oh, come, sweet nymphs, to cheer the bride!
Why should she bide with old Sig Sloomysides?
    Take *me,* Lizzy my love!
I was the first one to toss her;
And, "You're the most likeable lad that's come
    my ways yet," said she.

Matthew, Mark, Luke, John—and the Donkey.

And still a light moves long the river. And stiller the mermen ply their keg.

Its pith is full. The way is free. Their lot is cast.

So, let us give the stage to John o' Dreams.

[Thus ends the Tristram and Iseult passage with a forward roll to the next book. It is true that what HCE has just dreamed is something remembered from his own past—but it is also a dream of some else's present. This "somebody else" in the role of successful lover was just such a fine fair-haired hero as his own son, Kevin (Shaun), would one day be. The dream may be said to signify a shift of emphasis of HCE's spirit from the flesh-case now broken on the floor to that younger flesh-case, full of future, now asleep upstairs.]

BOOK III

THE BOOK OF THE PEOPLE

[It is difficult to make the transition from Earwicker's dream of the bliss of Tristram and Iseult to the material of Book III, but the clue is supplied on pages 556-57. One fine night, while Katherine the Slop was basking on her pillow, she thought a knock came to the downstairs door, and down she went to see who it might be, and glory be to the saints in heaven, there was a creak up the staircase, and when she raised her candle to see, glory! down she went on her knees—as if it were the wreck of the *Hesperus,* or old King Gander O'Toole of the Mountains, or his ghost, she seen, slipping off over the sawdust lobby out of the back room in his honeymoon trim, holding up his finger with the clookey in his fistball for her to be still, and the whites of his pious eyeballs swearing her to silence. That is to say, the old man, after his dream on the floor (Bk. II, chap. 4), gathered himself together and went creaking up the stairs to bed. Old Kate, hearing the noise below, came down and saw him, disgracefully exposed. But he proceeded to his room. Book III opens with the old man at last in bed with his wife.

[The material of Book III is largely the dream of Mr. Earwicker between the late hour of his arrival in bed and the first crack of dawn. The principal figure of this dream is Shaun, envisioned as a great man of the future, carrying forward the mighty tradition of his ancestors and winning with blithest ease the battles lost by his father. But this Shaun of the father's fondest wishes is not really a very great or very substantial figure, for all his heroic hulk. He is maudlin, brutal, grandiloquent, and trite, short winded in the end and quick to collapse. The people accept him only with reservations, and after his moment of fruitless triumph sit over him in judgment.

[Each of the books of *Finnegans Wake* has its peculiar logic. Book I, the book of the forgotten past (the prehistory of mankind, the infancy of the individual), the book of the dark energies of the unconscious, is filled with obscure, swelling figures, rich with germinating power, vigorously bubbling and rapidly breaking into fresh figures reproductive of themselves. Book II is the book of the present. Architecturally it is the central block of the volume. It is devoted to Earwicker's tavern as it is known today. Its figures are not half-remembered potencies of the past, but living actualities, fully rounded, dense with implications. Book III is the book of the *desired* future; not the future *really* germinating in the nursery upstairs (that will be the matter of Book IV), but the mirage-future of the idealizing daydreams of the half-broken father. It is a future that will not survive the touch of daylight-actuality; its personages are thinner than the stuff of life; they lack resiliency; they are pat and dull.

[Book III is divided into four chapters. In Chapter 1 Shaun stands before the people and recommends himself to their votes, hurling vituperation against his opponent, Shem. He abruptly fades. In Chapter 2 our same hero, now called Jaun (Don Juan), finds himself before the twenty-eight schoolgirls and their princess, Iseult. With overly caressing paternal intimacy he lectures them on life and love, and enjoys their large-eyed adulation. Again he abruptly fades. In Chapter 3 this Jaun, now Yawn, is stretched recumbent over the midmost hilltop of Ireland. He is already exhausted. The Four Old Men arrive with their Donkey to sit over him in inquest. The long chapter is shot with voices offering testimonies against him. Gradually the hulk of Yawn disintegrates under the acids of the analysis. Finally it melts entirely into the great Form of forms which was its substratum all the time, namely, HCE, the dreaming father at the side of his sleeping ALP. Chapter 4 reveals the primal couple in their dreary bed.]

Book III, Chapter 1: Shaun before the People

[This chapter opens with the night sounds of bells tolling an unidentifiable hour, and the voice of the watch. We view the parental couple in bed. There is a third presence in the room, a threatening incubus. It is the incubus of life defeat. This terrible presence is the immediate stimulus to the father's compensatory dream of a successful son.]

(403) Hark! The hour!

And low stole o'er the stillness the heartbeats of sleep.

White fogbow spans the arch embattled. Mark the man, Mark: the nose of the man is self-tinted, wrinkled, ruddled. His cap is a gorse cone. He is Gascon Titubante, whose features are moving before my memory. The woman, the next exhibit, is his Anastasia: she prays in low Delft. But what named blue-toothed man is yon who stares? Jugurtha![1] He has the becco[2] of a wild Indian. He hath hornhide.[3] And his eye is now for you. (The most beautiful woman of the violet vale.) Snatcher! Come not near! Black! Switch out.

[The vision of Jugurtha fades. The figure of Shaun appears. He exhibits credentials and announces his plans for the good of the people. These insinuate questions which draw from him indignant rebuttal. To illustrate clearly the distinction between himself and his rival, he recounts the fable of "The Ondt and the Gracehoper." When the people ask to know the contents of the letter he carries, he replies with a tirade against the author, Shem, and the language that he used. Shaun declares he could write a much better letter

[1] Jugurtha: Numidian king, 112–106 B.C. Uttered the words, after his first visit to Rome: "A city for sale, and doomed to perish as soon as it finds a purchaser." Here he represents the threat of the darker forces to the imperialistic ego. Called forth, for a moment, by the stroke of the hour, he embodies in demonic and unpropitious form the total sense of this moment to HCE.

[2] Becco: beak, nose; *becco* (Italian): cuckold. The dark man will take from the empire-builder his bride—the Queen of Life.

[3] Hornhide: horn suggests cuckolder again.

himself: "The orthodox book, if given to light, would far exceed that bogus." Finally, with a tear for his mother, sleepy, in the manner of a dream, he disappears.]

Methought as I was dropping asleep, in nonland, at zero hour, I heard the peal of vixen's laughter among midnight chimes. (404) And as I was jogging along in a dream, I dreamed of the old earth whispering of Shaun. "Shaun! Shaun! Post the post!" And as the sound grew louder, lo! gradually, his light emerged from the dark, his belted lamp, and he loomed, dressed like an earl [4] in just the correct wear; his costume somewhat international: classy MacFrieze coat and Irish-terrier collar free-swinging from his shoulders, thick welted brogues hammered to suit the scotsmost public and climate, his jacket of wool well provided by Providence with big buttons of Russian red, invulnerable burlap waistcoat, popular choker, loud tie, and damask overshirt, a star-spangled zephyr with crinkly-doodle front, with his motto embroidered over it in peas, rice, egg yolk, turnips, and soup, to wit: R. [for royal] M. [for mail] D. [for Dublin]: hard cash on the nail; everything the best; none other than (405) Shaun himself!

What a picture primitive!

Would I were as wise as the Four Old Men, but, alas, I am only as their Donkey! But methought Shaun stood before me, so fired smart, in much more than his usual health. No mistaking that beamish brow. He was immense. For he was just after having a great time of it in a porter house, St. Lawzenge O'Toole's, leave your clubs in the hall and wait on yourself, where he had recruited his strength, in the sight of lovely eyes, by meals of spadefuls of mounded food: orange, bacon, eggs, rice-plum pudding, cold steak peatrefired, (406) half a pound of round steak very rare, with a side of rice-peas and Yorkshire à la mélange, and bacon with a pair of chops and goulash-gravy and pumpernickel and a gorgeous bulby onion, and then finally after his snack of saddlebag steak with old phoenix porter and sweet Irish praties and stew and mock turtle soup and Boland's broth, his soup with nightcap, with sec-

[4] Earl = jarl. Shaun has assumed the great, billowing costume of HCE.

ond course eggs and bacon, with broad beans, steak, loin of veal, more cabbage and peas; P.S.—a finger-hot Rhein genever to give the *Pax cum spiritu tuo*. Thrice thankful. Bread and seaweed and jam, all free of charge. And best wine *avec*. For his heart was bigger than himself. All St. Jilian's of Berry give him praise for the cheer he furnishes them. But it is ever of thee, Anne Lynch, that he is dreaming. He will flourish on tea and butter at the sign of Mistress Vanhomrig. Mind you, I don't mean to say for the moment that he was gluttonous, but, on the whole, when not off his oats (407) he grubbed his tuck all right.—And he was so jaunty. And he was plainly out on the ramp and mash—for he spoke:

When lo, I heard a voice, the voice of Shaun—vote of the Irish (and no purer boy ever chanted mid the clouds of divine nomination: *Tu es Petrus*)—a breeze over the ozone sea, a call (Moore Park! Moore Park!) [5] to scented night life.

His lifted hand—his helpful hand—made a gesture, and it said: "Greetings, lads and lassies." He yawned (that was yesterday's meal of pigeon pie and champagne), addressing himself in rehearsal, and complaining it was so close—his moment of appearance before a houseful of deadheads. (408) Having moistened his lips, on the quiet, and rubbing his teeth clean with his two forefingers, he sank down to rest at once, exhausted as a winded hare (disgusted with himself that his weight was too much for him) upon the native heath he loved.

[And now begins his dialogue with the people:]

SHAUN: "Well, I'm dashed, seeing myself in this trim! How all too unwordy I am! Unworthy to be the bearer extraordinary of this posthumous missive on His Majesty's service. It should have been my other, my enemy—for he's the *head*—my twin. He looks rather thin imitating me. I'm very fond of him, Fish-hands Macsorley! We're the music-hall pair that won the prize at the Guinness festival. I ought not to laugh at him on this stage, but he's such a

[5] Moore Park: the call-notes of an Australian bird; also, name of the meeting place of Swift and Stella.

260

game loser. I lift my disk to him. He lived his whole life trying to interpret the thoughts and doings of Woman. As for me, I am no helot-worshiper, but I revere her. (409) But, Gemini, he's looking frightfully thin! I heard the banshee singing, so down among the dustbins let him lie. I am the *heart* of it, yet I cannot recollect ever having deserved the postmastership of a nation. St. Anthony Guide me." [6]

THEY: "But have we ever asked you, dear Shaun, who it was gave you the permit?"

SHAUN: "Good-by now!" And he gave a tug at his candy-lock. "It is my heaviest cross and daily lot.—I'm off relief kitchens. Only a few weeks ago, I was meeting with a pair of men out of Glasshouse, named MacBlacks—or MacBlakes [7]—and they were talking me into their theory about no five-hour factory life with insufficient pay and accident insurance. Indeed, I take the greatest pleasure in announcing how I have it from none other than St. Columkille's [8] prophecies: 'After Sun., Mon., Tues., Wed., Thurs., and Fri., comes Sabotage.'"

THEY: "Then you might be so by order?"

SHAUN: "It is not that I want to do it, but I am told to do it, from above, by Book and Cook; (410) it is put on me from on high, out of the book of breedings; it is an inherited coercion, and I have no egotistic advantages in view.—I am about fed up with going circulating about, and I was thinking of some out-of-the-way place where I might isolate i from my multiple Me's, but where on earth to turn I do not know: I am hopelessly off course."

THEY: "We expect you are hopelessly off course, honest Shaun; but a whisper reaches us that in the end it may well turn out to be you who will bear this open letter."

[6] Pious Catholics put the letters S.A.G. (St. Anthony Guide) on the back of envelopes to insure their safe delivery.

[7] Followers of the poet Blake, one of the first to excoriate the industrial degradation of man.

[8] The reference here is to the Book of Kells. Columkill was a little town founded in the ninth century beside the monastery of Kells by St. Cellach, and named in honor of St. Columba, otherwise known as Columkille (Dove of the Church). The prophecy is of doomsday.

SHAUN: "As to that, I have the gunpowder, and that is a lot to say."

THEY: "Would you mind telling us where, mostly, you are able to work?"

SHAUN: "Here! Being too soft for proper work I mostly was able to walk—between three masses a morn and two chaplets at eve. I am always telling those three pedestrians, Top, Sid, and Hucky, (411) how it was foretold for me, by brevet, that I should be disbarred after Holy Orders from unnecessary servile work, lest I get into trouble. And I have certain maxims for getting on; viz. —never back a woman you defend, never get quit of a friend on whom you depend, never make face to foe till he's rife, and never get stuck to another man's pfife. And I pray that His will may be done. I am good at the root—a believer."

THEY: "But you have painted our town green, with your Wearing of the Green."

SHAUN: "Yes, I confess I have. How did you guess it? Down with Saxon rule!—It would not be my first coat-changing. (412) New worlds for all!"

THEY: "How sweet thy song! But is it our property or our national virtue you would take from us?"

SHAUN: "A foul insinuation! Another time please confine your insinuations to someone else! What would I be doing with your virtue? So let's drop that.—And let me tell you that under the past officeholder too much private stationery was eaten up, largely by those pension goats.—I intend to compose a savings book, in the form of a pair of goat-sheep boxing gloves, around this matter of the Welsh Fusiliers and their scapegoat, for my publishers, Nolan and Brown, so long as (413) there is a salary to keep me going.

"And the statement would read about as follows: 'A letter to the Very Honorable Sometime Sweepyard at the Service of the Writer:—The late Mrs. Sanders and her sister, Mrs. Shunders, both medical doctors and as alike as two leggs. She was the nicest person, only too fat, used to babies and totty-dean verbiage. She was well under ninety and had a taste for poetry. P. L. M. Mevrouw von Andersen was the one who staked her to her first big party and gave her presents.—This is my last will and testament, duly written before witnesses—oh, what must the grief of my mind be for two little coolies worth 20,000 quid—here witnessed with best wishes to Pepette for next match, from their dearly beloved Rugger, M.D.D.,O.D.' " [9]

THEY: "Absolutely killing you are, together with your Cadenus.[10] And go along now, so that we may complete our White Paper. *Two* Venuses? Queer! but go on. The whole truth. And so what happened next to your pile of money?"

SHAUN (*He peered rather close at the fake stone of his ring*): "All of it (414) was spontaneously handed over by me, in the name of Mr. van Howten of Tredcastles, Clondalkin.[11] Permit me to tell you, I never spent it. It went, anyway, like hot cakes. And this brings me to my fresh point: I am presenting you with a barrel of Guinness's. Drink!"

THEY: "Give us a song!"

SHAUN: "I would rather spin you a fable, one of Aesop's Grimm gests of Jacob and Esau. Let us consider the case—" (he coughed and cleared his throat: husstenhasstencaffincoffintussemtossemdamandamnacosaghcusaghhobixhatouxpeswchbechoscashlcarcarcaract [12]) "—the case of 'The Ant and the Grasshopper': [13]

" 'The Gracehoper was always dancing and happy, or else making overtures to Floh, Luse, Bienie, and Vespatilla, inviting them to play with him, even if only in chaste. He would curse deliciously with his antennae, until she was red for shame, and furnish her with spider-web hose. Or he would be always making up funny

[9] Overtones of Swift, brooding on the death of Vanessa.
[10] Cadenus: the name assumed by Swift in his poem to Vanessa, "Cadenus and Vanessa." Here the Cad theme appears connected directly with the lover aspect of the Dean.
[11] Cf. p. 111, "the hate turned the milk on the van Houtens."—Clondalkin is a Dublin suburb on the Grand Canal, southeast of Lucan.
[12] The thunder voice of the father is heard through the cough of the son.
[13] Cf. La Fontaine, Bk. I, Fable 1, "The Grasshopper and the Ant."

funereels about Besterfather Zeus, the Aged One, (415) inside his sheath wormcasket; and Dehlia and Peonia, his nymphs, coaxing him; and Auld Lady Plussiboots to scratch his head and cackle his transitus; and all of them with tambourines and castanets dancing their *danse macabre* to the ra, the ra, the ra, the ra, attended to by a Mutt and Taff boxing match and a troop of sozzlers singing "The Cotter's Saturday Night," and "Humpty Dumpty Sat on a Wall," but "Ho, Tim Finnegan's Wake!"[14] For if science can mute us nought about the Great Sommbboddy, perhaps art may sing us something about the Little Newbuddies that ring his paunch: for O'Cronione lies acrumbling in his sands[15] but his sunsunsuns still tumble on.[16]

" ' "Gracious me! What a sight for the gods!" vented the Ondt, who, not being a summer fool, was thoughtfully making silly faces at himself before the isinglass of his window. "We shall not come to the party, for he is not on our social list. Nor to old Ba's burial either, the sluggard." He lifted hands and prayed: "May my reign flourish as broad as Beppy's realm, as high as (416) Happy's heaven. May it grow and flourish."

" 'The Ondt was a cosmopolitan, well-built, and spacious fellow, very solemn and chairman-looking.—Now, when the silly Gracehoper had jingled through a jungle of love and debts, and jangled through a jumble of life in doubts, wasting his substance among bumblebees and ladybirds, he fell sick and knew not where to turn for food and help. What a plight! He repented his folly and was melancholy.

" 'He had eaten himself out of house and home; he had lived heartily. But when the winter storms came, he went out from his house and he took a round stroll; and the winds were tearing everything to pieces.

[14] I.e., the Gracehoper is wasting his time composing a work on Finnegan's wake.

[15] Chronos: time—the sands of time.

[16] "John Brown's body lies..."

It is impossible to study the Creator Himself, yet art (the work of the Gracehoper) can celebrate His creation.

(417) " 'Blind as a batflea, he tossed himself in the vico,[17] wondering where would he light; and next time he meets the Ondt he will be lucky if he beholds not a world of differents.—Behold His Majesty the Ondt upon his throne, smoking Havana cigars, handsomely clothed, relaxing in his sun parlor, seated before his tasty plate, as happy as a boy basking on the Libido, with Floh, Luse, Bienie, and Vespatilla. "Emmet and demmet and be jiltses crazed and be jadeses whipt!" sneezed the jealous Gracehoper, at his wit's end. "What do I see?"

" 'The Ondt, that perfect host, was having a wonderful time, blissful as a happy Mohammedan among houris. He was amusing himself chasing Floh, and tickling Luse, and tackling Bienie, and jucking Vespatilla. The veripatetic figure of the Gracehoper, signifying chronic despair, was too much for the company. (418) "Let him be the Weeper, with his parasites dropping away from him; I'll be the jolly one now! Let him be the one to write off his phoney stuff; I'm the one to make the melody that mints the money. *Ad majorem Dei gloriam*—and for pounds, shillings, pence! Capsizer of his own boat, now he seeks advice from me, the lord of loaves, whom he formerly despised. So be it! Let him receive now the weight of my wisdom."

" 'The thing pleased the Ondt; he laughed and he laughed; and he made such a noise the Gracehoper feared lest he misplace his throat.

" ' "I forgive you, Ondt," said the Gracehoper, weeping. "Take care of the girls; I commit them to your care. I played the piper, so now I must pay. And I accept your reproof, for, like Castor and Pollux, we are complementary twins. The prize of your save is the price of my spend. Ere those flirts now gadding about you quit your Mookse-like mocking for my Gripes-like groping, a stretch of time must elapse. But take stock of my tactics, and all's well; for as I view by your far-look, so should you hale yourself to my heal. (419) Regard my thin wines, while I see your whole bread chest. In *my* laughable universe you'd hardly find such prodigious beforeness with so much behind. Your feats are enormous,

[17] He gave himself up to fate.

your volumes immense; your genius is world wide, your space is sublime! But, Holy St. Martin, why can't you beat time?" ' " [18]

And Shaun concludes with the sign of the cross: "In the name of the former and of the latter and of their holocaust, all men."

THEY: "What a great teacher you are! How far-flung your folklore and how grand your vocabulary! You've a wonderful way with you. Your talk is easy to listen to. But could you read this open Shem-letter for His Christian Majesty?"

SHAUN: "Hand it to me! Greek! I'm as Roman as Pope could christen me. I am capable of translating anything, backwards or forwards, with my eyes shut and with the tips of my fingers. But, alas, it is hard on the corns. I agree with your remark *re* the purloined notepaper, for I am in just the position to say: It is not a nice production; it is a worthless scribble. Besides, it's actionable— all about crime and libel. The foulest filth (420) and flummery, reduced to writing by the mother of Mr. Unmentionable, and really telling us nothing new. It is simply the old story of the two girls in the bushes and the three fellows in the shrubs.—And then to think of him hawking his pictures around to the Frenchies and Germans in the kitchen: 'This is my mother and here's my father!' And the Dutchies dying laughing. An infant sailing eggshells on the floor of a wet day would have more savvy."

The letter: carried of Shaun, written of Shem, for Alp, mother of Shem, for Hek, father of Shaun.[19] It has wandered far. Its addresses cannot be located. (421) Sender: Boston (Mass.).

THEY: "Kind Shaun, much as we hate to say it, but, since you rose to the use of money, have you not used language ten times

[18] Underneath the sly insect play of this fable, the Gracehoper restates Shem's philosophy: there are advantages to Shaun's possessions and the thrift that begot them—all of which the Gracehoper appreciates—but he would not relinquish his own life style to enjoy them. He can see the Ondt's point of view, but why cannot the Ondt see his?—The fact that *Shaun* recites this fable would seem to indicate that he knows very well the charm of Gracehoper existence, but realizes that he is incapable of enjoying it, and therefore insists the more on imposing his own storekeeping pattern on the world.

[19] Here the mother's patronage of Shem and the father's of Shaun is clearly stated.

worse than the pen marks used with such hesitancy by your celebrated brother?"

SHAUN: "Celebrated! *HeCitEncy*! Notorious, I would rather say. I've no room for that fellow on my roster. As I hourly learn from Rooters and Havers, he is on his last legs. Mammy was put up to it by him.[20] He ought to be (422) placed in irons. For it is well known that he has the D.T.'s, and consumption, and syphilis. Rot him! I will describe you in a word, thou—homo! With his unique hornbook and his Prince-and-the-Pauper's pride,[21] blundering all over the two worlds! I'd famish before buying him a Mussulmans' present: He's no half-cousin of mine! The pig!"

THEY: "Please, then, unravel the substance of his letter in your own sweet words, and with yet another Aesop's fable."

SHAUN (*taking, as his hunger got the better of him, a bite out of his triune hat*): "I thought you all knew the story. It's an old one and well known. Blindman's Buff [Beerman's Bluff] began it. It's about Old Knoll and his borrowing; then the two lilies of the field; then the Three. I regret to announce that, after laying out his literary bed, for two days she kept squalling out to her (423) jameymock farceson,[22] in Shemish, about the Balt and his Royal Divorces —the whole Tale of the Tub; and he, the cribber, fast to his chair, with pen in hand, taking it all down in that idioglossary he invented.[23] Imitator! I was present at the whole thing.—Whenever I think of that unbloody housewarmer, Shem Skrivenitch, be gorry, I declare I get a pain in the jaw. You know, he's peculiar: he was gray at three, when he made his bow to the public, and was barnacled[24] up to the ears when he repented at seven. He's weird and medieval, down to his vegetable soul. That's why he was forbidden

[20] Shaun is discussing the important matter of Shem's inspiration, derived from ALP.

[21] Mark Twain, *The Prince and the Pauper*.

[22] James Joyce and Macpherson. Finn MacCool was father of Macpherson's Ossian.

[23] Here is the clearest description of the composition of the letter.

[24] Mrs. James Joyce, nee Barnacle. This paragraph is a parody of Joyce's life.

to mate under the Helpless Corpses Enactment. He was expelled from school for itching. Then he caught erysipelas and joined the Jesuits. (424) Once, when he just missed being killed, the freak wanted to join the clergy as a Dominican. He used to be avoided. Then he went to Cecilia Street, on his own, to pick up Galen. [Went to Paris to study medicine.] Shame!—I have the utmost contempt for him. Frostbitten! Conscientious objector! Your pudding is cooked!"

THEY: "But why do you hate him so? Vouchsafe to say. You will now, won't you? Why?"

SHAUN: "For his root language: [25] Ullhodturdenweirmudgaardgringnirurdrmolnirfenrirlukkilokkibaugimandodrrerinsurtkrinmgernrackinarockar! Thor's for you! [26]

THEY: "The hundred-lettered name again, last word of perfect language!—But you could come near it yourself, we should think."

SHAUN (*He swigged a slug from his cane*): "Peace! Peace! You missed my drift. What I mean is, every damned letter in it is a copy. It's the last word in plagiarism. And what's more, it's downright lowbrow systematic and schismatic rabblement." (425)

THEY: "Still, in a way, not to flatter you, we fancy that you are so brainy and well read, you could go him one better yourself, if you only would take the time and trouble."

SHAUN: "Undoubtedly. It would be a foul day I could not. I am

[25] Shaun's reason for hating Shem seems peculiar, even mysterious, until we probe deeply into its implication. The "root language" of Shem is filled with thunder echoes of the divine judgment. Shem's words are the hammer of Thor which could destroy the civilization of which Shaun is the representative. Joyce is here following Vico's notion that all language has its origin in man's effort to formulate the meaning of the primal thunderclap. Shem's language threatens to make that meaning clear, and is thus fraught with judgment on Shaunian society. Shaun's fear of Shem's language shows that he, Shaun, very well knows the secret and power of his brother.

[26] The thunder noise is here ascribed directly to the thunder-god Thor. This variant of the word is full of syllables suggesting the monsters that are to go against the gods at the time of Ragnarok: Midgard serpent, Fenris wolf, Surt. And we recognize Molnir, Thor's hammer, and Loki, father of the monsters.

liable to do it any time I like (bet you fippence off my boot allowance). It is an open secret, how ingenious I am at clerking. I'd pencil it as easy as I'd eat a row of beans.—The orthodox book, if given to light, would far exceed that bogus by Guy Fawkes, my Siamese brother. And one of these fine days I may be moved, like Ormuzd,[27] to invent it, mark my words: and it will open your eyes for you—only I would never spend so much trouble on it as he spent. Why? Because I am altogether too good to lower myself to that sort of thing. And I swear to you (426) I will commission to the flames any incendiarist or Ahriman howsoclever, who would endeavor to set any mother of mine on fire."

With that, the big strong man nearly broke down in tears, overpowered by himself with the love of the tearsilver that he twined through her hair, for, sure, he was the soft slob of the world. But he brushed the tear aside, laughed it off with a wipe of his pudgies and a gulp apologetic.—He was in deepest earnest, although his jaw was becoming too sleepy for talking any further. He looked up, up, up, scrutinizing the planets of the heavens to feel out what age he might find. His thumbs fell into his fists, and, losing balance, like a flash of lightning over he careened (oh, the sons of the fathers!) and, as the wisest postlude course he could playact, he collapsed and rolled buoyantly backwards in less than a twinkling via Rattigan's Corner, out of earshot, with his highly curious mode of slipshod motion (427) and by Kill Esther's leaps and falls, in the direction of MacAuliffe's, the medieval torture chest, Open The Door Softly, down in the valley, and before he was really uprighted he spoorlessly vanished, like a popo down a papa, from circular *circulatio*. Amen.

Going, going, gone! [The Shaun image fades out of the dream.]

And the stars were shining. And the earth night strewed aromas. His pipe music crept among the darkness. A reek was waft on the air. He was ours, all fragrance, and we were his for a lifetime. O dulcet dreamings languidous!

---

[27] Ormazd (Ahuramazda), Persian divinity of light, opposed to Ahriman (Angra mainyu), divinity of darkness and evil, as Shaun to Shem.

It was charming! But charming!
And the lamp went out.

[Now a final keen for departed Shaun:]
Well, it is regrettable that thou art passing hence, my brother
able Shaun, ere the morning light calms our hardest throes; from
carnal relations and familiar faces to the inds of Tuskland and
the ousts of Amiracles; more is the pity—you were the walking
saint and the toast of the wake.—Face whose disappearance is regretted, winner of the gamings, choice of the ages, spokesman of
our silences! Well, be mindful of us, poor twelve-o'clock scholars,
while you are out there in Cockpit.—Be coming back to us. We
miss your smile. (428) Our people here in Samoan isle will not
forget you; and the elders, the four of them, will be discussing how
you would be thinking, how the dickens it all began, and how
you would be behaving under such-and-such a circumstance.—Ireland calls you. Turn your coat and tarry among us, only once
more. May the best of all things come your way.—Well do we
know you were loath to leave us, blowing your horn, right royal
post; but sure, pulse of our slumber, you will ship across the Moy-
land Sea and round up in your own escapology some canonizator's
day or other, like the good man you are, and from that till this in
any case, may the tussocks grow quickly under your tramp-thickets
and the daisies trip lightly over your battercrops.

Book III, Chapter 2: Jaun before St. Bride's

[This amusing and easy-to-read chapter opens several miles along
the road, with Shaun, now under the name of Jaun, halted to fetch
breath and loosen his brogues. We find him leaning against an
ancient pillar-stone reminiscent of his long-remembered father. Almost immediately he encounters the twenty-nine little girls of St.
Bride's Academy. Greeting them with a few remarks anent their
personal appearances, he proceeds to deliver a queerly trite and
long-winded sermon, advising them to be careful, to look out for

fancy men, to keep early hours, to exercise without brazenness, to watch out for furnished lodgers, college boys, etc., to read our standard press, and to go when the gong for marriage rings. Then he speaks sentimentally of his proposed departure over sea. Far away he would think, with deepest love, of her, the leap-year girl Iseult.

[There follows a Swiftian courting interlude, while Jaun, gazing upward, sings from his music book. The uninspired sermon concludes with a warning that the finis of our times is almost at hand.]

(429) Having finished the first leg of his night stride, Jaunty Jaun next halted to fetch a breath and to loosen his brogues at the weir by Lazer's Walk. He was amply altered for the brighter, though still the graven image of his squarer self, perspiring but happy, his foot still asleep on him. And he was propped up against a butter-blond warder of the peace, one Constable Sigurdsen,[1] who, buried upright like the Osbornes, had tumbled to sleep at night duty, equilebriated amid the embracings of a monopolized bottle.

(430) Now there were twenty-nine hedge daughters out of Blessed St. Bride's national nightschool (for they seemed to remember, it was still a leap year) learning their antemeridian lesson of life, beseated under the tree beside a pond, attracted to the sight of the pillar-stone. They paddled away with their fifty-eight little feet, all barely in their teens, though repelled by the snores of the intoxicated sleeper, who looked stuck in the sod, murmuring in his native Dutch: "Dotter dead bedstead my diggy smuggy flasky."

Jaun (after he had doffed his hat and bowed to that chorus of good-willed girls, all making a tremendous girlyfuss over him, their *jeune premier*—all but that one, Finfria's fairest—he was just

[1] Jaun is leaning against an ancient pillar-stone, a petrification of HCE in the opposed roles of policeman and drunk (63–4, 67). The name Sigurdsen unites the policeman (Lally) and HCE's man of all work (Knut, Behan, Joe): Knut is called Saunderson (221), Sockerson (370), Soakerson (566); the constable, Sistersen (186), Seckesign (530), Seekersenn (586). Behan caught HCE at the gate, Lally testified against him.

the killingest lady-killer) (431) next went on to drop a few remarks anent their personal appearances, asking this one had she read her Irish legends, gently reproving that one because the ham of her hom could be seen below her hem, whispering to another that the hook of her hum was open at her back. For Jaun was becoming the most purely human being that ever was called man, in love with everything and everyone. Jaun, after those few preliminaries, made out through his love look the apparition of his fond sister Izzy. He knew her by her way of blushing, nor could he forget that he was her brother, besides her godfather, and he thought the world of her.

Prelude to Jaun's sermon:

"Sister dearest," Jaun delivered himself with express cordiality, as he began to take leave of his little school, "we honestly believe you sorely will miss us when we go to discharge our duty; for it is about time for us to shove off on our long last journey.—This is all in accord with your teachings, Sis, in which we were raised; your old-world tales of home-spinning and daddyho, these tales which captured our heart, narrated by you to perfection; you, our pet pupil and mainstay of our house, when we two boys were tossing ourselves in bed, (432) striving to share our hard suite of affections with thee."

Introduction to Jaun's sermon:

"I rise, O fair assemblage, after this introit of exordium.—I was asking advice on the strict T.T. from father Mike, P.P. (by the by, he was telling how he had been conferring, *tête-à-tête,* with two viragoes intactas about what an awful life he led, and what a lawful day it was for a consommation with an effusion, and how he'd marry any old time). I am giving youth now his advice, in his own inspired words. Settle down and listen! Follow me close! Now: During our brief absence adhere to as many as probable of the Ten Commandments.—Where are we? What's the first hymn to be sung? Several Sundays after Whitsuntide. I'll sack that sick server the minute I bless him! I've all the saints in the calendar to

choose from. (433) Here she is: Isabel, virgin, white.[2] *Oremus!*
Words taken, my dearly beloved, from the pen of the Penman."

Body of Jaun's sermon:

"Never miss Mass. Never eat pork on Good Friday. Never let a
hog of Howth trample under foot your linen of Killarney. . . .
Never lose your heart away till you win your diamond back.
Never sing risqué songs at commercial travelers' smokers. (By
the way, is it you has been biting all these biscuits?) First thou
shalt not smile. Twice thou shalt not love. Lust, thou shalt not
commix idolatry. Never park your brief stays in the men's con-
venience. . . . Especially beware (434) please of being at a party
to any demoralizing home life. . . . Leg-before-Wicked lags-be-
hind-Wall where here Mr. Wicker whacked a great fall. . . . Put
your swell foot foremost. . . . Never lay bare your breast secret to
joy a Jonas in the Dolphin's Barn car. . . . But now reappears
Autist Algy, the pulcherman, stated to be well (435) known in
and near the city of Buellas Arias, taking you to the playhouse to
see the *Smirching of Venus* [3] and asking, in a very low, bearded
voice, with a nice little manner and a very nice little way, won't
you be an artist's model and pose in the nude before four old masters and the usual dozen cameramen. . . . Stick wicks in your ear-
shells when you hear the prompter's voice. . . . Keep early hours
and the worm is yours. . . . Tobacco's taboo and toboggan's a
back seat. . . . Don't acquire a penchant for that habit of frequenting and chumming together with the couples of Mr. Tunnelly's
hallways, with the end to commit acts of (436) indecency under
the curfew act. . . . Disinfected and legal love is desirable, but beware of the taverns and hall doorways.—When parties get tight
for each other, they lose all respect together. You'll pay for each
Saturday night each Sunday morning. We won't meet in heaven

[2] Shaun is in the role, for a moment, of a priest preparing to say Mass.
He is looking up the instructions for this particular Sunday: what saint's
day it is, what color vestments are to be worn, what prayers are to be
read, what hymns sung, etc. Then, suddenly, we find him in the pulpit,
about to begin his sermon.

[3] *The Merchant of Venice.*

till you give the Kells Fire Club the go-by. If you've a notion to raise Cain I'll spank you soundly. (437) Don't go ridewheeling with your heels up on the handle bars. But if you need a little moving about, go onto the dirt track and skip. Good health is worth more than the perfumes of Punt. Eat well. And watch out for furnished lodgers, college boys, etc.—the too friendly friend sort, who makes himself so at home and spanks the ivory that lovely: for he may prove your undoing should you, while Jaun is from home, get used to basking in his lover's lap. (438) Suppose the camera caught you! becoming guilty of unladylike intoxication with a prominent married member of the vice-reeking squad, and in consequence of the subpoenas being embarrassed by becoming a detested company-keeper of the demimonde of Lucan's night-life.—Once for all, I'll have no college swankies (439) trespassing on your danger zone in the dancer years. If ever I catch you at it, I'll give it to you hot, high, and heavy."

[Jaun pauses a moment to test and celebrate his singing voice, then continues:] "Dear sister, take a brotherly advice: don't commit yourself if they tingle you, either say nothing or nod. Be vacillant over those vigilant who would like you to believe black on white.—And I'll burn the books that grieve you. Read, instead, our standard press. (440) The very latest, the Good Catholic books approved by our bishops. Sifted science will do your arts good!—Perform little works of mercy. Guard your treasure. (441) And when the gong rings for marriage, go. Eat all the lard you care for; meat on Ember days, remember, is allowed to workers and their families.—Guard that gem, Sissy, there's nothing to touch it. Let me catch any scoundrel making improper advances!" Jaun clenches his manly fists. (442) "He's a marked man from that hour. I don't care a tinker's dam who the mucky is, it will be a poor lookout for that insister. Because we'll damn well show him what the Shaun way is; we'll go a long way toward breaking that outsider's face for him for making up to you. We'll reduce him to a pulp. (443) And after that, I'll probably turn him over to the police; and what do you bet I mightn't even wipe the street up with him, pending my bringing proceedings before a bunch of magistrates and twelve good gleeful men. He'll have something then to think about. I'll contrive to half kill your Charley-you're-my-darling for you and send him to his maker—particularly should he turn out to be a man in brown about town, of about fifty-six or so, with a toothbrush mustache and jaw crockeries and of course no beard, sipping some Wheatley's on a bar stool, with a good job and pension in Guinness's, bluey-green eyes—a bit scummy—developing a series of (444) angry boils, seeking relief in alcohol. I hereby admonish you.[4] And lest there be any misconception as to whom to fasten the marriage knot on, when the little baby's squalling in the cradle what the dirty old bigger'll be squealing through his coffin, you better keep the gunbarrel straight as I recommend you to, or I'll be all over you myself for knocking my name, yourself, and your babybag, down at a sacrifice to a third-rate cowhandler. The pleasures of love last but a fleeting, but the pledges of life outlusts a lifetime. If I catch you in any nonsense, I'm the one will know how to discipline you. You'll go no more with Wolf the Ganger. (445) If you two go to walk upon the railway, I'll goad to beat behind the bush. I'll lash you to ribbons. I'll spank you till you cry for pardon. For 'tis I that have the pair of arms that carry the wallop.

"Unbeknownst to you, I would return o'er sea.—Far away, I shall think, with deepest love, of thee. Our poet, Fred Wetherly, puts it better.—You fill a big corner in my heart.—Earwicker's my breed, so may we (446) multiply like the sands. I want you. If I've proved myself a man of honor let me see your isabellis. How I shall cover you with kisses if I survive. I will be come come coming, when, like massive mountains to part no more, you will kiss me back; and that great moment of return is bound to be.

"Come slum with me. We shall render social service, completing our union by adopting fosterlings. We'll circumcivicize all Dublin County. (447) Meliorism in mass quantities.—Write me your essays, my scholars, on morti-natality in the life of jewries and the sludge of King Haarington's at its height, running boulevards over

[4] Watch out particularly for HCE.

275

the whole of it. I'd write it all myself if only I had my pen. Bear in mind all the fine public works carried out by our priest-mayor-king-merchant. Compare them with public works elsewhere. Contrast the Citizen with the Pagan. Explain why there is such a number of orders of religion in Asia. Where is the greenest island off the coast of Spain?—Ascertain the facts for yourself by embarking on a field trip. Take the tram and stand on, say, Aston's, along with a copy of the Seeds and Weeds Act (448) and take a good long gaze into any shop window, and in the course of about thirty-two minutes' time turn on your heels toward the previous causeway, and you will be astonished to see how you will be, meanwhile, coated with cakes of slush occasioned by the traffic jam. Therefore one may well ask: Where's the housedrudge and cleaner, Kate? When will the face of our so muck-loved Dublin get its well-belavered white, like Liverpool and Manchester? Who'll fix up all these Irish places?—Do you know what, little girlies? I am advised by the snoring vote-seeker to quit for good and all, until provision is made, under privy sealed orders, to get me an increase of automobile oil and footwear and money for a cure at Bad Anywhere (though where it's going to come from this time—), as I certainly think that that's about the bloody boundary limit." [5]

Courting interlude:

"Sis dearest," Jaun added, with voice-noise somewhat murky, as he turned his back on her and opened his book to give note and (449) score, while his uncertain eye, cast upward, followed an imaginary swallow, "oh, vanity of Vanessy! Personally, I'm in no violent hurry. Haste makes waste.—I'll hunt with any of them; but I'd turn back, as lief as not, if I could only find the girl of my heart's appointment, the One True Catholic and Apostolic, my Lady of Lyons,[6] to guide me by gastronomy under her safe con-

---

[5] Jaun complains that the voters are weary of him and want him to retire on a pension. But where the money is to come from, this time, he does not know.

[6] Lyons: a British restaurant chain; i.e., "If I could only find a nice Catholic girl with a job in a restaurant." (Cf. Stuart Gilbert's careful analysis of

duct. That's more in my line.—I'd ask nothing kinder of fate than to stay where I am, with my tinny of brownie's tea, under the protection of St. James Hanway [7] and with Jacob Pershawm for my incense-bearer, and with Peter Rock, that friend of my bosom; leaning on my elbows out here in the Park, among pheasants, my ears and hair standing up like those of a frightened rabbit, till well into the bosom of the night, picking fireflies out of the hedges and catching misty dew on the tip of my tongue. I could wait patiently until the moment of lawful wedlock, finding meanwhile nice things to do: listening to the birdcalls and cracking jokes with the frogs until dawn; and then, leaving my picnic litter behind me,[8] I'd follow through my upturned telescope the rugby-ball lullaby moon rolling herself to sleep in the west: I'd await the sunrise— the golden egg laid for me by my nocturnal goosemother (450) down under in the shy orient. And what wouldn't I give to share a feast of fishing flies with the finny ones, I racing down the swansway, leaps ahead of the eels, carp, and perch; or, when I prefer to be alone, I should recline against my stone, my pipe in my face,[9] match in my cupped hands, and the aroma of my beloved Turkish smoking tobacco in my nostrils, with the perfume of the jasmines and the odors of the great tree about me, fishing.— I'd teach my twenty-nine little birds to pipe pleasant airs: do, re, mi, fa, sol, la, si, do, till the woods re-echoed. Do, mi, re, do! [10]— I may not be able to sing the more difficult passages but you'll never catch me off key. I'm at home singing 'The Lily of Killar-

this courting passage in *Our exagmination round his factification for incamination of Work in Progress,* London, n.d., pp. 64–67. The following passage in our text has drawn heavily on Mr. Gilbert's resourceful elucidation.)

[7] James Hanway (1712–86): first man to carry an umbrella in London. Was stoned ("lapidated") by pedestrians.

[8] Compare the midden heap of p. 110, etc.

[9] G, B, and D are the "pipe notes" of the scale. The space notes are F, A, C, and E. Cf. again the article by Stuart Gilbert cited in footnote 6, *supra.*

[10] These notes of the scale are represented in the text by a punning translation: Do—I give; re—a king; mi—to me; fa—she does; sol—alone; la—up there; sì—yes, see; do—I give.

ney.'—But enough of greenwood gossip. Business is business. (451)
I'll bet you, if I wanted to I'm the one could make easy money on
investments. I'm the go-getter that'd make it pay. I tell you, the
best football line in the country wouldn't hold me. By the old
Salmon of River Liffey, ye god of little fishies, nothing would stop
me. Yep. How's that for scats, *mein Schatz?*" [Jaun is now urging
his sister Isabel (Iseult) to sing, higher and higher.] "Be bold! It's
only natural to funk; it's daring fear that is divine. Up you go—
high, higher, highest.—I'd certainly spoil you altogether if you were
my bride; I'd plant you in the lap of lechery, having run my shoe-
string into near a million or so.—Only I'd be awful anxious about
rain (452) and drafts in the morning [Jaun is catching cold; he
says 'borting' instead of 'morning'] that might be detrimental to
my lyrical health, and that's the truth—for I could never tell a lie
—hachoo [a sneeze]!

"Sissibis dearest, as I was reading to myself not very long ago
in Tennyson's 'Morte D'Arthur,' seated upon my three-legged
stool (tripos) preparing for my final honors exam at Cambridge
(tripos), thinking how long I'd like myself to be continuing here,
snapping pictures, dreaming, listening to phonograph and radio—
'tis transported with grief I am this night sublime, moved to go
forth from our no-story house upon this benedictine errand, the
most glorious mission recorded in the annals of our efferfresh-
painted Liffey. The Vico road goes round and round to meet where
terms begin. Still on-appealed to by the cycles and unappalled by
the recoursers, we feel all serene as regards our dutiful task. I am
proud, for 'tis a grand thing to be going to meet a king, not an
everynight king, but the overking of Erin himself.—Before there
was a patch at all on Ireland, there lived a lord at Lucan. And I
have complete confidence in the newly wet fellow that's bound to
follow. Tell mother that. 'Twill amuse her."

Conclusion of Jaun's sermon:
"Well, to the dickens with the whole business, I'm beginning to
get sunsick. I'm not half Norwegian for nothing. Freezing time is
due. The finis (453) of our times is not so far off as you might
wish.—And I don't want you to be fighting duels over me, as you

278

gulp down stout and mackerel in a sewing circle, turning break-
fasts into last suppers—steaming the damp ossicles [malleus, incus,
stapes] of your ears, praying to Jaun while Ole Clo goes through
the wood with his dog, toting in the chestnut burrs for Goodboy
Sommers, and Mr. Blownose hugs his kindlings (when, as a matter of fact, it's my gala benefit), robbing leaves out of my tabloid
book. May my tongue fester if I have ever seen such a miry lot of
weepers! Let it just be a plain chair by the fire for absent Shaun
the Post, and I'll make ye all an eastern hemisphere of myself the
moment you name the way. *Sursum-corda's* [11] all round, while I
stray, and let ye not be getting grief out of it.—Lo, improving ages
wait ye in the orchard of the bones. Sometime, very presently now,
the odds are we shall all be hooked and happy, communionisti-
cally, among the elysian fields of the elect in the land of lost time.
Lay up treasures for yourself in heaven! So drink it up, ladies,
fasting time is by. (454) We must now part. Parting's fun. Good-by,
sweetheart, good-by. Sure, my treasures, a letterman does be often
thought reading the between-lines that do have no sense at all. I
sign myself, Inflexibly yours, Ann Posht the Shorn.—To be continued."

Postlude to Jaun's sermon:

Something funny must have occurred to Jaunathaun, for he
emitted a great big laugh at the thought of how they'd like to be
rolling his hoop and they were all just on the point of laughing
too, when suddenly he wheeled right round sternly to see what
was loose. So they stood still and wondered. After which he pon-
dered; and finally he replied:

"There is something more: it's prayers that count; prayers in the
suburbs of the heavenly gardens, once we shall have passed through
to our snug eternal reward. Shunt us! Shunt us! Shunt us! [12] If
you want to be felixed come and be parked. No petty family squab-

[11] *Sursum corda:* Let us lift up our hearts. A versicle in the Mass. Shaun
is beginning to play up, sentimentally, the theme of his departure. They
are not to weep or quarrel over his memory. He represents himself as a
Christ figure making ready to go forth upon his father's business.
[12] Sanctus contaminated with Shanti.

bles Up There. (455) You will hardly recognize the old wife in the new bustle and the former sinner in his latter-day paint. You take Joe Hanny's tip for it!—To borrow and to burrow and to barrow! That's our *c*rass, *h*airy, and *e*vergreen life, till one final howdiedow Bouncer Naster raps on the bell with a bone and his stinkers stank behind him with the scepter and the hourglass. We come, touch, and go, from atoms and ifs, but we're presurely destined to be odds without ends. . . . What a humpty-dump seems our miserable earth here today, as compared beside the Here-we-are-again Gaieties of the Afterpiece, when the Royal Revolver of this world lets fire for the pandemon to end and the Harlequinade to begin, properly SPQueaRking.[13] Mark Time's Finish Joke. Putting Allspace in a Notshall.

"Well, but give me good home cooking every time! But I feel twice as tired as I felt before, when I'm after eating a few natives. Give us another cup of your scald. That was damn good (456) scald. I enjoyed your luncheon fine. Tenderest bully ever I ate, with the boiled protestants,[14] only the peas were a bit too salty. And give me Cincinnati's cabbage with Italian cheese, and save that olive oil for thy summer day. No soup, thanks. But I'll try yon gray fur coat. Next I'll try a duck with cauliflower. Mass and meat mar no man's day. *Ite, missa est.*[15]—All the vitamins are beginning to sozzle in chewn—fudge, steak, peas, bacon, rices, onions, duckling, and xoxxoxo and xooxox xxoxoxxoxxx [16]— and soon I'll

[13] S.P.Q.R.: *Senatus Populusque Romanus* ("the senate and people of Rome"); also, small profits, quick returns. Cf. p. 229.

[14] During the year of the potato blight (1846), converts to Protestantism were fed potato soup; Protestants are called, therefore, "soupers," and potatoes, "protestants."

[15] "Go, the mass is ended." Words announcing conclusion of Mass. Behind all the references to oil, wine, and vestments Joyce has been converting Shaun's sermon into a kind of celebration of the mass. Shaun has also been consuming various Protestant sects, masticating them with great pleasure. Shaun's gormandizing is connected with the themes of the Wake and the Eucharist.

[16] The fudge, etc., thought of as broken by the masticating teeth, are spelled "kates," "eaps," etc. Thoroughly masticated, the foods appear as

be off on my letterman's rounds again. My next problem: how to collect postage from Thaddeus Kelly, Esq., for undesirable printed matter. But I know what I'll do; I'll knock it out of him. (457) Blackmail him I will, in arrears, or my name's not penitent Ferdinand.

"Well, here's looking at ye! If I never leave you biddies, I'll be tempted to become a Passionate Father. My hunger's weighed. My anger's suaged. Sit tight, little lay mothers, till the grim reaper draws nigh, as a blessing in disguise. Devil I care if any Claude Lightfoot [17] was to hold me up, I'd let him have my pair of galloper's heels in the belly. Console yourself, dearest, there's a refund coming to you out of me, so mind you do your duty on me. You'll miss me more as the weeks wing by. . . ."

Iseult's reply:

She whispers her reply, flushing, but flashing from her dove-and-dart eyes: "Yes, pet, we were so happy; I knew something would happen. I understand. But listen, draw near, dearest. I want to whisper my wish. I'm ashamed over this last-minute gift of memento note paper,[18] which is all I call my own, but accept this wee widow's mite (458) torn here by my hands. X.X.X.X. It was blessed for young Father Michael, my pet parish priest, by your friend the Pope. And listen, bear it with you from morn till life's end; and when you use it think of me, not of Sister Maggy. And be sure you don't catch cold and pass it on to us. And this, a sprig of blue, so you'll remember your Veronica.[19] Of course, please to write, and leave your little bag of doubts behind you, and send the message back by pigeon's breath [spirit of the Holy Ghost] in case

xoxxoxo and xooxox xxoxoxxoxxx. If the x's here are consonants and the o's vowels, these hardly identifiable last items are probably "cabbage" and "boiled protestants."

[17] Hero of one of Father Finn's books for boys.

[18] Iseult gives Shaun a box of writing paper as a parting gift, with the plea that he write to her.

[19] Under the sentimental clownery of this scene appears very dimly the figure of Christ on his *via crucis*. Shaun has spoken of and actually eaten his Last Supper; his way is lined with women whom he exhorts not to weep, among them Veronica.

I couldn't think who it was. I will tie a knot to remind me to write you on my best paper; and don't trouble to answer unless by special, as I am collecting his pay [20] and want for nothing, so I can live solely for my beautiful curls.—I will practice oval oh's and artless ah's before my mirror. (459) And I will say my rosary for you to the Almighty, with nurse Madge, my looking-glass girl.[21] You'll love her coarse clothes and black stockings. Simply killing. I call her Sosy because she's society for me. But she's nice for enticing my friends. She breaks in my shoes for me when I've arch trouble. She's terribly nice.—And I'll be true to you in my own way; I will long long to betrue you along with one who will so betrue you that not once will I betreu him not once will he be betray himself.—Can't you understand? Oh, bother, I must tell the truth! My latest lad's love letter, I'm sure I done something with. I like him lots cause he never cusses. Pity *bonhomme*. Pippet. I shouldn't say he's pretty, but I'm cocksure he's shy. He fell for my lips, my lewd speaker; I felt for his strength.[22]—Dear professor, you can trust me, though I change my name; never will I give your lovely face of mine away to my second mate. (460) So don't keep me in misery, or I'll murder you, but meet me by next appointment near The Ship, at Mountjoy Square. Sweet pig, he'll be furious.—The Dargle will run dry sooner than I'll forget you. I will write down all your names in my gold pen and ink. While memory's leaves are falling I will dream (but don't tell him, or I'll be the death of him) under the trees and 'twill carry on my hertzian heart-waves to thee, beyond the Bosporus. Here I'll wait for thee all the time you're away. (461) I'll bury my cheeks in

[20] This seems to say that her divorce from Glugg is yielding alimony.

[21] Iseult and her looking-glass reflection suggest the Two Temptresses and also Iseult and Kate, the maid. The paragraph emphasizes differences between upper and lower class pronunciation, which together with other hints indicate that Iseult is High Church and the maid Roman Catholic. Shaun being Christ has left these in his wake.

[22] The ecclesiastical allegory continues in Iseult's promises that though she may take up with other lovers she will remain basically faithful to her Shaun. Overtones of the Stella and Dean Swift relationship are strongly sounded.

vanishing cream and buy myself some flowers for your return. Always, about this hour, I steal secretly away with my tall Russian, Pinchapoppapoff, who is going to be a general: but last thing at night, after my golden wedding in my upstairs room, I just want to see will he, or are all Michaels like that; I'll strip before his fond stare and poke stiff under my ironbound bed with my chinese chambermate for the night's foreign males, and your name of Shane will come forth between my lips, when I next open my eyes just awakened by his toccatootletoo.[23] So now, seated with Mag at the organ, we are going to say one little prayer before going to bed. Coach me how to tumble, Jaime, and listen, with supreme regards, Juan, in haste, warn me which to ah ah ah . . ."

". . . MEN," Jaun responded, with his chaliced drink now well in hand.

Jaun's last words:

"Ever gloriously kind! And I truly am (462) eucharized to you. Well, ladies and gentlemen, a toast and a song to Erin go Dry. Weep not, Esterelles, though Jonathan be in his fail! To stir up love's young fizz, I tilt with this bride's-cup, this stirrup-cup champagne [the sacramental wine], and while my teeth are nipping her bubbles, I swear I ne'er will prove I'm untrue to your liking.

"So good-by, my poor Isley! I'm leaving my proxy behind for your consolation, lost Dave the Dancekerl. He will arrive incessantly in the fraction of a crust [the bread]. He's the mightiest penumbrella I ever flourished, beyond the shadow of a doubt! [24]— But soft, I tremble. Behold the man. The return of the Paraclete. I knew I smelt the garlic leek.[25] Why, bless my swits, here he is, darling Dave,[26] like the cat-o'-nine-lives, just in time, as if he fell

[23] Iseult, as the Faith Christ left behind him, is going to be generous with her ecclesiastical favors to wooers of all denominations. High Church, Low Church, Latin, Greek, and Russian—she will embrace them all in His name.
[24] Shaun as Christ at the Last Supper (drinking wine and breaking bread); Shem as the Paraclete who is to follow.
[25] Garlic is a symbol of immortality.
[26] Dave the Dancekerl is cognate with the Holy Ghost, the Paraclete; Shem is the Dervish Dancer made ecstatic by the fire of Pure Spirit.

out of space, all draped in mufti, coming home to our mountains on quinquasecular cycles,[27] after his French evolution,[28] (463) blushing like Pat's pig.—He's not ashamed to ca.ry in his left hand the testimonials he gave his twenty years for.[29] He's my altar's ego in miniature, as usual a Romeo as I am, forever cracking quips on himself, merry, he'll soon bring the rosy blushes mid dewy tears to any living girl's laughing cheeks. He has novel ideas and he's a jarry queer fish betimes, but I'm enormously full of that foreigner. Got by the one goat, suckled by the same nanna, one twitch, one nature, makes us old-world kin. I hate him for his patent henesy [heresy] but I love his old rum-blossom nose. Isn't he after borrowing all before him? He is looking aged and thin; he's been slandering himself, but I pass no remark. Hope he hasn't the cholera. Sure there's nobody to hold a candle to him for sheer dare. Dave (464) knows I've the highest respect for that intellectual debtor. And we're the closest of chums. Ho, by the old snakes, someone has shaved his skull for him. He took off his hat to let the fans behind him see me proper. He's very thoughtful that way when he isn't drunk. Hold hard till you hear him clicking his bull's bones. [Jaun turns to welcome Dave the Dancekerl:] You're welcome back. Put your hat on. Give us your hand. How are things? I'm proud of you. (465) You've surpassed yourself. [Jaun introduces him to Julia Bride:[30]] Be introduced to my aunt, Julia Bride, dying to have you languish in her bosky dell. Don't you recognize him? Come on, spinster, do your stuff. Don't be shy, man. She has plenty of room for both of us, push. Have a good time. Embrace her at my frank incentive and tell her how I do be asking for her. Let us be holy and evil, and let her be peace on

[27] Cf. Quinquagesima Sunday.
[28] This refers to Shrove Tuesday, the day before the beginning of Lent. "French evolution": it has been transformed into Mardi gras, a day of wild festivity.
[29] A reference to the twenty years of St. Patrick's novitiate. His role is here identified with that of the Holy Spirit.
[30] St. Patrick is being introduced to Ireland, the Holy Ghost to the Church.

the bough. Sure, she fell in line with your tripartite photos,[31] when we were stablehands together. Always raving how we had the wrinkles of a snail-charmer. Take her; I'd give three shillings to shadow you kissing her from me liberally as if she was a crucifix. You'll be a perfect match. (466) Why, they might be Babau and Momie! Give us a pin for her and we'll call it a tossup. Can you reverse positions? Put me down for all ringside seats. I can feel you being corrupted. Recoil. I can see you sprouting scruples. Get back.—My hero, if you want to win a woman, shuck her all she wants. Could you wheedle a little encore out of your harp, hey? He's so sedulous to sing always, if prompted. And I'll string second to harmonize. With your dumpsey diddely dumpsey die, fiddely fa.[32] Or, let's scrap and then be chummy.—Begob, there's not so much green in his Ireland's eye! But he could be near a colonel with a voice like that. (467) The misery billyboots I used to lend him before we split.[33] But I told him make your will be done and go to a general and I'd pray confessions for him. Did you note that worried expression in his low voice? And did you hear the rattle-making when he was preaching to himself? And do you twig the wilted shamrock on his dirty shirt? My old father's uncle

[31] Tripartite Life of St. Patrick; doctrine of the Trinity; triple crown of the Pope.

[32] A brief pass at the diverse attitudes of Roman and Protestant churches as regards singing. The congregational singing of the Protestant faiths is contrasted with the chanting of the Roman clergy and choir.

[33] This matter of the borrowed boots reminds us of the relationship between Stephen Dedalus and Buck Mulligan in *Ulysses*. Mulligan is coarsely parodying Christ's priest; Stephen is brooding on the heresy of Joachim of Floris, according to whom the present age of Christ's church is to be superseded by an idyllic period when the Holy Ghost will dwell immediately in each human heart. Ecclesiastical mediation between Man and God will then have become superfluous.

In Shaun's chapters, as in *Ulysses,* questions of theology are regarded from the standpoint of an unreligious century. In a postrevolutionary, half-atheistical mood, Mulligan-Shaun burlesques the role of Christ, Stephen-Shem the Holy Spirit. The profound symbols of the long-forgotten Patriarchal Age have simply lost their power; even the respect in which they were held during the Age of the Sons has been lost. They are empty shells, lightly kicked around. This is the moment just before the thunderclap of wrath.

who was garroted, Caius Cocoa Codinhand, used to talk that language of his, jap-latin, with my uncle's owlseller, Woolfe Woodenbeard, as brisk as I'd eat mutton chops and lobsters. But it's all Greek to me.[34] Sam knows miles better than me how to work the miracle, and I see he's improving—he's dropping the stammer—since I bonded him off to try and grow a muff and place the ocean between his feet and ours, after he was capped out of Berlitz School for the sin against the past participle, and earned the reputation of cutting chapel and being as gauche as Swift. B.A.A.[35]—'Twas the quadra sent him, and Trinity too. He'll pretty soon hand-tune your ear for you, while I'm far away, writing memoirs (468) of my English hosts and taking my medical examinations.[36] In the beginning was the deed, Faust justly says, for the end is with woman, flesh without word; while the man is in a worse case after intercourse than before, since he has subordinated himself to her biologic concern with the future. Thou art paltry, flippant, and serious, Miss Smith, so fix yourself up pretty: show you shall, and won't he will! His hearing is in doubting, just as my seeing is on believing. So dactylize him up to blankpoint and let him blink for himself where you speak the best ticklish."

From the stress of their thunder and lightning a little one will be born.

"Well, I hear 'tis time to be up and ambling. I've got to go to the toilet. Tempos fidgets. The shack's not big enough for me now. (469) The earth's atrot! The sun's a scream! The air's a jig! The water's great! I'm going. Somewhere I must get far away from Banba shore. I'll travel the wide world over." He suddenly falls and rises again. "I hurt myself neatly that time. Come, my good frogmarchers. We felt the fall, but we'll front the defile. Was not

[34] Mulligan-Shaun (The Christ Shell of the Age of the People) is saying that he had an ancestor who could talk metaphysics with the All-Soul, but it's all Greek to him.

[35] References to Joyce's self-exile, Berlitz School teaching, and apostasy.

[36] References to the activities of Mr. Oliver St. John Gogarty, Joyce's chief model for Mulligan and Shaun.

my old mother a running water? And was not the bold one that quickened her the sea-borne Fingale? All aboard, farewell awhile to her and thee, the brine's my bride to be. Lead on Macadam, and danked be he who first sights Halt Linduff.[37] So long! It's now or never, sis-kinder! Here goes the enemy! One, two, three—you watch my smoke!"

Jaun's departure:

After poor Jaun the Boast's last fireless words, twenty-eight-add-one with a flirt of wings were pouring to his assistance, prepared to cheer him should he leap or to curse him should he fall, but, repulsing all attempts (470) at "first hands on," our greatly misunderstood one gave himself some sort of hermetic prod or kick to sit up and take notice, while the girls voiced approval by dropping knee-deep in tears over their concelebrated midnight sunflower, and clapping together joyously the plaps of their tappyhands, with a cry of genuine distress, they viewed him, the just one, their darling, away.

A dream of favors. They wail. It is psalmodied today; yesterday's song of sorrow answering tomorrow night's wail.

[Their litany resounds:] Oasis, Oisis, Oasis, Oisis, Oasis, Oisis. Tree of marvels! [Shaun is compared here to many kinds of tree.] —Meanwhile, Pipetto, Pipetta has misery unnoticed.

But then the strangest thing happened. Backscuttling for the hopoff Jaun just then I saw to collect from the gentlest weaner among the weiners the familiar yellow label into which he let fall a drop; smothering a curse, he choked a guffaw, spat expectoratiously, and blew his own trumpet. And next thing was, he licked the back and stamped the oval badge of belief to his brow with a genuine dash of piety. He waved a hand-across-the-sea, while the pacifettes waved their arms widdershins; [38] (471) but in righting himself, between Stellas and Vanessas, he toppled, and, making a brand-new start for himself, his hat blew off in a love blast (re-

[37] Macbeth to Macduff. Compare Glugg and Chuff, p. 252.
[38] Circling counterclockwise.

ward for finder!) and Jaun Redhead, bucketing after, made away
at the double (the headless shall have legs!), scurried round with
an easy rush by the bridge beyond Ladycastle, and then away with
him, let off like a grayhound, with a posse of tossing hankerwaves
to his windward and a tempest of good things teeming into the
funnel of his shrimp-net, along the highroad of the nation—following which he was quickly lost to sight. While the ancient pillar-stone muttered, full of woe: "Where maggot Harvey kneeled
till bags? Ate Andrew coos hogdam farvel!"

Farewell to Haun:

May the good people speed you, rural Haun, (472) aye, and
heart in hand of Shamrockshire! May your brawny hair grow rarer
and fairer, our own only white-headed boy! Good by nature and
natural by design, had you but been spared to us, Hauneen lad!
My long farewell I send you. Gone is Haun! Our Joss-el-Jovan!
Our Chris-na-Murty [Krishnamurti]. You who so often consigned
your distributory tidings of great joy into our never-too-late-to-love
box. Thy now paling light lucerne we ne'er may see again. Our
pattern sent! There are a dozen of folks still unclaimed by the
death angel, who will fervently pray that they may never depart
this earth till (473) their hero boy comes marching home on the
crest of the wave. Life will be a blank without you.

But, boy, you did your nine-furlong mile in record time—so too
will our phoenix sunward stride. Aye, already the somberer opaci-
ties of the gloom are vanished. Brave footsore Haun, Work your
Progress.—The silent cock shall crow at last. The west shall shake
the east awake. Walk while ye have the night, for morn morrow-
eth, whereon every past shall full fast sleep. Amain.

Book III, Chapter 3: Yawn under Inquest

[The figure of Shaun, titanic and extensive, brutal, empty, long-
winded, and sentimental, repeats in grotesque parody the patterns
established long ago by the father. Shaun is not creative. He is the

end, not the beginning, of a mighty destiny. He represents the last stage of a vast historical development; his is the period of the fully expanded and exhausted blossom. For all his world-filling bulk. he lacks durability. Whereas HCE was always up again and around. Shaun will quickly fade.

[After the solemnities of the Theocratic Age and the pomp of the Aristocratic, Shaun represents the frank vulgarities of the demagogue (Bk. III, chap. 1). After the pious seed-sowing of the Patriarchs and the gallant love play of the heroic Lords and Ladies, Jaun is simply a Victorian lady-killer bachelor, prurient, prudent, prudish, and didactic (Bk. III, chap. 2). In the present chapter we find him already exhausted, grandly sprawling across a hillock in County Meath, which is the umbilical center of the Green Isle of the World. Known now as Yawn, he has carried into full decline the ageless dynastic line of his fathers.

[The representatives of the People arrive to sit over Yawn in judgment. Their systematic and ruthless inquisition presses through to the very roots of his existence form, discrediting (after the manner of the Democratic Critics) the whole history of his kingly line. This investigation is begun by the Four Old Men. They arrive and squat about the form, then immediately develop a pointed series of questions (474–77). First they ask concerning the relationship of Yawn to the old criminal of the past (477–82). Next they wish to explore the problem of his relationship to Shem the Penman (482–91). When they have completed these preliminary studies of his personal connections, the figure of Yawn slightly disintegrates, and from a deeper level of his being the voice of ALP breaks forth, to betray the whole scandal of the incident in the Park (491–96). During a feverish attempt on the part of the Four to obtain clearer information concerning the Wake, the figure of Yawn disintegrates still further—practically disappears. From within the earth itself, on which he has been resting, resound cries of hunt and battle. The investigation suddenly breaks through to a strange zone of primeval existence (496–501).

[After a great moment of silence, a witness utters a straightforward statement about that day-night where the first couple met, the midden, the flagstone, the ashtree, the thunder, the incident in the Park, the ball at the Tailors' Hall, and the funeral games (501–19). But then the witness himself "confusticates" this story with a second account which he claims to have received from Tarpey, one of the Four Old Men. He is forced to recant his first and swear to the second statement (519–22). When he becomes confused, a bone somewhere suddenly slips into place and strange yet familiar voices issue from his presence, whereupon the inquest reaches a third stage (522–28). An efficient young group of Brain Trusters take over the cross-examination to summon forth, with gratifying success, first Kate (530–32), then HCE himself (532–50). The great man obliges with a long and complete statement of his majestic history.]

(474) A wail went forth. Pure Yawn lay low, on the mead of a hillock, dormant. His dream monologue was over, his drama parapolylogical was yet to be. Yawn in a semiswoon lay awailing.

Hearing that churring call, the four senators came to where he lay. They came from their four directions, (475) afraid to wonder what sort of crossword puzzle he might be. There were ells on ells of him. They climbed the hillside in order: Matthew Gregory, Mark Lyons, Luke Tarpey, Johnny MacDougal—and the Ass (476).

The leader stopped, lifting a hand for silence. Who lay before them but Yawn, all asprawl amongst the poppies, asleep!

The four of them squatted about him, watching for the issuance of his soul through any one of the orifices of his body, and whispering to each other.

(477) "Is he drunk?" they asked. "Is he rehearsing someone's funeral?"

And as they were spreading abroad their nets, there was one word of agreement among them: "Let's get going."

For it was in the back of their minds how they would be spreading their nets to mesh his issuing fish breath; while, as hour gave wav to hour, Yawn himself was keeping time with his trip-tongue, mouth open, the way dew and moon mist would be melting into his mouth.

Inquest. Stage I: Words of Yawn himself

"Why?" asks one of the squatting four.

"It was before your day," replies a voice from within the prostrate presence.

"I see," assents the questioner. "But after what space of time did it happen? Was it in the land of lion's odor?"

One of the questioners reassures him: "We are friends! First, if you don't mind, name your historical antecedents."

"The orangery," the voice replies. "This same prehistoric barrow.[1] (478) In this barrow are letters sent by Thunder for my darling, Typette."

Another inquisitor changes the subject. "To come nearer home," says he, "I am told by our donkey-interpreter here, that though there are 606 words in your national vocabulary describing secular kingship, you have not a single vocable for spiritual majesty and no clue of a road leading to salvation. Is that the case?"

"How?" replies the voice, and continues in French. "That may well be. Nevertheless, I have found the clover-key in the fields."[2]

Asked who he is, the voice replies: "Trinathan partnick dieudonnay."[3] And having given this name, the voice asks: "Have you seen her? Typette, my tactile O!"

They demand to know whether he is now in his father rick [the "peatrick" of page 3; Old Ireland; Abraham's Bosom], and whether he is cold. "I know that place better than anyone," one

[1] Midden dump with letter and orange peels, p. 110.

[2] The German for "clover" is *Klee; clé* in French is "key." St. Patrick converted Ireland to belief in the Trinity by exhibiting a shamrock which he had plucked in a field. Yawn's claim to being Patrick and the representative of the one true church is developed in the following pages.

[3] Trinathan: triune Jonathan. Partnick: Patrick part Nick. Dieudonnay: given by God.

of the questioners interrupts. "Sure, (479) I used to be over there frequently at my grandmother's place in Tir na n-Og [the Celtic land of eternal youth; paradise; Ireland itself as the land of dream], when the hounds were giving tongue. I never knew how rich I was, strolling and strolling, carrying my interpreter, the Ass with the unpronounceable tail, along the shore. Do you know my cousin, Mr. Jasper Dougal, who keeps a tavern?"

"Deed I do," Yawn replies. [But the question has touched a sore spot. The tavernkeeper is his father. He suddenly senses, behind the inquisition, an unfriendly purpose. He becomes afraid.] "But what are you bothering me for?" he whines. He pleads: "Do not throw me to the wolves!"

"One moment!" [The old man is going to press his question.] "Birds have informed us as to the where, how, and when of the burial of the carcass, the bad whisky of the dump, and the committal of nuisance. It would be interesting to send a cormorant around this blue lagoon just to see what he would learn. [I.e., There has been a heinous crime committed in this neighborhood and all the evidence is not yet in, but we think we know what will happen to your Old Man's reputation should we find it!] You told my learned friend, a moment since, about this barrow. I now suggest to you that long before that barrow there was a boat, a burial boat, the *Pourquoi Pas* bound for Weissduwasland, our ship that ne'er returned; the orange-boat. What can you tell us about it?"

"Consider the runes and barrows," comes the evasive answer. "Each must away when he hears the go-horn, S.O.S. Why not? (480) The Norse slaver's raven flag was out. Crouch low, you pigeons three! Say, call that girl with the tan dress on! Call Wolfhound! Wolf of the sea!"

"Very good now. That tallies with the Ass's story. I want to go further with this problem of the parent ship, weather permitting, and discuss its departure from a certain port far away from these green hills. Well then, to come to the question of the Midnight Middy on his Levantine sea: From Daneland sailed the ox-eyed man. Now mark well what I say."

"Big Spadebeard, perfidious Welshman: a destroyer in our port. He signed to me with his bailing scoop; laid bare his breast paps to suckle me. *Ecce Hagios Chrisman!*" [I.e., He is not my true father, but my foster parent. He took me to his bosom when he arrived here in our port. I have no part in his guilt.]

"*Hootchcopper's enkel!*"

"Who is he? Who is this lad?"

"*Hunkalus Childared Easterheld.* It's his lost chance, Emania. Ware him well."[4]

"Did you dream you were eating your own tripe, acushla, that you tied yourself up that wrynecky fix?"[5]

"I see now. We have broken through to the beast cycles. You took the words right out of my mouth. A child's dread for a dragon vicefather! *Hillcloud encompass us!* You mean you suckled like a wolf-cub and learned to howl yourself wolfwise? Do your best to recall."

"The cubs are after me. The whole pack."

"Saints and gospels! The old animal runs again! Find the fingall harriers."

"What? Wolfgang?[6] Whoah! Talk very slow."

(481) "*Hail him heathen, heal him holystone!
Courser, Recourser, Changechild? . . .
Eld as endall, earth? . . .*"[7]

[4] Cf. p. 379. Echoes of an American Negro song, "Titanic": "It's your last trip, Titanic, fare thee well." "Emania": capital of North Ireland in the days of the ancient heroes. The inquest is trying to push through to the story of HCE. At first only hazy and ominous, half-evasive memories can be reached. The heavy atmosphere of fatal and heroic associations will clear only slowly to reveal, at the root of all, the full figure of the great all-nourisher and father.

[5] Reineke Fuchs, Reynard the Fox, hero of the medieval beast cycles. HCE's fox associations here assert themselves. The fox figures in the *Tunc*-page illumination of the Book of Kells.

[6] Wolfgang von Goethe, whose Reinecke Fuchs is the best-known modern version of the cycle.

[7] Shaun gives forth a runic anagram containing the initials and history of HCE. (The question marks appear in Joyce's corrections to the printed text.)

"Did this ancestor of yours live in paradisal early Ireland, where death entered not, or during prehistoric times, before the days of modern whoredom?"

"It is all a dream. On a nonday I sleep. I dream of a someday. Of a wonday I shall wake."

"I understand now your runic verse. The same thing recurs three times differently, descending from the abstract to the concrete, from that historic brute, Finn Do-nothing, to this same vulgarized suburban gentleman of yours, Mr. Tupling Toun with his bathrooms and subways. We are speaking always of the One Father, but in terms of his various locations at various times."

"Our Daddy, the Holy Baboon, who is both patriarch and totem animal. He committed the Original Sin, I continued it, and it remains for the future. More shame to us all. You could not heave a stone over a wall here in Dublin, those ancient pagan days, but it would bound off the back of some fornicating couple. That is the man I go in fear of, Tommy Terracotta; and he could be all your and my daddies, the brother of the founder of the father of the finder of the pfander of the pfunder of the furst man in Ranelagh. Father, Son (482), and Holy Ghost."

"Breathe softly his name?"

"Me das has Oreilles. Persse." [8]

"Pig Pursyriley! But where does his story unfold itself?"

"At the tram stop on the Lucan-Dublin line! The fourfold loop line of world regeneration."

[The Father theme having been sounded, the inquest now will go to work on the problem of the Twins:]

"MacDougal or his wild Asian ass! [9] I can almost identify you,

[8] King Midas has ass's ears. His barber whispered this carefully guarded fact into a hole in the ground. Soon after, all the near-by reeds were whispering the story to the world. HCE's guilty secret, remurmured in solitude by an intimidated lad (37-8), was flung back from all sides in the Persse O'Reilly balladry and gossip. (This adds a new overtone to the Earwig and perceoreille motifs.)

[9] This paragraph is addressed to Johnny MacDougal, the last of the Four Old Men (Gospel according to St. John). Carrying Christ's cross and wear-

John of County Mayo, by your cross and crown of thorns. That melancholy air you have from the west coast of Ireland is no use to you either, John, my Don Quixote. Number Four, fix up your arm of the spread eagle and pull your weight." [Ask your share of the questions that will crucify this Yawn.]

"Do you know a young student of psychical chirography named Kevin?" Matt Gregory asks the still-silent Johnny MacDougal. "He was shooting the guinea hen that found the Document Number One, an illegible penned by an uneligible"

"Do I know the sainted sage?" MacDougal replies. "Sometimes he would keep silent a few minutes, as if in prayer, and clasp his forehead; and during that time he would be thinking to himself, and he would not mind anybody who would be talking to him or selling fish. But I don't need prompting from you, Matty Armagh."

[During the next pages Shaun will be put under terrific pressure by his examiners. They will question him about the manuscript dug up by the hen. Shaun in his role of Kevin had taken credit for discovering this manuscript (110), whereas actually it was Shem as Jerry who had retrieved it from the beak of the hen. Self-aggrandizing duplicity is the very kernel of Shaun's nature; if this can be cracked he will disintegrate. He therefore resists, with every dodge and artifice, the probings of the Four Old Men. He evades with indirections and sophistries, pretends that he cannot speak English, and seizes upon irrelevant aspects of the question under discussion. By the stubborn quality of his resistance we gather that he is being threatened in the profoundest part of his soul.

[Gradually we begin to realize that Joyce, up to his old tricks, is weaving a multiple allegory. The self-defensive Shaun is among other things the Anglo-Catholic church. And who are the Four Old Men? They are the representatives of a Catholicism antedat-

ing his crown of thorns, he is urged by the others to do his share in the questioning of Shaun. Throughout *Finnegans Wake* he is depicted as lagging behind with the Ass. The Ass of the Four Gospelers slowly reveals itself to be Christ himself.

ing even that of medieval Europe—the Irish Catholicism of the Book of Kells. This manuscript of the Four Gospels, from the age of the Irish saints, is written in a Latin slightly different from that of the Vulgate. The Four, with this archaic book as authority, challenge the pretensions, not only of Henry VIII, but also of Henry II. By innuendo and subtle inquisition they are forcing Shaun to acknowledge that his inherited primacy is as fraudulent as his claim to credit for the hen manuscript. He wriggles, stutters, and evades, but the probing goes on.]

"He is cured by faith who is sick of fate—that's the point of our Book of Kells. What can't be coded can be nevertheless understood, if one uses one's ears instead of eyes. Now, the doctrine obtains that we have a cause caus-(483)ing effects, and effects recausing aftereffects. I would suggest then that we give a twist to the Penman's tale. The story is about Shaun, but the hand that wrote it is Shem's. There is a strong suspicion that this Kevin was a counterfeiter. He would go preaching to the Turks and baptizing the Indians, and bringing the word of Resurrection to all who would entrust their new appearance to his Easter millinering. Have you any hesitancy in your mind about him?"

"No," replies the voice of Yawn. "Let this bolt in my hand be my gage.—But why bring up that blarneying Penman Shem? What can such a wretch say to me; or what have I to do with him? Am I my brother's keeper? I know not. But the First Mover knows, by whom I came into being. When I was ordained in the presence of my brother, (484) he urged me to confess cleanly; which I (the person in whom I now am) did not do. But why, O my brother, did you say you would be so delighted to back me to Humphrey and Nephew for a post in his night office, and then go telling the other catachumens you would celebrate my deathday? Well, I'm fed up with you lay-created cardinals. I recite hereby my 'Improperia'[10] against you: 'I saved you from the

---

[10] "The Reproaches": a Good Friday service, consisting of a series of antiphons after each of which the Trisagion (Sanctus, Sanctus, Sanctus) is sung as a respond. The antiphons are sentences represented as sung by Christ to his people to remind them of his love and of their ingratitude.

enemy and you turned me loose to the whole town of Dublin. I taught you, and you circumdeditioned me. . . . My caste is a cut above yours. See the labor of my generations. Look at my jail brand, marked upon me. (485) I can praise myself for my patrician coat of arms with its crest and its caudal motto: *Ich dien*. [Motto of the Prince of Wales.] Mine is the first personal name heard in God's doomsday book. *Hasta la vista,* or, in German, Sukkoth [Hebrew: Feast of Tabernacles]."

"Suck it yourself, Sugarstick," MacDougal retorts absurdly. "You'd think we was asking to look at your sore toe or something. Are we speaking English or are you speaking German? Now, what about your old man through the ages, with his 'Ho halloo!' before there was a sound in the world? How big was his best friend?"

"Me no angly mo, me speakee Yellman's lingas. He numba one belong she."

"Hell's Confucium and the Elements! That's not Shaun the Post talking! (486) Halt this sob story about your lambdad's tale! Are you Roman Patrick, 432?" [11]

"Quadrigue my yoke, [4]

"Triple my tryst, [3]

"Tandem my sire." [2]

"History as her is harped. Tantric Tristram.[12] Hattrick Patrick. Mere man's mime: God has jest. The old order changeth and the last is like the first. Every third man has a chink in his conscience

The present outburst comes from Yawn against Shem and the Four, in response to the charge just quoted by his inquisitors from the writings of the Penman. Shaun's language here sounds very much like Shem's. We begin to suspect that he and his brother may be essentially one.

[11] A.D. 432, the supposed date of St. Patrick's arrival in Ireland. Yawn replies with a riddle which conceals the date, 432, and hints of his family.

[12] The Tantric philosophy of medieval India is best known for its sexual symbolism; the whole universe is generated by the embrace of the god Shiva and his consort. This is precisely the embrace of HCE and ALP, stressed, in all its implications, in the Tristram theme. The inquest is approaching the problem of the genesis of the cosmos out of HCE. (There are many plays on Tantra in *Finnegans Wake*. Joyce's earliest reference to Tantra occurs in *Ulysses,* Random House ed., p. 499; Paris ed., p. 481.)

and every other woman has a jape in her mind. [All history and all mystery lie hidden in this body of Yawn.] Now, Minucius Mandrake, fix on the pupil of my eye. I am placing this initial T-square of burial jade upright to your temple a moment. What do you see?"

"I see a black French pastrycook . . . carrying on his brainpan . . . a cathedral of love jelly for his . . . *Tiens,* how he is like somebody!"

"A pious person. What sound of Tristram-distress assails [Iseults] my ear? I place the ⊢, this serpent with ramshead,[13] to your lip a little. What do you feel, liplove?"

"I feel a fine lady . . . floating on a still stream of Isis-glass . . . with gold hair to the bed . . . and white arms to the stars."

"I invert the initial of your tripartite, adze to girdle, ⅃, on your breast. What do you hear, breastplate?"

"I hear a hopper behind the door slapping his feet in a pool of bran."

"And so the triptych vision [i.e., the vision of the history of man] passes. Out of a hillside into a hillside. Fair-shee fading. Again I am delighted by the picturesqueness of your images.— Now I feel called upon to ask, did it ever occur to you (487) that you might be substituted by a complementary character, voices apart? Think! The next word depends on your answer."

"I'm thinking. I was just trying to think when I thought I felt

[13] Serpent with Ramshead, a type of ornament occurring in ancient Celtic religious monuments. (MacCulloch, *Celtic Mythology,* Marshall, Jones, 1918, Plate VII.) The inquisitors are pressing to Yawn's forehead, mouth, and heart a mystic symbol intended to stir his memory of the past. As they change the position of the symbol, it sounds deeper and deeper levels. First it resembles a T-cross: this suggests the age of Christianity and its missionary, St. Patrick (the French Pastry Cook). Patrick resembles Shaun himself. Next the symbol ⊢ looks like serpent with a ramshead. This suggests the pre-Christian period of Celtic warriors and myths, the age of Cuchulinn, Finn MacCool, and the Fairy Queens. The Queen figure resembles Shaun's mother-and-sister. Finally the symbol is made to look like a phallic monolith: ⅃. Such monuments date from pre-Celtic times: a simple age of semiprimitive agriculture and fertility dances. The old fertility dancer resembles Shaun's primeval father.

a flea. I might have. I cannot say. Once or twice when I was in Wodenburgh with my brother, I imagined myself trying on his suit. A few times I chanced to be stretching the life right out of myself in my imagining. I swear I seem to be not myself, when I realize how I am going to become."

"Oh, is that the way you are, you creature? In the becoming was the word. Hood maketh not the friar. The voice is the voice of Jacob, I fear. Are you Roma or Amor? You have all our empathies, Mr. Trickpat, if you don't mind answering to my straight question."

"I won't mind answering to your strict cross-questions; but it would be as unethical for me now to answer as it would have been nonsensical for you then not to have asked. Same no can; home no will; I am on my way. Mine is the Way and I will return. You knew me once, but you won't know me twice. I am *simpliciter arduus,* ars of the school, Free-day's child in loving and thieving."

"Part of that answer appears to have been taken from the writings of St. Synodius, (488) that first liar. Tell us, therefore, whether the indwellingness of that which shamefieth be entwined of one or atoned of two."

[The inquisitors are pressing the point of Shaun's relationship to his brother. Shem and Shaun are "equals of opposites." The text is shot with anagrams which, read backward and forward, yield the two. "Roma" and "Amor" is a case in point: "Roma," Imperial Rome, is Shaun and "Amor," Christian love, is Shem. But in the Church (politically effective, yet preaching the Word of Him whom the Empire crucified) the two are mixed—as, indeed, they are in all and everything. The two brothers are but the two faces of Man; where the one is visible the other cannot be wholly absent. Hence, one of the first discoveries of the Four Old Men over Yawn was that this gigantic son of HCE sometimes spoke with a voice hardly distinguishable from that of his brother (483). When they now seek to know which of the two he really is, the whole enigma of the brother identities shatters into wild fragments and vanishes without leaving them the wiser. Under such names as

Gottgab (Dieudonnay) and Baggut, Bruno and Nola, Brown and Nolan, the Twin Hero is revolved. His identity and his relationship to the Father elude the probers with a thousand grins.]

"Dearly beloved brethren," Yawn replies. "Bruno and Nola, book and stationery life partners off St. Nassau Street, were explaining it yesterweek. Bruno and Nola are at once identical and eternally opposite, and mutually provocative. *Per omnia saecula saeculorum.*"

"One can hear just beyond the two the lion roar of Finn Mac-Cool [whose divers traits they share]. Is it a case of bear-lion? or of Nolens but Volens? of uniting pity but severing pleasure?"

"Oh, yes!" Yawn will explain himself. "I never dreamed of being a postman. But I am talking not about myself but about my deeply beloved, my alibi-brother, Negoist Cabler, of this city, the scapegoat, expelled for looking at churches from behind, who is sender of the *H*ullo *E*ve *C*enograph in prose, starving today, opening tomorrow. Won't you join me in a small 'Hail Mary' for that well-met cabalist? (489) There be some who mourn him, concluding him dead, and more there be that wait astand. Let us pray for that poor brother that he may yet escape the gallows and still remain our faithfully departed. I want to know if he lives somewhere in the antipodes of Australia, safe on his hush money. Has he hopped it, or what? I remember when we were like bro and sis over our castor and porridge. We are ashamed of each other. He is in a poverty-stricken condition. I loved that man, my *semblable,* my *frère.* I call him my half brother because he reminds me of my natural brother."

"As you sing it," declares one of the Four, "it's a study: that letter self-penned to one's other; that neverperfect everplanned."

"This nonday diary, this allnights newseryreel."

"My dear sir! In this wireless age any old rooster can pick (490) up Boston. But why waxed he so anguished, so vexed?"

"A parambolator rammed the small of his back and he's been feeling a kink ever since."

"Madonna and child! Idealist leading a double life. But who is the Nolan?" Yawn is asked.

"Mr. Nolan is pronominally Mr. Gottgab ["Dieudonnay," in German]."

"I get it! Eureka!" Johnny MacDougal exults at last. "He stands pat for you before a direct object in the feminine. Now will you just search through your memoirs for this impersonating pronolan, fair head on foul shoulders. Would it be an expatriot about your medium height, with sandy whiskers?"

"I surprised him lately for four and six,[14] bringing home the Christmas bundles. Now he is doing the dirty on me in Blessed Foster's Place. She's written to him, but she's lived by me, Jenny Rediviva! Toot! A letter for you, Mr. Nobru [Bruno]. Toot toot! A letter for you, Mr. Anol [Nolan]. This is the way we . . . of a redtettetterday morning."

"When your contraman is looking for righting, that is not a good sign?"

"It's a sure sign that it's not."

"What though it be for the sow of his heart?"

"If she ate your windowsill you wouldn't say sow."

"Would you be surprised if I asked, have you a bull with a whistle in his tail to scare other birds?"

"I would."[15]

(491) "Were you with Sindy and Sandy attending Goliath, a bull?"

"I was simply attending a funeral."

"Tugbag is Baggut's. Two destinies. I see. We can deal with that phase of the problem. But you spoke of a certain tryst. I wonder now, without releasing secrets, have I heard mention his name anywhere? Strike us up a song about him."

A stanza is sung from the ballad:

> Mark! Mark! Mark!
> He dropped his drawers in the Park,
> And had to borrow off the archbishop of York!

[14] Cf. p. 82. Shem is now in the HCE role, Shaun in that of the Cad in the Park. This is the pattern of the Festy King case, pp. 85 ff.
[15] The sense of these exchanges escapes us. The inquest is moving through the problem of the brother pair to that of the father.

"Brobdingnag's out for a stroll?"

"And lilypet-Lilliput's [16] on the grass. An eternal actuality, again taking place in time. From the sallies [two girls] to the allies [three spies] through their central power [HCE]?" [17]

"Pirce! Perce! Quick! Queck!"

Inquest. Stage II: Words of ALP

[The first bastion of Yawn's resistance has been breached. The problem of the brother polarity has been aired and linked to the mystery of the scandal in the Park. From a deeper level of Yawn's subconsciousness a female voice now is heard. It has the ring of ALP. Indeed, it soons turns out to be she in the role of temptress in the Park, telling a circumstantial tale of the events which led up to that rape (491–93). Her story is peppered with references to British Imperialism in India, England's supremacy in the cotton-weaving commerce with the East, and England's consequent collision with Germany. That is to say, the old story is retold, but with special emphasis on its modern merchant-imperialistic phase.

[When ALP has had her say as India (the darker of the Two Temptresses in the Park), one of the Four Old Men, in a prayer re-echoing the periods of the Egyptian Book of the Dead, bids the other temptress aspect to let herself be heard (493). She speaks forth now with the voice of Ireland, bewailing the indignities thrust upon her (493–94). She describes the scene in the Park in terms of the heavenly constellations spread vast for the whole world to see, at which outburst one of the Old Men exclaims that she is drunk, and then recapitulates the entire story of the life of ALP with HCE in terms of mountains, animals, ancient kings, and modern industrial czars.

[16] Brobdingnag: the land of giants in Swift's *Gulliver's Travels;* reference, of course, is to HCE, the father. Lilliput: the land of midgets; reference to ALP in Temptress role. We are coming to the problem of the father through the story of the scandal in the Park.

[17] "Sally in our Alley"; Allies vs. Central Powers; Military sally. Approaching the problem of HCE in the Park, we press first through the smoke of his battle associations.

"And he said he was only taking the average grass temperature for green Thursday, the scalawag! Do you know him? He loves the theater. Congratulations to Mr. Hairwigger who has just had twin little kerls! He was resting in bed, wailing about the war; but at the first thunderclap put on his soldier suit, when the boys of Erin wouldn't join up."

(492) "How do you explain that? He is not a big man. Ask him this some time. And what about that urinating incident in the Park, for which he was baited and jeered?"

"Indeed he was baited! Uproariously! In seven different ways! And falsely, too."

"And his little diva, in Celtic Twilights, singing him Russian through the bars?"

"I beg to deny the above statement. My dear revered gentleman was confined to the guardroom. I was bringing a specimen [18] to my doctor. I visited him in jail. He was sitting humpbacked, in dry filthy heat, suffering from emotional vulvular. My reputed husbandship (493) took a brief one in his shirtsails out of the alleged given bottle of mineral water, telling me how his picture was in the Sunday papers. He never batted an eye before paying me his duty; he simply showed me his propendiculous load-poker, which was produced in his man's way by this wisest of the nine gems of Vikramaditya, with a lewd remark."

"Which was said by whom to whom?"

"I can't remember."

"Fantasy, all is fantasy!" one of the old inquisitors remarks. "There is nothing nuder under the cloth-weaving moon! When

[18] The specimen she was bringing is both beer and urine; figuratively, HCE became intoxicated, seeing the girls urinating in the Park. Cf. p. 8, note 8.

his little wife bumpsed her dumpsy-diddle down in the new woolen sark he had got for her, she made the peerless German girlies sit up in all their pride, fanned, flounced, and perfumed with frangipani: England's victory is Germany's end. Arkwright [19] runs the show now!"

In the style of the Egyptian "Opening of the Mouth," the overseer of the house of the oversire of the seas, Nu-Men, triumphant, calls upon Ani Latch of the postern to shout.

Her Irish voice then cries: "My heart, my mother! My heart, my coming forth of darkness! They know not my heart! What a surprise, dear Mr. Preacher, (494) I to hear from your astronomical majesty! Yes, there was that Rainbow of Promise up above the flabbergasted firmament. Talk about iridecencies: Ruby and Beryl and Chrysolite, Jade, Sapphire, Jasper, and Lazul [the seven Rainbow Girls were all there].

"When the constellation Ophiuchus [the Serpent Holder] is visible above the horizon, then muliercula [his little woman] occluded by the pisciolinnies, Nova Ardonis and Prisca Parthenopea, is a bonny feature in the northern sky. Ers, Mars, and Mercury are at that time surgent below the rim of the Zenith part, while Arctura, Anatolia, Hesper, and Mesembria weep in their mansions over North, East, South, and West." [20]

[One of the Four Old Men breaks in to belittle her testimony:]

"Eva's got a talking jag on! The Ural Mount he's on the move and he'll quivvy her with his strombolo! Here he comes, creeping through the liongrass and bulrushes, camouflaged as a sacramental pudding! Three cheers and a heva heva for the name of Dan Magraw!

[The whole matter is now reviewed through a new version of the letter of ALP:]

"The giant sun is in his emanence. But which is the chief of

[19] English inventor of the spinning frame (1732–92).
[20] HCE being visible, his little woman is occluded by the Two Temptresses, while the Three Soldiers lurk, and the Four Old Men in their four quarters weep.

those white little fairies by which he is surrounded? Do you think I might have been his seventh? He will tickle my elbow. What about his age? says you. What about it? says I. His sins I will confess, blushing, but I shall not deign to retort to base libels. The canailles, dynamite is too good for them! Two over-thirties in shore shorties dared to write to me as follows: 'Will you warn your husband, barking at beggarmen, chewing his chain? R.S.V.(495)P.' And then there is the before-mentioned Sully, that blackhand, writer of most annoying anonymous letters and scurrilous ballads in Parsee French, who is Magrath's thug—and he is not fit to throw guts down to a bear! Telling me that when a maid is nought a maid he would go anyposs length for her! [21] If they cut his nose they had seven good reasons. Lynch Brother and Company, as I say, are prepared to stretch him, inasmuch as I am delighted to be able to state, that a handsome sovereign was freely pledged, along with a kish of fruit, to both the lady performers of unquestionable display,[22] by that lecher at his Saxontannery. The motto of that lecher's saloon: O'Neill saw Queen Molly's pants [*Honi soit qui mal y pense*]. The much-admired engraving on its wall represents the complete manly parts of our chief magistrate during the alleged recent act. Now you see! R.S.V.P.—Your wife, Ann."

[But the Old Judges are not going to accept her report at its face value:]

"You wish to take us in, Frau Maria, by degrees; but I am afraid you are misled."

(496) "*A*las for *l*ivings' *p*ledjures!" she sighs

[21] This pattern of references to Sully and the blackmailers is characteristic of the angry-grateful letters of ALP which appear in these last chapters of the book. They represent her version of the episodes of Hosty's ballad and the hue and cry. Sully, Hosty, and Shem all melt together here.

[22] There are many hints throughout *Finnegans Wake* that the two girls may have been put up to their trick by HCE's political enemies. The whole scandal is intimately connected with his defeat in a recent election. In the letters of his wife, which appear in these last pages of *Finnegans Wake,* this aspect of the case receives due attention.

"That old humbugger was boycotted, snubbed, and in debt, as I'm given to understand. There wasn't a soul would come next or nigh either him or his guest bungalow for rime or ration after that."

"All ears did wag," she concurs.

"Recount."

"I have it here at my fingers' ends," says she. "This liggy piggy wanted to go to the jampot. And this leggy peggy spelt pea. And these lucky puckers played at Peeping Tom O'Toole. Ma's da. Da's ma."

Inquest. Stage III: Exagmination

[The gossipacious voices of the various aspects of ALP have carried the inquest well into that zone of rumor which surrounds, like an impassable ocean, the island figure of the father. The Four Old Men, pressing hard for headway, now direct their questions to a gallery of jury-voices. The replies conjure up the Wake scene. But the scene is strangely amplified and magically transformed; the body on the bier seems to be, not Finnegan of primeval times, but HCE in the full glory of his empire. And the celebrants at the wake are not the "hoolivans of the nation," but the shahs, sultans, and rajas of Britain's Orient, the head-hunters and witch doctors of Britain's Oceania and Africa, and the ambassadors from Britain's vassel states of Europe and America. The full depth-in-time of the Wake image and the full force of its vision of death-in-life suddenly assert themselves in a passage that quickens and illuminates the whole round of *Finnegans Wake*.]

"Now, to change the subject and get back to daddy—if so be you may identify yourself with the him in you. Was he trading in tea before he went on his bier, or didn't he one time do something seemly heavy in sugar? First, like Noah from his ark, he sent out the dove, Christopher Columbus, and it came back with only a jailbird's unbespokables in its beak; then he sent out the crow, Caron, and the police constables are still looking for him.[23] He can never be bothered, but he may be waked. (497) His producers, are they not his consumers? Declaim your exagmination round his factification for incamination of Work in Progress!"[24]

"Arra, man—weren't they arriving from all quarters for his festival: scalp-hunters and head-hunters, a scarlet trainful, totaling in their aggregate ages 1132 of them, from Rathgar, Rathanga, Rountown, and Rush, from America, Asia, Africa, and Europe, and even the valley of New South Wales and from Vico, Mespil Rock. and Sorrento; coming, for the lure of his weal and the fear of his epidemic, to his salon of hope; afraid he was a gunner but afraid to stay away? Weren't they coming for to contemplate in manifest and pay their first-rate duties before the both of him, at and in the licensed boosiness premises of his delightful bazaar and reunited magazine hall, by the Magazine Wall, *Hosty's and Co.,* Exports, for his 566th birthday;[25] the grand old Magennis Mor, Parsee and Rahli [Persse O'Reilly], taker of the tributes, their Rimski-Korsakov and Peter the Great? His holdings were many and sundry: Dunker's durbar, boot kings and india-rubber empires, and shawhs [shahs/shawls] from Paisley, and muftis [muftis/

[23] This sentence speaks of the whole history of European empire as though it were the work of HCE. First he sent out the Spaniards with Christopher Columbus, and now the lands which they discovered are entirely under the lock and key of the Anglo-Saxon. Next he sent out the French (Caron was French Director General of India in the days of the East India Tea Company, d. 1674), but is still busy trying to gather in the French colonies outstanding.

[24] *Our exagmination round his factification for incamination of Work in Progress:* title of a symposium discussion of Joyce's book composed when *Finnegans Wake* was still in the writing and was being published in *transition* under the provisional title of *Work in Progress.* Joyce here identifies himself with HCE; his book with the empire of HCE; his critics and disciples with the jury of the trial.

[25] The figure on the bier unites the two aspects of the full hero: the conqueror aspect and the conquered. He is both HCE and the singers of the ballad. The number 566 indicates that this is a moment midway in the career of the hero; on pages 13–14 the number 1132 was given as the full round of "Finnegan Aeon," and the number 566 as the halfway point. The hero's wake is the midpoint in his spiritual career.

muffs] in muslim, and sultana raisins, and jordan almonders, and
a row of jam sahibs, etc., etc., etc. And there was present at the
scene, J. B. Dunlop, the (498) best tyrent of our times; and there
were a swank of French wine stuarts and Tudor keepsakes; and
there was the Viceroy for the current counter, riding lapsaddle-
longlegs up the oak staircase on muleback, hindquarters to the
fore and kick to the lift, hanging onto his truly natural anthem:
"Horsibus, keep your tailyup"; and as much as the hall of the
vacant throneroom could safely accommodate of the houses of Orange and Betters—permeated by Druids, Brehons, Flawhoolags,
Agiapommenites, and Antiparnellites, Ulster Kong, Munster's
Herald, etc., etc.—all murdering Irish out of their boon companions, after plenty of his fresh stout and his good balls of malt,
socializing and communicanting in the deification of his members,
for to salvage their hero bit of him: him, Dodderick Ogonoch
Wrack, busted to the world at large, on the table round, a dozen
and one-by-one tallow candles round him in a ring, lying high as
he lay in all dimensions, in court dress and ludmers chain, with
his butt-end up, expositoed for sale after referee's inspection,
*h*ealed, *c*ured, and (499) *e*mbalsemate, most highly astounded at
thus being reduced to nothing."

"And all his devotees, tripping a trepas,[26] Keening: 'Mulo[27]
Mulelo! Homo Humilo! Dauncy a deady, oh! Dood, dood, dood!
. . . Rest eternal give unto him, O Lord! Bad luck's pepperpot
loosen his eyes!'"

"But there's lots of flame in Funnycoon's Wick. The King is
dead, long live the Keying!"

"God save you, King! Master pattern of the Hidden Life!"

"God serve you, kingly Oedipus Rex!"

[The cross-questioning suddenly sharpens and the situation
changes abruptly. The voice celebrating the fun at the funeral having suddenly melted away, the Four Old Men now hear from an
invisible watcher sitting on an age-old knoll. He is one of those

[26] A sacred dance in ¾ measure.
[27] A Celtic Mule-god.

fairy presences such as occasionally speak to mortal ears; he stems from within the fairy hill where the giants of Finn MacCool's day are now and forever drinking together the beer of immortality. Such fairy visitants are generally great singers; this one declares he can outmatch the master singers (ollaves) of the jury and can sing a better song than the one that they have just sung.

[The inquest is on the point of a great breakthrough into a deeper, more luminous zone of forms. This challenging, churlish, ominously confident speaker is an outpost of the giant father himself, indeed, may well be an avatar or transformed, mocking ventriloquism of that very presence. No sooner has he made his first premonitory remark, than the Four Old Men begin to overhear from below ground the strangest, wildest cries. It is as though their inquisitorial anatomizing of the figure of Yawn had carried them through his prostrate hulk into the body of the hill on which he lies. Echoes of the long-forgotten come shattering out of the deep grave mound of the past. All is at first confusion; the Four are agog with excitement.]

"Impossible tissue of improbable liars! Do you mean to sit there where you are now, Sorley boy, repeating yourself?" they demand.

"I mean to sit here on this old knoll where you are now, Surly guy, replete in myself, as long as I live, in my homespuns, like a sleeping top, with all that's buried of sins inside me. If I can't upset this pound of pressed ollaves I can set up zounds of sounds upon him." Thus the invisible personage impudently replies.

"Oliver! He may be an earth presence. Was that a groan, or did I hear the Dingle bagpipes Wasting war and? Watch!"

"Tristis est anima mea! Prisoner of Love! Bleating Hart!"

"Rath of God and Donnybrook Fair? Is the world moving in this mound, or what babel is this, tell us?"

"Who-is-he who-is-he who-is-he who-is-he who-is-he linking in? Who-is-he who-is-he who-is-he?"

(500) "The snare drum! Hold your ear to the ground! The dead giant: man alive! They're playing thimbles and bodkins. Clan of the Gael! Hop! Who's within?"

"Dove-gall and fin-shark: they are riding to the rescue!"

309

"Zinzin. Zinzin." [28]

"Crum abu! Cromwell to victory!"

"We'll gore them and gash them and gun them and gloat on them."

"Zinzin."

"Oh, widows and orphans, it's the yeomen! Redshanks forever! Up, Lancastrians!"

"The cry of the roedeer it is! The white hind. The hound hunt-horning."

"Christ in our *Irish Times!* Christ in the *Irish Independence!* Christ, hold the *Freeman's Journal!* Christ, light the *Daily Express!*"

"Slog and slaughter! Rape the daughter! Choke the Pope!"

"Zinzin."

"Sold! I am sold! Brinabride! My esther, my sister, my Brinabride, good-by!"

"Pipette dear! Us! Us! Me! Me!"

"Fort! Fort! Bayreuth! March!"

"Me! I'm true. True! Isolde. Pipette. My precious!"

"Zinzin."

"Brinabride; get my price! Brinabride!"

"My price, my precious?"

"Zin."

"Brinabride, my price! When you sell, get my price!"

"Zin."

"Pipette! Pipette, my priceless one!"

"Oh! Mother of my tears! Believe for me! Fold thy son!"

"Zinzin. Zinzin."

"Now we're getting it. Tune in and pick up the foreign counties! Hello!"

(501) "Zinzin."

"Hello! Tittit! Tell your title!"

"Abride!"

---

[28] This theme is associated throughout with the noise of jubilee at the wake: it accompanies the Fall theme; it is the sound of a dry leaf scratching Earwicker's bedroom window.

"Hello, hello! Ballymacarett! Am I through, iss? Miss?"
"Tit! What is the ti . . . ?"

SILENCE

[A new clarity and precision come into the cross-questioning at
this point.] There is a call for the curtain, the juice, the footlights.
The Four attempt to get their connection. They listen to radio advertisements. They find themselves getting in deeper. They call for
the Sibyl. They are again in the magnetic field.

[It is disappointing to discover, after all the excitement, that the
scene is still that of the trial of HCE. A witness is undergoing
swift and sharp examination. But there is an encouraging lucidity
about the statement of the present witness. We feel that we are
coming, at last, to the truth. He is describing the time and place
of the first meeting of the first couple. He himself, it appears, was
there.]

It was a fair day. There were bonfires that night. It was a high
white night. The lord of the heights was nigh our lady of the
valley. There was rain, mist, dew, (502) a little snow, gales, a moon,
and the weather was hot-cold moist-dry. There were whitecaps;
(503) and there was thunder under the blankets. This garden is
now awfully dirty.

The witness knows the well-known midden where the ill-
assorted first couple first met each other. They met in Fingal too,
beneath the bidetree, fairly exposed to the four winds, in the woods
of Woeful Dane Bottom. There was a flagstone there to the
memory of the grave, and with the warning, "Trespassers will be
persecuted." There was also an ashtree, the great tree, (504) standing in sunshine and in shadow. The witness saw it from his hiding place and took down what took place. It was a most extraordinary sight.

[What is now described is the great World Tree, or World Axis,
known to all mythologies. This is a primal symbol of Life. Eter-

311

nally growing, eternally casting its dead leaves and branches, masculine and feminine and neuter at once, all-sheltering, rooted in abyssal waters yet rising to the polestar around which all revolves, this majestic vegetable symbol of the power and glory of man and the universe is here represented as the figure of HCE and ALP in their eternal union.

[A stone is by the tree. The vast monolith or towering mountain is another well-known mythological symbol of the World Axis, or center of all. In the stone it is not the dynamism but the durability of the cosmos that is represented. Those eternal, all-governing, unchanging laws which control the processes of the universe and endure from everlasting to everlasting are symbolized in the immutable stone. The witness describes both tree and stone as aspects of the One. And this One is that great enigma of a presence toward which our whole inquest is moving.]

Growing upon her [the tree] are Tudor queensmaids and Idaho shopgirls and woody babies; flaming sunbirds sweeny-swing on the tipmost; Oranian apples play hop-to-ciel and bump-to-terre; Fenians snore in his [the tree's] trunk; crossbones strew its [the tree's] holy floor; Erasmus Darwin's and Adam Smith's boys, with their underhand lead pencils, climb to her crotch for the Origin of Spices, and charlotte darlings with silk blue ask-me's chatter in dissent to them; the Kilmainem pensioners are trying to stone down her cranberries; hand-painted hoydens are plucking husbands of him; cock robins are hatching out of his Eggdrizzles/ Yggdrasills; [29] sun and moon are pegging down honeysuckle and white (505) heather; tomtits are tapping resin there and tomahawks watching tar elsewhere; creatures of the wood approaching him to claw and rub; hermits of the desert barking their shins over her roots and his acorns; and pine cones shooting wide all sides out of him; and her leaves sinsinning [30] since the night of time,

[29] Yggdrasill, the World Ash of Germanic myth. The name means "Ygg's steed"; Ygg is a name for Woden, who is frequently identified with HCE.
[30] Here the sinsin, zinzin, wimwim, etc., of the Fall become the sound of rustling leaves.

and each and all of their branches meeting and shaking twisty hands all over again in their new world.—The tree was the shrub of Liberty; but the stone was the stone of the Law, named Death: finite mind mid infinite truth: the form masculine, the gender feminine.

As to why this great tree-man-angel was on his end? Well, he had been pretty cruel to (506) animals and was acting free, so the Master of the House thundered down at him. He was lagged through the coomb. And so that was how he came to be the First Prince of our Tree Fallers. The witness is asked how near he feels to this Head Promontory; he replies that on cold days he seems far, but on wet nights is close by.

[The spirit of the examination changes. The vast mythological imagery is dropped; the problem of the Fall in the Park is presented in the familiar terms of *Finnegans Wake*.]

Does the witness know a certain pagan called Toucher Tom, a man around fifty, struck on Anna Lynch's Pekoe Tea with milk and whisky, (507) all the more himself since he is not all there, being most of his time down at the Green Man, where he steals, pawns, belches, and is a curse, drinking gaily two hours after closing time? "Mad as brambles," the witness replies. "He has kissed me more than once." "Lately?" "How do I know?" He was a Methodist whose real name was Shivering William, (508) and he was wandering in his mind, too, and his clothes were coming down off him. "What a curious epiphany!" [31]

P. and Q., the two girls in the bushes, it appears, were in pretty much the same pickle. And while the witness was peeping (509) they were watching the watched watching; watchers all. The witness is asked whether he gathered much from what Tomsky let

---

[31] Epiphany: revelation of Godhead to mortal eye. The young James Joyce used to speak of art as an epiphany. Each of Joyce's works is conceived as an epiphany. Cf., the excellent article by Theodore Spencer, *"Stephen Hero: The Unpublished Manuscript of James Joyce's Portrait of the Artist as a Young Man." The Southern Review*, vii (1941), i, especially pp. 184–186.

drop, whether he would blame him at all stages, and whether his heliotrope hat was why maids all sighed for him. The witness replies that he would not be surprised. As to the deed committed by the man: "He outs his noli-me-tangere and has a lightning consultation, and he downs his pantaloons and did something that remains to be cleaned." (510) As to how many were married that morning; that'd be telling.

[Next event to be described is the ball at the Tailors' Hall, that fateful night.] Everybody in the world was drunk, two by two, true Norman fashion. A few plates were being shied about, and then followed that wapping breakfast at the *H*eaven and *C*onvenant, *e*h? They came from everywhere. But the priest and the bride-elect were sober. (511) Or perhaps the witness is wrong about the priest. Magraw was the best man. The witness heard him kicking the sexton while they were tickling his Missus in the hall. It was beyond the pretensions of the witness to establish personal contact with him. He thinks it was about the pint of porter. But this all was only in order that the childbearer might bloody well split her sides. " 'Twas woman to woman and man to man." [32] She was wearing bureau drawers to humor his hobbies—a floating panel, secretary sliding drawers, a bunch of klees on her shoulder, a brass sehdass on her ring, and forty crocelips on her curling tongue.[33] (512)—Drysalter, father of Izod, was in the pink, squeezing the life out of the Liffey; he came, he kished, he conquered. The house was Toot and Come Inn, by the bridge called Tiltass. (513) The date was A.D. They were all there, shouting and tripping: Laughing Hunter and Purty Sue, Jorn, Jambs, Isabel, the Four, the Twelve. (514) In short, it was some party. It was a Thundersday, at the inn called A Little Bit of Heaven, Howth. Pontifical mass was celebrated. When suddenly Schott fired furtively—the pawnbroker was right in there—everybody was right in there. A great scrap ensued. The old man was on his arse, (515)

---

[32] A refrain from the vaudeville song, "Finnegan's Wake."
[33] Dali, Klee, Croce: Joyce is describing the costume of the bride in terms of modern paintings and esthetic philosophies.

beating his chest in penance while his belle was being rung. He said nothing important while being kicked.

[Finally:] The witness is requested to reconstruct the funeral games; he has to be urged to do so. (516) He describes now first the man came up to the town's major, MacSmashall Swingy of the Cattleaxes, with a cock on and the horrid contrivance as seen above, whistling the "Wearing of the Blue" into a bone, and taking off his hat in his usual free and easy manner, saying good morrow to everybody and dragging his feet in the usual course, and he was so terribly nice, telling him clean his nails and fix himself up and comb his whiskers; and hang me, sir, if he wasn't wanting his body back before he'd take or save his life. Then, counting eleven to thirty-two seconds with his pocket browning, he kept cursing at him for the key of John Dunn's field fore it was sent for, wanting to know everything. All of which the man, who was only standing there on the corner of Turbot Street preparing to spit, knew nothing about. And that was how their angelic warfare started. (517) Then they called each other names, Box and Cox, huing and crying at each other, about 11:32 o'clock, (518) near the ruins of Drogheda Street. The illegal-looking turfing iron changed feet several times. They did not know the war was over. They were only rebelling and repelling one another by chance or necessity with sham battles, like their caricatures in an Irish novel, to celebrate the expulsion of the Danes. Yet this war has made peace. (519) And this went on, night after night, for years and years.

Inquest. Stage IV: Confustication

[The inquisitors have progressed mightily. They are now well in the field of the father's odylic force. Phantomatic reflexes of his all-creative but evasive presence have materialized and dissolved under their perseverant scrutiny. These have made manifest his ubiquity. The constellations in the heavens, the configurations of the land, the vast octopus of empire and the course of human events, the Tree and Stone of symbolic import, all have screened yet betrayed his presence; and all have been dispelled. The inquisitors have at last come to a body of direct and relatively clean-cut statement concerning the personal history of HCE himself. Apparently the informant is one of the soldier-witnesses. The inquest is on the point of clearing the last obscuring veil, the cross-questioning sharpens, the witness contradicts himself, and the whole process suddenly buckles in hopeless confusion.]

The cross-questioning sharpens. The witness is challenged and denounced. He declares he was told it all by a friend, Tarpey [one of the Four], as follows: He [Tarpey] (520) is walking in Phoenix Park and he meets Mr. Michael Clery, who says Father Mac-Gregor is desperate and for him, Tarpey, to tell Father the truth about the three shillings in the confessional and say how Mrs. Lyons promised to post three shillings to Mr. Martin Clery for Father Matthew to put up a midnight mass for nuisances committed by soldiers and nonbehavers and miss-belovers.

The witness is called upon to recant all that he professed in his first statement and to swear now to this one. He is asked how much cabbage or (521) peppermint he draws in payment for all this swearing. Whereupon a quarrel develops between the judges and the witness. It is Matthew, Mark, and Luke (the Synoptic Gospels) versus John. (522) The witness is asked which of two offenses he would select as the more likely charge: (*a*) playing bull before she-bears, (*b*) playing the hind legs of a clotheshorse. He is asked if any orangepeelers or green-goaters appear periodically up his family tree.—"Buggered if I know," he replies.

Abruptly the witness ejaculates a "Hah!"

"What do you mean, sir, behind your hah?" he is asked.

"Nothing, sir," he explains, "only a bone moving into place. I have something inside me talking to myself."

[There now speak forth from him, severally, five voices:]

(523) 1. [The voice of the girl detective of page 61:] "The evil, she says, "though willed, might nevertheless lead somehow to the general good."

2. "May it not be," asks another, "that the man is as much sinned against as sinning?"

3. "The race horse, Everready," says a third, "will stand at Miss MacMannigan's Yard."

An explanation is demanded, whereupon a fourth voice speaks with the pompous "-ation" pattern of the Twelve:

4. "Pro general continuation and in particular explication to your singular interrogation our asseveralation."

5. [The fifth voice is apparently that of Treacle Tom, one of the original causers of the ballad (39).] "Me, Frisky Shorty, and a few boys," says he, "were carrying on over the old middlesex party; (524) we asked the Rev. Mr. Coppinger about a certain piece of fire fittings; the Rev. Mr. Coppinger cited examples; for instance, the hypothetical case of a school of herring Mayriding off Bloater Naze, at midnight. They had been as happy as little kippers could be; and all of them, little upandown dippies, had given evidence of early bisexualism. This case was cited as an example by the Rev. Mr. Coppinger in answer to the request of me and Frisky Shorty for information anent the problem of a certain piece of fire fittings." (525) [A series of questions develops the fish image. HCE becomes the Great Salmon. One of the fishy temptresses is lively lovely Lola Montez, beautiful mistress of Wagner's Prince Maximilian. Rhine maidens and Liffey maidens and the Salmon in pursuit inspire a new verse for Hosty's popular lampoon:]

> There was an old salmon full of sperm
> Leaping fresh after every Tom and Lizzy:
> *Our Human Conger Eel!*

Hep! I can see him in the fishnet. Hold him! Play him!
Pull, sir! He'll cry before he's flayed. Lungfish!

He missed her mouth and stood into Dee. No, he skid like a skate and berthed on her byrnie, and never a fear but they'll (526) land him yet, slitheryscales on liffeybank, time and time again.

Problem: Were these anglers coexistent and compresent with or without their *tertium quid?*

Reply:

Three in one, one and three.
Shem and Shaun and the shame that sunders em
Wisdom's son, folly's brother.

The witness is dismissed and another called. The new witness thought he was lurking in the clover with two stripping bare-maids—while that other little girl, nearly gone on him, was admiring her image in the brook.

(527) "The latter resembles Iseult? A penny for your thoughts!"

[From Iseult herself comes the answer, as she scolds and consoles her own reflection in the mirror:]

"Listen, dearest, come rest on this bosom. So sorry you lost him, poor lamb. Of course I know you are a very wicked girl to go in the dream place at that time of day; it was a very wrong thing to do, even under the dark flush of night. Still, you are forgiven, and everyone knows you do look lovely in your invisibles. And of course it was downright wicked of him, meeting me disguised. How we adore each other! May I introduce? This is my futuous. (528) It will all take place, as arranged, at St. Audiens' Chapel. *Christe eleison, Kyrie eleison. Sanctus, sanctus, sanctus.* So, my sister, be free to me. I'm fading."

Alice through the looking glass? or Alice in Jumboland? Think of a maiden. Double her. Knock and it shall appall unto you. Is she having an act in apparition with herself?

Inquest. Stage V: Brain Trust Takes Over

[The Four Old Men have carried the case as far as they can. A bright, sharp, systematic group of younger investigators now takes over. With utmost certainty and authority they call up Kate (Kitty the Beads), the old woman guardian of the museum pieces. who was herself very close to the great man in primeval times.

And after she has said her say, they go directly and fearlessly to. the root of all, and summon HCE himself.

[This transition from the Four to the young group of Brain Trusters suggests the progression from nineteenth tc twentieth century science, scholarship, and statecraft. The problems broached by the elders are so deep and vast that only the most severe and consequential organization of human forces can cope with them. This is the last, the ultimate moment of historical progress. What the Brain Trusters summon forth is the prodigious, primeval power of the uttermost; upsurgent, welling, gushing forth inexhaustibly, it dissolves all in itself. The whole great world of the sons and the grandsons simply vanishes like a dream, and only the primordial, archetypal presence of HCE and ALP remains.

[Through some wireless interference comes a voice scolding:] "You're crackling out of your turn. Stay off my air. You've grabbed the lion's share since 1542, but we'll trump you yet. And, sir, my questions first. (529) We bright young chaps of the Brain Trust are empowered to know: whether the generals had their service books in order when discharged; how O'Bejorumsen came into possession of the bellywash; why the man was in the coomb; where the Three Soldiers were going; how he started his tavern; whether he is co-owner of a circus; (530) whether he has been complaining to police barracks about being molested; whether it was he who sent his son out for a jar of porter and then set is before his wife, bidding her mind the house while he rambled the road— Where's that auxiliary policeman, Seckesign, that reported the affair? Call Kitty, the janitrix, with her beads.

Inquest. Stage VI: Brain Trust Questions Kitty the Beads

"A paternoster for his Armenian atrocities. (531) And then a confiteor, as sanctioned by the Council of Trent, for his indulgence. —I massaged his shoulder muscles on the kitchen table till he was red in the face with love-soft eyebulbs and his kiddledrum steaming and rattling like the roasties in my mockamill. I ought to have scorched his back for him. He sizzled there, watching my picture as the refined soubrette, with my broached bust. And he never saw anything finer than he saw when I started so ladylike to leg a jig, highty tighty, kickakickkack. Fuddling fun for Fullacan's sake." [34]

"Halt," cry the Brain Trusters. "Enough of this. A final ballot now to remove all doubt. I'll get at this if I have to take down every mask in the country. (532) Search ye the Finn! Ho, evil doer, speak up! Arise, sir ghostus! Doff!"

Inquest. Stage VII: Brain Trust Hears from HCE Himself

[The voice of HCE in self-defense:] "Here we are again. I am bubub-brought up under an act long out of print. I was brought up under a dynasty long extinct: the first of Sihtric Silkybeard; but I am known throughout the world, wherever Anglo-Saxon is spoken, by saints and sinners alike, as a clean-living man; and they know that my game was a fair average. I cannot afford to be guilty of trespass on my wife with a girl friend. As a matter of fact, I tell myself I possess the ripest little wife in the world. She romped off first with the consolation prize in my serial dreams of faire women,[35] handicapped by two breasts in operatops, a remarkable little garment, fastened at various places. I keenly love (533) such, particularly when decorated with heliotrope tulips, as this is.

"She is my best-preserved wife, with the smallest shoe outside Chinatown. And our private chaplain can tell you about my clean character at the time I introduced her to our four-poster. Let Michael now follow Sutton and tell you how I amplify stout." [The broadcast begins to fade out under a jumble of advertisements, interference, and static.] "Thank you. That'll be all for (534) today. Call

[34] Compare the account given by the laundresses of Anna's attempts to amuse the old man, pp. 199, etc.
[35] Grainne's legendary race for Finn. Liffey's race. Tennyson's *Dream of Fair Women.*

320

it off. Good night everybody, and a merry Christmas. . . . New York. . . . Thanks."

[Four auditors, probably the Four Old Men, utter brief and obscure comments. Then the broadcast proceeds. Or rather, the control proceeds; for we are about to become aware of the fact that we are attending a spiritualistic séance. It is the voice of HCE again:]

"Calm has entered. It is a great entertainment. God's truth! I protest, there is not one teaspoon of evidence as to my wickedness, as you shall see. And I can quote you my thirty-nine articles here,[36] before those in heaven, to prove myself stiff and stanch forever. I can enter to the proper authorities my protest against the publication of libel by any tipsy loon or towny of Hiersse Lane. The cad! Sherlock is looking for him. Shame on his lying soul! (535) And mine it was to hold up to His Majesty the keys of our city.

"Someone was with us. Adversaries! And those missies? Obscenest nonsense! The hole affair is rotten as pig's filth. Enough!"

[The voices of the four auditors are heard:] "Is that you, Whitehead?" "Have you head noise now?" "Give us your misspelled reception, will you?" "Pass the fish, for Christ's sake!"

[Old Whitehead is speaking again:] "Open your ears. Pity poor Whitehead. Tell the world I have lived through a thousand hells. My age is thirty-nine; my hairs are white; my memory is failing; my joints are stiff; and I'm dear. I ask you, dear lady, to judge my tree by our fruits. I gave you to smell and to eat of the tree. Pity poor *H*aveth *C*hilders *E*verywhere with Mudder!"

[Announcer:] "That was Communicator, a former colonel. A disincarnated (536) spirit, called Sebastian, from Rio de Janeiro, may phone shortly with messages for my departed. Let us cheer him up a little and make an appointment for a future date. Hello, Communicator! Ever skeptical, he does not believe in our psychos and soul surgery. He has had indigestion for quite a little while. Poor Felix

---

[36] Thirty-nine Articles of the Anglican church. Cf. p. 283, where this theme was introduced through the shopkeeper-arithmetic of Kev (Shaun).

Culprit. Too bad about him. In tall white hat, with stick of iron, with buckled/Buckleyed hose, he would smoke carefully and husband his cigar. With us, his grandchildren and neighbors, incensed and befogged by him and his smoke. But he shall have his glad stein of our best beer in Oscarshal's wine tavern. His voice is still flutish and his mouth still scarlet, though his flaxen locks are peppered with silver. It was because of that he was sent into prison. Some day I may tell his story. It looks like someone else bearing my burdens. I cannot let it be."

[Communicator himself:] "Well, sir, I have bared my whole past. Give me even as little as two months by law, and my first business will be to protest to the proper authorities. Our Father, who art in heaven . . . Those who live in glass houses, they shall not peg stones. (537) I am here to tell you, I am planning to become a Celt. Anyone with anything against me need only speak up and I will pay my price. And as a matter of fact I undertake to discontinue entirely all practices; and I deny *in toto* to have agreed to share my mouthless Negress with my quarter brother, who sometimes is doing my locum for me on a grubstake. May the Fire of Frigg and the Sulphur of Woden strike me if I did take milady's maid. Such a deed were a frolic for my comic strip, to be brayed at by silly clowns at Donnybrook Fair. It would make one laugh. (538) If she has been discharged, I am uninterested; and if she is still slopping around, I am strongly of the opinion that it should not be. I do not believe a word of it. Nor have I engaged to resell or borrow the same by exchange. 'Twere a cruelty worthy of ancient Carthage. Utterly improbable! Not for anything, so help me Cash, would I become party to such viciousness.

"*Meine Herren!* The absurdity of it! This tale is of a piece with the story about the two girls. I would not know how to contact such wretched youngsters, or any sisters or heiresses of theirs. What a shrubbery trick to play! I will testify, under oath, to my virtue! (539) I always think of that great company of poets, Dante, Goethe, Shakespeare, Inc., as the models for my pious best policy; and if I have failed, by accident, in one way, I have made good in another.

Since my arrival, famine (540) has vanished from this place and vicious people are no more. We have a pleasant, comfortable, and wholesome land."

[The discourse is interrupted by an advertising slogan, repeated in four languages:] "Visit Drumcollogher."

"Things are not as they were. Let me briefly survey: Proclamation! Where the jay piped, now the whistle blows. The Black-and-Tans may be back, but love goes on. Social improvements have been numerous. My lord and my lady are safe now. All is in good order. (541) I had seven hills. The chart of my heart was my guide. I raised a cathedral, acquired wealth; I faced the Dutch, faced a thousand kings. The noise of strife resounded from all sides. I improved my city; (542) made my people happy. I protected decent womankind, and enjoyed their appreciation. In the humanity of my heart, I sent out highwaywomen to refresh (543) the weary, then broke the base fellows for the curtailment of their lower man. I extended my boundaries. I have been receiving ominous letters, petitions; lampoons have been plastered. But listen. I have established colonies far and wide: I have granted charters and founded plantations; and I receive all types under my protection. [There follow two pages of rooms-to-let advertisements, describing the dreary habitations which have flourished under the broad protection of this great empire-builder:] Fair home overcrowded, tidy but very little furniture, respectable . . . shares closet with six other dwellings. . . . (544) . . . Floor dangerous for unaccompanied old clergymen, thoroughly respectable, many uncut pious books in evidence. . . . (545) . . . Respectability unsuccessfully aimed at, copious holes emitting mice. . . .

"I have freed the enslaved; but lo! tall tales have been circulated about me. (546) Wherefore my sovereign lord has regard for me, and has given me my nickname and my shield. It were idle to inquire after my conception and birth; I claim to be spontaneous."

[The discourse is interrupted again by the four auditors, but then proceeds:]

"Had my faithful Fulvia gone rambling and been seduced, (547) there might be some point in trying to discover wherein her deceivers sinned. But she remained constant to fairness. And I waged love on her; and she wept."

[Another interruption, playing on the theme of tragic time.]

"But I was firm with her and did lead her overland, along the course of her Liffey, to Ringsend Ferry, where I lifted puntpole and bade the seas retire: and I abridged her maiden race, and I knew her fleshly and did her worship: whereupon the heavens thundered and the lightning flashed. And I cast my ten spans upon her, and I trade-marked her mine (548) and I put a name and wedlock round her, the which to carry till her grave. I did girdle her about with all loving-kindness and gave her fine presents of gewgaws and frocks; I pierced her beck (549) and our folk had rest from Blackheathen and the pagans, and I established lights along the coast; I settled with my bride, fed her well, showed her pageantries. (550) My worthies were applauded enthusiastically, far and wide."

[Another interruption from the auditors.]

"And I fed her on spices, gave her ointments and a currycomb; we had impressive portraits on the walls; she had time for play, and I, dizzed by our (551) interloopings, fell off in ballast: she reigned in the kitchen. All admired her chemises. I more than fulfilled my promises.—I bring the glad tidings to man. My tugs plied the canals. I built a country-city for my darling, with a convenient privy: I established universities: I was rosetted on two stelae/stellas of Little Egypt, had a trio of rock-cut readers, constructed twelve bridges, (552) set four provinces, set up twin minsters, pro and con; forced mankind to follow the way of destiny. I trailed my seven winds to maze her, reformed her church for her . . ."

["*Hoch!*" exclaim the four auditors.]

"And (553) I did teach her to read, spread softest mats before her, planted gardens and a vineyard with a magic-scene wall (rim-rim rimrim); brewed good ale for her, constructed roads whereon now fare men of all kinds, (554) and she laughed in her diddy domino to the switcheries of the whip.—Down with them. Kick. Play off."

Matthew! Mark! Luke! John!

Book III, Chapter 4: HCE and ALP—Their Bed of Trial

[John o' Dreams having dissolved, with the dawn, into the form of his sleeping father, the realities of the waking world begin to break through the tissues of dream. Just as the seductive nightmare, or "Alp," of German folklore may dissolve, at waking, into a mere wisp of straw or puff of down, so, many of the dream figures that have obsessed our sleeping hero are now reduced to the banal, familiar traits of the room and the bed-companion.

[It is the morning after the night of the winter solstice. A dry leaf still clinging to the tree outside the window has been scratching at the pane; and this sound has drawn the inexhaustible dream from the depths of the psyche, as the scratching of the hen drew that inexhaustible letter from the dung heap. In the sleepy state of earliest morning, in their bed of trials, the two attempt intercourse, as of old.

[A plaintive cry from the more troubled of the twins, Jerry, who has been frightened by a nightmare, brings the parental couple upstairs to his bedside. Half-sleeping he sees them standing in his room, the father in the background apparently with an erection. The soothing mother voice lulls the child back to sleep and the couple return downstairs to their own bed, where they embrace, in position of concord.

[There are witnesses of their act. Perhaps we are to think of the twins themselves opening the door a little and peeking through. Furthermore, their shadows on the windowblind flash their happiness far and wide. The hen cackles and the cock crows. This is the famous hen of the letter. The act of copulation is then concluded. We are not clearly told that it was unsatisfactory; we only read: "You never wet the tea."

[Vaguely, at the opening of this chapter, we strive to locate ourselves in time and space:]
(555) What was that? It was fog? Too many sleep. Let sleep. But whenabouts? Spread out our times in space.

So, night by night, while kinderwardens (the Four and their Donkey) minded their twinsbed,

(556) while little daughter Isabel slept like some lost happy leaf,

while Havelok, from yonsides the choppy, went gathering up the leave-things from allpurgers' night,[1]

while Kate the Slop heard a voice, came down (557) and caught him slipping upstairs,

when goodmen twelve tried and found him (558) guilty,

and the twenty-nine darlings had such a ripping time over Shaun,

father and moddereen are in their bed of trial.

[There sounds a little cry from Jerry, in the room of the twins, and the waking scene is suddenly before our eyes:]

Where are we at all? When and where?

Scene: a bedroom.

Interior of dwelling on outskirts (559) of a city. Ordinary bedroom set. Salmonpapered walls. No curtains. Blind drawn. Bed for two with strawberry bedspread. Facetowel on bookshrine. Woman's and man's garments distributed. Picture of Michael, with lance, slaying Satan, dragon with smoke. Lighted lamp. Man's gummy article, pink.

[And now the dumbshow is to be regarded from four standpoints:]

Dumbshow I. First position of harmony (*Matthew's view*)

Closeup. View from side. Man looking round, beastly expression, rage,[2] Episcopalian, any age. Woman sitting, haggish expression, fear,[3] undersized, Free Church, no age.

Her move: She hopped out of bunk and was off; nightlamp with her. His large limbs prodgered (560) after, to queen's lead. Huff. Blackout.

---

[1] Cf. pp. 380–82, HCE drinking up the dregs.
[2] Anger at having been disturbed by Jerry's cry.
[3] Anxiety for her little one upstairs.

Shifting scene: Room to sink. Stairs to sink behind room.

The old humbug looks a thing incomplete so. But it will pawn up a fine head of porter when finished. Checkered staircase: one square step only, notwithstanding they are stalemating backgammon upstairs.

It is an ideal residence for a real tar. There is a bell to airwake the master. Ominous house. Here noggins are poured.

Tell me something. The Porters are very nice people, are they not? Very. Mr. Porter is an excellent forefather; Mrs. Porter is a most kindhearted messmother. They are perfectly united. They are of a rarely old family and care only for what is allporterous.

(561) Here are two rooms upstairs for the Porter babes. In Number One sleeps little Buttercup with her (562) mirror and dolly.

In Number Two sleep the twins. Our bright bull babe, Frank Kevin, is on the heart-sleeve-side.

(563) The other, twined on cod-liver-side, has been crying in his sleep, and has wet his bed. He will vow to be of Blake's bleak tribes.—They are two very twinnish [4] little portereens. I wish to leave my blessing between the pair of them. Weeping shouldst thou not be, when man falls, but ever adoring the divine scheming.

Dumbshow II. Second position of discordance (*Mark's view*)

(564) A second position is now taken up by the view. View from behind. Male partially eclipses female. Rere-view of our park, our father's bottom, revealing road, prominences, thickets, leavesdroppings, (565) and bandstand.[5]

[With Slavic accent the motherly voice now comforts the little whimperer.] Why do you tremble at our shadow-show joke? It is just a Jabberwocky joke. Why? [6] I have heard her voice somewhere else before.

Slow music. Thunder in the air.

"You were dreaming, dear. There are no phantoms in the room

[4] *Bleeznyetz* (Russian): twin.
[5] HCE's bottom is described as though it were Phoenix Park.
[6] *Potchyemoo* (Russian): Why.

at all. My little boy.[7] Gothtown father will go far away tomorrow, the rocky road to Dublin, to do business. Spank."

"Is he asleep?"

"Son, it's only all in your imagination." Poor little brittle magic nation, dim of mind!

(Advertisement—When you are coaching through Lucalizod, on a visit to the sulphur spa, stop at his inn. It's dangerous out on the highways. (566) You will find here hard sledding, but good room and board.)

In the sleeping chambers (the court to go into half morning): the Four with their Donkey, all rocking in their chairs and sharpening up their pencils; the boots, Soakerson; the swabsister, Katya; those twelve to be standing by, with folded arms, who will afterwards be returning to their farms; the maid-brides all to be joyously declining into spinsterish old age; the dame dowager to stay kneeling as she is, as first mother; the two princes of the royal tower to lie as they are, without seeing; the dame dowager's duff gerent to present weapon and wheel about without being seen by them; the infant Isabella, from her corner, to do obeisance toward the duff gerent, as first father. (Then the court to come into full morning.)

"Behold, pork-ego. They are watching you. Return, pork-ego. This is hardly delicate."[8]

The veiling gauze lifts from heaven, and then, what an entrancing vision! That crag! Those hillocks! But what are you afraid of? —I fear lest we have lost our way: how dark and wild!—And what are you looking at?—I am looking at the stark pointing pole which I must see before my misfortune.—Can you read the legend thereon?—"To the Dun-(567)leary obelisk, so many miles no fur-

---

[7] *Moi malyenkee malcheek* (Russian): My little boy. Pun: "my melancholy male chick." Cf. p. 253: "[Glugg's] grandmother coughed Russky with suchky husky accent."

[8] A warning to HCE that children have eyes.

328

longs. To the General Post Office, endless patience. To the Wellington Memorial, half a league wrongwards. To Sara's Bridge, good hundred and nine. To the point, one yeoman's yard." He, he, he!—Do you leer at that?—Yes, I leer, because I see a hunting cap on the point; such a pink cap, when broken on roof staff, has long been the effigy of standard royal which shall cast welcome to the gunnings: the queen lying abroad, her liege shall arrive tomorrow; he shall come with beagles and terriers for a hunting on foxes; there shall be a great gathering; (568) the boys shall mark one atonement; the burgomaster shall greet the king; the king shall be charming; (569) church bells shall ring; 'tis holyyear's day! There shall be pontifications, a feast, mummers, (570) contests, and fireworks. But tomorrow never comes.

[The regal flourishes and the promises of a glorious festival on the morrow aptly suggest the mood of euphoria preceding intercourse. Everything is going to be lovely, the issue will be blessed and glorious. The king himself will come and the pope give benediction. This anticipated arrival of the king brings back the image of Book I, Chapter 2, when royalty halted itself at the cottage of goodman Humphrey, who came forth bearing a pole with a flowerpot on top of it. The phallic symbolism is explicitly developed in the present scene, when HCE, tumescent, follows his wife to the bedside of their little son.]

True. But tell me now more about the rich Mr. Pornter.—He is strong, in good health, stouter than formerly, and has long been a marrying man. He has fine sons—his mic son and his two fine mac sons, and a superfine mick won't they make between them. She, she, she! I am not leering; I pink your pardons; I am highly sherious.

Pardon, I must go somewhere: that prickly-heat feeling: let us go for a walk to No. 1 Sairey's Place, admiring the scenery of our first national route, 1001; where St. Sylvanus washed the tips of his anointed fingers.—Beware of looking back: it is stealer of the heart. I am anxious lest you be transformed into a pillar of salt. (571) These will-o'-the-wisps leap from a spring-well which makes the deaf to hear. Fronds floating on the spring-well cast spells upon

the branchings. There are Tantrist spellings on the branchings: [9]
"Elm; bay; this way; cull dare; take a message; tawny runes; ilex
sallow; meet me at the pine." Yes, they shall have brought us to
the water trysting. Then here in another place is the chapel of
eases. See! She is easing herself. I, Pipette, must also. Peace! This
is heaven. Listen: *H*orsehem *c*oughs *e*nough. *A*nnshee *l*ispes *p*rivily.
He is quieter now.—There is mumbling of words of marriage
and of challenge. Wait! Hist! Let us list!
For in the nether world our foes be at work. (572) A revolution
is preparing. The young girls will soon be heart-pocking on their
betters' doorknockers: and the young men troweling a grave-trench
for their four-in-hand forebears. [10]
Wait, the door is open. See! Careful.

Let us consider. [We are invited to study the full import of this
family scene of the parents visiting the bedchamber of their child.]
A professor of law, Dr. Alter-ego, presents us with this poser:
[The passage about to unfold (572–76) is probably the strangest
and most complicated in the book. Practically without warning a
relatively innocent glimpse into a bedroom opens out upon a morass
of indescribable decadence. The apparently healthy ocean of parental
love deteriorates into a sick sea peopled by monsters of incest and
perversion. Under Joyce's ray, the deepest reaches of the unconscious,
containing the debris of normal love attachments, are disclosed.
[What does it all mean? On one plane it illuminates the darkest
pits in the unconscious of HCE and ALP, who here are symbols
of every living man and woman. Their slightest, most furtive desires stand revealed as though fully enacted. More cynically and
on a historical plan, it is a parody indictment of the whole literature of romantic love from the time of Eleanor of Aquitaine to the

[9] The little boy, sleepily observing his parents in disarray, glimpses the
mysteries of sex as he might the verdure of a wood. The word Tantrist,
suggesting tourist, refers to the Tantric sex symbolism of India and Tibet.
See footnote 12 to the previous chapter.
[10] The younger generation represents the dynamic future threatening to
overturn the adult present.

modern Hollywood sex triangle. Strong echoes of the Provençal "Courts of Love," Ariosto, and the interminable medieval romances that drove Don Quixote mad are mixed with sick Strindbergian overtones. The whole compost is a devastating commentary on the male-female relationship of our day, and we are reminded thereby that it is precisely this chaos and turpitude which characterize the period of dissolution just preceding the Viconian thunderclap.

[The final twist of the screw is supplied by the *form* in which the revelation is made. It comes to us as a law case, "perhaps the commonest of all cases," says the professor who presents it to his class. One is struck with horror that such matters can be discussed in the boring terminology of everyday legal experience, and that this phraseology, and the social attitude it covers, should be the most characteristic expression of our time.

[The presentation of the law case falls into two parts. The first (572–73) relates in detail the ramifications of the loves of HCE, ALP, and their household. In this phase of the proceedings HCE is known as Honuphrius; ALP as Anita.]

Honuphrius is a concupiscent ex-service-major, who makes dishonest proposals to all. He is father of Felicia, Eugenius, and Jeremias. He is considered to have committed infidelities with Felicia and to have practiced unnatural coitus with Eugenius and Jeremias. He is the husband of Anita. He has instructed his slave (Mauritius) to urge an emulous friend (Magravius) to solicit Anita's chastity, while requiring her to deceive himself by rendering conjugal duty when demanded. He pretends publicly to possess his wife in thirty-nine different ways [11] whenever he has rendered himself impotent to consummate by artifice.

Anita is the wife of Honuphrius and the mother of Jeremias, Eugenius, and Felicia. She is informed by her tirewoman (Fortissa) that Honuphrius has confessed to instructing his slave (Mau-

[11] Yet again, the Thirty-nine Articles of the *H*igh *C*hurch of *E*ngland (cf. pp. 283, 534). The theme is here brought to its climax: "As HCE offers thirty-nine public pretenses when impotent, so the Thirty-nine Articles of the Anglican church; for the Anglican clergy is powerless to transubstantiate the bread and wine."—In the end James Joyce remains the son of Rome!

ritius) to urge his friend (Magravius) to solicit her chastity. Anita knows that the schismatical wife of Magravius (Gillia) has been debauched by Honuphrius and is now visited by Honuphrius' advocate (Barnabas) who was himself corrupted by Jeremias. Anita discovers incestuous temptations from Jeremias and Eugenius. Anita has been threatened by Magravius with molestation from a certain orthodox savage (Sulla), if she will not yield to him and also render conjugal duty to Honuphrius. She would yield to Honuphrius to save the virginity of Felicia for Magravius, but fears that by allowing his marital rights she may cause reprehensible conduct between Jeremias and Eugenius. She is dispensed by her priest (Michael), under pain of anathema, from yielding to Honuphrius. Four Excavators (Gregorius, Leo, Vitellius, and Macdugalus) warn her through her tirewoman (Fortissa) of strong chastisements by Honuphrius, and advise her to submit to Honuphrius. They describe, also, as a warning, the depravities practiced by the savage (Sulla) on the wife of Honuphrius' slave (Canicula).

Sulla would procure Fortissa for the Four Excavators. Fortissa has had illegitimate children by Honuphrius' slave (Mauritius). The priest, Michael, has formerly committed double sacrilege with Anita and wishes to seduce Eugenius.

The case has been reviewed by the following theorists: Ware, D'Alton, Halliday, Gilbert, Wadding, and D'Oyly Owens. The question is: Has Honuphrius hegemony and shall Anita submit?

[The second phase of the discussion (573–76) reviews the history of the case.]

The court rules that so long as there is a joint deposit account in the two names a mutual obligation is posited. The scrutiny of the couple's financial situation quickly opens out into a review of the history of Christianity in the British Isles, particularly since the days of Henry VIII (Hal Kilbride[12]) and the Counter Reformation. The Irish Catholic wife (now called Ann Doyle) is found to be the junior partner of a great corporation (the Roman Catholic

[12] Kilbride is named by the washerwomen of the last chapter of Book I as an early lover of ALP. Cf. p. 203.

332

church) known as Tangos, Limited. The senior partner of this firm (Rome-Vienna-Madrid) is variously known (according to the historical epoch under discussion) as Brerfuchs, Breyfawkes, Brakeforth, and Breakfast. The junior partner (Ireland) is variously known as Warren, Barren, Ann Doyle, Sparrem, and Wharrem. Now it seems that a rival firm (the Anglican church), known as Pango, Limited, was formed, whose fund trustee, a certain Jucundus Fecundus Xero Pecundus Coppercheap (HCE), sued the junior member of Tangos, Ltd., for tithes due. Payment was made in a crossed check signed by the senior member of the Tangos firm; the check was a dud, and was never negotiated, yet passes among Pango stockholders.

All the members of the jury as well as the judge are named Doyle, and disagree with each other in typical Irish fashion. Ann Doyle herself turns up in the jury, and offers to reamalgamate with a certain Monsignore Pepigi, who is the permanent trustee for the fund. Judge Jeremy Doyler rules that Pepigi has been a corpse since the days of Hal Kilbride and Ann a slave since the time of the Anglo-Norman conquest. The value of the check, therefore, which has been taken out of her hide, she cannot recover.

[Let us ask again what is the meaning. Not only romantic love but also Christian faith is snarled, knotted, and exhausted. All the wires have been so crossed that there is no clean flow any more, either of natural or of supernatural energy. These are the days of the worn-out forms. Our lawyers and our psychoanalysts can write it all down for you in the driest, calmest way. You must not be surprised. It is simply a fact. That is the way things are. But just try to untangle them!

[After this moment of appalling revelation, the scene resumes its apparent simplicity, and the chapter proceeds. HCE and ALP, having visited their sleeping son, are about to go downstairs again to bed.]

(576) "He sighed in sleep. Lest he waken, let us hide ourselves."
"While dream wings hide my manikin from fears, keep my big man of men."

To bed.

Protector, Giant Builder, give hand to our Adam and Eve. Cause of all causes; alpha and omega; source of grace; self-knowing *a priori;* give hand to our forced payrents, He and She: guide them down their laddercase of night-watch service and bring them at suntime flush with the lowest rung of their stepchildren; defend them from roamers and from loss of bearings, so long as they fulfill their duties to thee. (577) That he may cover her and she uncouple him; that one may crumple them and they recoup themselves—time and again, as per periodicity.

Stop! Did someone stir? It's only the (578) wind on the road outside—to wake all shivering shanks from snoring.

But who is this great man, dressed cozily for sleep? Can this be our hotelkeeper, rounding up on his family?

And who is this bodikin by him? Look at the way she's looping the lamp. Why that's old missus wipe-them-dry—happy tea area.

Where are they going, and why? They're coming through their Diamond Wedding tour: that Luxumburgher with his Alzette. (579) Down, up, under talls and threading tormentors, shunning the star-traps and slipping in sliders, from Elder Arbor to La Puirée, setting the clock back, sweetheartedly. And these are some of his slogans: *h*ot and *c*old and *e*lectrickery with *a*ttendance and *l*ounge and *p*romenade free. Renove that Bible. Scrape your souls. Commit no miracles. Postpone no bills. Share the wealth and spoil the weal. My time is on draught. Bottle your own. Lean on your lunch. No cods before Me. Import through the nose. By faith alone. Lots feed from my tide-table. Let earwigger's wivable teach you the dance.

Now may their laws assist them and ease their fall!

For the life they lived was turbulent: they met and mated and bedded and buckled and got and gave and reared and raised . . . and pawned our souls . . . and bequeathed us their ills and recrutched cripples gait . . . manplanting seven sisters, while one warmwooed woman scrubs . . . and never learned the first day's lesson . . . and feathered foes' nests and fouled (580) their own . . . and escaped from liquidation by the heirs of their death and

334

were responsible for congested districts . . . and left off leaving off, and kept on keeping on . . . and were cuffed by their customers and bit the dust; and now together they lie; yet they wend it back, light in hand, helm on high, to peekaboo through the thicket of slumbwhere, till he close the book of the dates and she sing her farewell tour.—And gentle Iseult whispering in the leaves to Finnegan to sin again and to make grim grandma grunt and grin again, while the first gray streaks steal silvering by for to mock their quarrels.

They near the base of the chill stair—that large incorporate licensed vintner and his *a*mbling *l*imfy *p*eepingpartner . . . they of the rann that Hosty made.

(581) He has been called bad names at indignation meetings and by the crowd roaring homeward, high hearted, from his tavern: invader and foreigner, the man from the ark and his Banshee's bedpan.

And didn't they abhor him? the unregendered thunderslog, the male man all unbracing to omniwoman! when they were looking on: the Four and their Ass; the Three; the Two. And his Monomyth, ah ho!—Say no more about it. I'm sorry. I saw. I'm sorry to say I saw.

And is there not among us another like that other, but not quite such another; not precisely the selfsame and still but one and the same, ever made amenable?

(582) Yet he begot 'em.

Wherefore, let us propose a vote of thanks to H. C. Experimenter!

We must put up with them, and they with us. We must face the inevitable; and so—there was a maid tempted a smith:

Dumbshow III. Third position of concord (Luke's view)
Excellent view from front. Female imperfectly masking male. He's the *d*ullakey-kongsby-ogblagroggers-wagginline.[13] Gaze at him now in momentum (583) and his poor little tartanelle. Their copulation.—Meanwhile the daughter sleeps, as do the twins.

[13] Noise of the night tram from Dalkey added to the figure of HCE.

The man in the street can see the coming event—their shadow on the blind photo-flashing it far too wide: it will be known through all Urania soon; here's the flood that's to come over help- less Irryland. While the Park's police peels peering by.

Copulation continued: at half past quick in the morning; at kicks o'clock in the morm. Her lamp was all askew, and a trumbly wick in her; (584) tipatonguing him on in her pigeony linguish, with a flick at the bails for lubrication, to scortch her, faster, faster. Three for two will do for me and he for thee and she for you.[14] Go easy-osey—for fear he's tire and burst his dunlops and waken her bornybarnies making his boobybabies,[15] treading her, when, keek, the hen in the Dorans' shantyqueer began in a kikkery key to laugh it off, yeigh yeigh neigh neigh, the wav she was wuck to doodledoo by her gallows bird.[16]

Cockadoodledoo! Cocorico!

We are pleased to return auditors' thanks. Exclusive pictorial rights (585) in next aeon's issue. Echolo choree choroh choree chorico! Thanks also to Miss Glimglow [the lamp], Master Met- tresson [the mattress], patient ringsend [the condom], and the thunder which first taught love's lightning the way. Come, if you please, kindly feel for her, while the dapple-gray dawn drags near- ing nigh.

Copulation concluded: Anastomosis.[17] O yes! O yes! Withdraw your member. Closure. The chamber stands abjourned. Humbo, lock your kekkle up! Anny, blow your wickle out. Tuck away the tablesheet. You never wet the tea.—And you may go rightoway back to your *A*unty *D*iluvia; Humphrey, after that!

Witness!
Rules of the hotel: Quiet please, (586) and decent decorum. Maid Maud blabs to her bosom friend who does all the chores; this ig-

---

[14] Popular song: "Tea for Two."
[15] Care lest he burst the condom.
[16] Cf. p. 110. Here the henyard noises break into the peace.
[17] Anastomosis: the union of one vessel with another belonging to a different system; inosculation. Cf. p. 615, "anastomosically assimilated."

norant sweeps it out, then it goes to the river and to the laundresses; finally everyone in Dublin knows.

Soon, all is as it was before, right as ever, in very old place. Were Patrolman Seekersenn to pass, about this time, he would have plenty of light shining through either one of uncle's windows. Were he to bring his boots to pause in peace on the road, he would hear only the flow of water, telling him all about ham and livery and inviting him to stay; (587) or he would hear only the wind among them trees.

Testimony of the witnesses: Me and my auxy, Jimmy d'Arcy, we had not much light with which to see. Who was he seen with? He treated the three of us to a couple of drinks, and, toasting our king, declared his standpoint was to belt and butcher him before the whole congregation. Was he true to me? Fred Watkins here calls him Honeysuckler. Who has sinnerettes to declare? Concerning our Phoenix Rangers' nuisance, the Two, and the Three—the party must be raw in cane sugar. Who trespasses against me? That's him with his wig on, Mr. Beardall, ex-burgomaster. Who fears all masters? (588) How we framed him: defenses down, we spied on him; she'll do it again during her music-hall visit after he's had his fill of alcohol.

Following up to see-point: You two Black-and-Tans, were you there? What was the weather? Could the waters only speak as they flow! Six trees were waving there, and all the trees in the wood trembled when they heard the news.

Account of his rise and fall: Two pretty mistletots ribboned to a tree; up rose liberator, and they were free! Four witty missywives wink-(589)ing under hoods made lasses and lads love Maypole-riding, and so dotted our green with tricksome couples. So pennies grew into pounds, and many made money, following the way of the world. And the cause of it all, he forged himself ahead: our *h*ugest *c*ommercial *e*mporialist, with his sons booing home from afar, and his daughters bridling up at his side.

How did he bank it up?—Taking advantage of others' blunders. But misfortunes overwhelmed him, (590) and he came to grief. So now he is weeping on his bankrump.

He is rejected by Lloyds.
What followed?

Dumbshow IV. Fourth position of solution (John's view)
Tableau final. View from horizon. Male and female unmask we
them. Dawn! After having drummed all he dun; worked out to
an inch of his core. More! Ring down. While the queen bee blesses
her bliss for to feel her funnyman's functions. Rumbling.

Tiers, tiers, and tiers. Rounds.

BOOK IV

RECORSO

[The cycle of a life has run its course. The hero in his soul's anguish dreamed of a future that would be gloriously mastered by his John o' Dreams son, but beheld the vision disintegrate and dissolve. In the end all reduced itself to a dowdy, unpromising present. The man and woman had reached the end of their fruitfulness. Love was no longer what it once had promised.

[Thus the clock now moves one tick past them to the opening of another cycle. The worn-out father and mother fall back one degree into the past. Not in the father's *dream* for his son, but in the actual fleshly son he once begot buds the future. This youth who will carry the burdens of tomorrow will be actually a lumpish chip of the old block, another incarnation of HCE. Book IV will show his incipient power seeding forth. The father, together with his day of deeds, will shift into the position of the comic old-timer Finnegan. His wife will become the widow of the giant of the past, the mistress Kathe, tip.

[This succession is in reality the sustaining idea of *Finnegans Wake,* demonstrable not only in the father-son nexus, but in the relationship of the four books each to the other. To state the matter in terms of Joyce's characters, it may be said that the central figure of *Finnegans Wake* is the HCE of Book II, the father-husband in life's prime. But his virile bulk is destined to be cracked by the pressure of time. Kevin (Shaun) is time's elected hammer, born to deliver the blow which will shatter HCE. Shaun himself will then step into his father's shoes. In Book II we saw the old

339

man beginning to crack; in Book IV we shall see the instrument (Shaun) who is pulverizing him. Books I and III represent HCE's envisionments, under pressure, of past and future. The cyclic plan of *Finnegans Wake* is made clear when we realize that Kevin (Shaun) will presently occupy the central position of Book II and generate his own Finnegan dream of a past and a future.

[*Finnegans Wake in toto* is the fourfold aspect of every living moment: the whole round is entirely present with every tick of the clock. Book IV is that aspect of the tick which translates "not yet" into "now." It opens with the dim cries of angelic voices calling. They are convening the mystical guardians of the new aeon to their positions. The avatars, or vehicles, of the new law are summoned to prepare to become manifest.]

(593) *Sandhyas! Sandhyas! Sandhyas!* [1]
Calling all downs. Calling all downs to dayne.[2] Array! Surrection. The smog is lofting. The olduman has godden up to litanate the bonnamours. Good morning, have you used Piers' *aube* [Pears' Soap, Persse O'Reilly's dawn]? Quake up, dim dusky; wake doom for husky! Guinness is good for you.

[1] The book opens with a strong coloration of Sanskrit, the language of those Hindu and Buddhist works which have supremely formulated the idea of the cosmic cycles of unending time. The mood of the last pages of *Finnegans Wake* is very nearly that of the vastly disillusioned yet profoundly acquiescent, and even subtly joyful East. The standpoint is far beyond the simple antinomy of optimism and pessimism.
Sandhyas is a Sanskrit word meaning "twilight, the period between aeons, period of junction." The daily prayers recited at dawn, noon, sunset, and midnight are called *sandhyas*. Joyce here in punning with the *Sanctus, Sanctus, Sanctus* of the Catholic Mass.
[2] "Calling all downs" suggests the "Calling all cars" of the police radio. In the cabalistic decade of p. 308 the word "Car" appears in the place of the four. Properly, this is the place of the Word, and this Word is the seed-pronouncement of which the whole universe is the visible expression. Each aeon, or world cycle, has its Word. The officers, or agents of the Word are those laws of nature which control the process of the cycle. "Calling all downs" is the voice of the Lord summoning to their tasks all the officers of the new aeon; they will descend, as though in mystical elevators, to the plane of manifestation.

A hand from the cloud emerges, holding a chart expanded.[3]

The sower of the seeds of light, lord of risings in the yonder world speaks:

(594) Vah! Suvarn Sur! Thou who agnitest! *Dah!* Be![4] Svadesia, save and guide us! We Durbalanars thee adjure.[5] Guide us from our house of death through kingdom come to Heliotropolis, city of the sun. A flash, and quickly it comes to pass; life comes to the hearths of the world; the stone in the center of the druids' circle is touched by the light of dawn. Past now pulls [i.e., karma becomes effective]. Dane the Great [the new Logos] may tread the path. So, let the cock crow, once, twice, thrice. (595) The death bone is pointed and the quick quoke, but life wends and the dombs spake.[6]

Twilight tour with professor-guide

[The tone abruptly changes. The apocalyptic imagery suddenly gives place to the dream-tour motifs of *Finnegans Wake*. The professor is with us again, pointing out the sights and monuments of

[3] This chart is the as yet unwritten page of the new cycle.

[4] "Vah" is here a word of command addressed to the Word which is to become flesh in the new cycle. *Vah* is Sanskrit, meaning "flow, experience, take in marriage, convey in a carriage, lead."

"Suvarn Sur" is a title of the Word made manifest. *Suvarna* is a Sanskrit word meaning "golden, of beautiful color." *Sur* is again Sanskrit, meaning "sun, god, sage."

"Agnitest" is the word "ignitest" modified by the Sanskrit *agni*, which means "fire," and is the name of the divine energy that burns in all things and is especially manifest in the sacrificial flame intermediating between man and the divine. "Agnitest" also suggests *Agnus Dei*, Christ as Lamb of the Sacrifice.

Dah (Sanskrit) means "burn."

[5] *Svadesia* (Sanskrit) means "self-guider, thou who movest spontaneously in thy proper course." *Durbala* means "of little strength." "We who are of little strength call upon Thee to save and guide us." Joyce puns on "Dubliners."

[6] On pp. 193 and 195 Justice and Mercy are represented as pointing, respectively, the death bone and the life wand. According to the cabala Justice and Mercy are the two antagonistic principles which produce, by their interaction, Life and Beauty. Here they are shown in juxtaposition at the opening of the cycle.

the history-ridden countryside. Nothing has happened yet, nevertheless all that will come to pass has happened before. We are shown the landscape. We then regard the microcosmic sleeper in his bed. We then listen to the song of a friarbird [7] which tells of the coming of HCE. Again we regard the sleeper who, vaguely troubled by a beam of morning light, stirs in his bed and rolls over.]

There stretches the hill beside the river. Presently we may hear the twenty-nine again, saying their good-nights to Livia. (Fortunately old Bruton has withdrawn his theory; you are absolutely right. You are not becoming bored?) We seem to be standing somewhere about Wellington's monument. Among horseshoes, charioteers, barrows, etc. While a successive generation has been in the deeps of Deeper-eras, buried hearts have been resting here.

The sleeper

So, let him sleep, the sap, till they take down the shutter from his shop.

Conk a dook he'll do. *Svap.* [8]

The tale told by the friarbird *(the four-o'clock)*

A natural child was kidnaped; or perhaps he conjured himself from sight by sleight (596) of hand; but he returns—the Sassenach, full of spawnish oil; quite a big bug: *parasama* [9] to himself; as Jambudvispa Vipra [10] foresaw him; sure, straight, slim, sturdy, serene, synthetical, swift.

He has achieved through ruse his inherited wish; he comes from

---

[7] The friarbird is an Australian songbird, called also the four-o'clock because of its note.

[8] *Svap* is Sanskrit, meaning "sleep."

[9] *Parasama* is Sanskrit, meaning "pre-eminently like"; HCE is pre-eminently like unto himself.

[10] *Jambu dvipa* is Sanskrit. It is the name of the great continent inhabited by man. This continent is surmounted by a mighty jambutree, which is, of course, the World Tree of pp. 504–5. Joyce here puns on Giambattista Vico whose historical cycles are identified with the cyclic rise and fall of the World Tree.

afar. (597) We have been having a sound night's sleep? It is just about time to roll over. *Svapnasvap*.[11] Because, there are two sides to turn to, west and east, the falling asleep and the waking up—a sort of systole-diastole which everybody all doze. Why? Such me.[12]

The time

Look! A shaft of shivery in the act—flash from a future of maybe. It is infinitesimally fevers—sleeper awakening.

The torporature is returning to mornal. It is perfect degrees excelsius—humid nature is feeling itself freely at ease. You have eaden fruit! You have snakked mid a fish! (598) Vanished! You had him on the tip of your tongue. Noctambulant, we have wandered through the nonexistent waters of the night-Nile. It was a long, dark, all but unending night: now day, slow day. The lotus bells.[13] It is our hour of risings.

In that european end meets Ind.[14]

There is something supernocturnal about him-it. In this vale without tares, this is that. All the formulations of the past are to be transcended. Where he gets up, there will be a great stretch of fancy—through strength toward joyance.

Those in the city, hearing, heard. The identity of the present with the past rings out: the urb it orbs! Then's now with now's then, in tense continuant. When the clock strikes, it will be exactly so fewer hours from the opening of the day of him and her.

(599) See you not the path our fathers founded? Our fathers of earliest ages, padding on their paws! Primeval conditions have gradually receded, but the emplacement of solid and fluid has, to a great extent, persisted through the Vicʌnian ages; so that, at the

[11] *Svapnasvap* is Sanskrit: sleeping-sleep.

[12] *Search me!* I cannot tell you why; but *such me,* that's the way I am.

[13] From the navel of the sleeping god Vishnu, whose dream is the universe, a golden lotus blossoms forth at the opening of each new cycle of existence. This lotus is the universe of his dream.

[14] This is the moment of *Sandhyas,* "Junction," when the opposites come together. Europe and India, empirical knowledge and intuitive wisdom, are now one.

place and time under consideration, a socially organic entity in a more or less settled state of economic equilibrium, after a certain hesitancy, is made possible and even inevitable.—Come on, old man, no more of that stuff for me; let's have a drink.[15]

(Take Tamotimo's Topical.—Advertisement.)

The place

[Step by step the conditions of the dawn moment are being revealed. The Time aspect has been discussed: it is the moment of the first shaft of light. The Place aspect now comes up for consideration; together with the problem of the gist of it all. The place is this fishy river pool where so many things have happened. Here are the great tree and stone. Here a great life festival might flourish, or just as well, a hermit's hut might stand.]

Beclouded heaven electing, the dart of desire has gored the heart of secret waters. And the popularest wood in the entire district is being grown. It is all very obscure, so that, beyond indicating the locality one can add very little. The gist of the pantomime (600) is simply this: in this Drury world-theater of ours, Father Time and Mother Spacies boil their kettle with their crutch. Which every lass and lad in the lane knows. (And though the old man of the sea and the old woman in the sky don't say nothings about it, still they don't tell us no lie.) [16]

Polycarp pool, of meadowy marge, the river of lives; the regenerations of the incarnations of the emanations of the apparentations of Funn and Nin: where Allbroggt gladsighted Viggynette; where Linfian Fall turned the first sod before Gage's Fane; where ex-Colonel House's heiress is to return to Dweyr O'Michael's pikehead. There a tree begins to bloomer. There a stone, immemorial, the only one in the swamp. Tree and stone tell Paudheen Steel the

[15] Earthly man protests against all this metaphysical clap-trap. There follows an advertisement for a refreshing drink.

[16] The union of Time and Space, World Father and World Mother, generates the universe of living forms. These cosmic powers do not tell us in so many words what the show is all about; but their mysterious presence itself implies something which cannot be denied, and which is taken for granted by buoyant youth.

Poghue and his perty Molly Vardant, that this is a proper site, either for the cardinal communal celebration or for the hut-caged (601) naked yogi.

Of Kevin

[We now come to the first form that is to issue pristine from the life-fertile waters. It will be fair with the perfection of an as yet unbroken harmony. Luminous, first fruit of the womb of night, it will sit like Brahma on the golden lotus that blossoms from the navel of Vishnu, the cosmic dreamer. Pure, with the innocence of sainthood, balanced in all virtues, the first child of the new aeon will be radiant with the dew of dawn.

[Who is he but saintly Kevin? He rises from the lake in the gentle guise of an early Irish saint, greeted by the joyful, angelic song of the twenty-nine girls.

[The celebration of Kevin is interrupted by a news report, broadcast by the Ass of the Four Old Men, describing the Funeral Games at Valleytemple: the Ass, as representative of an outworn aeon, reminds us that the present is the wake of the past. Whereupon a greasily smiling presence out of London puts ashore, Shaun the Post, giddy on ladies—to help us remember what this Kevin is one day to be.

[But to give the moment of innocence its due: with the rising of the sun, a little stained-glass window of a chapel in Chapelizod becomes illuminated, like a jewel, and therein is revealed the sweetly pictured life of the angelic hermit.]

Bring about that which is to be brought about and it will be. Look—the city of Is is issuant (Atlanta! At last!) from under the lake: our lake lamented, that greyt lack, Erie.

And from the throats of the twenty-nine goes up a sigh and prayer of praise, longsome the sapphire coast, echoing the sigh of the earth itself. They carol round Botany Bay [Darwin, reminiscent of Natural Selection] and what they sang about was Kevin, only he, little he!

So, now that the girls have sung, get up! You have irrigation work to do. Ascend out of your bed. Ireland awaits.

345

(602) One seeks the perfect specimen. Someone in particular? Or something ideal and general, hanging in the air?

What is Kevin [17] doing? A would-to-godder, his moral tack is his best of weapons. His face is the face of a son. A virgin, the one, shall mourn thee.—The Ass, abrowse in the Potter's field of the four coroners, visited by an independent reporter, "Mikes" the news of the great funeral games at Valleytemple.—Out of London, along the seaways, comes Mr. Hurr Hansen, Shoon the Puzt, hoping to fall in with a merry lot of maidens, (603) smiling greasily, fit as a fiddle. Oh, what an ovenly odour! Bring us this day our maily bag! —All the news and scandals: official with alter girl on a pillow; he was giddy on ladies, till Dr. Chart changed his backbone; it might be anything after dark; a libel action.

But what is Kevin doing? His legend, depicted in the stained glass, begins to show in the faint light. (604) The vine has fruited, but the public hatches are not quite open yet for mess. The angel of the lord has not yet declared unto Mary. Yet the Greek Siderial Railway will soon be starting. See what our first ray of dawn shall show:

(605) The miracles, death, and life of Kevin:—With priest's portable *altare cum balneo*,[18] at matin chime in celibate matrimony he arose; rafting to the yselt in the lakelet, and at the third morn hour building a honey-beehivehut, then at sextnoon collecting Gre-

<hr>

[17] In Joyce's text appears the Irish spelling, "Coemghen."

[18] Altar and bathtub combined. The hermit uses this *altar-tub* as a boat to take him to an islet in the middle of a lake. In this islet is a spring from which the saint collects water. He builds himself a hut, in the floor of which he digs a pit into which to pour the water; then he sits in the water to meditate. This passage is one of the most charming in the book.

The place of St. Kevin's hermitage is Glendalough, in the Wicklow Hills. The waters named in Joyce's text are rivulets and lakelets of this area. Here is where Anna Liffey is a young and dancing nymph. The washerwomen of Book I spoke of the monk who touched her with his lips to slake his thirst (p. 203).

The water in which Kevin sits to meditate is called, in the manner of St. Francis, "sister water." The act of the saint is a cherubical combination of baptism, the Mass, and marriage. The word "yee" at the end of this passage is the shiver of the saint as he squats in the chilly element.

gorian water and exorcising his holy sister (606) water, when violet vesper vailed he meditated, in the water, on the sacrament of baptism. Yee.

Twilight tour with professor-guide—Resumed

Note this rare view of the three bens (hills). The first to make his ablations in these parks was the mortal shown in the trial (607). The motto of the MacCool family is "Great sinner, good sonner." The gloved list was introduced into their sacerdotal tree before 1175. There are four town clocks which show Jacob (with pipe) and Esau (with borrowed dish) and then a procession of the apostles, at *e*very *h*ours of *c*hangeover; this hourly puppet procession represents the first and last riddle of the universe. It is the signal for Finnegan's wake, for the old Lord of Chapelizod to seek the shades of his retirement, and for young Chappielassies to tease their partners.

And it's high tigh tigh. Titley hi ti ti. Beg pardon. Excuse. Sorry.

Day gains. Hail, receding darkness. Thund, lightning thund. King Sol the First will show above Dublin Bar, to be greeted by the burgomaster.

(608) It is a mere trick of this vague of visibilities. There have been dissolving before you only (1) the draper, (2) the two drawper's assisters, (3) the three assessors—surprised by (4) the Sigurd Sigerson Sphygmomanometer Society [the Twelve].

From sleep we are passing. The chill cry of Stena is heard and the gladdening voice of Alina; bringing the brew with a future in it. I seem to remember—it was something like. There are signs that there is something still willing to be becoming upon this once-a-here-was world! Temtem tamtam, the Phoenician wakes.

One, two, three: into the wide-awake world from sleep we are passing. Four: come, hours, be over!

But still. Ah dear, ah dear! And stay!

(609) It was all so agreeable, touring the no placelike no time like absolent; touring in our gearless clutchless car; mixing up the

347

petty populace with the great gentry, like so many improbables in pursuit of the impossible, with Matthew, Mark, Luke, and John—and their Ass.

The Ass will be browsing among the girlyflowers in the neighborhood of Wynn's Hotel (opening shortly) when the Messenger of the Risen Sun shall settle upon the time and place. Meanwhile we are waiting for . . . hymn.

A.D. 432

[All is now in readiness for the crucial moment of Book IV; the crucial moment, indeed, of history; the moment of the renovating impulse. This crisis is represented by the arrival in Ireland of St. Patrick (*ca.* A.D. 432) and his debate with the Archdruid before High King Lughaire (pronounced Leary). The archdruid is called Bulkily, Balkelly, and Burkeley and speaks his piece in Chinese pidgin; Patrick speaks in Japanese pidgin and is called the Eurasian Generalissimo. We behold here a curious convergence of many themes.

[The name of the archdruid suggests, in the first place, the Irish metaphysician George Berkeley (1685–1753). The druid's strictly idealistic philosophy, too, is strongly Berkeleyan in character, with a flavoring of Kant. Practical, hard-headed St. Patrick, on the other hand, though unable quite to follow the trend of the druid's transcendentalist argument, knows well enough how to give a popular reply. As the representative of the Rock of Peter he is the protagonist of effective action. He simply cuts the gloriously involved Gordian knot of metaphysics with a sharp, good-enough retort, and wins from the populace a triumphant cheer. With that stroke, the deep night of druidical brooding is dispelled and the way is opened for the day of progressive action. The logic of *Finnigans Wake* itself, which is the logic of slumber and druidic myth, is overcome by St. Patrick's blow. This is the moment of transition into waking life: from here on the book slides quickly toward the opening of the eyes to day.

[The name of the archdruid suggests, in the second place, Buckley, who shot the Russian General; and this suggestion is supported by the designation of St. Patrick as the Eurasian Generalissimo. In the depths of sleep it was Buckley who won, but in the course of daylight history it will be the General.[19] The theme of imperialism developed in the Butt and Taff episodes (338–55) here becomes expanded and clarified. Rome, Russia, England, and Japan coalesce as representatives of successful statecraft, in opposition to the Gnostic, Individualistic, Irish, Taoist combination of the druid. The former is Shaunish, the latter Shemmish; the former is lord of the day, the latter of night.

[Just as Patrick's triumph comes at the point of waking, so his opposite's, Buckley's, came in the middle-depth of night. And if we turn back, now, to the very early encounter of Mutt and Jute, we shall see in it the prelude to Buckley's conquest: Mutt, the representative of the dark world, pointed out to Jute, the blond conqueror, the marvels of his dream landscape and elicited from him an exclamation of awe.

[As if to stress the continuity of the Mutt and Jute, Butt and Taff, and Druid-Patrick episodes, Joyce opens the present scene with a discussion between two queer fellows Muta and Juva, who are watching from a distance the arrival of the saint and his train of pack-bearers.]

Muta and Juva

Muta and Juva are watching the arrival. Dawn hangs like smoke over the Head of Howth. The day is now lord over sleep and commands the shadows to disperse. St. Patrick arrives with monks, porters, and ghariwallas. Meanwhile, the archdruid of Ireland stands tall (610) and disgusted. His name is Bulkily. From under a memorial the spirit of old Finn is resurrecting, i.e., the end-and-rebeginning is at hand. Finn stands incarnate in the figure of Leary, high king of Ireland. King Leary smiles. He has bet half his crown on the Burkeley boy [the druid] but half on the

[19] Actually there is no historical record of a Buckley shooting a Russian General. The victory is a dream victory, opposite and compensatory to literal actuality.

349

Eurasian Generalissimo [Patrick]; thus, doubly willing, he is doubly cynical. King Leary quaffs a drink, the dry-wet glass he never starts to finish at Wynn's Hotel.

Muta asks whether the lesson of history may be summed up in the cyclic formula: "From unification, through diversity and instinct-to-combat, toward appeasement." Juva agrees, but with the rational amendment that the process proceeds from the light of bright reason which day sends to us from on high.

Whereupon Muta and Juva, representing the expiring aeon, reach appeasement: Muta asks, "May I borrow that from you, old rubberskin?" Juva replies, "Here it is, and I hope its the death of you, Erinmonker!" But in the encounter of the druid-sage and missionary-saint, diversity is immediately again in force:

The Grand Natural Mooting: Sage and Saint

The grand national meeting is introduced as a colorful, rhythmical, fashionable horse race (611) during the course of which Patrick and the druid chat.

And here are the details of their debate.

Balkelly, archdruid: [20] "The phenomenal forms beheld by mortal eye are comparable to the refracted hues into which sunlight is broken by a prism. The mineral, vegetable, animal, and common-man inhabitants of the world are incapable of experiencing the whole source-light. But the true seer, in the seventh degree of the Wisdom of Being, knows the inwardness of reality, the *Ding an sich,* the essence of each thing; and for him all objects shine with that gloria of seed light which is within them. The entire world, for him, is an epiphany.[21]

Patrick, however, did not quite follow the drift. While the druid waxed in eloquence, the saint's eyes wandered to High King Leary, whom, by way of passing the time, he tried to envision as King

[20] The archdruid's paragraph opens with the word "Tune," linking his talk to the *Tunc* page of the Book of Kells (pp. 122, etc.). The druid stands over against Patrick as the later Irish saints against Pope Adrian IV, the Gripes against the Mookse, the Four Inquisitors against Yawn, etc.

[21] Epiphany: see footnote 31 to chap. 3 of Bk. III, *supra.*

Harvest: with kilt like spinach, (612) torque like cauliflowers, eyes like thyme chopped with parsley, stone of ring like an olive lentil, war scars on face like chopped senna: *H*ump *c*umps *E*bbly-bally: a veritable Feast of Tabernacles.

Patrick's reply:[22] "It is a mistake to say that knowledge *a posteriori,* even for a seer, can attain to the celestial. When you speak of the essential knowledge of the true seer, it is as though, by a paralogism and circumlocution, 'My' were to be spoken of as 'Me,' or a handkerchief were to be taken for the owner of the handkerchief. If we are to permit to you such seeming 4-3-2 agreement, then we may also accept for common man the Sacred Heart as adequate sound-sense symbol for the fire cast therein by the sunlight of the Father, the Son, and the Holy Ghost. Amen."

That was the very thing, begad. The druid was completely nonplussed. His throw had lost. Thud.

(613) "God save Ireland!" hailed the populace, awed. And the heavens resounded: *"Per eumdem Dominum Nostrum Jesum Christum Filium Tuum."*

And the entire company, saints and sages, kings and carls, was moved.

Transition

[The victory of St. Patrick is the sunrise of a new day, scattering the profound night shadows of the self-contemplating, mythological age of dream. All eyes will open now to the solid realities of waking life, and these will be regarded rationally, as discrete from each other, three-dimensional, and opaque. The wild fluidity of the subtle night figments, their strange yet appallingly familiar, unfathomable portent, their identity with each other and with the dreamer who beholds them, their insidious phosphorescence, swiftly now will scatter and sink into the pits below the depths of what is known.

[And yet, nothing has really changed. It is only the manner in

---

[22] Patrick's paragraph opens with the word "Punc," i.e., *Punkt,* period, that's an end to it.

which things are regarded that has changed. Their relationships to each other have thereby been transformed. And this transformation promises a new era.

[But even this great promise is something that has been known before. Even the new relationships are the standard relationships of waking consciousness. The individual who emerges out of the pits of sleep and drinks the waking-up drink of his morning coffee will open his eyes to a world of old, old friends. The morning paper will rehearse the ancient story.

[Hence, this chapter of renewal leads forward to the old theme of the Letter, which is Joyce's prime symbol of the recurrence of the past.]

So that's the great news for today. The great crisis has come to pass. 'Tis gone forever to fix Eurasia in trance. Now for a far bigger pancosmos. And let every crisscouple be crosscomplementary: ham and eggs for all.

Yet is no body present that was not here before.—Only order othered. *Fuitfiat!* [As it was, let it be!]

Benediction on the land of Ireland when saint and sage have had their say.

Ralph the Retriever ranges in a wild weed waste of a world. Catkins luxuriate among skull hollows. The nauseous cup must be drunk before breakfast; then you'll be as paint and spickspan as a rainbow.

*H*ealth! *C*hance! *E*ndless necessity! *A*rrive, *l*ickypuggers, in a *p*oke. There is bound to be a lovely day for marriages in the open. Morning and Evening will bury the hatchet. But first: straighten out these disorderly affairs, settle down to decent sexual relationships.

(614) All will be incessantly coming back. Every article will be needing several rinsings. For nought that is has bane. Habit returns. So get to work at all this washing. Today persists in tomorrow. Forget—remember.

Our wholemole millwheeling vicociclometer receives the separated elements of precedent decomposition for the purpose of subsequent recombination, (615) so that the old Adamic structure of our Finnius may be there for you when cup, platter, and pot come piping hot. As sure as herself pits hen to paper and there's scribblings scrawled on eggs. Scribblings such as those of the letter:

The Letter

[This final and most extensive development of the Letter continues in the mood of the last letter passage of pages 494–95. It rehearses some eight themes: (1) it opens with a greeting to Dear Dirty Dublin, (2) it expresses thanks for favors received, (3) it scolds those muckrakers who have trespassed on the reputation of the great man, (4) it mentions incidents out of his life, (4') it rails against him, (5) it gives news of the writer of the Letter, her past, her present, and her children, (6) it speaks of a funeral and wake, (7) it develops what might be called "the Boot Lane Complication"—a version of the scandal and arrest peculiar to these statements of ALP and characterized by references to a thug, Sully, and a bottle of urine-pilsener-medicine, (8) it suggests that the reader look in his own letter box for a post-card view of the whole affair.

[The sequence of the statements may be summarized as follows:]

1. Greeting: Dear Dirtdump [Dear Dirty Dublin], Reverend Majesty!

2. Thanks: We have enjoyed these secret workings of natures; delighted this last time.

3. Muckrakers, shut up! A fine day will come.

4. He: Born on the top of the long car, as merrily we rolled along; looking at us, as if to pass away in a cloud; woke up in a sweat beside us, and daydreamed we had a lovely face.

5. That was the prick of the spindle to me, that gave me the keys to dreamland.

(616) *4. He:* That coerogenal Hun and his knowing the size of an eggcup; first a salesman, then Cloon's fired him (Advertisement for sausages); the mitigation of the king's evils was one of his earliest wishes.

(617) 2. *Thanks:* 111 plus 1001 blessings to you for all the trouble you took.

5. *Us:* We are all at home in Fintona, thank Danis to whom we will be true.

4'. Who would want to remember a mean stinker like Foon MacCrawl?

5. Tomothy and Lorcan [à Becket and O'Toole, Shem and Shaun] changed characters during blackout.

6. Music ought to wake him; funeral shortly; please come.

4'. I wish I was by that dumb tyke and he'd wish it was me under heel.

(618) 5. *Us:* Our shape as a young girl was much admired (Advertisement for beauty shop).

7. *Boot Lane Complications:* Thugs off Bully's acre, got up by Sully; she had a certain medicine brought her in a victualer's bottle. Shame! The waxy, angry one is now in the hospital and may never come out.

8. Look through your leather box for a view of St. Patrick's Purge—to see under grand piano Lily on the sofa pulling a low (and then he'd begin to jump a little to find out what goes on when love walks in).

3. *Denials:* Not true that we were not treated grand when the police arrived; we never were chained to a chair; no widower followed us about with a fork.

4. *He:* A great civilian, gentle as a mushroom and very affectable.

7. Sully is a thug, though a fine bootmaker by profession; would we were here earlier to lodge complaint on Sergeant Laraseny.

(619) Whoever likes that urogynal pan of cakes, one apiece, it is thanks to Adam, our former first Finnlatter, for his beautiful cross-mess parcel.

3. Their damn cheek, wagging about the rhythms in my twofold bed. Reply:

4. We've lived in two worlds: (*a*) it is another he who stays under the Hill of Howth, (*b*) the here-waker, who will *e*rect, *c*onfident and *h*eroic, when a wee one woos, is his real name same.

5. She: About fed up now with nursery rhymes, she rigs up in regal rooms with the ritzies.

Signed: *Alma Luvia Pollabella.*

The final monologue

[The night of HCE is far behind. The letter-memoirs of the widow let us know that all is past. With the approach of day the mystical sleep identity of HCE and ALP has been sundered; each remains only himself, separate, three-dimensional and alone. The man form has rolled over; the woman now flows rapidly away from him. Her final monologue, one of the great passages of all literature, is the elegy of River Liffey as she passes, old, tired, soiled with the filth of the city, through Dublin and back to the sea.]

Greetings, city. Liffey speaking. A leaf for my golden wending. Rise up, (620) man of the house! You make me think of my former lovers. The children are still asleep. Remember the night you begot the girl. What will be—is. (621) Come, step out of your shell! Yes. I'll take my shawl. Give me your hand. There are bad things in your past, but we'll lave it so. We'll take our walk before the bells ring. (622) The birds are cawing luck to you. Next election you'll be elected. It seems ages since; remember our boy and girl days! We have loads of time before the hunting party calls again. (623) We might call on the Old Lord: his is the House of Laws. I shall behave there as the prankquean. We can sit and watch the sunrise, and see if the letter you're waiting for be cast ashore: it was a hard letter to write. (624) When the waves give up yours, the soil may mine for me. I wrote me hopes and buried me page till a kissmiss coming. Scale the top, Master Builder, 'twas little your ground-planning brought. On limpid marge I've made me home—only don't start your old stunts again. Grand old marauder! If I knew who you are! First time you called. Your brother's slander against you. The (625) night you mistook me for two other girls. The false beard in your bag! I can point out to you the scenery of the circular road: Cadmillersfolly, Bellevenue,

355

Wellcrom, Quid Superabit—villities, valleties! Change the plates for the next course. Ask the Four Old Men. It's all so often, and all the same to me. New times, old customs. This is the way. (626) I'm a little faint; let me lean on you. Island Bridge! Remember? The fellow who followed me with the Fork. The ways you had. I was everyone's pet then. But you're changing, (627) son-husband, turning from me for a daughter-wife. She'll come. She'll be as sweet as I was. Be happy. I could have stayed up there forever in me great blue mother: it's something fails us; first we feel, then we fall.—And let her rain now if she likes, for my time is come. I done me best when I was let. A hundred cares, a tithe of troubles, and is there one who understands me? All me life I have been living among them, but now they are becoming loathed to me. I thought you were great: you're but a puny. I would go back to my people. Back to my wild (628) father sea. My leaves have drifted from me, but one clings still. I'll bear it on me, to remind me of . . . Yes. Whish! A gull. Gulls. Far calls. Coming, far! End here.—Us then. Finn, again! Take. The keys to. Given! A way a lone a last a loved a long the

CONCLUSION

Thus ends the Book of Doublends Jined. Like a millrace it sweeps down and out of sight, to strike again the paddle wheel of revolving time. As the dark torrent disappears from view, we are left standing on the bank, bewildered, yet strangely refreshed by the passage of these miraculous waters. Life, drained from the inexhaustible hills, has been measured, proved and named without mercy; cynic depths have been sounded and the very sewage of existence has become part of the flood. Yet the river odor has been congenial to the human nostril, and the rhythm of the waters has been felt as familiarly, and with the same amoral acceptance, as the heartbeat within our own body.

What is the fascination of this book? Why are we magnetized by its secret? And again we ask, by what warrant does the author make his message so hard to decipher—and by what act of creative largess does he compensate us so richly for our labors?

Clearly, a new kind of communication—unique, original, and difficult—has been encountered in these pages. On the merely stylistic level, *Finnegans Wake* represents the logical end of Joyce's literary development. From the beginning, he strove to let the essential nature of the subject matter dictate and shape his style: *Dubliners* he wrote "for the most part in a style of scrupulous meanness," [1] to match the society it portrayed; in *A Portrait of the Artist as a Young Man* the style matures with the growth of the hero. In *Ulysses* it follows the modalities of the advancing day across a city of burned-out clichés. And in *Finnegans Wake* it sinks

[1] James Joyce in a letter to Mr. Grant Richards, quoted by Herbert Gorman. *James Joyce,* Farrar and Rinehart, 1939, p. 150.

with the sun and enters the world of night logic, there to take on the crowding shapes of dream.

Joyce, progressing through these stages, obviously became dissatisfied with the one-dimensional declarative sentence and conventional vocabulary. Pioneer and transinsular spirit, he could not repose contentedly within the bounds of experience and expression delimited by the Anglo-Saxon tongue. As a Celt he had already complained of these limitations in the *Portrait;* as a cosmopolitan genius he learned to bend to his craft purposes the recorded tongues of the world. With a greed unmatched in the history of literature he seized all language for his province. He had sucked Latin in with the milk of his Jesuit education; with Greek, Sanskrit, Gaelic, and Russian he was on terms of scholarly intimacy. He spoke Italian in his own home; French and German were second mother tongues to him. Obscure dialects, argots, and the slang of many nations clung to his ear like limpets. As a young man he had learned Norwegian in order to study Ibsen; oddments from Finnish, Arabic, Malay, Persian, and Hindustani are plentifully sprinkled through *Finnegans Wake.* While he outrivals Sinclair Lewis in his ability to burlesque the American Babbitt, he knows also the caress of the Neapolitan diminutive. From a teeming thesaurus of vitally experienced words he selects the aptest to convey his nuance of mood or idea—and keeps on doing so with such passion and rapidity that the reader stands rooted in bewilderment as the multisemantic barrage whizzes past his ears.

Not content with this traffic in staple words, Joyce hangs numberless outriggers of association on every syllable. It is here that even the resourceful dictionary scholar loses his bearings. To take an obvious instance: in the famous "Washers at the Ford" chapter, Anna summons maids to her boudoir for HCE's delight. Into "boudoir" Joyce inserts the letter *l,* and converts the word to "boudeloire," thus adding a river association "Loire." Clinging to the word also are the French associations, *bouder,* "to pout," and *boue,* "mud." Coquettes pout in a boudoir, and the Loire is certainly muddy. Mud, fertile river mud, the delta mud of the Nile, the life mud of the early agricultural civilizations, is throughout

Finnegans Wake associated with the river mother ALP. The mud packs of her boudoir now will freshen up the pouting temptresses, who are to coax the old thunder father from his gloomy brooding. Often a Joycean word will mean more than the sum of its parts, just as a musical chord means more than the sum of the notes composing it. An example occurs in "persequestellates" in which "pursues" vibrates with overtones of Persse O'Reilly, Stella, love quest, and persecutions. No wonder Joyce does not read as easily as Trollope or Louis Bromfield.

Still another protractor for opening out words and sentences is Joyce's use of rhythms to touch off half-remembered reverberations from the childhood of the individual and the race. Thus Shaun the great clergyman world-wanderer describes his love for his motherland in a ridiculous parody of the rhythm of Father Prout's "The Shandon Bells." The book resounds with echoes of popular songs, ranging from "Ole Man River" to "Does Your Mother Know You're Out?"—and over the haunting rhythms of the "Angelus," the Lord's Prayer, and the Angelical Salutation, Joyce plays his Finnegan themes *da capo al Phoenix*.

This complex fabric of semantics, associative overtones, and stem rhythms is merely the *materia prima* of Joyce's communication. To this, add an enormous freight of mythological, historical, and psychologic reference. It would be well-nigh hopeless to attempt to trace the design of any page were it not that a thread of logic runs through every paragraph. True, the thread always frays out into lateral associations which in turn disappear into almost inaccessible tenuities of meaning. Yet the main lines can all be followed. Joyce provides an answer to every riddle he propounds. In every passage there is a key word which sounds the essential theme. This word is supported, augmented, commented upon by other expressions in the same passage. Taken together, they not only indicate the mood but convey the meaning. The task of opening the way into any passage thus divides itself into three stages: (1) *discovering* the key word or words, (2) *defining* one or more of them, so that the drift of Joyce's thought becomes evident, (3) *brooding* awhile over the paragraph, to let the associations running out from the

359

key centers gradually animate the rest of the passage. Presently the whole page will be alive with echoings and amplifications, re-echoings and sudden surprises.

Amidst a sea of uncertainties, of one thing we can be sure: *there are no nonsense syllables in Joyce!* His language means so much that any intelligent reader can shave off some rewarding layers of meaning. The clarity and scope of the discoveries will depend almost wholly on the perception brought to bear; as the Master himself says: "Wipe your glosses with what you know."

II

One of the chief tasks of the creative artist is to provide new sustenance for the insatiable gorgon within him. By doing so, he incidentally satisfies the hungers of his generation. It is in keeping with the history of genius that Joyce's personal need for an advanced medium should have coincided with the emergence of powerful new tendencies in Western culture and communication.

During the past half-century a whole new dimension of human experience—the unconscious mind—has been recognized and explored. Without assigning total credit to Freud, Jung, or their disciples, the fact remains that the unconscious is today a well-established entity. But although creative and clinical circles have been aware of this new dimension, there existed no literary technique for projecting it until Joyce developed the forms, first of *Ulysses* and then of *Finnegans Wake*. Conventional language, even in the hands of a great writer, was absolutely inadequate to the task Joyce set himself. He had to smelt a new vocabulary and invent new devices, new grappling hooks, to dredge up the flora and fauna of the hitherto unplumbed abyss.

Indeed, Joyce actually plunges into a region where myth and dream coalesce to form the amniotic fluid of *Finnegans Wake*. Joyce well knew that this deepest level of creation could not be tapped by the siphons of conventional literature. He believed also that somewhere in the noncerebral part of man dwells an intelligence which is the most important organ of human wisdom. He knew further that it operated most typically during the mysterious process of sleep. And for these reasons, he chose night logic, expressed in dream language, as his method of communication.

To translate this dream logic into waking logic is the task that confronts the reader of *Finnegans Wake*. Even when the dream is nearest the surface, the task is not easy. The displacements, transpositions, and mergings of dream images tantalize the interpreter as he snatches at comprehension. But the task is further complicated by the fact that it is the business of a dream not only to reveal but to *conceal* meaning. Our dreams cloak in acceptable disguise messages too horrid with guilt, too stained with unsocial blood, to be admitted to the chambers of day. Only during sleep do these apparitions stream forth to enact hooded mimes of fear and desire. Both for himself and for the world, Joyce is releasing terrific psychic pressures in *Finnegans Wake*. What no man would dare acknowledge publicly, he covertly declares.

The dynamic of obsessional guilt, personal and racial, animates these pages. Author and reader identify themselves with the burdened hero who stutteringly attempts to deny, but must be forever confessing. Indeed, the baffling obscurity of *Finnegans Wake* may be due to the author's determination to muddy the track of his narrative with a thousand collateral imprints, lest we trace him to the scene of his own life-secret, which he yet describes in compulsive half-revelation.

Besides being a Dream Confessional, *Finnegans Wake* is also a Treasury of Myth. Myths, like dreams, are an upworking of the unconscious mind—and Western scholarship has recently become aware of their essential homogeneity throughout the world. *Finnegans Wake* is the first literary instance of myth utilization on a universal scale. Other writers—Dante, Bunyan, Goethe—employed mythologic symbolism, but their images were drawn from the reservoirs of the West. *Finnegans Wake* has tapped the universal sea.

The complexity of Joyce's imagery—as distinguished from that of his language—results from his titanic fusion of all mythologies; and his genius shows itself in his application of these to the special traits of the modern day. *Finnegans Wake* is fellow to the Puranas of the Hindus, the Egyptian Book of the Dead, the Apocalyptic writings of the Persians and the Jews, the scaldic Poetic Edda, and the mystical constructions of the Master Singers of the ancient Celts. In such anonymous productions of the human spirit, shaped by many hands and minds, there is to be found an astonishingly constant under-pattern of archetypal characters and themes. These are the characters and themes of *Finnegans Wake*. They are the forces of the human soul. They speak for themselves with the authority of a timeless, fearless presence, which has survived every kind of disillusionment and living death, embraces every variety of human vice and virtue, and has ridden gloriously on every crusade—indeed, on both sides of every crusade.

Joyce early understood that unless we transcend every limitation of individual, national, racial, and hemispherical prejudice, our minds and hearts will not be opened to the full stature of Man Everlasting. Hence his zeal to shatter and amalgamate the many gods. Through the lineaments of local tradition he sends an X-ray, and on the fluorescent screen of *Finnegans Wake* projects the permanent architecture of all vision and life. For him Krishna, the Buddha, Osiris, Dionysus, Finn MacCool, the Christ, and Mohammed are substantially one; but one with these also, though unconscious of the fact, is the modern citizen of Dublin crossing the green of Phoenix Park. Beneath our constricting coats and vests we are Man the Hero, triumphant over the snares of life and over the sting of death, sublime behind the tailorings, the petty harryings, marryings, and buryings of the endless round in this valley of tears and joy.

James Joyce did not subscribe to the journalistic fallacy that everything should be made easy to understand. He knew that there are levels of experience and consciousness that can be reached only by a prodigious effort on the part of the creative artist, and comprehended only after a comparable effort on the part of the audience. Nietzsche's description of his own creative struggle, "I write in blood, I will be read in blood," is applicable tenfold to Joyce. His youth had been nurtured on such sacramental fare that he was nauseated by the sweetish, sawdust loaf offered to the populace as true bread.

And now the great miracle occurs: even though the race does not cerebrally grasp the full charge of the message, the artist's labor has not been in vain. A subtle radiance emanates from his work and seeps into the unconscious of his age. As George Edward Woodberry says:

> "No echo of the Holy Ghost
> This heedless world has ever lost."

Ulysses, that once unintelligible book, after two decades of official suppression and public neglect, now runs into popular editions. Is it too much to expect that *Finnegans Wake* will win its own audience with the years?

III

In some quarters it is the fashion to dismiss Joyce with various charges, all pivoting on the word "decadent." He is a solipsist talking to himself in a nutshell kingdom of his own. He is a sick spirit addicted to pathologic gnawings of no possible interest to those of us with splendid, robust minds. He is a man for whom time stopped with the death of Tristram, and whose idea of a pleasant experience is to jog his bookish liver with a canter on Vico's nag. Lastly, he is a man who has lost his faith and whose world is a living doomsday, a bleak pit of pessimism.

If Joyce is sick, his disease is the neurosis of our age. Lifting our eye from his page we find in every aspect of society the perversion, the decay, and the disintegration of religion, love, and morality that he has described in *Finnegans Wake.* The hypocrisy of political promises, the prurient preoccupation with sex, the measuring of all values by mercantile standards, the fascination of lurid headlines gossip and its effect on a literate but basically ignorant bourgeoisie—all these are mirrored to the life by this liveliest of observers. Yet there is not a syllable of tirade in *Finnegans Wake.* The lesions of the modern soul, the ulcers of the modern state, are to Joyce but the recurrent fever sores of life in ferment. He is a

clinician who knows that although individuals, indeed whole societies, may be desperately ill, there is a principle of health in the
human germ-plasm that survives pestilence, wars, and dissolutions.
If Joyce's viewpoint is pathologic, then any rosier lens is sentimental.

Every reader must of course decide for himself whether *Finnegans Wake* is the secretion of a spirit in decay. For our own part,
we are convinced that this saga of man's tragicomic destiny is not
a symptom of disintegration, but a powerful act of reintegration,
yielding more for the present, and promising more for the future,
than any work of our time.

In particular we find in *Finnegans Wake* that ebullience and
form-building energy which are the master signs of the creative
spirit in full career. That Joyce was cynical and embittered cannot
be denied; he outsulphurs Swift in his caustic indictment of politics,
religion, imperialism, and the social hypocrisies that accompany
these. Emphatically, *Finnegans Wake* is not a book of sweetness
and light, yet the underlying note is one of positive affirmation.
Not, to be sure, the paean of an ecstatic Pippa, nor the kalsomine
rationalization of a Leibnitz! The affirmation of *Finnegans Wake*
is the Yea of acceptance that Stephen Dedalus uttered when he
saw a young girl wading like a glorious bird in the shallows of a
stream. She appeared to him as an angel, summoning him to life:
to live, to err, to fall, to rise, to re-create life out of life, on and on.
James Joyce married the girl, so to speak, not to reform her but
because he loved her.

The Yea of such a work is not the sponsoring of this or that
hope or the embracing of transient plans for the renovation of the
world. Joyce's "Yes" is more permanent and primary. And *Finnegans Wake* is written from the level of that eternal Yea. Joyce im-
plants this positive golden seed in his female characters, Molly
Bloom and Anna Livia Plurabelle. In *Ulysses,* the drab sterility
and disheartening labyrinths of Dublin's frustration are swallowed
by Molly Bloom at the end, and made to live in her as a vast
symbol of a life impulse deeper than the throb of Dublin's daily
anguish. Molly's "Yes," at the end of the book, is not justified by

any of the recorded events of the day; it comes from a zone beneath the level of the records, precedent to the records, timeless, primary, and the source of all the cities that ever will bloom.

In *Finnegans Wake*, Anna Livia Plurabelle is the carrier of the Eternal Yes; she is the secret of the continuation of the jollification. Men, cities, empires, and whole systems bubble and burst in her river of time. Day-world defeats and losses, the sins of the parents, the clash of brother with brother, the death of heroes and collapse of empires are beheld as parts of form-producing, form-sustaining, form-dissolving life itself. All the contending parties, the victors and the losers, the angels and the devils, the builders and the destroyers, are mothered and cherished by her. Them she affirms and celebrates as she slips between the river banks on her dream journey to the sea of renewal.

To Anna, fittingly, is given the last word of the dissolving dream. Seemingly, this last word loops back to join immediately with the first. But in that suspended tick of time which intervenes between her dissolution into the vast ocean and her reappearance as "riverrun," a brave renewal has taken place. We know that she will be drawn up in dew and descend in rain upon the Wicklow Hills, and that the sun of a whole new day will run its course before she again leads us back to Howth Castle and Environs. A great deal will happen to everyone and everything during this day. And when the night comes again, bringing its release from sun logic, it will be discovered that the daylight personages, objects, and events—swallowed and digested during waking hours—will be curiously transformed. The dream and the strange black book that celebrates it will have more to say the second time, inflecting more exquisitely and abundantly the timeless story of that slow combustion which ever consumes and sustains itself in the interior of the spinning atom, in the living world, and in the soul of man.

FOR THE BEST IN PAPERBACKS, LOOK FOR THE (penguin)

In every corner of the world, on every subject under the sun, Penguin represents quality and variety—the very best in publishing today.

For complete information about books available from Penguin—including Pelicans, Puffins, Peregrines, and Penguin Classics—and how to order them, write to us at the appropriate address below. Please note that for copyright reasons the selection of books varies from country to country.

In the United Kingdom: For a complete list of books available from Penguin in the U.K., please write to *Dept E.P., Penguin Books Ltd, Harmondsworth, Middlesex, UB7 0DA.*

In the United States: For a complete list of books available from Penguin in the U.S., please write to *Dept BA, Penguin, Box 120, Bergenfield, New Jersey 07621-0120.*

In Canada: For a complete list of books available from Penguin in Canada, please write to *Penguin Books Ltd, 2801 John Street, Markham, Ontario L3R 1B4.*

In Australia: For a complete list of books available from Penguin in Australia, please write to the *Marketing Department, Penguin Books Ltd, P.O. Box 257, Ringwood, Victoria 3134.*

In New Zealand: For a complete list of books available from Penguin in New Zealand, please write to the *Marketing Department, Penguin Books (NZ) Ltd, Private Bag, Takapuna, Auckland 9.*

In India: For a complete list of books available from Penguin, please write to *Penguin Overseas Ltd, 706 Eros Apartments, 56 Nehru Place, New Delhi, 110019.*

In Holland: For a complete list of books available from Penguin in Holland, please write to *Penguin Books Nederland B.V., Postbus 195, NL-1380AD Weesp, Netherlands.*

In Germany: For a complete list of books available from Penguin, please write to *Penguin Books Ltd, Friedrichstrasse 10-12, D-6000 Frankfurt Main I, Federal Republic of Germany.*

In Spain: For a complete list of books available from Penguin in Spain, please write to *Longman, Penguin España, Calle San Nicolas 15, E-28013 Madrid, Spain.*

In Japan: For a complete list of books available from Penguin in Japan, please write to *Longman Penguin Japan Co Ltd, Yamaguchi Building, 2-12-9 Kanda Jimbocho, Chiyoda-Ku, Tokyo 101, Japan.*

FOR THE BEST LITERATURE, LOOK FOR THE 🐧

FOR THE BEST LITERATURE, LOOK FOR THE 🐧

☐ A SPORT OF NATURE
Nadine Gordimer

Hillela, Nadine Gordimer's "sport of nature," is seductive and intuitively gifted at life. Casting herself adrift from her family at seventeen, she lives among political exiles on an East African beach, marries a black revolutionary, and ultimately plays a heroic role in the overthrow of apartheid.

354 pages   ISBN: 0-14-008470-3 $7.95

☐ THE COUNTERLIFE
Philip Roth

By far Philip Roth's most radical work of fiction, *The Counterlife* is a book of conflicting perspectives and points of view about people living out dreams of renewal and escape. Illuminating these lives is the skeptical, enveloping intelligence of the novelist Nathan Zuckerman, who calculates the price and examines the results of his characters' struggles for a change of personal fortune.

372 pages   ISBN: 0-14-009769-4 $4.95

☐ THE MONKEY'S WRENCH
Primo Levi

Through the mesmerizing tales told by two characters—one, a construction worker/philosopher who has built towers and bridges in India and Alaska; the other, a writer/chemist, rigger of words and molecules—Primo Levi celebrates the joys of work and the art of storytelling.

174 pages   ISBN: 0-14-010357-0 $6.95

☐ IRONWEED
William Kennedy

"Riding up the winding road of Saint Agnes Cemetery in the back of the rattling old truck, Francis Phelan became aware that the dead, even more than the living, settled down in neighborhoods." So begins William Kennedy's Pulitzer-Prize winning novel about an ex-ballplayer, part-time gravedigger, and full-time drunk, whose return to the haunts of his youth arouses the ghosts of his past and present.

228 pages   ISBN: 0-14-007020-6 $6.95

☐ THE COMEDIANS
Graham Greene

Set in Haiti under Duvalier's dictatorship, *The Comedians* is a story about the committed and the uncommitted. Actors with no control over their destiny, they play their parts in the foreground; experience love affairs rather than love; have enthusiasms but not faith; and if they die, they die like Mr. Jones, by accident.

288 pages   ISBN: 0-14-002766-1 $4.95